# Islam and Democracy in the 21st Century

# Islam and Democracy in the 21st Century

TAUSEEF AHMAD PARRAY
*Assistant Professor of Islamic Studies, Higher Education Department,
Jammu & Kashmir, India*

*With a Foreword by*
M. A. MUQTEDAR KHAN
*Professor, Department of Political Science and International Relations,
University of Delaware, USA*

# OXFORD
UNIVERSITY PRESS

Oxford University Press is a department of the University of Oxford.
It furthers the University's objective of excellence in research, scholarship,
and education by publishing worldwide. Oxford is a registered trade mark of
Oxford University Press in the UK and in certain other countries

Published in India by
Oxford University Press
22 Workspace, 2nd Floor, 1/22 Asaf Ali Road, New Delhi 110002, India

© Oxford University Press India 2023

The moral rights of the authors have been asserted

First Edition published in 2023

All rights reserved. No part of this publication may be reproduced, stored in
a retrieval system, or transmitted, in any form or by any means, without the
prior permission in writing of Oxford University Press, or as expressly permitted
by law, by licence or under terms agreed with the appropriate reprographics
rights organization. Enquiries concerning reproduction outside the scope of the
above should be sent to the Rights Department, Oxford University Press, at the
address above

You must not circulate this work in any other form
and you must impose this same condition on any acquirer

ISBN-13 (print edition): 978-9-39-105033-7
ISBN-10 (print edition): 9-39-105033-6

ISBN-13 (eBook): 978-9-35-497305-5
ISBN-10 (eBook): 9-35-497305-1

ISBN-13 (OSO): 9789354973062
ISBN-10 (OSO): 935497306X

DOI: 10.1093/oso/9789391050337.001.0001

Typeset in Minion Pro 10.5/14
by Newgen Knowledge Works Pvt. Ltd.
Printed and bound in India by
Replika Press Pvt. Ltd.

*With Affection, Appreciation, Admiration to:*

*Beloved Family (Parents, Better Half, and Siblings): For Their Admiration, Adoration, and Attention;*
*Friends & Well Wishers: For Their Friendship and Amity;*
*Teachers & Mentors: For Their Intellectual Upbringing, Mentoring, and, Above All, for Making Me What I Am; and*
*Shah-i-Hamdan Institute of Islamic Studies (University of Kashmir) and Department of Islamic Studies (and Its Library), Aligarh Muslim University: For Everything*

# Contents

| | |
|---|---|
| *Foreword* | ix |
| *Preface* | xiii |
| *Acknowledgements* | xix |
| *A Note on Transliteration, Translations, Copyright Permissions, and Other Conventions* | xxiii |
| *Abbreviations* | xxvii |
| Introduction on Contextualizing Islam–Democracy Discourse and Its Currents and Trends | 1 |
| 1. Democracy, Democratization, and the Muslim World | 23 |
| 2. Democratic Notions in Islam | 47 |
| 3. Nineteenth- and Twentieth-Century Muslim Intellectuals on Islam–Democracy Compatibility: Voices from Arab World | 112 |
| 4. Nineteenth- and Twentieth-Century Muslim Intellectuals on Islam–Democracy Compatibility: Voices from South Asia | 135 |
| 5. Twenty-First Century Muslim Thinkers on Islam–Democracy Compatibility—I | 183 |
| 6. Twenty-First Century Muslim Thinkers on Islam–Democracy Compatibility—II | 243 |
| 7. Democracy and Its Muslim Critics: Objections and Observations of the 'Opponents' | 288 |
| Epilogue | 309 |
| *Book Description (Publisher's Description)* | 317 |
| *About the Book (Author's Description)* | 319 |
| *About the Author* | 321 |
|    *Brief Profile* | 321 |
|    *Detailed Profile* | 321 |
| *Bibliography* | 323 |
| *Index* | 357 |

# Foreword

## Islam and Democracy and the Revival of Islamic Political Philosophy

Islam, like other major religions, has struggled to come to terms with structural, political, and normative developments precipitated by the advent of modernity. Modernity is a human condition that has replaced the feudal and agricultural economy with capitalist and neoliberal mode, replaced political governance by divinely anointed kings and emperors with elected rulers legitimized by human consent, kingdoms and tribes with nation-states, and to a great extent theology with science and philosophy. The development of human consent as a source of normative authority has caused the emergence of human rights regimes and the evolution of democratic governance. It is here that the so-called divine authority and sovereignty, in the form of the revealed law tradition (Shari'ah heritage), comes into conflict with the positive developments in modern law and governance.[1]

Muslim intellectuals who strongly privilege tradition rejected modernity as undesirable and even unnatural values coming from the West. A new breed of Muslim intellectuals, like Maulana Maududi in South Asia and Syed Qutb, bought into modernity and tried to modernize Islam by essentially using Arabic terms for modern ideas (e.g. *Hakimiyyah* for sovereignty and *Shura* for democracy) and tried to articulate a highly politicized version of Islam. They embraced modernity while trying to maintain a facade of rejection. Without any serious discussion or reflection they embraced the idea of a modern state and tried to Islamize it by using 'Islamic' as a prefix and invented the 'Islamic state'. These intellectuals are known as Islamists and their politicized Islam is widely referred to as political Islam.[2] The most interesting, intellectually speaking, contribution has come from Islamic modernists who have argued for the compatibility of Islam and modernity, Islam and human rights, and Islam and democracy. They have given birth to a truly contemporary Islamic political philosophy.[3]

I have provided a sustained critique of Islamist political thought elsewhere, and do not wish to revisit it here.[4] Islamists have also had an opportunity to come to power in many places and so we have both theory and practical evidence of the power of their ideas. In my view, Islamist thinkers have, through debates and discourse along with the modernists and traditionalists, helped generate a modern Islamic political philosophy with the issue of Islam and democracy as a central theme. It is because of the conversation about Islam and democracy that Muslims now have a thriving political and philosophical tradition. Dr Tauseef Parray's book, *Islam and Democracy in the 21st Century*, is critical to this new tradition because it consolidates the ideas and contributions of a wide range of Muslim thinkers in one place. This book is central to Islam and democracy, and any future research on the topic can and should begin with this book.

For several years now, Dr Parray has commented on the contributions of other scholars. It is time he took a firm position and engaged the issues that Muslims face rather than the issues Muslim thinkers have engaged. As democracy itself suffers setbacks in the West with the rise of populism and authoritarianism, the democracy *problematique* is not merely confined to the democracy deficit in the Muslim World but includes the limits of democracy as it recedes in traditionally democratic strongholds like Europe and North America.[5] Why is democracy losing its appeal? Even if theoretical arguments that Islam and democracy are indeed compatible become the dominant view in the Muslim World, will democracy become more popular there while populism undermines it everywhere else?[6] One of the drivers of the globalization of democratic values was the phenomenon of globalization itself. Now with the rejection of globalist values, as evidenced by the desire of many demagogic leaders to build walls between nations, exit from established unions and treaties, can the Muslim World democratize as globalization declines and the liberal democratic global order weakens? If not democracy, what? These are questions that contemporary Islamic political thinkers need to address and answer.

I believe that the future of governance will be determined by the ability of states and cities to provide good and smart governance.[7] Perhaps the age of ideology will recede and be replaced by the age of technocracy, where efficient and smart delivery of public goods will be more important than the legitimization of who and how of governance. In a forthcoming project, I have sought to move the conversation away from Islamic government to Islam and good governance, placing less emphasis on ideology and more on good governance.[8] The point is the project of contemporary Islamic political philosophy is well on its way and those of us who tried to revive it in the past twenty years are now joined by fresh talent like Dr Parray. I see this book as a beginning of a new impetus to this new tradition that will both invigorate it and expand its scope. My congratulations to Dr Parray for providing us with this thoughtful and comprehensive point of departure to the century-long conversation on the compatibility of Islam and democracy. This book is beneficial to students of Islam and politics, Islam in politics and politics in Islam, and also to those political leaders and policymakers who are looking for normative ideas to underpin their visions and their policies.

Muqtedar Khan, PhD
Professor, Department of Political Science and International Relations,
*University of Delaware*, USA

## Notes

1. Fazlur Rahman, *Islam and Modernity: Transformation of an Intellectual Tradition* (Chicago, IL: University of Chicago Press, 1984); Muhammad Khalid Masud et al. (eds.), *Islam and Modernity: Key Issues and Debates: Key Issues and Debates* (Edinburg: Edinburgh University Press, 2009).
2. John L. Esposito (ed.), *Political Islam: Revolution, Radicalism, or Reform?* (Boulder, CO: Lynne Rienner Publishers, 1997); Idem. (ed.), *Voices of Resurgent Islam* (New York: Oxford University Press, 1983).
3. Khaled Abou El Fadl, *Islam and the Challenge of Democracy: A Boston Review Book* (Princeton and Oxford: Princeton University Press, 2004). M. A. Muqtedar Khan, *Islamic Democratic Discourse: Theory, Debates, and Philosophical Perspectives* (Lanham, MD: Lexington Books, 2006).
4. M. A. Muqtedar Khan, 'The Political Philosophy of Islamic Resurgence', *Cultural Dynamics* 13, 2 (2001): 211–229. Idem., 'What Is Political Islam?' *E-International Relations* 10 (2014); Idem., 'Islam, Democracy and Islamism After the Counterrevolution in Egypt', *Middle East Policy* 21, 1 (2014): 75–86.

5. Larry Diamond, 'Facing up to the Democratic Recession', *Journal of Democracy* 26, 1 (2015): 141–155. Marc F. Plattner, 'Is Democracy in Decline?', *Journal of Democracy* 26, 1 (2015): 5–10.
6. Benjamin Moffitt, *The Global Rise of Populism: Performance, Political Style, and Representation* (Stanford, CA: Stanford University Press, 2016).
7. John Graham, Timothy Wynne Plumptre, and Bruce Amos, *Principles for Good Governance in the 21st Century* (Ottawa: Institute on Governance, 2003).
8. See Muqtedar Khan, *Islam and Good Governance: Political Philosophy of Ihsan* (New York: Palgrave Macmillan, 2019).

# Preface

About quarter of a century has passed since the publication of John L. Esposito and John O. Voll's seminal work *Islam and Democracy* (1996): A major initial work on the 'compatibility' of Islam and democracy—both in theory and practice. In this book, the authors argue that in the Muslim world, 'Religious resurgence and democratization are two of the most important developments of the final decades of the twentieth century', and among these 'dual aspirations', 'the most important questions revolve around the compatibility of Islam and democracy' as both have fashioned 'new realities that affect the relationship between Islam and democracy'.[1] Abdulaziz Sachedina, in 2001, attempted to depict Islam as a religion or a system with strong impending for upholding 'pluralistic, democratic institutions' by undertaking 'to map some of the most important political concepts in Islam that advance better human relationships, both within and between nations' and by 'uncovering normative aspects of Muslim religious formulations... to suggest their critical relevance' in the twenty-first century.[2] On the similar lines, Noah Feldman (in 2003) argued that 'Can Islam and democracy cohere—either in principle or in practice?' is no more a 'crucial question' because it has been debated immensely, from the 1990s, in numerous works, by Muslims and non-Muslims alike; and it is incongruous to perceive or discuss 'Islamic democracy' as a 'contradiction in terms'.[3] Khaled Abou El Fadl's *Islam and the Challenge of Democracy* (2004)—a long essay, with brief responses from a number of scholars, originally published in the *Boston Review* (2003)—engaged the reader in a rich discourse on the challenges of democracy in the contemporary Muslim world.[4]

A decade after Esposito and Voll's seminal work, Muqtedar Khan in his *Islamic Democratic Discourse* (2006)—analysing the democratic discourse in Islam in legal, historical, and philosophical perspectives as well as on regional and global levels—proposed that the 'discourse on Islam and democracy and its constituent debates is just one theme of the grand narrative on Islam and the West' and envisaged that the 'new interest in

Islam and democracy will certainly revive old ideas and generate new interpretations'. Consequently, he viewed 'Islamic-democracy-in-practice' as a challenge both for Islamic political theory and Muslim political theorists.[5] In *Democracy in Islam* (2007), Sayed Khatab and Gary D. Bouma attempted to provide a balanced standpoint on, and 'to resolve', the question of Islam–democracy compatibility.[6]

Similarly, in 2009, Nader Hashemi in his *Islam, Secularism, and Liberal Democracy*, amidst analysing the theoretical relationship between religion and democracy, specifically Islam's relationship with liberal democracy, maintained that the 'problem of religion's relationship with democracy is not an exclusively Muslim phenomenon', but it is one of those problems that other religions and religious traditions, 'Christianity in particular—have had to struggle with' in the past. And in the twenty-first century, Hashemi recognizes 'the establishment and organization of democracy in the Muslim world' as 'arguably the great problem of our [present] time'.[7] In 2013, Hashemi anticipated: 'The debate on Islam and democracy has generated considerable controversy and acrimony over the years. It has been one of the key political and intellectual debates of the post-Cold War era, rising in importance after the tragic events of September 11, 2001 and then again after the 2011 Arab Spring'. 'Like other religious traditions … Islam is neither more nor less compatible with modern democracy than Christianity or Judaism'.[8]

Almost a decade after 9/11, Irfan Ahmad (in 2011) reiterated: 'An important global debate has been about the interface between Islam and democracy … [which] has intensified in the wake of "Democracy's Third Wave" ending in 1990' (1974–1990); and gave rise, predominantly, to 'two major poles in the debate … Compatibility and Incompatibility Paradigms'.[9] In 2015, Paul Kubicek, in his *Political Islam and Democracy in the Muslim World*, rather than asking 'if and how Islam undermines democracy' focused on 'to uncover how democracy has taken root in Muslim-majority countries', from Asia to Africa.[10] Esposito, Tamara Sonn, and Voll, in *Islam and Democracy after the Arab Spring* (2016), suggested that in the 1990s, the argument was 'whether or not Islam and democracy are compatible'; and in the second decade of the twenty-first century, 'the relationships between Islam and democracy are in a new phase reflected in the evolution of the political systems' of Muslim countries like Pakistan, Iran, Indonesia, and Tunisia. 'The basic questions now [in contrast to 1990s] go beyond the simplistic question of "essential" compatibility, and involve the nature of the democratic experiences in the Muslim world'.[11] Offering a normative reconceptualization of a modern Islamic governed state, Joseph J. Kaminski, in his *The Contemporary Islamic Governed State: A Reconceptualization* (2017), argued that the 'question of Islam and its compatibility with democracy has been examined in great detail in the past, but has recently taken on new salience'.[12] On the verge of completion of the second decade of the twenty-first century, Md Nazrul Islam and Md Saidul Islam in their *Islam and Democracy in South Asia* (2020),[13] reflected on, and presented a critical analysis of, the complex relationship between Islam and democracy both in theory and practice—exploring normative and philosophical viewpoints of this discourse and by focusing on Bangladesh as a case study in the South Asian context.

These are just a few examples, from among a galaxy of scholars/thinkers on Islam–democracy discourse, which provide some significant and definite insights into the trends, tendencies, and developments that have ensued in this discourse. There is copious literature—in the form of books, monographs, book chapters, articles, papers, essays, etc.—which deliberate on different aspects of Islam–democracy (*in*)compatibility. Having a look at these works—whether focusing on the theoretical perspectives and/or empirical studies, from the Muslim world (Asia to Africa)—one finds a similar question (posed and answered) in all these works: *Is Islam Compatible with Democracy*? These insights also reveal, among others, that Islam–democracy discourse is as relevant today as it was (a few decades before) in the past. These examples, within a plethora of literature on Islam and democracy (and/or Muslims and Muslim societies vis-à-vis democratization), are relevant even in the third decade of the third millennium. Be it the 1990s, 2001 (9/11), or 2011 'Arab Spring' scenario, it has become, in Irfan Ahmad's maxim, a *signature question*, to ask, explore, and examine, *Is Islam Compatible with Democracy*?[14], and/or interrelated questions like: 'Islam and Democracy: Are they Compatible?'; 'Islam and Democracy: What is the Real Question?'; 'Islam and democracy, an oxymoron?'; 'What is Islamic Democracy?'; 'What elements are present in the Islamic tradition in service of democracy?'; etc.

It is in this line of thought, and a continuation of this decades-old discourse, that this work attempts to answer these questions as a way of opening further discussion on Islam and democracy in the twenty-first century. Having been engaged and involved with Islam-democracy discourse from about-a-decade-now, and originally based on my PhD dissertation (2009–2014, which I did at the Department of Islamic Studies, *Aligarh Muslim University*, India), and on my publications (in journals, periodicals, and other portals), over the years (2010–2021), on diverse aspects of Islam and democracy theme, the present work deals with Islam–democracy (*in*)compatibility, on the theoretical grounds, with a focus on some noted modern Muslim thinkers, of last-two-and-half-centuries—from the nineteenth to twenty-first centuries. The prime concern of this book is to analyse and examine the relationship between the socio-political concepts and institutions of Islam—like *Shura* (Mutual Consultation), *Khilafah* (Caliphate), *Ijma'* (Consensus), *Ijtihad* (Independent Interpretive Reasoning), *Bay'ah* (Oath of Allegiance), *Maslaha* (Public Interest), *Ahl al-Hall wa al-'Aqd* (the 'Wise Ones'), and *Mithaq al-Medina* (the Constitution of Medina), etc.—and the principles of (modern) democracy by covering a wide range of Muslim scholars down the ages—ranging from the pioneering modernists of the Arab world (Rifa'a al-Tahtawi to Malek Bennabi) and South Asia (Abul Kalam Azad and Muhammad Iqbal to Syed Abu'l 'Ala Mawdudi and Fazlur Rahman) to present-day thinkers and prominent figures (including, but not limited to) Fathi Osman, Wahiduddin Khan, Yusuf al-Qaradawi, Khurshid Ahmad, Rachid al-Ghannouchi, Abdolkarim Soroush, Javed Ahmad Ghamidi, Abdelwahab el-Affendi, Khaled Abou El Fadl, Muqtedar Khan, etc. It seeks to examine thoroughly the elements of compatibility and congruence between Islam and democracy, while not overlooking the basic difference(s) that exist between the Western approach to democracy and Islamic political thought (as highlighted by 'hard-core'/radical Islamists like Sayyid Qutb, Taqiuddin al-Nabhani, Abd al-Qadim Zallum, or academicians and analysts like Malaysia-based Abdul Rashid Moten and Canada-based Abid Ullah Jan, etc.). It engages—while looking at the 'real question' in this hotly debated discourse—with the thoughts and insights of Asef Bayat, Nader Hashemi, Irfan Ahmad, etc., as well.

Beginning by contextualizing the question of Islam–democracy discourse within the broader perspective, the book, in its various chapters, focuses on democracy, democratization, and the Muslim world;

democratic notions in Islam; nineteenth and twentieth-century Muslim intellectuals (of Arab World and South Asia) on Islam-democracy compatibility; views and visions of twenty-first-century Muslim thinkers on Islam–democracy compatibility; and democracy and its Muslim critics (the 'Opponents'). It ends with some concrete reflections on this crucial and complex issue vis-à-vis the challenges (for the contemporary Islamic political thought) in Islam and democracy discourse. The focus, overall, is to highlight the discourse of Islam-democracy compatibility, theoretically; and, thus, a continuation of century-long-search for establishing the prospects of an authentic and viable 'Islamic democracy'. It, thus, takes the discussion on Islam and democracy many steps further, by treading through the text, tradition, history, as well as interpretation(s) and visions of some eminent scholars (down the ages) for understanding the theoretical relationship between Islam and democracy.

Tauseef Ahmad Parray (PhD; Postdoc)<br>January 2022/Jumad al-Thani, 1443<br>Pulwama, Kashmir (J&K)

## Notes

1. John L. Esposito and John O. Voll, *Islam and Democracy* (New York: Oxford University Press, 1996), pp. 3, 6–7, 202.
2. Abdulaziz Sachedina, *The Islamic Roots of Democratic Pluralism* (New York: Oxford University Press, 2001), pp. 11, 139.
3. Noah Feldman, 'The Best Hope', in Khaled Abou El Fadl, *Islam and the Challenge of Democracy: A Boston Review Book*, Joshua Cohen and Deborah Chasman (eds.) (Princeton & Oxford: Princeton University Press, 2004), pp. 59–62, p. 59.
4. Abou El Fadl, *op. cit.*
5. M. A. Muqtedar Khan, 'The Politics, Theory, and Philosophy of Islamic Democracy', in M. A. Muqtedar Khan (ed.), *Islamic Democratic Discourse: Theory, Debates and Philosophical Perspectives* (Lanham, MD: Lexington Books, 2006), pp. 149–171, pp. 150, 157.
6. Sayed Khatab and Gary D. Bouma, *Democracy in Islam* (New York: Routledge, 2007).
7. Nader Hashemi, *Islam, Secularism, and Liberal Democracy: Toward a Democratic Theory for Muslim Societies* (New York: Oxford University Press, 2009), p. 5.
8. Nader Hashemi, 'Islam and Democracy', in John L. Esposito and Emad El-Din Shahin (eds.), *The Oxford Handbook of Islam and Politics* (New York: Oxford University Press, 2013), pp. 68–88, p. 83.

9. Irfan Ahmad, 'Democracy and Islam', *Philosophy and Social Criticism [PSC]*, 37, 4 (2011): 459–470, pp. 459–460.
10. Paul Kubicek, *Political Islam and Democracy in the Muslim World* (Boulder, CO: Lynne Rienner Publishers, 2015), p. 8.
11. John L. Esposito, Tamara Sonn, and John O. Voll, *Islam and Democracy After the Arab Spring* (New York: Oxford University Press, 2016), pp. 238–239.
12. Joseph J. Kaminski, *The Contemporary Islamic Governed State: A Reconceptualization* (London: Palgrave Macmillan, 2017), p. 11.
13. Md Nazrul Islam and Md Saidul Islam, *Islam and Democracy in South Asia: The Case of Bangladesh* (Cham, Switzerland: Palgrave Macmillan/Springer Nature, 2020).
14. Ahmad in *PSC*, p. 460.

# Acknowledgements

Writing acknowledgments for an academic work is always a precarious venture, as it is very tough to remember the names of mentors, friends, or well-wishers who deserve recognition and gratitude but whose names do not appear on these pages. Therefore, I would begin by expressing my profound gratitude, immense indebtedness, and sincere thanks to all those beautiful souls and minds for providing me suggestions, advises, and for encouraging my academic endeavours and activities. They have been providing me their valuable suggestions, encouragement, and above all, inspiring my academic endeavours and efforts: to all of them a big thanks from the depths of my heart.

I have many people to thank for their support, in one way or the other, in writing this book. I owe an exceptional debt of gratitude and appreciation to many people: to Professor Sayyid Ahsan (*Aligarh Muslim University*, India) for his supervision and guidance during my PhD; to national and international PhD Thesis evaluation committee members (especially Professor Muhsin Usmani of *EFLU*, Hyderabad) for their evaluation reports and constructive comments; to Professor Muqtedar Khan (*University of Delaware*, USA) for his constructive suggestions, encouragement and for writing a perceptive *Foreword* to this book; and to Professor(s) Asma Afsaruddin (*Indiana University*, Bloomington, USA), Abdullah Saeed (*University of Melbourne*, Australia), Joseph J. Kaminski (*International University of Sarajevo* [*IUS*], Bosnia), and Louay Safi (*Hamad Bin Khalifa University* [*HBKU*], Qatar) for their 'Endorsements'; to Professor(s) Abdur Raheem Kidwai (*AMU*, India) and Kaminski for their suggestions, instructions, and encouragement; to Dr(s) Mohammad Dawood Sofi, Showkat Ahmad Dar and Saajid Shaffi, Mohammad Ismail, Muhammad Irfan Shah, and Mujtaba Farooq for many things—for reading parts of this work, for providing material when contacted, and for their comments, suggestions, and valuable feedback whenever approached (among these, Saajid and Irfan deserve more gratitude: they know very well the reasons). I am also much grateful to the anonymous reviewers of the *Oxford University Press*, New Delhi, for their comments, and critical feedback, on this manuscript which helped in making this a better book. I am deeply grateful to all of you for your valuable insights and suggestions—acknowledging, of course, that all shortcomings in this book are my own.

Profuse thanks are also due to my friends, relatives, and family—my parents, 'better half', siblings—and words can hardly express and articulate it. I am highly grateful and indebted to my beloved parents, 'better half', and siblings for their love, adoration, affection, care, and for being a source and spring of support, uninterrupted encouragement, and for countless things. It is their prayers and patience which made this academic challenge all the easier.

I would like to express, from the core of the heart, my gratefulness to all my teachers, especially those who taught, and mentored, me during the Masters/PG (2006–2008) at Shah-i-Hamadan Institute of Islamic Studies, *University of Kashmir, Srinagar,* and during PhD (especially my dissertation supervisor, Professor Sayyid Ahsan) at Department of Islamic Studies (DoIS), *AMU*, Aligarh—my 'academic home' during the years 2009–2014: *Aligarh Days*, for me, were truly remarkable and are memorable and worth to cherish.

This work is a highly revised, meticulously modified, enormously re-organized, and in certain cases précised, version of my PhD dissertation, 'Islam and Democracy: A Study of the Views of Contemporary Scholars of India and Pakistan' (submitted, in 2014, to the DoIS, *AMU*). During, and after my PhD, some portions of this work were published in different journals (and in certain magazines and other portals). Parts of many of these journal articles, review essays, and conference proceedings are reprinted and reused with written permission in this work. Though I tried to contact all the copyright holders for grant of permission to reuse the published material, however, in a couple of cases, it was not possible. Therefore, I express my sincere thanks to all the editors and/or organizations (not only) for granting me permission to reuse the published material, but for giving space to my writings over these years, which helped me to gain more insights, and delve deep into this hotly debate discourse. A list of all these writings is provided in the Bibliography (Parray, 2010–2021) and the copyright holders who granted permission are mentioned (at the end) below in the alphabetical order.

Furthermore, I have received a lot of support, guidance, and benefits, from my family, teachers, and friends. It is in lieu of all the affection, appreciation, and admiration, that I dedicate this work, collectively, to all of them.

Many thanks are extended to the Publisher, OUP, and the Team associated with it from the very first day (the proposal of this book was submitted) to its completion: Dr Sugata Ghosh, Rekha Natarajan, Nandini Dey, Dr Prasun Chaterjee, Prakash Pranshu, and especially Ms Nandini Ganguli (Acquisitions Editor, History, Philosophy, and Religion Academic Publishing), and everyone associated with this project, for overseeing the publication of this work.

Last, and in no way the least, I will feel privileged if the readers will offer any suggestions and constructive criticism for improving the contents of this work. Feedback, in any form, is always welcome.

I sincerely pray to Almighty to accept this work as a modest contribution on behalf of this student of knowledge, and reward me with all that is good, virtuous, and beneficial: *Aameen*!!

Tauseef Ahmad Parray (PhD; post-doc)
Assistant Professor, Islamic Studies,
Higher Education Department, J&K
(tauseef.parray21@gmail.com)
January, 2022/Jumad al-Thani, 1443
Pulwama, Kashmir (Jammu & Kashmir)

# A Note on Transliteration, Translations, Copyright Permissions, and Other Conventions

## On Transliteration and Other Conventions

For transliteration of the Arabic terms/words and names, I have adopted a simplified Arabic-to-English transliteration method. This is done keeping in view the readership, which includes both specialists as well as non-specialists. I have avoided the use of diacritical marks—macrons and/or dots. However, I have used the symbol (') for *'ayn* (as, e.g. in *'Umar, 'Uthman, Shari'ah, Ijma', al-'Alwani*, etc.). The same is the case with the *hamza* ('), as in the Qur'an. The *h* indicating *ta' marbuta* is also retained, as, for instance, in *Shari'ah, Khalifah/ Khilafah, Maslaha*, throughout the book. In addition, few Anglicized words, like Qur'anic, Shura-cracy, have been frequently used. All dates are generally given in the Common Era (CE), unless otherwise mentioned (as, e.g. in a quotation where either only AH or both CE/AH are mentioned).

## On Citation of the Translations of the Qur'an and the Referencing Style

Quotations from the Qur'an usually follow M. A. S. Abdel Haleem, *The Qur'an: A New Translation* (2005 [2004]) and Abdullah Yusuf Ali, *The Holy Qur'an: Text, Translation and Commentary*, 2nd ed. (1977 [1934]). I have used (unless otherwise mentioned) these two translations with some minor modifications, wherever necessary, for clarity and context.

For this work, I have drawn profoundly, utilized amply, and benefitted much—as will become evident from the extensive Bibliography—from various works (mostly in English and Urdu) related to different aspects of the theme under study. All these works are cited in *The Chicago Manual of Style*, with some alterations, like using shortened and/or abbreviated forms *for*: lengthy titles, journal/magazine names; *op. cit.* and *loc. cit.* for works cited frequently, and other such technicalities.

## On Using Abbreviations

Abbreviations are used for the works which have been cited frequently or have lengthy titles, as well as the titles of journals, magazines, newspapers, etc. A list of all these abbreviations is provided below.

## On Copyright Permissions (for My Previous Publications)

The present work is a highly revised version of my PhD dissertation. During, and after PhD, many portions of this work were published in different journals (and in certain magazines and other platforms). I tried to contact all the organizations/publishers/editors (copyright holders) for granting permission for reusing the published material. Those who granted the permissions, very graciously, for reusing the previously published material either in full or as excerpts, are enlisted below in the alphabetical order:

**Centre for Mediterranean, Middle East & Islamic Studies** (CEMMIS), *University of the Peloponnese* (UoP), Greece, for their permission to reuse material from my essay 'Three Living Arab-American [Western Muslim] Academicians on Islam-Democracy Discourse', published in *Point of View* [PoV] on 28 January 2015, pp. 1–7: www.cemmis.edu.gr (courtesy Dr Sotirios Roussos, Department of Political Science and IR, *UoP*)

**Centre for Social Action and Development (CSAD)** Lucknow, India (courtesy Professor Nadeem Hasnain) for their permission to reuse material from my (i) 'Allama Iqbal on Islam-Democracy Discourse ... '; (ii) 'Review of the Literature on Islam–Democracy Compatibility Theme ... '; (iii) 'Muslim Reformist Thought in 21st Century ... '; and (iv) 'Islam-Democracy Reconciliation in the

Thought/Writings of Asghar Ali Engineer', published in *Islam and Muslim Societies—A Social Science Journal* [*IMS*] in 4, 2 (2011): 9, 31, and 12, and 5, 1 (2012): 23–29, respectively (www.muslimsociet ies.org)

**Department of Islamic Studies (DoIS), Aligarh Muslim University (AMU), India,** for their permission to reuse material from my 'Modern Muslim Scholars' on Islam-Democracy Discourse: Views of Azad, Iqbal, and Maududi', *Journal of the Institute of Islamic Studies* [*JIIS*], 40 (2011): 27–50 (courtesy Prof. Abdul Hamid Fazili, In-charge Chairman, DoIS, AMU)

**Department of Sociology,** *University of Kashmir* (KU), J&K, India for their permission to reuse material from my 'Globalization, Democracy, and Muslim World ...', published in *Journal of Society in Kashmir* [JSK], 4 (2014): 1–20 (courtesy Prof. Aneesa Shafi, Editor-in Chief, *JSK*)

**Hamdard Foundation Karachi, Pakistan** for their permission to reuse the material from my 'Text, Tradition, and Interpretations of Shura ... ' published in *Hamdard Islamicus—Quarterly Journal of Studies and Research in Islam* [HI], XXXIV, 3 (July–September 2011): 7–24 (courtesy Dr M. Wasie Fasih Butt, Editor, *HI*)

**Hatam Group Publishers, Malaysia** (courtesy Prof. Anees Ahmad, Managing Editor, *Journal of Humanity and Islam*: *JHI*) for their permission to reuse material from my (i) 'Operational Concepts of Islamic Democracy: Khilafah, Shura, Ijma', and Ijtihad'; and (ii) 'Review Essay: The West and Islam: Western Liberal Democracy versus the System of Shura, Mishal Fahm Al-Sulami (2003)', published in *JHI*, 1, 1 (April 2011): 11–27 and 52–59

**Institute of Political Economy,** *University of Asia and the Pacific (UA&P)*, Philippines (courtesy Dr May Zuleika Q. Salao, Editor-in-Chief, *The Roundtable*/Director, *Political Economy Program at UA&P*) for their consent through email to republish the contents from my 'Democracy in Islam: Views of Modern Muslim Scholars', *The Roundtable*, special issue on 'Islam and democracy', 9, 1 (2011): 4–10

**International Digital Organization for Scientific Information (IDOSI), IDOSI Publications, UAE** (www.idosi.org) for their consent through email to republish the contents from my 'Islamic

Democracy' or 'Democracy in Islam: Some Key Operational Democratic Concepts and Notions', *World Journal of Islamic History and Civilization* [*WJIHC*], 2, 2 (2012): 66–86

**International Institute of Islamic Thought** (IIIT), USA for their written permission, as Publisher and Copyright Holder, to use material from my (i) 'Democracy in Islam: Views of Several Modern Muslim Scholars' and (ii) 'A Survey of Four Indo-Pakistani Scholars' Perspectives on the Islam-Democracy Discourse', published in *American Journal of Islamic Social Sciences* [*AJISS;* renamed now *American Journal of Islam and Society: AJIS*], 27, 2 (2010): 140–148 and 29, 1 (2012): 146–159, respectively (courtesy Mr Obay Altaleb, Associate Director and Ms Huda D. Kamareddine, Journals Coordinator, Department of Publication & Translation/Managing Editor, *AJIS*, IIIT)

**Middle East Studies Institute** (MESI), *Shanghai International Studies University* (SISU), Shanghai, China (Journal: *Journal of Middle Eastern and Islamic Studies in Asia* [JMEISA]; now renamed as *Asian Journal of Middle Eastern and Islamic Studies* [*AJMEIS*]) for their written permission to use the contents from my (i) 'Global Muslim Voices on Islam-Democracy Compatibility and Coexistence ... '; and (ii) 'Iranian Intellectuals on "Islam and Democracy" Compatibility ... ', *JMEISA*, 6, 1, (2012): 53–86 and 7, 3 (2013); 43–64, respectively (courtesy Dr Song Niu, Deputy Editor-in-Chief, *JMEISA/AJMEIS*)

**Students Islamic Organization (SIO), Calicut** (Kerala, India) for their permission to reuse the material from my "Articulating an 'Islamic democracy' in 21st Century: Views and Visions of some Living Muslim Intellectuals of Indo-Pak Subcontinent", published in *Islamic Academic Conference Proceedings* (2012), pp. 267–274 (courtesy Mr Suhaib C. T., Sub-Editor, *SIO*, Calicut)

**Viva Books Pvt. Ltd. New Delhi, India** (courtesy Mr Sreetilak Sambhanda, Executive Vice-President, Publishing and Learning) for their permission to reuse the material from (i) ' "Islamic Democracy" or "Democratic Islam" ... ', 4th chapter of my *Mediating Islam and Modernity: Sir Sayyid, Iqbal, and Azad* (2019, pp. 81–104); and (ii) 'The Qur'anic Text on Shura ... ', 2nd chapter of my *Recent Trends in Qur'anic Scholarship* (2020, pp. 26–47)

# Abbreviations

| | |
|---|---|
| AJIS | American Journal of Islam & Society |
| AJISS | American Journal of Islamic Social Sciences |
| AJMEIS | Asian Journal of Middle Eastern and Islamic Studies |
| AJQS | Aligarh Journal of Quranic Studies |
| AMU | Aligarh Muslim University |
| ANALISA | Analisa: Journal of Social Science & Religion |
| ASBIDER | ASBIDER—Akademi Sosyal Bilimler Dergisi |
| BJMES | British Journal of Middle Eastern Studies |
| BSOAS | Bulletin of the School of Oriental and African Studies |
| CEMMIS | Centre for Mediterranean, Middle East & Islamic Studies (Greece) |
| Cont. Islam | Contemporary Islam—Dynamics of Muslim Life |
| CSAD | Centre for Social Action and Development |
| CSID | Centre for the Study of Islam and Democracy |
| DISNA | Dr Iqbal Society of North America |
| DoIS | Department of Islamic Studies |
| EB | Encyclopedia Britannica (online) |
| EB15 | The New Encyclopedia Britannica, 15th ed. |
| EC | Encompassing Crescent (New York) |
| EI2 | The Encyclopedia of Islam, 2nd Ed., 12 Vols. |
| EIMW | Encyclopedia of Islam and the Muslim World, 2 Vols. |
| EPW | Economic and Political Weekly |
| EQ | Encyclopedia of the Qur'an, 6 Vols. |
| GK | Greater Kashmir (Daily Newspaper, Srinagar, J&K) |
| HI | Hamdard Islamicus—Quarterly Journal of Studies and Research in Islam |
| HT | Hizb al-Tahrir al-Islami/Hizb ut-Tahrir |
| IAIS | International Institute of Advanced Islamic Studies |
| IBSUSJ | International Black Sea University Scientific Journal |
| ICMR | Islam and Christian–Muslim Relations |
| ICR | Islam and Civilizational Renewal |
| IDOSI | International Digital Organization for Scientific Information |
| IEQ | The Integrated Encyclopedia of Qur'an |
| IIIT | International Institute of Islamic Thought |
| IIMM | Islam: Its Meaning and Message |

## ABBREVIATIONS

| | |
|---|---|
| IIUI | International Islamic University Islamabad |
| IIUM | International Islamic University Malaysia |
| IJAPA | The International Journal of the Asian Philosophical Association |
| IJMES | International Journal of Middle East Studies |
| IMS | Islam & Muslim Societies—A Social Science Journal |
| IQ | The Islamic Quarterly |
| IS | Islamic Studies |
| ISTAC | International Institute of Islamic Thought and Civilization, Malaysia |
| IUST | Islamic University of Science and Technology, Awantipora, J&K |
| JAOS | Journal of the American Oriental Society |
| JHI | Journal of Humanity & Islam |
| JI | Jihat al-Islam |
| JIA | Journal of Islam in Asia |
| JIIS | Journal of the Institute of Islamic Studies, Aligarh |
| JMEISA | Journal of Middle Eastern and Islamic Studies in Asia |
| JMI | Jamia Milia Islamia, New Delhi |
| JMMA | Journal of Muslim Minority Affairs |
| JoD | Journal of Democracy |
| JPHS | Journal of the Pakistan Historical Society |
| JSK | Journal of Society in Kashmir—Annual Journal of Department of Sociology, Kashmir University |
| KAN-CQS/CQS | K A. Nizami Center for Quranic Studies, Aligarh |
| KR | Kashmir Reader (Daily Newspaper, Srinagar, J&K) |
| KU | University of Kashmir, J&K |
| Liberal Islam | Charles Kurzman's Liberal Islam—A Sourcebook |
| MCI | John L. Esposito and John O. Voll's Makers of Contemporary Islam |
| MD | Muslim Democrat |
| MEI | Middle East International |
| MENA | Middle East and North Africa |
| MEQ | Middle East Quarterly |
| MER | Middle East Report |
| MERIA | Middle East Review of International Affairs |
| MES | Middle Eastern Studies |
| MES | Muhammad: Encyclopedia of Seerah |
| MESI | Middle East Studies Institute, Shanghai |
| MICE | Medieval Islamic Civilization: An Encyclopedia, 2 vols. |
| MJMES | McGill Journal of Middle East Studies |
| Modernist Islam | Charles Kurzman's Modernist Islam—A Sourcebook |
| MQ | Mufti Muhammad Shafi's Ma'ariful Qur'an |

| | |
|---|---|
| MW | The Muslim World (Hartford Seminary, USA) |
| MWBR | The Muslim World Book Review (Islamic Foundation, UK) |
| OEIP | The Oxford Encyclopedia of Islam and Politics, 2 vols. |
| OEIW | The Oxford Encyclopedia of Islamic World, 6 vols. |
| OUP | Oxford University Press |
| Oxford History | John Esposito's Oxford History of Islam |
| PEIPT | Princeton Encyclopedia of Islamic Political Thought |
| PSC | Philosophy and Social Criticism |
| RC | Religion Compass |
| RMES | Review of Middle East Studies |
| SIO | Students Islamic Organization (Calicut, Kerala) |
| SISU | Shanghai International Studies University, Shanghai) |
| SOAS | School of Oriental and African Studies, London |
| TAM | The American Muslim |
| TCS | Theory, Culture & Society |
| Td.Q | Amin Ahsan Islahi's Tadabbur al-Qur'an |
| Tf.Q | Mawlana Abul Ala Mawdudi's Tafhim al-Qur'an |
| Tj.Q | Abul Kalam Azad's Tarjuman al-Qur'an (Urdu) |
| TM | Daryabadi's Tafsir-i-Qur'an: Tafsir-i-Majidi |
| TQ | Abdul Majid Daryabadi's Tafsir-i-Qur'an, 4 vols. |
| TTQ | Abul Kalam Azad's The Tarjuman al-Qur'an (English) |
| UCLA | University of California, Los Angeles |
| Voices | John Esposito's Voices of Resurgent Islam |
| Western Muslims | Tariq Ramadan's Western Muslims and the Future of Islam |
| WJIHC | World Journal of Islamic History and Civilization |
| WO | World Outlook |

# Introduction on Contextualizing Islam–Democracy Discourse and Its Currents and Trends

Towards the culminating decades of the twentieth century, a number of questions regarding Islam–democracy compatibility have gravely engaged experts, professionals, analysts, and intellectuals worldwide. Some of these questions are: 'Is Islam compatible with democracy?' If yes, then 'on what grounds'? And 'what elements are present in the Islamic tradition in service of democracy?' Over the recent years, the issue of Islam–democracy compatibility has been indisputably surfacing as a critical and crucial challenge for the Muslim world and has turned out to be a key question in the contemporary Islamic political thought. The issue has not only received a vigorous attention from the Muslim academics/intellectuals but has been discussed, debated, and deliberated by numerous Western academics and experts as well. Despite the emergence of this issue in the 1980s and 1990s, it gained much prevalence in the post-9/11 era—when Islam was branded as a 'violent' religion, with hardly any concern for the universal values like peace, tolerance, justice, democracy, freedom, etc.—and also in the aftermath of the 2010–2011 uprisings in the Arab world—referred to as the 'Arab Spring'.

In his *Democracy in America* (1831), Alexis de Tocqueville (d. 1859; French political thinker and historian) discussed what he calls the 'great political problem of our times'. The 'organization and the establishment of democracy in Christendom', according to Tocqueville, 'is the great political problem of our times'.[1] By now, this almost-two-centuries-old-observation is still relevant, especially in the context of debates and discussions revolving around religion–democracy relationship in the Muslim world. This observation reminds us, in the words of Nader Hashemi (*University *of Denver*, USA), that the 'problem of religion's relationship with democracy is not *an exclusively Muslim phenomenon*' but one of those problems that other religions and religious traditions—'Christianity in particular—have had to struggle with [in the past]' (italics added).[2] Commenting on Tocqueville's observation from a twenty-first-century Muslim point of view, Hashemi argues:

> To the extent that Tocqueville's observation is correct, it could be extrapolated that in the same sense that the 'great political problem' facing Europe in the nineteenth century was the *question of democracy in Christian lands* [and in the same way, in] the twenty-first century, arguably the great problem of our time is the *establishment and organization of democracy in the Muslim world*.[3] (Italics added)

Graham E. Fuller (American author and political analyst) puts it as: 'No religion is inherently "compatible" with democracy: Judaism, Christianity, Buddhism, and Islam are all concerned with issues that have little to do with democracy.... Islam is not a fixed thing ... [but] is a living phenomenon of Muslims who constantly interact and evolve with the world around it. Indeed, the real question is not whether "Islam is compatible with democracy" but rather what is the relationship between *Muslims* and democracy. We are discussing not what Islam is but what Muslims want'.[4] (Italics in original)

The process of democratization in the Muslim world has received diverse reactions and responses. Of these multiple responses, three main approaches and responses bear considerable significance: (i) the 'Ultraconservatives' and 'Extremists', in this regard, uphold a rejectionist approach arguing that Islam comprises its own specific system and institutions wherein democracy hardly occupies any space; (ii) some others—loosely labelled as 'Secularists'—advocate of relegating religion to private life for the successful implementation of democracy in the Muslim societies; (iii) still others, mostly 'Reformists/ Modernists' (and some 'Moderate Islamists' as well)—which are labelled, loosely, as *Muslim Democrats*[5]—argue that Islamic political philosophy can easily assimilate democracy. The champions of this reformist trend—majority of whom are Muslim intellectuals, academicians, and moderate religious leaders—open up the possibilities for reconciling some socio-political principles of Islam with democracy. With a reformative approach, these intellectuals advocate Islam–democracy compatibility by taking into account the traditional Islamic concepts like *Shura* (mutual consultation), *Ijma'* (community consensus), *Ijtihad* (independent personal reasoning), *Bay'ah* (oath of allegiance), and *Maslaha* (public interest), and similar other ideas and ideals—with their roots in the primary sources of Islam. For them, such viable Islamic concepts can be employed to establish and sustain parliamentary forms of government meanwhile executing checks and balances among the essential branches of the government, that is, the executive, legislative, and judiciary.

Living in both Muslim and non-Muslim countries/societies, these reformist/moderate Muslim thinkers/intellectuals,[6] in majority espouse the democratic principles based upon the (re) interpretations of the (political notions of the) *Qur'an*. The essential components of modern democracy, for these intellectuals, including principles of accountability, consultative bodies, elected rulers, equality, freedom, human rights, human welfare, justice, the rule of law, and tolerance have their very foundations in the primary sources of Islam—the *Qur'an* and the *Sunnah* of the Prophet (pbuh).

## Scope of Islam-Democracy Discourse in the Twenty-First Century

During the time of liberation from the clutches of European colonialism (i.e., the first half of the twentieth century), the Muslim world faced two instantaneous and major tests in the form of reinstating their governance and in facing modernity. In other words, 'form of governance' and the 'era of modernity' were the two crucial challenges for the Muslim world to tackle with. However, during the early twentieth century, many Muslim scholars explored the prospects and diagnosis of establishing and instituting an 'Islamic democracy'—for they had only two options: either to follow a model of the Western world (the colonizers) or to come up with an alternative. While some countries opted for the former (like Turkey), others could not succeed in developing a new governing model; many others came with novel models, like Pakistan—a South Asian 'sovereign state' which became an 'Islamic Republic' in 1956—that came into existence after the independence of India from the British colonialism in 1947 and was created, as the first 'Islamic democratic state'.

Though the concept of 'Islamic democracy' was introduced at the very outset of the twentieth century, yet the discourse gained prominence only from the final decades of last century, especially during the 1980s and 1990s. This impression and notion is shared, among others, by John L. Esposito and John O. Voll (*Georgetown University, USA*), James Piscatori (*Durham University, UK*), Gudrun Kramer (*University of Berlin, Germany*), Noah Feldman (*Harvard University, USA*), Roswitha Badry (*University of Freiburg, Germany*), Nader Hashemi (*University of Denver, USA*), Uriya Shavit (*Tel Aviv University, Israel*), Irfan Ahmad (*Australian Catholic University, Australia*; presently a Senior Fellow at Max Planck Institute, Germany), and many others.

For instance, Esposito and Piscatori, back in 1991, argued that in the Middle East, 'the 1950s and the 1960s were dominated by Arab nationalism and socialism, the 1970s and 1980s witnessed the rise of 'Islamic fundamentalism', challenging secular ideologies', while the 'continued strength of Islamic revivalism in the 1990s and the increased participation of Islamic movements in electoral politics' brought into focus 'the question of the compatibility of Islam and democracy'.[7]

Two years later (in 1993), Kramer asserted the view that Islam–democracy debate 'witnessed some fresh thinking and considerable movement on the ground' from the 1980s, as a growing number of Muslim intellectuals and Islamist activists, 'called for pluralist democracy, or at least for some of its basic elements: the rule of law and the protection of human rights, political participation, government control, and accountability'. In her theory, many speak of *Shura* as 'the idealized Islamic concept of participation-qua-consultation', others refer to 'Islamic democracy', and many others 'do not hesitate to call for democracy'.[8]

Similarly, two years after 9/11, Feldman[9] wrote: 'Can Islam and democracy cohere—either in principle or in practice? This crucial question—debated in scores of Arabic books, articles, and fatwas since the ... 1990—is [in the present times] no longer merely of abstract or regional interest' because it has been debated tremendously, from the mid-1990s, in English works—produced by Muslims and non-Muslims alike—as well. So, in the twenty-first century, it is absurd to perceive and discuss, 'Islamic democracy' as a 'contradiction in terms'.[10] Putting forth another interesting understanding, Badry is of the opinion that 'intensive research' was carried on *Shura* and its harmony with western democracy 'in the 1970s and 1980s', but it failed in advancing any 'theories of an Islamic democracy' that time.[11] Hashemi, in his writings, has put forth the view that though the debate on Islam and democracy emerged after 1980s, but it generated considerable controversy and acrimony from the events of 9/11, and has gained momentum from the 'Arab Spring'.[12]

In a study published in 2010, Shavit too accepts and supports the view—though he traces the origins of contemporary Islamist scholarship on *Shura* and democracy back 'to the end of the 19th century and to the reformist movement in Islam'[13]—that it became a full-fledged discourse in the 1990s: 'The contemporary polemics on the compatibility of Islam and democracy in Muslim-Arab writing was the focus of much scholarly attention in the West as well as in Arab scholarship since the early 1990s'.[14] Irfan Ahmad, almost a decade after 9/11, reiterated that 'the interface between Islam and democracy', which is now an important global debate, 'intensified in the wake of 'Democracy's Third Wave' ending in 1990' (1974–1990); and gave rise, predominantly, to the signature question: Is Islam compatible with democracy?[15]

Providing such a range of references, observations, and positions of some influential voices is indispensable and necessary. The reason is simple: the generally accepted and established trend in the Islam-democracy compatibility discourse—or in comparing the similarities between *Shura* and democratic values—is that the discourse started, referring generally to the works in Arabic and English, from the final decades of twentieth century (1980s and 1990s). However, what is overlooked is that majority of the Muslims live in South (East) Asian regions—with Indonesia, Pakistan, Bangladesh, Malaysia, etc., being the most Muslim populated countries. Furthermore, looking back to early 1900s, especially in the context of the Subcontinent, one realizes that Muhammad Iqbal (d.1938) and Abul Kalam Azad (d.1958), among others, were writing and advocating for the democratization of Islam, as were the modernist thinkers of Middle East, like Jamal al-Din al-Afghani (d. 1897) and Muhammad 'Abduh (d. 1905), etc. For example, Azad—particularly through his weekly magazine *al-Hilal*—emphasized the concept (and interpretations) of *Shura* and labelled it *Islamic democracy*.[16]

Iqbal estimates the significance of *Ijtihad* with an unswerving belief in the egalitarian approach and character of Islam that hardly guarantees any special or distinctive status to clergy or aristocracy. Pertinently, he argued for its democratization and institutionalization in a proper legislative assembly, hence, attempting to hook up the concepts of divine and popular sovereignty. To interpret the democratic ethics in Islam, he introduced the term *'spiritual democracy'* and tried to explain that the concept of *Ijma'* (engaging the consensus of Muslims and Muslim elite) in Islam corresponds with the modern principle of democracy.[17] In his 'Islam as a Moral and Political Ideal', an article published in the *Hindustan Review* (1909), Iqbal asserted that 'best form of Government' for the Muslim community/society 'would be democracy, the ideal of which is to let man develop all the possibilities of his nature by allowing him as much freedom as practicable'.[18]

In the second half of the twentieth century, a large number of books were published on Islam–democracy theme. For example, in his 'Islam and Modern Democracy' (1958), Fauzi M. Najjar (*Michigan State University*, USA) examined the compatibility between 'the basic teachings and institutions of Islam [as a religion and social philosophy]… with the essential teachings and basic assumptions of Western democracy'.[19] In 1980, Najjar explored 'Democracy in Islamic Political Philosophy' by focusing on the works of prominent political philosophers (of the medieval era) like al-Farabi and Ibn Rushd.[20] In 1989, Larry Diamond et al. published a series of books on 'Democracy in Developing Countries' with one volume dedicated to *Democracy in Asia*:[21] in this volume, they provided an 'exhaustive examination of all the historical, cultural, social-economic, political, and international factors that might affect the chances for stable democracy', with case studies from Pakistan, Turkey, Malaysia, and Indonesia, and their 'experiences with democracy'.[22]

Between 1992 and 1993, Bassam Tibi (a German political scientist and Professor of International Relations) explored the concepts and themes of the Islamic system of government (*al-nizam al-islami*), *Shura*-democracy nexus, and the implementation of the *Shari'a* as opposed to secularism (*'ilmaniyya*) in his 'Major themes in the Arabic political literature of Islamic Revivalism, 1970–1985' (published in *Islam and Christian–Muslim Relations*, 1992 and 1993).[23]

Charles Kurzman, in his anthology on *Liberal Islam* (1998),[24] provides an interesting list of writings of Muslims on the compatibility of Islam and democratic government; viz., Indonesian Muhammad Natsir, Humayun Kabir of India, S. M. Zafar of Pakistan, Iranian Mahdi Bazargan, and

Ali Bülac of Turkey.[25] In her *Islam and Democracy: Fear of the Modern World* (1992),[26] Fatema Mernissi (the Moroccan feminist scholar) provides a brilliant analysis and gives religious, philosophical, and historical reasons of the incapability of the Muslim world to put in action a real democracy. Azizah Y. al-Hibri, in her thought-provoking essay, 'Islamic Constitutionalism and the Concept of Democracy' (1992)[27] discussed the role of democracy in the Muslim world. This essay remains so far a well-documented case for the compatibility between *Shariʿah* based (Islamic) and democratic form of governance.

Exploring the relationship between religion and politics generally, Timothy D. Sisk, in his *Islam and Democracy: Religion, Politics, and Power in the Middle East* (1992),[28] examined the global wave of democratization in the late twentieth century, as background to different interpretations of political Islam. Bringing together many of the experts on Middle Eastern politics to analyse the process of democratization in MENA (Middle East and North Africa), Ghassan Salame's *Democracy without Democrats* (1994)[29] was one of the first works to deliberate on modern democracy in the Arab and Muslim world and its connection with Islam. (In 2021, Usaama al-Azami of *University of Oxford* published *Islam and Arab Revolutions—The Ulama between Democracy and Autocracy*, which highlights the role of prominent religious scholars and how they responded to the Arab uprisings of 2011.)[30]

In 1996, John L. Esposito and John O. Voll in their *Islam and Democracy*[31] examined the relationship between Islam and democracy with six case studies—Algeria, Egypt, Iran, Malaysia, Pakistan, and Sudan—and depicted an excellent portrait and representation of the status of democracy in the Muslim world.[32] Two decades later, in 2016, an updated and enlarged version of this book (by Esposito and Voll, along with Tamara Sonn) was published as *Islam and Democracy after the Arab Spring*[33]—revisiting and reconsidering, in the light of the Arab Spring uprisings and their apparent failures, the question of Islamic approaches to democracy by examining the current state of democratization efforts in seven countries as a way of opening further discussion on Islam and democracy in the twenty-first century.

Abdulaziz Sachedina's *The Islamic Roots of Democratic Pluralism* (2001),[34] written subsequently after 9/11, attempted at depicting Islam as a religion or a system with strong potential for sustaining pluralistic, democratic institutions befitting the demands of the twenty-first century and suggested that 'Islam's overlapping social and religious ideals can inspire the creation of pluralistic, democratic institutions in a best Muslim global community of the twenty-first century'.[35] Another significant work published in 2003 was *Islam and Democracy in the Middle East*:[36] Edited by Larry Diamond, Marc F. Plattner, and Daniel Brumberg, it is a collection of essays, published over the years in *Journal of Democracy*, which provide a comprehensive assessment of the struggle for affirming the compatibility of Islam and democracy in MENA (especially). Likewise, Mishal Fahm Al-Sulami in his *The West and Islam: Western Liberal Democracy versus the System of Shura* (2003)[37] analysed the relationship between Western and Islamic political ideas and focused on the similarities and differences between Western liberal democracy and *Shura*. In the same year, *United States Institute of Peace* (USIP)—a Washington-based think tank—published a special report on 'Islam and Democracy', which was an outcome of a workshop (co-sponsored by the *Center for the Study of Islam and Democracy*, Washington), on the same theme. The major questions addressed were: Why the majority of Muslim countries are not democratic? Whether there is an inherent contradiction or incompatibility between Islam and democratic principles?[38] Another important effort on this theme was by Ömer Çaha, 'A Theoretical Discussion on the Compatibility of Islam and Democracy' (2003).[39]

Khaled Abou El Fadl's *Islam and the Challenge of Democracy*—a long essay with brief scholarly responses from a number of scholars (like Esposito, Hashemi, Feldman, Muqtedar Khan, Saba Mehmood, Muhammed Fadl, Bernard Haykel, etc.), later developed into a book (2004)[40]—engages the reader in a rich discourse on the challenges of democracy to the contemporary Muslim world. Massimo Campanini, in 2005, explored the 'Democracy in the Islamic Political Concept', by arguing that 'although democracy is not an 'Islamic' concept, there is an 'Islamic' theory of democracy', and one cannot 'appreciate the notion of Islamic democracy without considering the development of Islamic juridical thought'.[41] Exploring the multi-faceted relationship between Islam and democracy, *Islamic Democratic Discourse* by M. A. Muqtedar Khan (2006)[42] also analyses the democratic discourse in Islam in legal, historical, and philosophical perspectives as well as on regional and global levels.

Similarly, based on Islam's authoritative sources, Sayed Khatab and Gary D. Bouma's *Democracy in Islam* (2007)[43] discusses meticulously the very topical issue of Islam's compatibility with democracy. In an attempt to yield a balanced viewpoint of the burning issue of democracy and Islam in the modern world, it 'sets out to resolve' the question of whether Islam is compatible with democracy, which 'has been a puzzle for some and a source of frustration for others'.[44] Zoya Hasan in her edited work, *Democracy in Muslim Societies: The Asian Experience* (2007)[45] presented a study of six Asian Muslim countries, Pakistan, Bangladesh, Iran, Turkey, Indonesia, and Malaysia, and the process of democratization therein. It seeks to discuss and explore the character of the political transformation and democratic transition as well as assess the extent of actual democratization in these six countries. Azam S. Tamimi's 'Islam and Democracy from Tahtawi to Ghannouchi' (2007)[46] deliberates on the views and visions of Islam and democracy in the thought of some of the prominent modernist thinkers of the Arab world. Taking Iran, Turkey, and Indonesia as case studies, Nader Hashemi in his *Islam, Secularism, and Liberal Democracy* (2009)[47] analyses the theoretical relationship between religion and democracy, specifically Islam's relationship with liberal democracy, in a way that advances theory and practice regarding their relationship.[48] In a similar attempt, Shiping Hua's *Islam and Democratization in Asia* (2009)[49] deliberates on the compatibility of democracy and Islam in the Muslim world and, more specifically, in Asia, covering both theoretical and practical aspects.

There is copious literature—in the form of books, book chapters, papers, essays, etc.—which deliberate on different aspects of Islam–democracy (in) compatibility;[50] some examples, from 2000 to 2021, are: Khurshid Ahmad (2000);[51] Mark Tessler (2002);[52] Fatih A. Abdel Salam (2004; 2005);[53] Mumtaz Ahmad (2005);[54] John O Voll (2007);[55] Asef Bayat (2007);[56] Carole Reckinger (2007);[57] Roswitha Badry (2008);[58] Omar Ashour (2008);[59] Larry Diamond (2010);[60] Haifaa Jawad (2010);[61] Uriya Shavit (2010);[62] Irfan Ahmad (2011);[63] Muhammad Hashim Kamali (2013);[64] Ana Belén Soage (2014);[65] Abdulkadir Mubarak (2016);[66] Md Nazrul Islam and Md Saidul (2017);[67] Thomas Isbell (2018);[68] Alfred Stepan (2018);[69] Khalid Butt and Naeema Siddiqui (2018);[70] Leina McDermott (2019);[71] Md Nazrul Islam and Md Saidul (2020);[72] Halim Rane (2021);[73] and the list continues.

Offering a normative reconceptualization of a modern Islamic governed state, Joseph J. Kaminski, in his *The Contemporary Islamic Governed State* (2017),[74] explores topics of bureaucracy, law, democracy, women in politics, and economic justice, and presents case studies from Turkey, Egypt, Tunisia, and Malaysia. It argues that the 'question of Islam and its compatibility with democracy has been examined in great detail in the past, but has recently taken on new salience'.[75] Paul Kubicek's *Political Islam and Democracy in the Muslim World* (2015)[76] and Md Nazrul Islam and Md Saidul Islam's *Islam and Democracy in South Asia* (2020),[77] yet reflect another endeavours on Islam–democracy compatibility issue. Rather than blaming Islam for the lack of democracy in the Muslim world, Kubicek examines the role of Islam and Islamic oriented actors in several countries of Africa, South and Southeast Asia, and the Middle East (like Turkey, Malaysia, Pakistan, Bangladesh, Mali, Indonesia, and Senegal) of relatively 'successful democratization'. It 'purposefully avoids essentializing Islam as inherently antidemocratic or democratic', and rather than asking 'if and how Islam undermines democracy', the focus and objective of this study are 'to uncover how democracy has taken root in Muslim-majority countries' and, in particular, the role of Islam in this process.[78]

*Islam and Democracy in South Asia*, which focuses on Bangladesh as a case study, presents a 'critical analysis of the complex relationship between Islam and democracy in South Asia and Bangladesh', with two chapters on the theoretical aspects—exploring normative and philosophical viewpoints—of this discourse.[79]

All this indicates, in the words of Halim Rane (*Griffith University, Australia*), that there is 'a long history of Islamic scholarship advocating democracy'[80] and the whole scenario is summarized by him beautifully in these words:

> Democracy in Islam and the Muslim world has been a topic of intense debate among Muslim scholars for well over a century and an area of focused research among Western academics for several decades. The study of democracy in the Muslim world received renewed interest since the Arab Spring in late 2010 and throughout 2011. For many scholars, Muslim and non-Muslim, a central question concerns Islam's compatibility with democracy, including the extent to which

democratic principles exist with the Islamic tradition and also the extent to which Islamic principles can be implemented within a democratic framework. Within these contexts, volumes have been written about Islamic democracy and political Islam, respectively.[81]

There are many other works related to this theme and the process of deliberations and discussions on the issues related to Islam and democracy is going on vis-à-vis the changing world geo-political scenario. At the same time, it is also noteworthy that various scholars and writers—being varied but marginal—have made serious attempts to argue that both are irreconcilable and contradictory. From Francis Fukuyama's thesis on the *End of History*[82] and Benjamin Barber's argument about *Jihad vs. McWorld*[83] to Robert Kaplan's suggestion about the *Coming Anarchy*[84] and, most influentially, Samuel P. Huntington's essay and subsequent book on *The Clash of Civilization*,[85] all have collectively reinforced and strengthened, in different ways, the idea that the Muslim faith and Islamic civilization are incongruent and divergent with liberty, democracy, human rights, gender equality, and other 'emancipator' principles. The opinions of Mark Tessler, Bernard Lewis, Yussef M. Choueiri,[86] and the above-mentioned scholars have been summarized by Md Nazrul Islam and Md Saidul Islam in these lines:

> These scholars argue for Islam's incompatibility with democracy because democracy requires openness, competition, pluralism, and a tolerance of diversity, whereas Islam encourages intellectual conformity and an uncritical acceptance of authority. They also stress that the Islamic tradition does not go in line with democratic ideals because the former vests sovereignty in God, Who is the sole source of political power and from Whose divine law must emanate all regulations governing the community of believers.[87]

While as Elie Kedourie (d. 1992: British historian of the Middle East, University of London), back in the 1990s, asserted the view that

> [T]he notion of popular sovereignty as the foundation of governmental legitimacy, the idea of representation, or elections, of popular suffrage, of political institutions being regulated by laws laid down

by a parliamentary assembly, of these laws being guarded and upheld by an independent judiciary, the ideas of the secularity of the state, of society being composed of a multitude of self-activating groups and associations—all these are *profoundly alien to the Muslim political tradition*. (Italics added)[88]

Islam and democracy discourse has taken new shapes/phases in the second decade of the twenty-first century despite its being in currency in the academic world since 1980s. Notwithstanding the echoing of 1990s debates signifying the antiquated views of some fundamentalist and hardcore Islamists that Islam and democracy are incompatible, majority of the Muslims assume democracy as feasible and suitable. To cut a long story short, Islam–democracy (in) compatibility discourse is still a lively and debatable issue with a global currency: 'there is a long history of Islamic scholarship advocating democracy.'[89]

## The Present Work: Scope and Structure

Political analysts, experts, and academics have significantly contributed to the Islam–democracy discourse over the recent decades. In this regard, while some works deal with this issue considering its future prospectus and other facets, a major portion of the literature studies the reaction, response from or relationship of Islam (and Muslims/Muslim societies) with democracy and democratization, in Muslim majority regions, Asia as well as in the Middle East. Western academics as well as Muslim scholars have been engaged in deliberating and discussing this phenomenon meticulously. However, an overall exploration of the literature produced in this direction reveals the paucity of a compact volume evaluating and discussing the relevant views/deliberations of these experts/analysts/academics (pertaining to Islam–democracy discourse). The current study, hence, attempts to fill this void from an academic point of view.

The prime concern of the current work is to analyse and examine the views of (selected) Muslim scholars of the last-two-and-half-centuries concerning the relationship between the socio-political concepts and institutions of Islam—like *Shura* (mutual consultation), *Khilafah*

(Caliphate), *Ijma'* (consensus), *Ijtihad* (independent interpretive reasoning), *Bay'ah* (oath of allegiance), *Maslaha* (public interest), *Ahl al-Hall wa al-'Aqd* (the 'Wise Ones'), and *Mithaq al-Medina* (the Constitution of Medina), etc.—and the principles of (modern) democracy. The study seeks to bring a meticulous study of the domains of compatibility, consistency, and co-existence between Islam and democracy, meanwhile recognizing the basic difference(s) distinguishing Islamic political thought from the Western concept of democracy.

Consisting of seven chapters, excluding 'Introduction' and 'Epilogue', the present work attempts to tread through diverse theoretical Islamic texts like the Qur'an and the Hadith and other more contemporary works by eminent scholars on the hotly debated issue of Islam–democracy (*in*)compatibility. It endeavours to create a discursive terrain for theorizing the notions of convergence vis-à-vis the notions of divergence inherent in the debates surrounding Islam and democracy. The Introductory chapter contextualizes, with the current trend and scenario, the discourse of Islam–Democracy (*in*)compatibility. In this chapter, the readers will find a comprehensive discussion on Islam–democracy discourse through a concise literature survey—under the heading 'Scope of Islam–Democracy Discourse in the Twenty-First Century'. It also provides an outline of the scope and structure of the work, under the second heading 'The Present Work: Scope and Structure'.

Chapter 1, 'Democracy, Democratization, and the Muslim World' provides, first, a brief conceptual description of 'democracy' as a political system (as it is understood and described by the political theorists) so that to delineate the persisting and prevailing features of democracy. This brief overview helps in contextualizing the necessary framework for finding out the similarities and differences between the two systems under consideration—namely Islam and democracy. This is followed by a discussion on 'defining' democracy in the Islamic context, for which it is important to answer *Whose Islam?* and *What Islam?*; i.e., to deliberate on the varied interpretations of contemporary Islam, and to highlight the Reformist/Modernist interpretation of Islam—that brand, version or description, of Islam which supports the compatibility thesis on the issue under discussion. This helps in understanding, and in contextualizing the 'Process of Democratization and the Islamic Heritage'.

Chapter 2, 'Democratic Notions in Islam', discusses some operational key concepts/institutions of democracy in Islam, like *Shura* (Mutual Consultation), *Khilafah* (Caliphate), *Ijma'* (Consensus), *Ijtihad* (Independent Interpretive Reasoning), *Bay'ah* (Oath of Allegiance), *Maslaha* (Public Interest), *Ahl al-Hall wa al-'Aqd* (the 'Wise Ones'), and *Mithaq al-Medina* (the Constitution of Medina). These 'notions' are regarded, *en masse*, the operational key concepts of democracy in Islam, basis of 'Islamic democracy', and/or the source of an effective foundation for comprehending the relationship between Islam and democracy in the contemporary world. Though the reformists/modernists reinterpret and construe all these notions and norms as the basis of 'Islamic democracy', however, it is the concept and institution of *Shura*, which is considered and reinterpreted (predominantly and indisputably by all) as the central and dominant source of democratic constituent in Islam. Therefore, in this chapter, more focus is on the theory, practice, and modern interpretations of *Shura*—both as a concept and as an institution.

Two major trends have been so far dominating the discourses of Islam–democracy relationship: Compatibility and Incompatibility trend/approach. The advocates of these trends have received specific labels, ranging from 'Proponents' and 'Opponents', and 'Muslim Democrats' and 'Muslim Isolationists', to 'Supporters' and 'Rejectionists'. However, it needs to be asserted that the compatibility trend is most significant and substantial, superseding the influence of the incompatibility approach. The current work focusing mainly on the compatibility trend/approach, dedicates the subsequent four chapters (3–6) to the theme while discussing the incompatibility pole/trend in Chapter 7.

Contextualizing Islam–democracy discourse within the broader context, Chapters 3 and 4, 'Nineteenth and Twentieth Century Muslim Intellectuals on Islam-Democracy Compatibility' deliberate on Islam and democracy reconciliation by providing an assessment of the views of some prominent pioneering Muslim modernists of the last two centuries 'Arab World' and 'South Asia', respectively. Providing a valuable contribution and some important insights to this hotly debated discourse, the prominent Arab thinkers included in Chapter 3 are: Rifa al-Tahtawi (d. 1873), Jamal-Din al-Afghani (d. 1897), Muhammad 'Abduh (d. 1905), Rashid Rida (d. 1935), and Malek Bennabi (d. 1973). The prominent voices, from South Asia, included in Chapter 4 are: Muhammad Iqbal (d.

1938), Abul Kalam Azad (d. 1958), Syed Abu'l Ala Mawdudi (d. 1979), Fazlur Rahman (d. 1988), and Amin Ahsan Islahi (d. 1997). Chapter 4 also includes a brief assessment of the views of scholars of *Traditionalist* bent, especially belonging to 'Deoband' school of thought, including Mawlana Ashraf 'Ali Thanawi (d. 1943), Mufti Shabbir Ahmad 'Uthmani (d. 1949), Mufti Muhammad Shafi (d. 1976), Abdul Majid Daryabadi (d. 1977), and Qari Muhammad Tayyib (d. 1983).

Chapters 5 and 6, 'Twenty-First Century Muslim Thinkers on Islam–Democracy Compatibility' (I and II), in the extension of previous discussions, deliberate on Islam–democracy relationship in the light of the views/interpretations of some globally reputed twenty-first-century academicians, political leaders/activists, and analysts. The selected figures in Chapter 5 include: Mohamed Fathi Osman (d. 2010), Dr Israr Ahmed (d. 2010), Asghar Ali Engineer (d. 2013), Mawlana Wahiduddin Khan (d. 2021), Sadek J. Sulaiman (d. 2021), Yusuf al-Qaradawi (b. 1926), Professor Khurshid Ahmad (b. 1932), Muhammad Khalid Masud (b. 1939), Rachid al-Ghannoushi (b. 1941), Abdulaziz Sachedina (b. 1942), and Abdolkarim Soroush (b. 1945). In Chapter 6, the selected voices are: Javed Ahmad Ghamidi (b. 1951), Abdelwahab el-Affendi (1955), Louay M. Safi (b. 1955), Khaled Abou El Fadl (b. 1963), Radwan Masmoudi (b. 1963), Muqtedar Khan (b. 1966), and Kamran Bokhari (b. 1968). The Islamic political concepts of *Shura*, *Bay'ah*, and Medina Constitution, etc., in their view, serve as the foundations of democratic governance in Islam. Chapter 6, also includes a comparative analysis of nineteenth and twentieth-century modernist thinkers with the intellectuals and analysts of the twenty-first century, under the heading 'A Comparative Analysis: Early Modernists *vs*. Twenty-First Century Intellectuals' in order to underscore the phases and trends, as well as relevance and significance of the Islam–democracy discourse.

Ensuing to the discussion pertaining the Islam–democracy compatibility, Chapter 7, 'Democracy and its Muslim Critics: Objections and Observations of the "Opponents"', assesses the arguments of the rejectionists approach or the 'hard-core'/'radical' Islamist scholars/leaders and organizations who advocate Islam–democracy incompatibility. It brings forth and contextualizes within the broader perspective of Islam–democracy discourse, the views, and approaches of Sayyid Qutb (d. 1966); Taqiuddin al-Nabhani (d. 1977) and Abd al-Qadim Zallum (d.

2003)—both associated with *Hizb al-Tahrir*); academicians like Abdul Rashid Moten (Malaysia); and other writers/analysts like Canada-based Abid Ullah Jan. This is followed by a succinct overview, with a specific focus on the insights of Asef Bayat, Nader Hashemi, Amr Sabet, etc., on *Islam and Democracy: What Is the Real Question?*

An 'Epilogue', culminates the work while furnishing some substantial reflections on this crucial, complex, and hotly debated discourse. The epilogue is meant to deliver a sum and substance of the findings of this study vis-à-vis the challenges (in the contemporary Islamic political thought) ahead.

## Notes

1. Alexis de Tocqueville, *Democracy in America*, translated by Henry Reeve (New York: Vintage Books, 1990), vol. 1, p. 325, as cited in Nader Hashemi, *Islam, Secularism, and Liberal Democracy: Toward a Democratic Theory for Muslim Societies* (New York: Oxford University Press, 2009), p. 5.
2. Hashemi, *loc. cit.*
3. Ibid.
4. Graham E. Fuller, *The Future of Political Islam* (New York: Palgrave Macmillan, 2003), pp. 121–122.
5. The phrase *Muslim Democrats* is borrowed from Muqtedar Khan, 'The Politics, Theory, and Philosophy of Islamic Democracy', in M.A. Muqtedar Khan (ed.), *Islamic Democratic Discourse: Theory, Debates and Philosophical Perspectives* (Lanham, MD: Lexington Books, 2006), p. 153, who uses it for describing those Muslim intellectuals—whether secular or liberal, fundamentalist or hard-line Islamists—'who argue that Islam and democracy are compatible'; while as, those 'who claim that democracy is un-Islamic', and therefore, oppose this compatibility, Khan calls them *Muslim Isolationists* [hereafter cited as Khan, 'The Politics']. This phrase is also used, among others, by Vali R. Nasr, 'The Rise of Muslim Democracy', *Journal of Democracy*, 16, 2 (April 2005): 13–27. In this work, the phrase 'Muslim Democrats', is used loosely for all the Muslim writers (intellectuals/thinkers/academicians/and others) who have written in favour of Islam and democracy or some of its aspects—whether modernists, reformists, secularists or so-called (moderate) Islamists or fundamentalists. Although it may be—and of course is—problematic for using this phrase in general for all those who favour fully or partly (to some extent) Islam–democracy compatibility, here, keeping in view the focus of this work, it makes some sense.
6. This will be further deliberated in the next chapter.
7. John L. Esposito and James P. Piscatori, 'Democratization and Islam', *The Middle East Journal* [*MEJ*], 45, 3 (1991): 427–440, p. 428.

8. Gudrun Kramer, 'Democracy and *Shura*', in Nissim Rejwan, *The Many Faces of Islam: Perspectives on a Resurgent Civilization* (Gainesville, FL: University Press of Florida, 2000), pp. 127–130, p. 127. Originally published as Gudrun Kramer, 'Islamist Notions of Democracy', *Middle East Report* [*MER*], 183 (July–August 1993): 2–8; also reproduced in Joel Beinin and Joe Stork (eds.), *Political Islam: Essays from Middle East Report* (Berkeley: University of California Press, 1997), pp. 71–82.

9. Noah Feldman is presently Felix Frankfurter Professor of Law at Harvard Law School, Chairman of the Society of Fellows, and Founding Director of the Julis-Rabinowitz Program on Jewish and Israeli Law, at *Harvard University* (USA). He specializes in constitutional studies, law and religion, and the history of legal studies. He is the author of nine books, including *After Jihad: America and the Struggle for Islamic Democracy* (New York: Farrar, Straus and Giroux, 2003), *The Fall and Rise of the Islamic State* (Princeton: Princeton University Press, 2012 [2008]) and *The Arab Winter: A Tragedy* (Princeton: Princeton University Press, 2020). For details, see his profile at https://hls.harvard.edu/faculty/directory/10257/Feldman (last accessed on 25 December 2021).

10. Feldman, 'The Best Hope', in Abou El Fadl, *Islam and the Challenge of Democracy*, p. 59. Originally published as Noah Feldman, 'The Best Hope: A response to "Islam and the Challenge of Democracy"', *Boston Review*, 28, 2 (April–May 2003), available online at https://bostonreview.net/issue/aprilmay-2003// (last accessed on 22 May 2022). Here references are from the (2004) book version.

11. Roswitha Badry, '"Democracy" Versus "Shura-cracy": Failures and Chances of a Discourse and Its Counter-Discourse', in Tzvetan Theophanov et al. (eds.), *30 Years of Arabic and Islamic Studies in Bulgaria* (Sofia: University Press St. Kliment Ohridski, 2008), pp. 329–345, p. 342.

12. Hashemi, *Islam, Secularism, and Liberal Democracy, op. cit.*; Idem., 'Islam [and Democracy] since 9/11', in Benjamin Isakhan and Stephen Stockwell (eds.), *The Edinburgh Companion to the History of Democracy* (Edinburgh: Edinburgh University Press, 2012), pp. 441–451; Idem., 'Islam and Democracy', in Esposito and Shahin (eds.), *The Oxford Handbook of Islam and Politics*, pp. 68–88; Idem., 'Change from Within', in Abou El-Fadl, *Islam and the Challenge of Democracy, op. cit.*, pp. 49–54.

13. Uriya Shavit, 'Is *Shura* a Muslim Form of Democracy? Roots and Systemization of a Polemic', *Middle Eastern Studies* [*MES*], 46, 3 (2010): 349–374, p. 350 [hereafter cited as Shavit in *MES*].

14. Ibid., p. 351.

15. Irfan Ahmad, 'Democracy and Islam', *Philosophy and Social Criticism* [*PSC*], 37, 4 (2011): 459–470, pp. 459–460; see also, Samuel Huntington, 'Democracy's Third Wave', *Journal of Democracy* [*JoD*], 2, 2 (1991): 12–34.

16. See, Mawlana Abul Kalam Azad, *Islami Jamhurriyah* [Islamic Democracy] (Lahore: Al Hilal Book Agency, 1956); Azad, *Al-Hilal*, 1, 8 (September 1912): 1, 9; and 3, 1 (2 July 1918): 9–11 (Calcutta, India).

17. See, Muhammad Iqbal, *The Reconstruction of Religious Thought in Islam* (Lahore: Iqbal Academy Pakistan and Institute of Islamic Culture, 1986); John L. Esposito, 'Muhammad Iqbal and the Islamic State', in John L. Esposito (ed.), *Voices of Resurgent Islam* (New York: Oxford University Press, 1983); and Aziz Ahmad, *An Intellectual History of Islam in India* (Edinburgh: Edinburgh University Press, 1969).
18. Shaikh Muhammad Iqbal, 'Islam as a Moral and Political Ideal' (Parts I & II), *Hindustan Review*, Allahabad, India, 20, 119 (July 1909): 29–38 and p. 20, 120 (Aug 1909): 166–171, p. 169, Reprinted in (i) Syed Abdul Vahid (ed.), *Thoughts and Reflections of Iqbal* (Lahore: Sheikh Muhammad Ashraf, 1992); (ii) Charles Kurzman (ed.), *Modernist Islam:1840–1940—A Sourcebook* (New York: Oxford University Press, 2002), ch. 41, pp. 304–313, p. 311 [hereafter cited as Iqbal in *Hindustan Review*].
19. Fauzi M. Najjar, 'Islam and Modern Democracy', *The Review of Politics*, 20, 2 (1958): 164–180, p. 166.
20. Fauzi M. Najjar, 'Democracy in Islamic Political Philosophy', *Studia Islamica*, 51 (1980): 107–122.
21. Larry Diamond Juan Linz and Seymour Martin Lipset (eds.), *Democracy in Asia* (New Delhi, India: Vistaar Publications [A division of Sage], 1989).
22. Ibid., pp. xiii, xiv.
23. Bassam Tibi, 'Major Themes in the Arabic Political Literature of Islamic Revivalism, 1970–1985: The Islamic System of Government (*al-nizam al-islami*), *shura* Democracy and the Implementation of the *Shari'a* as Opposed to Secularism ('*ilmaniyya*)', *Islam and Christian–Muslim Relations* [ICMR] 3, 2 (1992): 183–121 and 4, 1 (1993): 83–99.
24. Charles Kurzman (ed.), *Liberal Islam: A Sourcebook* (New York: Oxford University Press, 1998).
25. References to the respective chapters of Natsir, Kabir, Zafar, Bazargan, and Bulac, are provided in the coming chapters of this work.
26. Fatema Mernissi, *Islam and Democracy: Fear of the Modern World*, (trans.) Mary Jo Lakeland (New York: Addison-Wesley Publishing Company, 1992).
27. Azizah Y. al-Hibri, 'Islamic Constitutionalism and the Concept of Democracy', *Case Western Reserve Journal of International Law*, 24, 1 (1992): 1–27. It was published in book form as well by American Muslim Foundation, New York, 1992.
28. Timothy D. Sisk, *Islam and Democracy: Religion, Politics, and Power in the Middle East* (Washington: United States Institute of Peace, 1992).
29. Ghassan Salame (ed.), *Democracy without Democrats? The Renewal of Politics in the Muslim World* (London & New York: I. B. Tauris, 1994).
30. Usaama al-Azami, *Islam and Arab Revolutions—The Ulama between Democracy and Autocracy* (London: Hurst & Co.; New York: Oxford University Press, 2021).
31. John L. Esposito and John O. Voll, *Islam and Democracy* (New York: Oxford University Press, 1996).

32. Few more English works on Islam–democracy debate, published during the 1990s, include: Esposito and Piscatori, 'Democratization and Islam'; R. al-Solh, 'Islamist Attitudes Towards Democracy: A Review of the Ideas of al-Ghazali, al-Turabi and Amara', *British Journal of Middle Eastern Studies* [*BJMES*], 20, 1 (1993): 57–63; John L. Esposito and John O. Voll, 'Islam's Democratic Essence', *Middle East Quarterly* [*MEQ*], 1, 3 (September 1994): 3–11, available online at http://www.meforum.org/151/islams-democratic-essence (last accessed on 15 June 2010).
33. John L. Esposito, Tamara Sonn, and John O. Voll, *Islam and Democracy After the Arab Spring* (New York: Oxford University Press, 2016).
34. Abdulaziz Sachedina, *The Islamic Roots of Democratic Pluralism* (New York: Oxford University Press, 2001).
35. Ibid., p. 139.
36. Larry Diamond, Marc F. Plattner, and Daniel Brumberg (eds.), *Islam and Democracy in the Middle East* (Baltimore: John Hopkins University Press, 2003).
37. Mishal Fahm Al-Sulami, *The West and Islam: Western Liberal Democracy versus the System of Shura* (New York: Routledge Curzon, 2003).
38. United States Institute of Peace, *Special Report: Islam and Democracy*, 93 (September 2002): 1–12, p. 1.
39. Ömer Çaha, 'Islam and Democracy: A Theoretical Discussion on the Compatibility of Islam and Democracy', *Alternatives: Turkish Journal of International Relations*, 2, 3–4 (2003): 106–134.
40. Abou El Fadl, *Islam and the Challenge of Democracy*, op. cit.
41. Massimo Campanini, 'Democracy in the Islamic Political Concept', *Oriento Moderno*, 24 (85), 2/3 (2005): 343–352, p. 352.
42. Khan, *Islamic Democratic Discourse*, op. cit.
43. Sayed Khatab and Gary D. Bouma, *Democracy in Islam* (New York: Routledge, 2007).
44. Ibid., p. 1.
45. Zoya Hasan (ed.), *Democracy in Muslim Societies: The Asian Experience* (New Delhi: Sage Publications, [in association with] Observation Research Foundation, 2007).
46. Azam S. Tamimi, 'Islam and Democracy from Tahtawi to Ghannouchi', *Theory, Culture & Society*, 24, 2 (March 2007): 39–58 [hereafter Tamimi in *TCS*]; Idem., *Rachid al-Ghannouchi: A Democrat within Islamism* (New York: Oxford University Press, 2001).
47. Hashemi, *Islam, Secularism, and Liberal Democracy*, op. cit.
48. See also, Hashemi in Esposito and Shahin, *op. cit.*, p. 76, in which he argues that there are 'three issues that have been central to the debate on Islam and democracy: (1) the question of Islamism, (2) the role of Western policy, and (3) the question of liberalism'.
49. Shiping Hua (ed.), *Islam and Democratization in Asia* (New York: Cambria Press, 2009).

50. For details, see, Tauseef Ahmad Parray, 'Review of the Literature on Islam–Democracy Compatibility Theme: 1990 to 2009', *Islam & Muslim Societies—A Social Science Journal* [*IMS*], 4, 2 (June 2011), 31 pp, available at http://www.muslimsocieties.org/Vol4-2/Review_of_the_Literature_on_the_Islam.pdf. For a complete list of my previous publications on this theme, see, Parray, Tauseef Ahmad (2010–2020) in the Bibliography.

51. Khurshid Ahmad, 'Islam and Democracy: Some Conceptual and Contemporary Dimensions', *The Muslim World* [*MW*], 90, 1 and 2 (2000): 1–21 [hereafter cited as Ahmad, *MW*].

52. Mark Tessler, 'Islam and Democracy in the Middle East: Impact of Religious Orientations on Attitudes toward Democracy in Four Arab Countries', *Comparative Politics*, 34, 3 (2002): 337–354.

53. Fatih A. Abdel Salam, 'Islam, Democracy and Secularism: The Question of Compatibility', in *Insight Islamicu*s: *An Annual Journal of Studies and Research in Islam* (University of Kashmir, Srinagar, India), 5, 1 (2005): 85–101. Also published as 'The Questions of Compatibility between Islam, Democracy and Secularism', *Tafhim: IKIM Journal of Islam and International Relations*, 1, 3, (2004): 107–127. References are from the *Insights* version [hereafter cited as Abdel Salam in *Insight Islamicus*].

54. Mumtaz Ahmad, 'Islam and Democracy: The Emerging Consensus', *The Journal of Turkish Weekly*, 20 June 2005, http://www.iiu.edu.pk/wp-content/uploads/downloads/ird/downloads/Islam-&-Democracy-Emerging-Concensus.pdf (last accessed on 15 June 2018).

55. John O. Voll, 'Islam and Democracy: Is Modernization a Barrier?', *Religion Compass*, 1, 1 (2007): 170–178.

56. Asef Bayat, *Islam and Democracy: What Is the Real Question?* (Leiden: Amsterdam University Press, 2007).

57. Carole Reckinger, 'Islam and Democracy, an oxymoron?' *Politik*, Forum 272 (December 2007): 21–23.

58. Badry, 'Democracy versus Shura-cracy', in Theophanov et al., *op. cit.*

59. Omar Ashour, 'Democratic Islam? Assessing the Bases of Democracy in Islamic Political Thought', *McGill Journal of Middle East Studies* [*MJMES*], 9, 1 (2008): 7–27

60. Larry Diamond, 'Why Are There No Arab Democracies?', *JoD*, 21, 1 (2010): 93–104

61. Haifaa Jawad, 'Islam and Democracy in the 21st Century', in Gabriele Marranci (ed.), *Muslim Societies and the Challenge of Secularization: An Interdisciplinary Approach* (London: Springer, 2010), ch. 4, pp. 65–81.

62. Shavit in *MES* (2010).

63. Ahmad in *PSC* (2011).

64. Muhammad Hashim Kamali, 'Islam and Democracy', in *Islam and Civilizational Renewal* [*ICR*], 4, 3 (July 2013): 437–439.

65. Ana Belén Soage, 'Shūrà and Democracy: Two Sides of the Same Coin?', *Religion Compass*, 8, 3 (2014): 90–103.
66. Abdulkadir Mubarak, 'Democracy from Islamic Law Perspective', *Kom: Journal of Religious Sciences*, V, 3 (2016): 1–18.
67. Md Nazrul Islam and Md Saidul Islam, 'Islam and Democracy: Conflicts and Congruence', *Religions*, 8, 6 (2017): 1–19.
68. Thomas Isbell, 'Separate and Compatible? Islam and Democracy in Five North African Countries', *AFRO Barometer*, Dispatch no. 118 (14 February 2018): 1–11.
69. Alfred Stepan (ed.), *Democratic Transitions in the Muslim World: A Global Perspective* (New York: Columbia University Press, 2018).
70. Khalid Manzoor Butt and Naeema Siddiqui, 'Compatibility between Islam and Democracy', *South Asian Studies—A Research Journal of South Asian Studies*, 33, 2 (July–December 2018): 513–527.
71. Leina McDermott, 'Exploring the Compatibility of Political Islam and Democracy', *World Outlook [WO]*, 56 (Fall 2019): 110–115.
72. Md Nazrul Islam and Md Saidul Islam, *Islam and Democracy in South Asia: The Case of Bangladesh* (Cham, Switzerland: Palgrave Macmillan/Springer Nature, 2020).
73. Halim Rane, 'Democracy and Muslims', in Ronald Lukens-Bull and Mark Woodward (eds.), *Handbook of Contemporary Islam and Muslim Lives*, 2 vols. (Switzerland: Springer Nature, 2021), ch. 52, pp. 1067–1088.
74. Joseph J. Kaminski, *The Contemporary Islamic Governed State: A Reconceptualization* (London: Palgrave Macmillan, 2017).
75. Ibid., p. 11.
76. Paul Kubicek, *Political Islam and Democracy in the Muslim World* (Boulder, CO: Lynne Rienner Publishers, 2015).
77. Islam and Islam, *Islam and Democracy in South Asia*, op. cit.
78. Kubicek, *Political Islam and Democracy in the Muslim World*, p. 8.
79. For details, see 'Islam and Democracy in South Asia: An Introduction' (ch. 1) and 'Islam and Democracy: A Philosophical Debate' (ch. 4) in Islam and Islam, *Islam and Democracy in South Asia*, pp. 1–23 and pp. 67–101.
80. Rane, in Lukens-Bull and Woodward (eds.), *Handbook of Contemporary Islam and Muslim Lives*, p. 1086.
81. Ibid.
82. Francis Fukuyama, *The End of History and the Last Man* (New York: Free Press, 1992).
83. Benjamin Barber, *Jihad vs. McWorld: How Globalism and Tribalism Are Reshaping the World* (New York: Ballantine Books, 1996).
84. Robert Kaplan, *The Coming Anarchy: Shattering the Dreams of the Post-Cold War* (New York: Vintage Books, 2000).
85. Samuel Huntington, *The Clash of Civilizations and the Remaking of World Order* (New York: Simon and Schuster, 1996). It is pertinent to mention here that during this period, other prominent Western intellectuals who warned of a

coming Islamic threat were Bernard Lewis, 'The Roots of Muslim Rage', *Atlantic Monthly*, 266 (September 1990): 47–60; Idem., 'Islam and Liberal Democracy', *Atlantic Monthly*, 271 (February 1993): 89–98; Giovanni Sartori, 'Rethinking Democracy: Bad Polity and Bad Politics', *International Social Science Journal*, 43 (August 1991): 437–450.
86. Tessler in *Comparative Politics* (2002); Bernard Lewis, *The Shaping of the Modern Middle East* (New York: Oxford University Press, 1994); Youssef M. Choueiri, 'The Political Discourse of Contemporary Islamist Movements', in Abdel Salam Sidahmed and Anoushiravan Ehteshami (eds.), *Islamic Fundamentalism* (Oxford: Westview Press, 1996), pp. 19–33.
87. Islam and Islam in *Religions*, p. 3; Idem., *Islam and Democracy in South Asia*, p. 68.
88. Elie Kedourie, *Democracy and Arab Political Culture* (Washington: The Washington Institute for Near East Policy, 1992), pp. 5–6.
89. Rane, in Lukens-Bull and Woodward (eds.), *Handbook of Contemporary Islam and Muslim Lives*, p. 1086.

# 1
# Democracy, Democratization, and the Muslim World

Prior to initiating the Islam–democracy discourse, it will be more pertinent to elucidate the concept of 'democracy' as understood and explained by the political theorists/scientists. However, this discussion (on democracy) needs to be an outline of the concept rather than an extensive presentation of the historical development of the theories or the diverse forms of democracy as practiced in different societies. The discussion is aimed at establishing a contextual framework to comprehend the similarities and differences between the two political systems under study, that is, the Islamic political thought and democracy.

## Democracy: A Conceptual Description

Of all political concepts, democracy, unquestionably, is one of the most ancient and complex one, for there is no consensus on any of its definitions. Democracy has been discussed as a form of government, of state, of society, a way of life or philosophy, an ethical value system, etc., so no definition of democracy can comprise the vast history that the concept connotes.[1]

The simplest and most commonly accepted meaning (though it is being questioned now)[2] of the term 'democracy' is that it is derived 'from the Greek words demos (people) and kratia (rule or authority), hence "rule by the people".[3] It had its beginning in certain of the city-states of ancient Greece in the fourth century BC, notably in the Athens.[4] The term came into English language in the sixteenth century from the French 'democratie',[5] entailing a political community in which there is some form of political equality among the people.

The term democracy has several meanings in the contemporary usage. Democracy is a form of government in which: (a) the right to make political decisions is exercised directly by the whole body of citizens, acting under procedures of majority rule (known as direct democracy); (b) the citizens exercise the same right not in person but through representatives chosen by and responsible to them (known as representative democracy); and (c) the power of the majority is exercised within a framework of constitutional restraints designed to guarantee all citizens the enjoyment of certain individual or collective rights, such as freedom of speech and religion (known as liberal/constitutional democracy).[6]

According to Carl L. Becker, the term democracy refers primarily to 'form of government by many (people) as opposed to the government by the one', or to the government by 'a tyrant, a dictator, or an absolute monarch';[7] while, for Giovanni Sartori, democracy is a 'principle of legitimacy' which indicates both a 'set of ideals and a political system'. For him, the standard definition provided by most authors describes modern democracy as 'a system based on competitive parties', in which the governing majority respects the 'rights of minorities', and is focused on the concepts of 'representation, majority rule, opposition, competition, alternative government control and like'.[8] Similarly, Gizachew Tiruneh defines democracy as a political procedure that allows the presence of political rights, civil liberties, and a majoritarian decision-making or voting mechanism, and which permits the continuous achievement of a more 'equal distribution of political power'.[9] Abraham Lincoln (1809–1865), the 16th U.S. president—who seemed to be influenced by Greek democracy—in his Gettysburg Address, defined democracy as the 'government of the people, by the people, and for the people'.[10] This statement, though simple and brief, has a deep meaning and a variety of implications. James Bryce, in his modern democracies, describes democracy in its stricter, classical sense, as 'denoting a government in which the will of the majority of qualified citizens rules'.[11]

Thus, democracy is a contested term, and to delimit its scope, it is apt to employ definition of Axel Hadenius: 'a general principle of popular sovereignty, a principle of freedom, and a principle of equality'.[12] The three principles, respectively, reveal that the explicit preferences of the people as the basis of legitimate 'political decision making;' the free and unimpeded will of the people to be expressed in political decision-making; and that all individuals' opinions and preferences should be treated alike and considered as equal.[13]

To show the extent of the various definitions of democracy, it is suffice to refer to certain classifications under which they may be grouped. For instance, M. Rejai categorizes them into four groups:

> Traditionally definitions of democracy have been grouped under two headings: 'normative' (or 'classical') and 'empirical'. The former definitions are primarily concerned with certain values or norms; the latter attempts to describe and explain political reality. Closer examination reveals that, as a third category, a number of definitions are neither strictly normative nor purely empirical but combine elements of the two. This group we shall designate 'normative-empirical'. Finally, a fourth category—'ideological'—is added to the list. It differs from the first three by placing its emphasis on a collective mental outlook, on certain shared beliefs, attitudes, and habits.[14]

Though democracy was not directly instituted in the Middle Ages, many 'democratic ideas' were prevalent throughout the period. In 1215 CE, the Magna Carta[15] opened the door to a 'more democratic system' in England. Nobles forced King John to sign this 'Great Charter that created the English Parliament', or law-making body, and stated that the written laws held a higher power than the king, thereby limiting the power of the Royal family and giving some of that power to the people.[16] Magna Carta is considered as the first document in Western history where the rights of certain individuals were recognized.

It was in the seventeenth and eighteenth centuries that three revolutions—viz., the 'Revolution of 1688' or 'Glorious Revolution' of England[17] the 'American Revolution' of 1776;[18] and 'French Revolution' or the 'Revolution of 1789'[19]—which collectively contributed to the emergence of modern democracy in the western world. Besides these revolutions, many political philosophers also contributed significantly to the emergence of modern democracy by developing their theories. For example, Thomas Hobbes (1588–1679), an English philosopher and political theorist, is best known for his publications on 'individual security and the social contract'.[20] John Locke (1632–1704), an English political and educational philosopher, is viewed as the 'initiator of the Age of Enlightenment and Reason in England and France' as well as an 'inspirer of the U.S. constitution'.[21] Locke developed his theory of 'Social Contract', stating that 'the state of nature' was one of 'peace, equality and freedom'.[22] Baron de Montesquieu (1689–1755), a French philosopher whose major work *The Spirit of Laws* was a major contribution to political theory, abandoned the classical divisions of his predecessors into 'monarchy, aristocracy, and democracy', and produced his own analysis and assigned to each form of government an animating principle: 'the republic, based on virtue; the monarchy, based on honor; and despotism, based on fear'.[23] His theory 'inspired the declaration of the Rights of man and the constitution of U.S.'.[24] Jean Jacques Rousseau (1712–1778), a French politico-philosopher, proposed, through his theory of 'General Will', that all men were 'equal'. His treatises 'inspired the leaders of French revolution'.[25]

These political philosophers/theorists played an important role in popularizing the ideas of constitution, liberty, and democracy. Hobbes and Locke's theory of 'Social Contract'—aiming to preserve the natural rights (of man)—and Rousseau's theory of 'General will' proved a boost for democracy, and Montesquieu theory of 'separation of powers' proved helpful in thwarting autocratic rule.

Larry Diamond et al. mention seven features common to any democracy: individual freedoms and civil liberties; the rule of law; sovereignty resting upon the people; equality of all citizens before the law; vertical and horizontal accountability for government officials; transparency of the ruling systems to the demands of the citizens; and equality of opportunity for citizens.[26] The history of democracy—from past to present—has been summarized, very precisely but comprehensively, in Elliot and Summerskill's *A Dictionary of Politics* as:

> [Democracy is derived] from the Greek *demos*, people, and *kratein*, to rule, meaning government by the people. Democracy may be either direct, ... , or indirect... Direct democracy was practiced in some of the city-states of Ancient Greece; indirect democracy, ... , was developed in England in the 17th century and was imposed on France and North America, as a result of revolution, in the 18th century. [ ... ] Democracy

in the sense of the word generally accepted in Western [context] ... is based on the theory of separation of powers [a principle dividing the powers of government into three branches: legislature, executive, and judicial] ... [and free elections]. [I]n addition to separation of powers and free elections, other characteristics of western democracy are the rule of law ... ; freedom of opinion and speech, freedom of association, and protection from arbitrary interference on the part of authorities.[27]

While as Carl L. Becker summarizes the history of democracy in these lines:

Civilization was already old when *democracy* made its first notable appearance among the small city-states of ancient Greece, where it *flourished brilliantly* for a brief century or two and then disappeared. At about same time... *democracy* appeared in Rome and other Italian cities, but even in Rome it did not survive.... In the twelfth and thirteenth centuries certain favorably placed medieval cities enjoyed a measure of *self-government* but... *Parliamentary government* of England [result of Glorious Revolution of 1688] does not antedate the late 17th century; the great American experiment is scarcely older. Not until the nineteenth century did *democratic government* make its way in any considerable part of the world—in the great states of continental Europe, in America, in South America, in Canada and Australia, in South Africa and Japan. (Italics added)[28]

Democracy, as it has developed in the Western civilization, is considered as a social and political philosophy with moral and economic dimensions and is varied and assorted in theory as well as practice.

Bereft of any globally accepted model, democracy is an *essentially contested concept* as per W. B. Gallie (Walter Byrce Gallie: 1912–1998, Scottish social/political theorist and philosopher).[29] Given the diversity in its connotations, meanings, operational modes, it would be intellectual as well as cultural beyond the pale to advocate of a specific Western model of democracy as an ideal and universally accepted model of polity.

In a nutshell, from its origins to the contemporary times, the concept of democracy has changed and developed in the shade of a variety of social, economic, and politic developments.

## Defining Democracy in the Islamic Context

Emerging roughly in the 1980s, Islam–democracy discourse has engaged both Muslim as well as Western scholars and has been rigorously deliberated and debated over the recent decades. The issue of compatibility between Islam and democracy has led to the appearance of diverse reactions/responses including proponents and opponents or Islamists and modernists. This diversity arises out of the variance in understanding and interpreting the relevant postulates/concepts of the Islamic foundational sources. Eventually, for the opponents, Islam, as *Din* is a perfect/complete code of life with guiding principles relevant to every aspect of life including politics and hence, democracy could hardly be entertained in it. However, the proponents consider that certain political notions and universal values embedded in the basic sources essentially carry democratic nature. For instance, Saba Mahmood[30]—in her response to Abou El Fadl's *Islam and the Challenge of Democracy*[31]—opines:

> Abou El Fadl joins a growing number of scholars who have been writing on this theme in the last three decades [and they fall in different categories]: some of these writers are in the Muslim world and others in Europe and the United States. These thinkers represent a wide spectrum of political perspectives: some support the reformist trend within the Islamist movement (for example, Tariq al-Bishri in Egypt, the Tunisian scholar Rashid al-Ghannouchi... , and Abdolkarim Soroush in Iran), and others espouse a more straightforward secular-liberal line (such as Said Ashmawi in Egypt, Nurcholish Madjid in Indonesia, and Aziza al-Hibri in the United States).... Curiously, in these explorations by Muslim scholars, Islam bears the burden of proving its compatibility with liberal ideals, and the line of question is almost never reversed.[32]

In other words, Muslim discourse on political liberalization and democratization has embraced a broad spectrum of positions and perspectives, because contemporary Muslim intelligentsia disagrees on a unified position on the issue. For Hiafaa Jawad (University of Exeter, United Kingdom),[33] John Esposito,[34] and others, their positions were polarized, and continue to be so, in at least three (3) directions: Secularists, Rejectionists, and Reformists.[35] For Esposito, 'Secularists' argue 'for the separation of religion and the state', as they are in favour of a wholesale adoption of Western liberal system, believing that Islam (as religion) should be separated from politics. 'Rejectionists' (both 'moderate and militant Muslims'), a trend which is represented by those conservative and some radical religious forces that adopt a negative view of any shape or form of democratic system, maintain that democracy is a Western product, and thus should be completely avoided. For them, 'Islam's forms of governance do not conform to democracy'. Extremists and Conservatives, like the 'Rejectionists', condemn 'any [and every] form of democracy as *haram* (forbidden), an idolatrous threat to God's rule and divine sovereignty' (*Hakimiyah*), for they believe that 'popular sovereignty contradicts the sovereignty of God, with the result that the alternative has often been some form of monarchy'.[36]

Muslim reformers/reformist thinkers—the third broad perspective represented by those moderate voices who argue in favour of adopting a middle path: many Muslim intellectuals, academicians, and moderate religious leaders—believe that there is scope for reconciling some Islamic socio-political principles with democratic political order. They 'reinterpret key traditional Islamic concepts and institutions' like *Shura, Ijma', Ijtihad, Maslaha, Ba'yah*, etc., 'to develop Islamic forms of parliamentary governance, representative elections, and religious reform'.[37] And in the contemporary Muslim politics, the reformist interpretation has often been used to legitimatize and justify various forms and systems of government—ranging from monarchy to democracy—and in Esposito's words:

> Throughout history, Islam has proven dynamic and diverse. It has adapted to support the movement from the city-state of Medina to empires and sultanates; ... Islam continues to lend itself to multiple interpretations of government; it is used *to support limited democracy and dictatorship, republicanism and monarchy*.... Islam possesses intellectual and ideological resources that can provide the justification for a wide range of *political models*. (Italics added)[38]

In his scholarly survey of political themes in the Muslim world in the contemporary times, Abdelwahab El-Affendi identifies three categories of Muslim attitudes towards democracy; *those who* (i) enthusiastically supported it and tried to prove its compatibility with Islam; (ii) rejected it as alien to Islamic norms; and (iii) accepted democratic procedures but voiced philosophical objections to aspects of democracy and proposed limits on it to conform with Shari'ah law. It is this last group, which is arguably the largest in number and is most closely identified with mainstream Islamist organizations, whose intellectuals and leaders have extensively written about and wrestled with the question of democracy.[39]

Nevertheless, before deliberating on this discourse in detail, it is necessary here to throw light on the reformist/modernist 'interpretation' of Islam: that is to say, the questions *Whose Islam?*/Islam according to whom?, and *What Islam?*/what interpretation of Islam?—or in John Esposito's lexis *Islam or Islams?* (or 'interpretations of Islam')[40]—need to be answered here, because, in the contemporary world, there are various interpretations of Islam. To be precise, there are multiple faces of contemporary Islam; and 'reformist/modernist' interpretation represents only one strand of a 'complex and multi-layered phenomenon' that collectively constitutes 'Islam'.[41]

## *Whose Islam?* and *What Islam?*: The Multiple Faces of Contemporary Islam

There are different interpretations and ways of living Islam; however, many scholars have broadly categorized these different faces/strands of contemporary Islam, based on the varied interpretations of the Islamic law and Islamic history, into four groups. According to Esposito, these four broad faces of contemporary Islam are secular, conservative (or traditionalist), neo-revivalist (or fundamentalist/Islamist), and neo-modernist/reformist.[42] For William Shepherd and Mehran Kamrava too, contemporary Islam, in the broadest of terms, has four main faces—though their terminology is different from that of Esposito. These are popular Islam, political Islam, fundamental Islam (or Islamic fundamentalism), and intellectual Islam. Intellectual Islam, having its own internal divisions, consists of two broad and fluid strands: 'Conservative'/'Neo-Revivalist' and 'Reformist'/'Modernist'.[43]

It is pertinent to mention here that Abdullah Saeed (*University of Melbourne*, Australia) has identified[44] eight (8) 'broad trends among

Muslims today', based on the 'broad orientations of Muslims today towards law, theological purity, violence, politics, separation of religion and state, practice, modernity or *ijtihad* are taken as a basis for the classification of the trends'.[45] These 'preliminary' categories include: Legalist Traditionalists; Theological Puritans; Militant Extremists; Political Islamists; Secular Liberals; Cultural Nominalists; Classical Modernists; and Progressive *Ijtihadis*.[46] Correspondingly, another noteworthy categorization, and justification of the same, is provided by Meena Sharify-Funk, who puts it as:

> Drawing on nineteenth-century usage of the classical Islamic concept of *islah* ('reform') some scholars construe 'pro-anything Western' interpretations as *'reformist Islam'*. In contrast, those who see open-mindedness with respect to issues such as democratization, civil society development, human rights, and gender equality (to name just a few) as a counterpoint to a broader phenomenon of Islamic extremism use the language of *'moderate Islam'*. Those who believe that these issues are quintessentially modern speak of a *'modernist Islam,'* while still others use such terms as *'liberal Islam', 'critical Islam',* or *'progressive Islam'*. Though the media tend to use all of these labels interchangeably, each of them is laden with implicit theoretical as well as strategic or rhetorical content. (Italics added)[47]

In this work, it is this reformist/modernist strand of Islam vis-à-vis the discourse of political liberalization and democratization in Islam and of Muslim societies/countries that is predominantly highlighted and appraised. What this reformist/modernist Islam is, needs to be answered, because to say simply that 'Islam' *is* and/or *is not* compatible with democracy is perhaps a bit misleading when we consider this simple fact; and, here, it needs some clarification.

## Reformist/Modernist Interpretation of Islam and Its Advocates

Reformist/modernist interpretation of Islam—or Islamic modernist and reformist discourse[48]—represents only a strand of the complex phenomenon that collectively constitutes 'Islam'. The depiction of Islam and its role in human polity propounded by these modernists/reformists branded as *Muslim Democrats*, by Muqtedar Khan, in the context of Islam and democracy compatibility theme[49]—distinguishes them radically from the orthodoxy—the age-old traditional view of Islam emerging in recent years as the dominant version/interpretation among the multitude of interpretations of Islam.[50] Accentuating on 'the need to renew Islam both at the individual as well as community levels', the Muslim modernists/reformists espouse of a 'process of Islamization or re-Islamization that begins with the sacred sources of Islam', the *Qur'an* and the *Sunnah* of the Prophet (pbuh), and more interestingly, 'embraces the best in other cultures'. Articulating of 'a dynamic process', the modernists/reformists aim at bringing a 'new Islamic renaissance (*nahda*)' through a selective and self-critical trajectory.[51] By contrasting 'God's revelation and human interpretations', 'eternal' principles of Islamic law and the 'contingent and relative', or 'immutable principles and regulations that were human constructs conditioned by time and place', the modernists/reformists appear to act as 'more creative and wide-ranging in their reinterpretation of Islam and less tied to the traditional interpretations of the ulama ['*Ulama*: religious scholars]'.[52] Their call for the modernization of Islam distinguishes them from the rest of the strands; and for them, (re) interpretation and innovative *Ijtihad* are cornerstones of a 'dynamic theology'—the essence of true Islam.[53]

Here it may be pointed out that Islam–democracy discourse—or the 'Muslim discourse on political liberalization and democratization'[54]—is just 'one theme of the grand narrative on Islam and the West'. Some of the important themes of this discourse include: the threat of Islam; Islam and its relation with secularism, modernity, development, globalization, pluralism, etc.[55] For Khan,

> The grand narrative on Islam and the West has posited several binaries to distinguish between essentialized notions of Western and Islamic civilizations. Both Muslim as well as Western historians and political commentators have meticulously constructed narratives about 'the Islamic civilization' and 'the Western civilization', and in these endeavors their dominant strategy has been to identify, highlight and even exaggerate real and perceived differences between the two cultural

and historical entities. Interestingly secular as well as religious scholars from both sides are involved in maintaining this discourse of difference. The only exception are the Islamic modernists [and/or reformists, who] ... break away from the grand narrative to register their dissent through appreciation of democracy and arguing that there is more in common between Islam and the West.[56] They insist that what Islam and West share is vast and profound in comparison to what separates them.[57]

The central goal that these reformist Muslim thinkers[58] have set for themselves is to 'reformulate and reinterpret' popular notions of Islam in ways that are consistent with and supportive of the tenets of modern life. To put in other words, their central goal is to make Islam relevant by articulating a jurisprudence that addresses contemporary issues and concerns. Islam is not the problem, they maintain, and neither is modernity. The problem is with 'mutually exclusive interpretations' of Islam and modernity. Such interpretations, they claim, are fundamentally wrong.[59] And as 'democracy' is an integral part of modernity and a challenge for Islam, it is in this direction, that Islam and democracy discourse is so important and so recurrent.

Before going into details, here it is necessary to point out that although throughout the previous few decades, the proponents of the Islam–democracy compatibility have been debating the link between Islam and democracy, and the process of democratization in Muslim societies, etc.; but in recent years, and especially after the events of 9/11, and the subsequent policy of 'war on terror', this trend started 'to gain supremacy, respect and broad grassroots support as a result of its genuine and rational efforts to find a suitable solution to the relationship between Islam and democracy';[60] and has thus not only intensified but is still going on with much fervour and eagerness.

Another reason is that Islam is the world's second-largest religion globally as well as in Europe, and the third-largest religion in America, having its followers all through the globe—with 57 majority Muslim-populated countries worldwide, including Indonesia, Malaysia, Bangladesh, Pakistan, Egypt, Iraq, Nigeria, Turkey, etc.[61] That is, the 'world of Islam is "global": "its capitals and communities are not only Cairo, Damascus, Mecca [Makkah], Jerusalem, Istanbul, Islamabad, Kuala Lumpur, and

Jakarta but also London, Paris, Marseilles, Bonn, New York, Detroit, and Washington.'[62] But in the post-9/11 world, Islam has been frequently used and described as a 'violent/terrorist' religion having the least concern with peace, human rights, justice, tolerance, pluralism, democratic values, etc., and in the words of Haifaa Jawad,

> The equation of Islam with political violence, ..., the unquestioned and uncritical accusations of Islam as a religion that advocates dogmatism and prohibits pluralism and freedom of expression, provoked widespread discussion (within and outside Muslim world) about the relationship between Islam and democratic principles. It also raised critical questions about the place of tolerance, human rights issues, and the role of religious leaders in Islam and Muslim countries. Currently these issues have become the focal points of worldwide public debate.[63]

Although the crisis of the events of 9/11 was very severe and relentless in its implications for the Muslim world, it did nonetheless pave the way for constructive internal debate among Muslim scholars throughout the Muslim lands, employing the Arabic saying *Something good can come out from something bad* and indeed that is what has happened, argues Jawad; as serious Muslim intellectuals and scholars have decided to take the matter into their own hands in an attempt to come up with credible solutions to the whole issue.[64] In the words of Oliver Roy, since the so-called war on terror started with the dramatic events of 9/11, a previously scholarly debate has entered the public discussion in the form of 'reductionist' question: Is Islam compatible with secularism and hence democracy?[65]

## The Process of Democratization and the Islamic Heritage

In the Islamic tradition, concepts and institutions like *Khilafah, Shura, Ijma', Ijtihad*, etc., values and legal principles like freedom, justice, equality, human rights, peace, tolerance, public welfare, etc., are utilized by scholars for providing an effective foundation of democracy in Islam— or 'Islamic democracy'. In other words, efforts are being made to develop

'Islamic forms of parliamentary governance, representative elections, and religious reform'.[66] Throughout the world—from Asia to MENA, and from Europe to America—the majority of the modernist/reformist Muslim intellectuals accept the *'term'* democracy—its positive features and values—and insist on consistency and compatibility between Islam and democracy with a re-interpretation of Islamic political key concepts and values, institutions and legal principles, embedded in the primary sources of Islam—the Qur'an and the Prophet's *Sunnah*; albeit democracy here is conceived with certain qualifications and limits prescribed by the Islamic Law (*Shari'ah*).

In the last few decades, religious resurgence and democratization are two of the major developments. Although the Muslim world's debate over democracy, as well as its definitions and fundamentals, has continued for a long time, it has acquired an impetus in recent years. Over the past two decades or so, it has emerged as a highly influential and debated discourse among some prominent Muslim thinkers all over the Muslim world; and as Esposito puts it:

> Questions about the compatibility of Islam and democracy have, then, been contentious issues in recent decades among rulers, policymakers, religious scholars (*ulema* ['*Ulama*]), Islamic activists (Islamists or fundamentalists) and intellectuals in the Muslim world and the West. And these questions have grown in importance in recent decades, as diverse sectors of society—[of diverse (ideological) orientations and of different positions, like] secular and religious, leftist and rightist, educated and uneducated—have increasingly used democratization as a basis for judging the legitimacy of governments and political movements.[67]

In the discourse of Islam–democracy relation, many questions are raised, and some of them—which are common and frequent as well as significant and important—are:

- Is democracy compatible with Islam?
- Is there any relation between Islam and democracy? If yes, then
- What elements are present in Islamic tradition in the service of democracy?
- On what grounds are Islam and democracy compatible?

From an Islamic perspective, discussing or deliberating democracy and the concept of democratic participation hardly necessitates that the term/concept 'democracy' has its origins in the foundational texts of Islam. However, this implies that (i) the Islamic tradition contains (some universal) notions/concepts, values, and institutions that justify and serve as the Islamic perceptions of democracy; and (ii) the positive characteristics of democracy—for example, the rule of law, government responsibility, the general welfare, freedom, justice, equality, and human rights—likewise, find much correspondence and compatibility with Islamic spirit and legacy. Such and many other principles are inherent in an Islamic political setup, as Khurshid Ahmad pleads:

> The Islamic political order is based on the concept of *Tawhid* [Monotheism/Unity of Allah] and seeks its flowering in the form of popular vicegerency (*Khilafah*) operating through a mechanism of *Shura* [mutual consultation], supported by the principles of equality of humankind, rule of law, protection of human rights including those of minorities, accountability of the rulers, transparency of political processes and an overriding concern for justice in all its dimensions: legal, political, social, economic and international.[68]

This also infers that the political and sociological foundations of the modern democratic system are compatible with Islam.[69] Such an approach dealing with the Islam–democracy compatibility relegates the typical dry and limited lexical or linguistic connotations to oblivion. Here, in its wider context, democracy is characterized with certain merits: (i) towards the self, (ii) towards the other, and (iii) a combination of the sociopolitical conditions that are necessary for world peace, international relations, and the formation and development of the welfare of individuals and society. Democracy has three main perspectives as per Malek Bennabi (d. 1973)—a remarkable twentieth-century Algerian Muslim thinker: 'as a feeling toward oneself, as a feeling towards others, and as a cluster of social and political conditions necessary for the formulation and the blossoming of similar feelings in the individual'.[70]

There are many definitions, interpretations, and connotations of the term 'democracy' in the modern world. Democracy, as discussed above, is a concept, which is no doubt universally accepted, but there is not a universally accepted model/variant of democracy. That is, '"democracy", as it has developed in the context of Western civilization and polity, is neither a monolithic concept nor a totally uncontested one. It is more appropriate to suggest that democracy remains a multi-faced phenomenon, both at the conceptual as well as operational levels'.[71] In a nutshell, no definition of democracy can comprise the vast history that the concept connotes. In fact, the term 'democracy' is capable of multiple interpretations and applications and on the basis of its contested nature Gallie calls it an 'essentially contested concept'.[72] In this contested nature of democracy, throughout the world, scholars and analysts are actively involved in the efforts to create a more effective democratic structure(s) of democracy.

The same challenge is facing the Muslims currently as the Muslim intellectuals have rigorously embarked upon interpreting and elucidating democracy in light of Islamic tradition and ethos. Their efforts are meant to concretize a reliable and viable Islamic form of democracy for which they take recourse to the age-old Islamic traditions, notions, and concepts including among others, *Shura, Khilafah, Ijtihad, Bay'ah,* and *Maslaha*—considered as the pivotal concepts of Islamic polity. Islam–democracy discourse, thus, engages 'a broad spectrum of perspectives ranging from the extremes of those who deny a connection between Islam and democracy to those who argue that Islam requires a democratic system'.[73] The latter extends the argument that under the conditions of the contemporary world, 'democracy can be considered' not only 'a requirement of Islam', but is 'an appropriate way to fulfill certain obligations of the faith in the contemporary world' as well.[74]

There are various scholars/thinkers who have actively engaged in defining, discussing, debating Islam, its institutions, systems, and concepts vis-à-vis the modern challenges (and 'Islam and democracy' being one of them); and writing prolifically on Islamic doctrines, law, politics, science, and economics. The Islamic modernist movements and their legacy produced 'generations of reformers', throughout the Muslim world, especially from the Middle East to South Asia: Jamal al-Din Afghani and Muhammad 'Abduh in the Middle East to Sir Syed Ahmad Khan, Muhammad Iqbal, and Abul Kalam Azad in South Asia. The major 'founders of neorevivalist movements from the pioneers (Hasan al-Banna, Mawlana Abul Ala Mawdudi, and Sayyid Qutb) to present-day movements' constituting the 'backbone [and moral fiber] of the second and third generation of Muslim intellectuals and activists across the Muslim world'; among them: Sudan's Hassan al-Turabi and Sadiq al-Mehdi; Tunisia's Rachid al-Ghannouchi; Iran's 'Ali Shari'ati and Abdulkarim Soroush; Algeria's Dr Ali Abbassi al-Madni; Pakistan's Professor Khurshid Ahmad; Egypt's Hasan Hanafi, M. Saleem al-'Awwa; Malaysia's Mohammad Kamal Hasan, Osman Bakar, and Anwar Ibrahim; Indonesia's Dr Nurcolish Madjid, and Abdurrahman Wahid, etc.[75]

This broad spectrum does provide important insights into understanding the 'complex' relationship between Islam and democracy in the contemporary world. 'Despite the great dynamism and diversity among contemporary Muslims', as Esposito and Voll put it, 'there are core concepts that are central to the political positions of virtually all Muslims'.[76] In other words, contemporary Muslim scholars present certain concepts from within the Islamic tradition as the 'operational' key concepts of democracy in Islam; and what 'varies' is 'the definition of the concepts—not recognition of the concepts themselves'.[77] Most politically conscious people around the globe express their aspirations for political participation, freedom, and equality in terms of democracy. The issue of democratization is contested globally and has become the dominant discourse of politics. In this regard, for example, Esposito and Voll put forth this argument:

> In theory, there may be a number of methods for *increasing participation of the people in government* and for providing a sense of viable popular empowerment. However, at the end of the twentieth century, the *most widely accepted way* of expressing these desires is the *demand for democracy*. It is the broad heritage of concepts and images associated with *democracy* that provide the *foundations for democratic revolutions* and movements around the globe. (Italics added)[78]

It is, however, imperative to mention here that while defining democracy from an Islamic perspective, Muslim scholars have different perceptions about its precise meaning and connotation. The general perception, for them, is that Islam and democracy are compatible, because 'if by democracy is meant a system of freedom, justice, equality and human rights, [then, in that framework] Islam has the inclination and capacity to work them better',[79] and that the Islamic teachings already contain these values and systems. In fact, these values are essential, crucial, and basic to Islam. In other words, these values and systems are innate and inbuilt in Islam, for the primary sources of Islam throw sufficient light on them. According to Khurshid Ahmad, if democracy means the right of a people to 'self-determination and self-fulfillment' that is what Islam and Muslims have been striving for, nothing more and nothing less. The real democratization, in his view, means giving the people a chance to freely fashion their affairs according to their ideals and ambitions and aspirations.[80]

Similarly, according to Fateh A. Abdel Salam (International Islamic University Malaysia), as the 'pure idea of democracy... is the government of the whole people by the whole people, equally represented', so it means that 'the people have the opportunity of accepting or refusing the men who are to rule them'.[81] Ahrar Ahmad (Black Hills State University, USA) is of the opinion that as democracy is a 'contested concept', so its 'meanings, practices, and outcomes' are very different. Therefore, he suggests that considering the 'spirit' than merely the 'process' of democracy, 'the relationship between Islam and democracy... is not inherently problematic even by Western standards'.[82]

For Abdelwahab El-Affendi (Doha Institute of Graduate Studies, Qatar), democracy means: (i) 'the self-rule of the people through their freely chosen institutions and representatives';[83] (ii) 'a system of government in which all members of the community are permitted to participate in public decision making in some manner found acceptable to all or to the majority';[84] and (iii) 'a stable system of governance, which seeks to guarantee the widest possible degree of political participation on equal terms'.[85] Furthermore, he adds that the 'substantive values' like 'liberty, equality, tolerance, public spiritedness', etc., are essentials of democracy, and it is on the basis of these values that he finds 'an *Islamic alternative to liberal democracy*' not only 'conceivable, [but] even desirable' as well. (Italics added)[86]

Furthermore, in his *Principles of State and Government in Islam*, Muhammad Asad (1900–1992; formerly Leopold Weiss, who lived in Pakistan and Spain) states that terms like 'democracy' are used 'within the context of Western historical experience', which reveal the fact that 'many of the political terms current today', including democracy, 'bear a meaning different from that originally given to them'. For him, 'concept of democracy', literally 'rule of, or by, the people' (people = citizens) for its originators (the Greeks), is 'vastly different from that' and is used for the 'socio-economic equality of all citizens' (a sense given by the French Revolution).[87] He thus views democracy as perfectly compatible with Islam:

> Viewed from this historical perspective, 'democracy' as conceived in the modern West is infinitely nearer to the Islamic than to the ancient Greek concept of liberty; for Islam maintains that all human beings are socially equal and must, therefore, be given the same opportunities for development and self-expression.[88]

For Egyptian-American legal-theologian, Khaled Abou El-Fadl (UCLA, USA)—one of the leading authorities in Islamic law in the United States and the world—in a democracy, 'the people are the source of the law, and the law in turn ensures the fundamental rights that protect the well-being and interests of the individual members of the sovereignty'. For him, though 'democracy poses a formidable challenge' for Islam, but at the same time, 'democracy is an ethical good, and that the pursuit of this good does not require abandoning Islam'.[89] He also emphasizes that 'the Qur'an does not specify a particular form of government' but identifies 'a set of social and political values that are central to a Muslim polity', including 'pursuing justice through social cooperation and mutual assistance', establishing 'consultative method of governance; and institutionalizing mercy and compassion in social interactions'. These are the values that are central to (constitutional) democracy.[90] He, very eloquently, argues that

> My central argument ... is that democracy—by assigning equal rights of speech, association, and suffrage to all—offers the greatest potential for promoting justice and protecting human dignity, .... A fundamental Qur'anic idea is that God vested all of humanity with a kind of divinity by making every person the viceroy of God on this earth [Q. 2: 30].... In particular, human beings, as God's vicegerents, are responsible for making the world more just. By assigning equal political rights to all adults, democracy expresses that special status of human beings in God's creation and enables them to discharge that responsibility.[91]

Furthermore, he sees democracy as 'an appropriate system for Islam because it both expresses the special worth of human beings—the status of vicegerency—and at the same time deprives the state of any pretense of divinity by locating ultimate authority in the hands of the people'.[92] And for Nader Hashemi, democracy is 'a system of political organization that fundamentally implies a horizontal relationship among individuals in society'.[93] These arguments will be developed and deliberated in the next chapter through an examination of the Islamic text (the Qur'an), Traditions (the Prophetic sayings and practices), and a deliberation of some key concepts and institutions of Islamic tradition.

## Notes

1. Literature on democracy is vast. Some of the major works that have been consulted here are G. B. Forrest, *The Emergence of Greek Democracy: The Character of Greek Politics, 800-400 B.C.* (London: World University Library, 1966); David Held, *Models of Democracy*, 3rd ed. (Cambridge: Polity Press, 2006); Robert A. Dahl, *A Preface to Democratic Theory* (Chicago: University of Chicago Press, 2006); Ricardo Blaug and John Schwarzmantel (eds.), *Democracy: A Reader* (New York: Columbia University Press, 2000); W. Y. Elliot and N. A. McDonald, *Western Political Heritage* (New York: Prentice-Hall, 1949); George H. Sabine, *A History of Political Theory*, 3rd ed. (New York: Holt, Rinehart, and Winston, 1961); Carl L. Becker, *Modern Democracy*, 10th ed. (New Haven: Yale University Press, [1941], 1951); Axel Hadenius, *Democracy and Development* (Cambridge: Cambridge University Press, 1992); V. Bogdanor (ed.), *The Blackwell Encyclopedia of Political Institutions* (New York: Basil Blackwell, 1987); Gizachew Tiruneh, 'Democracy', in William A. Darity Jr. (ed.), *International Encyclopedia of the Social Sciences*, 2nd ed. (Detroit: Macmillan/Thomson Gale Group, 2008), pp. 272–276; 'Democracy' in *The New Encyclopedia Britannica*, 15th ed. (Chicago: Encyclopedia Britannica, Inc. 1994), IV: 5 [hereafter cited as *EB*[15]]; Harold J. Laski, 'Democracy', in Edwin R. A. Seligman (ed.), *Encyclopedia of the Social Sciences*, Rep. (New York: The Macmillan Company, 1935 [1923]), V: 76–84.

2. For example, John Keane, *The Life and Death of Democracy* (London: Simon and Schuster, 2009), p. 113, locates the origins of democracy not in Greece but in the ancient assemblies of the Middle East. Calling for a rethinking of the roots of democracy he argues that 'democracy of the Greek kind had eastern roots and that therefore in a very real sense today's democracies are indebted to the first experiments in self-government by assembly of "Eastern" peoples traditionally written off as incapable of democracy in any sense' (p. 113), also cited in Nader Hashemi, 'Islam and Democracy', in John L. Esposito and El-Din Shahin (eds.),

*The Oxford Handbook of Islam and Politics* (New York: Oxford University Press, 2013), pp. 68–88, p. 69.
3. Bogdanor, *op. cit.*, p. 166.
4. 'Democracy' in *EB*[15], IV: 5.
5. Held, *op. cit.*, p. 1.
6. 'Democracy' in *EB*[15], *loc. cit.*
7. Becker, *op. cit.*, p. 6.
8. Giovanni Sartori, 'Democracy', in David L. Sills (ed.), *International Encyclopedia of the Social Sciences* (New York: The Macmillan Company and The Free Press, 1968), IV: 112.
9. Tiruneh, in Darity, *op. cit.*, II: 275.
10. Abraham Lincoln, 'The Gettysburg Address', in Blaug and Schwarzmantel, *op. cit.*, p. 91.
11. James Bryce, *Modern Democracies* (New York: Macmillan, 1931), I: 22.
12. Hadenius, *op. cit.*, p. 9.
13. Ibid.
14. Mostafa Rejai, *Democracy: The Contemporary Theories* (New York: Atherton Press, 1967), p. 23.
15. The full text of the *Magna Carta* (*The Great Charter*) is available at https://archives.gov/files/press/press-kits/magna-carta/magna-carta-translation.pdf (last accessed 21 May 2022).
16. Ibid.
17. See, for example, 'Glorious Revolution', *Encyclopædia Britannica (EB)*, available online at https://www.britannica.com/event/Glorious-Revolution (last accessed on 20 August 2018).
18. See, for example, Willard M. Wallace, 'American Revolution', *Encyclopædia Britannica (EB)*, available online at https://www.britannica.com/event/American-Revolution (last accessed on 20 August 2018).
19. See, for example, 'French Revolution: 1787–1799', *Encyclopædia Britannica (EB)*, available online at https://www.britannica.com/event/French-Revolution (last accessed on 20 August 2018); see also, 'Declaration of Independence [1789]', in *EB*[15], VI: 283–84; 'Rights of man and of citizen, Declaration of the', in *EB*[15], X: 68.
20. 'Hobbes, Thomas' in *EB*[15], 5: 959–960.
21. 'Locke, John' in *EB*[15], 7: 435.
22. Vide, Sabine, *A History of Political Theory*, pp. 527–532; Muhammad Shafiq, *Islamic Concept of a Modern State* (Lahore: Islamic Book Foundation, 1987), p. 90.
23. 'Baron de Montesquieu' in *EB*[15], 8: 284.
24. Ibid. See also, Sabine, *op. cit.*, pp. 558–559.
25. 'Rousseau, Jean Jacques', in *EB*[15], 10: 210.
26. Larry Diamond, et al., *Democracy in Developing Countries* (London: Adamantine Press, 1988), pp. 218–260.
27. Florence Elliot and Michael Summerskill, *A Dictionary of Politics* (Baltimore & London: Penguin Books, 1981), p. 84.

28. Becker, *op. cit.*, p. 10.
29. W. B. Gallie, *Philosophy and the Historical Understanding* (London: Chatto and Windus, 1964), p. 158.
30. Saba Mahmood, 'Is Liberalism Islam's Only Answer? [A Response to Abou El-Fadl's *Islam and the Challenge of Democracy*]', in Khaled Abou El Fadl, *Islam and the Challenge of Democracy: A Boston Review Book*, Joshua Cohen and Deborah Chasman (eds.) (Princeton and Oxford: Princeton University Press, 2004), pp. 74–77, pp. 74–75.
31. Cohen and Chasman, *Islam and the Challenge of Democracy*.
32. Mahmood, in Cohen and Chasman, *Islam and the Challenge of Democracy*, p. 74–75.
33. Haifaa Jawad, 'Islam and Democracy in the 21st Century', in Gabriele Marranci (ed.), *Muslim Societies and the Challenge of Secularization: An Interdisciplinary Approach* (London: Springer, 2010), pp. 65–81.
34. See, John L. Esposito, 'Contemporary Islam: Reformation or Revolution?', in John L. Esposito (ed.), *The Oxford History of Islam* (New York: Oxford University Press, 1999), ch. 15, pp. 643–690 [hereafter cited as Esposito, 'Contemporary Islam']; Idem., *Unholy War: Terror in the Name of Islam* (New York: Oxford University Press, 2001); Idem., 'Practice and Theory', in Abou El Fadl, *Islam and the Challenge of Democracy, op. cit.*, pp. 93–100.
35. See, Jawad in Marranci, *op. cit.*, pp. 65, 67, 69, and 70; Esposito, 'Contemporary Islam', p. 675. Esposito, in his *Unholy War*, p. 145, repeats almost the similar views, but divides them into five categories, viz., 'Secularists', 'Rejectionists', 'Extremists', 'Conservatives', and 'Reformers' (Reformists), wherein the approach of 'Rejectionists', 'Extremists', and 'Conservatives' is similar vis-à-vis Islam–democracy discourse; Idem., 'Practice and Theory', in Abou El Fadl, *op. cit.*, pp. 96–97.
36. Esposito, *Unholy War*, p. 145; Idem., 'Practice and Theory', p. 96.
37. Esposito, *Unholy War*, p. 145.
38. Esposito, 'Practice and Theory', pp. 95–96. *Cf.* Esposito, 'Contemporary Islam', p. 675.
39. Abdelwahab El-Affendi, 'On the State, Democracy and Pluralism', in Suha Taji-Farouki and Basheer Nafi (eds.), *Islamic Thought in the Twentieth Century* (New York: I. B. Tauris, 2004), pp. 180–203; Idem., 'The Modern Debate(s) on Islam and Democracy', *The Asia Foundation*, 2010, available online at https://westminsterresearch.westminster.ac.uk/item/90331/the-modern-debate-s-on-islam-and-democracy-a-literature-review (last accessed 15 June 2021). Affendi's views have been summarized by, and I cite from, Hashemi, 'Islam and Democracy', in Esposito and Shahin, *op. cit.*, p. 73.
40. John L. Esposito, *The Future of Islam* (New York: Oxford University Press, 2010), p. 11.
41. Mehran Kamrava, 'Introduction: Reformist Islam in Comparative Perspective', in Mehran Kamrava (ed.), *The New Voices of Islam: Reforming Politics and*

*Modernity—A Reader* (New York and London: I. B. Tauris, 2006), p. 3 [hereafter cited as Kamrava, 'Reformist Islam'].
42. Esposito, 'Contemporary Islam', p. 681.
43. For details, see, William Shepard, 'The Diversity of Islamic Thought: Toward a Typology', in Taji-Farouki and Nafi (eds.), *Islamic Thought in Twentieth Century*, p. 63; see also, Kamrava, 'Reformist Islam', pp. 6, 13–15. In the following pages, in this context, the terms 'Reformist(s)' and 'Modernist(s)' are used interchangeably.
44. For details, see, Abdullah Saeed, 'Trends in Contemporary Islam: A Preliminary Attempt at a Classification', *Muslim World [MW]*, 97 (July 2007): 395–404. *Cf.* Idem., *Islamic Thought: An Introduction* (London: Routledge, 2006), pp. 142–154.
45. Saeed in *MW*, p. 396.
46. Ibid., pp. 397–403. For example, among the scholars discussed in this work, he labels Jamal al-Din al-Afghani and Muhammad Abduh as 'Classical Modernists', Fazlur Rahman as 'Neo-Modernist' (and Rahman along with Khaled Abou El-Fadl and Tariq Ramadan, as 'Progressive *Ijtihadis*'), Yusuf al-Qaradawi as 'a legalist traditionalist thinker', and Syed Abu'l Ala Mawdudi as a 'mainstream political Islamist'. Saeed, *Islamic Thought*, pp. 139, 143, 144; Idem., in *MW*, pp. 397, 400, 401, 402.
47. Meena Sharify-Funk, 'From Dichotomies to Dialogues Trends in Contemporary Islamic Hermeneutics', in Abdul Aziz Said, Mohammed Abu-Nimer, and Meena Sharify-Funk (eds.), *Contemporary Islam: Dynamic, Not Static* (Oxon and New York: Routledge, 2006), ch. 4, pp. 64–80, p. 65.
48. Though both terms have different connotation, however, here I am relying on the definition/terminology used by Charles Kurzman in his *Modernist Islam: A Sourcebook* (New York: Oxford University Press, 2002). For Kurzman, the early 'modernist' Muslims (e.g. Afghani, Abduh, Rida, and Sir Sayyid), distinguished by distancing themselves from the 'secularists', like 'Ali Abd al-Raziq (d.1966), who 'downplayed the importance of Islam in the modern world, privileging nationalism, socialism, and other ideologies', and differentiating themselves from the 'religious revivalists', like Hasan al-Banna (d. 1949), Syed Qutb (d.1966), and Abul 'Ala Mawdudi (d.1979) 'who espoused modern values… but downplayed their modernity, privileging authenticity and divine mandates'. Later, in the twentieth century, the 'combination of modernist and Islamic discourses was revived in a subset of modernist Islam', labelled by Kurzman as '*Liberal Islam*', which sought 'to resuscitate the reputation and accomplishments of earlier modernists'. See, Charles Kurzman, 'Introduction: The Modernist Islamic Movements', in Kurzman (ed.), *Modernist Islam*, p. 4; Idem., (ed.), *Liberal Islam*. Herein, Kurzman regards the second wave of reform as 'subset of modernist Islam' or 'neo-modernist', which includes figures like Allama Iqbal, Fazlur Rahman, etc. In this context, in this section, I have used the terms modernist and reformist alternatively.

See also, Tauseef Ahmad Parray, 'Muslim Reformist Thought in 21st Century and Its Broad Themes: A Brief Study of "Democratic Pluralism" in the light of

A. Sachedina's *"The Islamic Roots of Democratic Pluralism"*, *Islam and Muslim Societies—A Social Science Journal* [IMS], 4, 2 (2011): 12 pages, available online at http://www.muslimsocieties.org; Idem., 'Exploring Nejatullah Siddiqi's Contribution to the *Maqasid al-Shari'ah* in the Urdu Literature', in *American Journal of Islamic Social Sciences* [AJISS], 34, 1 (Winter 2017): 80–103, 97.

49. M. A. Muqtedar Khan, 'The Politics, Theory, and Philosophy of Islamic Democracy', in M. A. Muqtedar Khan (ed.), *Islamic Democratic Discourse: Theory, Debates and Philosophical Perspectives* (Lanham, MD: Lexington Books, 2006), p. 153.
50. Ibid.; See also, Tauseef Ahmad Parray, 'Globalization, Democracy, and Muslim World: Some Contemporary (Theoretical) Perspectives', *Journal of Society in Kashmir—Annual Journal of Department of Sociology, Kashmir University* [JoSK], 4 (2014): 1–20, p. 7.
51. Esposito, 'Contemporary Islam', p. 684.
52. Ibid.
53. Kamrava, 'Reformist Islam', p. 14.
54. Esposito, 'Contemporary Islam', p. 675.
55. Khan, 'The Politics', pp. 149–150.
56. Khan, on this point, relies on these works: Kurzman (ed.), *Liberal Islam*; John Cooper, Ronald Nettler, and Mohmed Mahmoud (eds.), *Islam and Modernity: Muslim Intellectuals Respond* (London: I. B. Tauris Publishers, 1998)
57. Khan, 'The Politics', p. 149.
58. For a list of personalities/thinkers of this group, and their writings, see, for example, Cooper, et al. (eds.), *Islam and Modernity*; John L. Esposito and John O. Voll, *Makers of Contemporary Islam* (New York: Oxford University Press, 2001); Kurzman (ed.), *Liberal Islam*; Idem., *Modernist Islam*; Kamrava (ed.), *The New Voices of Islam*; Shireen T. Hunter (ed.), *Reformist Voices of Islam—Meditating Islam and Modernity* (New York: M.E. Sharpe, Inc., 2009).
59. Kamrava, 'Reformist Islam', p. 15.
60. Jawad, *op. cit.*, p. 70.
61. John L. Esposito, *What Everyone Needs to Know about Islam*, 2nd Ed. (New York: Oxford University Press, 2011 [2002]), p. 4.
62. Ibid., p. xvi.
63. Jawad, *loc. cit.*
64. Ibid.
65. Oliver Roy, *Secularism Confronts Islam* (New York: Columbia University Press, 2007).
66. Esposito, *Unholy War*, p. 145.
67. Esposito, 'Practice and Theory', p. 94.
68. Ahmad, *MW*, p. 2.
69. These ideas and insights are borrowed from Khattab and Bouma, *op. cit.*
70. Malek Bennabi, *La Democratie en Islam* [Islam and Democracy] (Alger: Mosquee de Beni Messous, n.d.), p. 10 [hereafter cited as Bennabi, *LDI*], as quoted by

Yahya H. Zoubir, 'Democracy and Islam in Malek Bennabi's Thought', *AJISS*, 15, 1 (Spring 1998): 107–111 [hereafter Zoubir, *AJISS*]. The English translation is of Zoubir.
71. Ahmad, *MW*, p. 1.
72. Gallie, *op. cit.*, p. 158.
73. John L. Esposito and John O. Voll, 'Islam and Democracy', *Humanities*, 22, 6 (November/December 2001), available online at www.artic.ua.es/biblioteca/u85/documentos/1808.pdf (last accessed on 21 May 2022).
74. Ibid.
75. Esposito, 'Contemporary Islam', pp. 680–681.
76. Esposito and Voll, *Islam and Democracy*, p. 23.
77. Ibid.
78. Ibid., p. 13.
79. Khattab and Bouma, *op. cit.*, p. 40.
80. Ahmad, *MW*, p. 20.
81. Fatih A. Abdel Salam, 'Islam, Democracy and Secularism: The Question of Compatibility', *Insight Islamicus: An Annual Journal of Studies and Research in Islam*, 5, 1 (2005): p. 86.
82. Ahrar Ahmad, 'Islam and Democracy', *AJISS*, p. 22.
83. Abdelwahab El-Affendi, 'Rationality of Politics and Politics of Rationality: Democratization and the Influence of Islamic Religious Traditions', in Azzam Tamimi and John L. Esposito (eds.), *Islam and Secularism in the Middle East* (London: C. Hurts and Co., 2000), pp. 151–169, 168.
84. Abdelwahab El-Affendi, 'Democracy and Its (Muslim) Critics: An Islamic Alternative to Democracy', in Khan (ed.), *Islamic Democratic Discourse: Theory, Debates and Philosophical Perspectives* (Lanham, MD: Lexington Books, 2006), pp. 227–256, 247.
85. Abdelwahab El-Affendi, 'The Modern Debate(s) on Islam and Democracy'. Available online at https://westminsterresearch.westminster.ac.uk/item/90331/the-modern-debate-s-on-islam-and-democracy-a-literature-review (last accessed on 15 June 2021).
86. Affendi, 'Democracy and Its (Muslim) Critics', pp. 243, 254.
87. Muhammad Asad, *The Principles of State and Government in Islam* (Berkeley and Los Angeles: University of California Press, 1961), pp. 18–19.
88. Ibid., p. 20.
89. Abou El Fadl, *Islam and the Challenge of Democracy*, pp. 4, 5.
90. Ibid., p. 5.
91. Ibid., pp. 5–6.
92. Ibid., p. 36.
93. Nader Hashemi, *Islam, Secularism, and Liberal Democracy: Toward a Democratic Theory for Muslim Societies* (New York: Oxford University Press, 2009), p. 10.

# 2
# Democratic Notions in Islam

Islam, as the Muslims believe, is a divine Religion (*Din*) and complete code of life that guides humankind in all aspects and spheres of life—social, political, economic, intellectual, spiritual, etc. Every aspect of human life, according to Islam, is *Tawhid*-centric, and without *Tawhid* (Unity/Unicity of Allah or Monotheism),[1] 'Islam is unthinkable'.[2] Likewise, in addition to being 'the core of religious experience', *Tawhid* is the quintessence of Islam, the principle of history, of knowledge, of ethics, of aesthetics, of the *Ummah*, of the family, of the political, social, economic, and world orders. Precisely, *Tawhid* is the basis and heart of Islam's comprehensive worldview.[3] Considering the doctrine of *Tawhid* as the bedrock of Islam and 'a dynamic belief and a revolutionary doctrine', Khurshid Ahmad argues that it points to the 'supremacy of the law in the cosmos' and presents a 'unified view of the world and offers the vision of an integrated universe'.[4]

The Islamic political theory, an intrinsic component of Islam as a 'system', is also based on the concept of *Tawhid*, seeking its flowering in the form of *Khilafah*; administered through the process of *Shura*; supported by certain values and principles like justice, equality, public welfare, the rule of law, human rights, the accountability of the rulers, the transparency of political processes; etc.[5] Despite this fact, there have been significant attempts by the experts, as pointed out previously, to locate the similarities and contradictions between the two while exploring various concepts and ideas pertaining to the Islam-democracy discourse. For a better understanding of this discourse, this chapter expounds and explains in detail some operational key concepts/institutions of democracy in Islam, like *Shura* (Mutual Consultation), *Khilafah* (Caliphate), *Ijma'* (Consensus), *Ijtihad* (Independent Interpretive Reasoning), *Bay'ah* (Oath of Allegiance), *Maslaha* (Public Interest), *Ahl al-Hall wa al-'Aqd* (the 'Wise Ones'), and *Mithaq al-Medina* (Constitution of Medina).

## Operational Key Concepts of Democracy in Islam

There are various notions—ideas and ideals—which are considered as the operational key concepts, and/or crucial to determine the main ideals of 'Islamic democracy'. These notions are also used by modernists for conceptualizing a conceivable, feasible, and possible foundation of democracy in Islam. All these notions and norms are (re)interpreted in a way to provide an effective foundation for comprehending the relationship between Islam and democracy in the contemporary world. Besides these, the principles and values of elected rulers, consultative bodies, accountability, tolerance, justice, equality, freedom, human rights, public welfare, and the rule of law—many of which are the watch-words of modern democracy—are not unknown, unfamiliar or new, to Islam but are embedded and rooted in the very primary sources of Islam. Contemporary Muslim scholars propound these concepts not only as the 'foundations for the Islamic perceptions of democracy', but as the basis of the process of 'democratization in Muslim societies' as well.[6] For Ahrar Ahmad, 'Islamic doctrine, as embedded in the text and traditions, is conducive to democratic thought in many compelling ways'.[7] He argues that

> The insistence on the equality of all believers, the emphasis on individual responsibility, the encouragement of consultative rule, the protection of private property, the requirement of establishing justice and pursuing the public interest, the celebration of learning, and the tolerance toward other faiths (particularly the revealed religions) are all strongly indicative of *substantive democracy*. (Italics added)[8]

These concepts and notions, from *Shura* to *Mithaq al-Medina*, have been elucidated and expounded in the following sections:

### *Shura* (Mutual Consultation)

The term *Shura,* derived from the Arabic root *sh-w-r,* has a broad spectrum of meanings, including 'mutual consultation', 'consultative decision-making', or the decision-making process of the Muslim community.[9] The

Arabic root *sh-w-r* connotes to make a thing known, point to a thing or to point out, to gather opinions, give a word of good counsel, to consult, consultation. *Shura* has 'a broad spectrum of meanings, including mutual to consult, mutual consultation, opinion, to express opinions with each other, consideration, advice, counsel, conference, and deliberation and discussions with other individuals or groups or "the decision-making process of the Muslim community"'.[10] *Shura*, as mutual advice or deliberation, is no more than a procedure of making decisions. It can be defined as the procedure of making decisions by consultation and deliberation among those who have an interest in the matter on which a decision is to be taken, or others who can help them to reach such a decision. In the Islamic political thought, *Shura* refers to the deliberations conducted with the aim of collecting and discussing different opinions on a particular issue in order to reach a fruitful decision. For Patricia Crone, *Shura*, a 'highly distinctive institution', is 'a procedure leading to a decision by people in charge of government'.[11]

Many scholars have deliberated on the meaning and context of the word *Shura*. For Mufti Muhammad Shafi, the Arabic words, '*Shura, mashwarah,* and *mashawarat* (counsel, consultation and mutual consultation) all mean the soliciting of advice and counsel in something that needs deliberation'.[12] For Amin Ahsan Islahi, *Shura* means 'taking deliberation from each other';[13] and for Asma Afsaruddin, it refers 'to an electoral council or a consultative body'. In her analysis, the predominant attitude and approach in the literature (whether theological, juridical, ethical, or administrative) is that '*shura* as mutual consultation in various spheres (political, communal, social, military, familial) is the preferred and desirable method of resolving matters'.[14] In the political jurisdiction, it is often considered as a 'duty incumbent on the ruler to confer, deliberate and discuss' with knowledgeable advisors.[15]

In the modern times, *Shura*—a concept, an idea, and a political institution—is considered as the source of democratic ethics in Islam; or is central to the Islamic democracy; and/or the very basis of democratic government in Islam. It is a direct outcome of the theory of vicegerency and the basic spirit of Islamic society. Therefore, what follows next is a brief historical development of this concept/institution, from pre-Prophetic times to the present, both in theory and practice.

## *Shura* in Theory and Practice

The root *sh.w.r.* occurs three (3) times in the Qur'an, each in a different form: as *tashawur*, a verbal noun meaning 'consultation', in Q. 2: 233; as *shawirhum*, an imperative meaning 'consult with them', in Q. 3: 159; and as *Shura*, it occurs in Q. 42: 38.[16] On each occasion, the attestation is related to important issues in human life; and as such has, as noted in the *Encyclopedia of the Qur'an*, important implications for social and political theory.[17] For Okvath and Iqbal, in *Integrated Encyclopedia of the Qur'an (IEQ)*, 'Consultation is the act of drawing forth of another's opinion, advice, counsel, or command'.[18]

Although the word *Shura* does not find any direct attestations prior to those in the Qur'an, yet, before the emergence of Islam, the Arabs engaged in practices of social and political deliberation, 'and a number of towns in Arabia had their own 'councils' where affairs of common interest were discussed and settled'.[19] That is, the Arab tribes of the pre-Prophetic period 'had a loosely-formed council of elders known as *shura* (also known as *majlis* or *mala*') which adjudicated intra- and inter-tribal matters by consultation'.[20] This council system of pre-Islamic Arabia has been described by S. A. Q. Husaini in these words:

> Among the desert-dwellers every clan or tribe in Pre-Islamic Arabia was nominally ruled by its own elder or Shaykh: but the Shaykh had to make his decisions in a Council of the Elder of the clan or tribe. Though the Council was not elected, ... , it acted as a check upon the arbitrary power of the Shaykh. ... The method [of election] by which the chief of the tribe or the 'Council' was elected cannot be expressed in terms of modern political although the vocabulary of modern political phraseology. The tribesmen got together and they talked, and eventually an opinion, emerged from their talk which was the opinion of all of them. The process can only be called selection by acclamation.[21]

The appointment of *Shaykh*, predominantly, 'was for life, but the position was not hereditary'; and this kind of *Shura* council can be, in modern terminology, considered as 'a primitive parliament, in that it elected and supervised the work of the executive power (the sheikh [*Shaykh*]) as well as representing the different view within the tribe (although an effort was made to arrive at decisions by consensus)'.[22] However, the chief (*Shaykh*) of the tribe was not the only person who 'controlled the tribal affairs', there was, besides him, 'a council beside him known as 'the tribe's council'.[23] And this was, as al-Sulami puts it, 'the basic political situation in pre-Islamic Arabia and the main elements of political order'.[24]

In Makkah, which had a superior position over other cities in the region of Hijaz, the Quraysh tribe had a meeting house, a kind of town hall known as *Dar al-Nadwah* (the council hall or the 'parliament' house or the 'Senate'), which was built by Qusay bin Kilab (d. 480 CE), who, in the fifth century CE made himself the master of Makkah, and gradually of whole Hijaz.[25] Established with the purpose of permitting people to participate in conducting the affairs of the Makkans, this 'council hall' was the gathering place of the nobles (*Mala'*) where 'all matters of import to the Quraysh' are said to have taken place up to the coming of Islam: 'marriages, councils of war, advice on public matters' as well as 'bestowing of standards of war'. It was also regarded as the point of departure and return of all Makkan trade caravans. According to Syed Amer Ali, Qusayy erected for himself 'a palace in which the principle chamber was used as a council-hall [hence the name *Dar al-Nadwah*] of the people, for the transaction of public business'. Qussay also made 'rules for the proper government of the people, for raising taxes and supplying food and water to the pilgrims who came from many parts of Arabia' to worship at the Kab'ah/Ka'ba. It was called so because Quraysh used to convene there to deliberate on issues of social and political concern; and it was an initial stage of a 'parliamentary system of government' in which the delegates of the Quraysh used to meet and decide their important affairs with mutual consent.[26]

In *Dar al-Nadwah*, consultations were held for wars and treaties and foreign guests were entertained. In fact, a number of different deliberations were conducted in this meeting house, including the consideration of the issues related to marriage, matters of commerce, and war and peace. The council used to meet only on occasions required, and not at regular intervals. The Hall consisted of the 'representatives of the different clans', each in charge of a 'particular portfolio, like *Siqaya*, *Liva* and

*Imarah*', etc.[27] The decisions on important problems and matters were taken by these representatives (of the clans) in a very free and cooperative atmosphere. According to Ibn Hisham, the Quraysh never decided on any important matter without consultation. To decide important matters, they used to meet together in the *Dar al-Nadwah* and decide.[28] Apart from this council house or senate, in Makkah, there were as many 'ward councils or communes' as there were tribes or clans, known as '*nadi*— corresponding to the *Saqifah* of Medinite tribes'.[29]

## The Qur'anic Attestations

The three attestations and evidences—i.e. the verses wherein the word *Shura*, or its other forms occur (as in Q. 2: 233; 3: 159; and 42: 38)—relate to different situations and categories of Muslims. These describe the most important issues of human life, and in the sense of consultation, it has 'important implications for social and political theory'.[30] All these instances (especially Q. 3: 159 and 42: 38) reveal the 'social and political dimensions of consultation' as well as demonstrate its inevitability at the individual and collective levels. As noted by, among others, Ahmad Mubarak al-Baghdadi (in the *Encyclopedia of the Qur'an*), reference in Q. 2: 233 applies particularly 'to the potential controversy between two divorced partners concerning the matters of weaning [or giving up of sucking of] an infant'; Q. 3: 159 is a 'special text related to the Prophet Muhammad [pbuh] in the shadow of occurrence of battle of Uhud' in which the Muslims suffered a reverse and nearly lost the battle and Q. 42: 38 applies 'to all Muslims'.[31] Among these, for instance, Q. 42: 38 suggests that in true consultation, the view adopted is communal, and the decisions made are shared in common rather than made by a single individual. The verse Q. 3: 159 is viewed as a foundational principle in Islamic government and leadership, and in the relationship between Muslim rulers and their subjects.[32]

These attestations show—as Ahmad al-Raysuni observes in his *Al-Shura: The Qur'anic Principle of Consultation*—that 'Consultation is a necessity in connection with private affairs, including issues pertaining to the individual, the individual in relation to other individuals, between husbands and wives, and parents and their children, and is clearly vital regarding public affairs and the major issues they raise'.[33]

All these instances (verses) reveal that Shura is both unavoidable in political life of the Muslims and is an invariable requirement in all walks of social and community life. For example, when the Qur'an narrates the issues and problems related to the matter of weaning, it gives due importance to the mutual consent. The verse proclaims: '*If they both decide on weaning, by mutual consent, and after due consultation* (tashawur), *there is no blame on them*'.[34] Abdullah Yusuf Ali, in the explanation of this verse, writes:

> As this comes in the midst of the regulations on divorce, it applies primarily to cases of divorce, where some definite rule is necessary, as the father and mother would not, on account of the divorce, probably be on good terms, and the interests of the children must be safeguarded. As, however, the wording is perfectly general, it has been held that the principle applies equally to the father and mother in the wedlock: each must fulfill his or her part in the fostering of the child. On the other hand, it is provided that the child shall not be used as an excuse for driving a hard bargain on either side. By mutual consent they can agree to some course that is reasonable and equitable.[35]

The second verse in which the root *sh.w.r.* occurs is Q. 3: 159, which states: '*Consult with them* (shawirhum) *about matters, then, when you have decided on a course of action, put your trust in God*'.[36] This verse gives a direct order to the Prophet (pbuh) in the context of an event in the Medinan society. It refers to the battle of Uhud. The verse has been of central interest both to the exegetes and general scholars alike.[37] The wisdom in this verse is that Allah commands the Prophet (pbuh) to consult the believers in the worldly affairs and governmental matters and to respect the opinion of the majority (of them). For example, Mufti Muhammad Shafi, in its interpretation, writes:

> '*and consult them in the matter*' means that the holy Prophet (pbuh) is to seek their [Companions] advice in matters of concern so that they are fully satisfied and emotionally at peace, as the Messenger of Allah (pbuh), by following this instruction, will be giving an external form to his intention of doing what is good for them. Thus, the acts of his asking them to sit in the consultations with him will an act of mollifying grace.[38]

For Islahi, in this verse (3: 159) along the guidelines of seeking Allah's forgiveness, the Prophet (pbuh) is advised to consult the Companions in matters requiring deliberation. Regarding religious matters, the Prophet (pbuh) was not in need of consultation as he was guided by Revelation. But in political and administrative matters, the Prophet (pbuh) used to consult Companions constantly. In this way, he himself laid the foundations of the institution of *Shura* (*Shurai'yat*), which has been an important feature of the Islamic political system.[39]

Ibn Abbas relates that when the verse '... *and consult with them in the matter*' was revealed, the Prophet (pbuh) explained, 'Beware Allah and His Messenger do not need it, but Allah has bestowed His mercy upon my ummah. One who consults the people never loses the right guidance, and one who ignores it is prone to misguidance'.[40] For Shafi, the expression '*wa Shawirhum fi-l Amr*' (and consult them in the matter) in the present verse means that the Prophet (pbuh) has been commanded to consult with or seek advice of his Companions in matters that need deliberation, which include those of authority and government.[41]

The special import of this verse worth considering, as highlighted by M. Yusuf Faruqi, is that the Qur'an adopted a distinctive approach of illustration by mentioning the *Shura* in between the two fundamentals of Islam—*Salah* and *Zakah*—which demonstrates the significance of the institution of *Shura* in socio-political life. It does not mean that the *Shura* is one of the pillars of Islam; however, the style of its description provides ample evidence of its special importance in the Islamic polity.[42] Azad and Mawdudi share the same view, arguing that 'in this verse, the Prophet (pbuh) is commanded to take deliberation from or consult the Companions in the matters of importance.'[43]

Finally, the word '*Shura*' occurs in 42: 38, which reads: '*conduct their affairs by mutual consultation (Shura)*'.[44] In this verse, Allah praises those Muslims who conduct their affairs through consultation; i.e. one of the best qualities and attributes of true believers is that they conduct their affairs by mutual consultation. The expression *wa amruhum Shura baynahum* means that in every matter which needs deliberation, whether it belongs to the field of authority and government or to something important other than these, the customary practice of the true Muslims is that they work through mutual consultation.[45]

Here *Shura* is understood in the context of verses 37–39 (of Q. 42) as one of a series of attributes of Muslims: they shun great sins and indecencies, forgive when angry, answer their Lord and persevere in Prayer. Their rule is to consult one another, spend out of what God provides and, when tyranny affects them, defend themselves. Almost all the *Mufasirrun* (Exegetes) have made a detailed discussion on this verse. For example, Azad writes:

> To take consultation or deliberation from each other is one of the best qualities of Muslims mentioned in this verse and the Prophet (pbuh) is commanded to take consultation from the Companions in Q. 3: 159. Except Obligatory Commandments (*ahkam al-nasusah*), the Prophet (pbuh) used to take and accept the deliberation of the noble Companions on every matter related to state and administration. Later *Shura* was made the very basis of [government during the period of the] Pious Caliphate. Abu Bakr was selected under the same procedure which proves that Islamic social order is a pillar of Islamic way of life, having peculiar importance in it.[46]

Mufti 'Uthmani, in its interpretation, writes that 'Allah likes working through deliberations, whether in worldly affairs or in religious ones. Regarding the matters of importance, the Prophet (pbuh) used to take counsel from the noble Companions. The Companions not only deliberated with one another on matters of war (*hurub*) and about other issues and Commandments (*Masa'il wa ahkam*), but the very foundation of Pious Caliphate was laid on the [principle of] *Shura*'.[47]

In the *tafsir* literature, one comes to know that *Shura* (consultation) is described and detailed as 'one of the foremost rule of law in the Islamic system of political administration and social set up. The institution of *Shura*, the intrinsic component of Islamic Polity, plays a cordial role in the socio-political system as it discusses most important issues of human life.'[48] In the words of Asma Afsaruddin,

> The predominant sentiment in the literature is that *shura* as mutual consultation in various spheres (political-administrative, communal, military, [and] familial) is the preferred and desirable method of

resolving matters. In the political realm, it is often considered a duty incumbent on the ruler to confer [deliberate and discuss] with knowledgeable advisors.[49]

The verses 3: 159 and 42: 38, especially, have been debated significantly, but variedly. There has been substantial debate among Muslim commentators surrounding the context and the meaning of this command. On the basis of these Qur'anic injunctions, modern Muslim scholars and theorists (whether traditionalists, modernists/reformists, or Islamists in orientation) venerate *Shura* as the example *par excellence* of Islam's inherent democratic impulse. Resonating the way to just and consultative power-sharing in contrast to arbitrary despotism (*istibdad*), 'the concept of *Shura* is conflated with modern notions of democracy—and thus it becomes *first and foremost key operational concept and element* in the relationship between Islam and democracy—or "Islamic democracy"'. (italics added)[50] In the words of Abdullah Saeed, *Shura* is 'a central concept in contemporary Muslim political thought' which is seen not only as the 'foundation for thinking about governance in an Islamic context', but is (re)interpreted and regarded as being 'very closely connected to the kind of ideas, values, and institutions of democracy and participatory systems of governance' and thus 'akin to democracy and democratic institutions'.[51] Or as Asma Afsaruddin, in her *Contemporary Issues in Islam*, puts it, 'the principle of *shura* or consultation, endorsed in the Qur'an as the basis for collective decision-making and administration of public affairs' is generally understood, in the present times, 'to provide the conceptual grounding for consultative governance and collective decision-making.'[52]

## Attestations in Ahadith (and Sunnah)

The Prophet (pbuh) explained and elucidated the principle of *Shura* to his Companions on many occasions and expounded on its practical implications in diverse ways. There are many *Ahadith* (Prophetic Traditions) with regard to the counselling and *Shura*, which throw light on the nature, purpose, and importance of it, in both public and private matters. Some of these are mentioned below:

Khatib Baghdadi narrates the following statement of Caliph 'Ali (RA): 'I asked the holy Prophet (pbuh) that if, after you, we face a situation about which neither the Qur'an has any specific ruling nor have you given any direction, how should we proceed?' The Prophet (pbuh) replied by saying: 'In such a situation, assemble the *'abidin* (Pious or God-fearing people) of my *Ummah*, and decide the matter by mutual consultation; do not take decision on any single individual's opinion'.[53]

Baihaqi has narrated in *Shu'ab al-Iman* on the authority of Ibn 'Umar (RA) that the Prophet (pbuh) said: 'Anyone who intends to do something, and he takes that action after consultation, Allah would guide him towards the best possible option'.[54] Jaber (RA) narrates that the Prophet (pbuh) said: 'When anyone from you seeks counsel from his brother, he should give his advices'.[55]

In compliance with the verses of the Qur'an (3: 159 and 42: 38), the Prophet (pbuh) invariably consulted the Companions, and on a few occasions when serious matters had to be decided, he summoned the general assembly of all Muslims. In all the military expeditions (*Futuhat*), the Prophet (pbuh) consulted his Companions. It was also the general practice of the Prophet (pbuh) to consult his Companions on all public matters.[56] For example, the Prophet (pbuh) consulted his Companions regarding the battle of Badr,[57] Uhud,[58] Ahzab,[59] campaign of Khaybar;[60] and at the event of Treaty of Hudaibiyyah, etc.[61] Thus, the Prophet (pbuh) often took counsel with his Companions on important matters, as well as in affairs of state. Among these, the consultation taken at the time of battle of Uhud (and as attested by Q. 3: 159) is considered 'one of the solid pieces of evidence showing the importance of the majority as a procedure of decision-making to resolve public affairs'.[62]

Consultations on other matters of communal interest—religious as well as social—were also frequently held during the Prophet's (pbuh) period. For example, the establishment of the institution of *Adhan* (call to the prayer),[63] the selection of the site for the Prophet's (pbuh) Mosque at Medina (*Masjid al-Nabawi*),[64] and the establishment of the fraternity (*Mua'khat*) were also made after consultation.[65]

Thus, the Prophet (pbuh) used to consult his Companions so much that Abu Hurairah (RA), the most prolific *hadith*-narrator, says: 'I have never seen anyone more consulting with his Companions than the Messenger of Allah (pbuh) himself'.[66] This summarizes the practice of *Shura* during the Prophetic period.

## Shura under the Rightly-Guided Caliphs (632–660 CE)

During the Prophet's (pbuh) time, 'the Revelation and the Sunna[h] continued developing, providing answers to the Muslims' doubts and queries'.[67] But after his demise, the Caliphs followed his footsteps to settle the community affairs, not only through mutual consultation, but they devised other methods as well. The Companions established the *Khilafah* immediately after Prophet's (pbuh) demise. This was the paramount issue facing the *Ummah*, which was settled with mutual consultation and Abu Bakr was chosen as *Khalifah* after a long discussion between the *Muhajirun* and the *Ansar* at *Saqifah* of Bani Sai'dah. The example, thus, set up by the Prophet (pbuh) was fully followed by the Rightly Guided Caliphs. The extent to which they followed the Islamic system of *Shura*, if studied in the light of authentic texts, would lead one to the conclusion that not only did these Caliphs follow the *Sunnah* but also gave it a concrete shape.

The procedure through which all the four caliphs were selected and elected was truly democratic and consultative in nature, although the procedure—methods of selection and approval—differed and varied in form, from the selection of one caliph to another, from Abu Bakr to Ali; and in the words of Abdul Rashid Moten:

> They resorted to a two-stage process of instituting a successor: (1) consultation, nomination, and selection by the representatives of the Ummah (*al-bay'ah al-khassah*), and (2), subsequent confirmation by the public through general acclamation or *al-bay'ah al-'ammah*. The first caliph, Abu Bakr, was selected by the notables and confirmed by the general *bay'ah* in the year 11 AH/632 CE. The second caliph, 'Umar, was nominated by the incumbent in the consultation with the leaders of the Ummah and was then referred to the general public for confirmation in 13 AH/634 CE. The third caliph, 'Uthman, was nominated by an electoral college and subsequently ratified by the Ummah in the year 23 AH/644 CE. On the assassination of the third caliph and the

ensuing chaos, the representatives of the Ummah approached 'Ali to assume the leadership position. 'Ali, however, insisted on the approval of the masses and was elected by accordingly in the year 35 AH/656 CE. These modes of succession were inspired by the Qur'anic principle of *Shura*. These have acquired a special significance and remained a basic principle of the constitutional theory of an Islamic political order.[68]

Thus, the Righteous Caliphate, in short, was characterized by 'an *elected republican constitutional government* based on the rule of law (*political democracy* and *Shari'ah* nomocracy); socio-economic egalitarianism (*social and economic democracy*); and the altruistic Shari'ah binding personality of the ruling elites (*ethical democracy*)'. (Italics added)[69]

Abu Bakr, after assuming the chair of *Khilafah*, discharged his political responsibilities and decided on collective affairs, which were not dealt with in the Qur'an and the Sunnah, through consultation with the major Companions who enjoyed the confidence of the majority Muslims and who were considered best among their peers in knowledge and piety. The following tradition recorded in *Sunan al-Darimi* depicts the attitude of Abu Bakr in this regard:

> Maimun b. Mehran narrates: When a dispute was brought before the caliph Abu Bakr (RA) he would first look for guidance in the Book of Allah and decided it in the light of relevant divine command if he found one. If he found out that the matter was not discussed in the Qur'an and came to know that the Prophet (pbuh) had set an example in that particular matter he would decide in the light of the Prophetic Sunnah. If, however, he did not find guidance in the Sunnah as well, he would then bring up the matter before the Muslims. He would ask them whether any among them knew if the Prophet (pbuh) had said something concerning the issue at hand. Sometimes many people came forward and told him that the Prophet (pbuh) had in fact decided such a matter. At this he would say: 'All gratitude is due to God. Here in the Ummah are men who have preserved the prophetic knowledge.' If however he did not find any Prophetic Sunnah dealing with the issue, he would call upon the leaders of the people and those prominent among them and seek their opinion. When all of them reached a decision, he would implement it.[70]

It is in the time of 'Umar, that we get a detailed picture of the working of the government by *Shura* (Consultation). During his Caliphate (634–644 CE), the most essential and fundamental thing was the establishment of the *Majlis al-Shura* (Consultative Assembly). Whenever a question (issue) came up for decision—writes Shibli Nu'mani in his *al-Farooq*, biography of the caliph 'Umar (RA)[71]—the Consultative Assembly was called and no question was decided without free debate and without the consent of the majority.[72] During his caliphate, members of both groups (*Ansar* and *Muhajirun*) always necessarily took part in the deliberations of the assembly, including 'Uthman, 'Ali, Abdul Rehman b. 'Auf, Mu'adh b. Jabal, 'Ubay b. Ka'ab and Zaid b. Thabit, etc.[73]

The everyday affairs, which were of less political significance, were decided by this council; however, when any crucial matter arose, the whole community of the emigrants and the hosts would be called for. Only after unanimous approval of both parties, the matter would be decided. The pay of the soldiers, organization of the secretariat (offices), appointment of civil officers, freedom of trade of foreigners, and assessment of import duties and such affairs (relating to state and its administration) were decided in the Consultative Assembly.[74] Nu'mani, on the authority of Baladhuri, has narrated the proceeding of one of such meetings in these words:

> There was a council of the emigrants whose meetings were held in the mosque. 'Umar (RA) used to attend its meetings. He would put before the council dispatches from far flung areas. One day he said: 'I do not know how to decide the issue of [imposing *Jizyah*] on the Zoroastrians?'[75]

The historians have chronicled numerous events and incidents when Caliph 'Umar held long discussions and consultations with his colleagues and tribal leaders; and in the light of their advice, he took his decision on that specific issue. For example, designation of Sa'ad b. Abi Waqas as the Commander of the Muslim army (for the battle of Qadissiyya);[76] 'Umar's decision, after due consultation, to go to Palestine to sign a treaty with them;[77] settlement of the lands of Sawad,[78] and the appointment of 'Uthman b. Hanif as governor of this region;[79] maintaining a war department and a register of the army;[80] the appointment of the governors and other officials;[81] the construction of *Amir al-Muminun's* Canal, which joined the Nile to the Red Sea;[82] introducing the New Calendar;[83] and some Juristic issues.[84]

Though 'Umar himself was a great jurist, he still brought most of the questions to the Consultative Assembly, where matters were discussed with the greatest freedom and expertise. Abu Yusuf and Shibli Nu'mani argue that 'Umar never adjudicated upon any question which had not been decided already.[85] Shah Waliullah, in his analysis, says:

> 'Umar (RA) would consult the Companions and continue discussing the issues with them until the differences were removed and the people were utterly convinced of the validity of a decision. It is only because of this vigorous process that all the [political and administrative] decisions and religious rulings issued by him have been followed by [future rulers] from all over the Muslim world.[86]

When 'Umar constituted the *Shura* to determine the *ikhtiyar* (literally authority/authorize; signifying election) of his successor, he gave clear instructions that the decision of the *Shura* would be mandatory. He said that in case of any difference of opinion among the members of the *Shura*, the decision of the majority would be binding on all.[87] These examples are sufficient to prove that 'Umar established a powerful democratic state—though none of the states around him was democratic—in which all matters were discussed freely and decided entirely with consultation. On the basis of these evidences, Majid Khan, in his *The Pious Caliphate*, rightly argues that 'Umar's reign was 'an exemplary period as far as the principle of the democratic way of government is concerned'.[88] A similar position is argued by Crone when she writes that 'the procedure [adopted by 'Umar] was anything but democratic'.[89]

Caliph 'Uthman followed the practice of his predecessors regarding the function of the judicial system. The caliph used to hold his court in the mosque to hear the cases. When a case was brought to him, he summoned 'Ali, Talha, al-Zubayr, and Abdur Rehman b. Auf, and asked the applicant and defendant to explain their case before them. After hearing the statements of both, he used to discuss the issue with the jury and in case they reached to a consensus, he would announce the judgment in the same meeting. However, in case of a difference of opinion, he postponed the announcement of judgment for further consideration and reflection.[90] According to Urooj Sadeq Ibrahim, in the outgoing period, when there was anarchy and disturbance throughout the country, 'Uthman could not hammer the spirit of consultation. To make a critical analysis, he called for the *Ansar* and the *Muhajirun* to whom he said, 'You are my partners and as representatives of the Muslims, give your advice what to do to cool down the abnormal situations'. On the advice of the Companions, he sent a few experienced persons to different parts of the country so that they might find out the real causes and their remedies.[91]

The fourth caliph, 'Ali who had been an active member of the *Shura* during all the earlier caliphs, and had full perception of the significance of mutual discussion and consultation demonstrated the same spirit when he was requested to accept the caliphate. Al-Tabari reports that when 'Ali was approached and invited to accept the mantle of the caliphate, he told his colleagues that the decision should not be made in a hurry, adding that let the people get together, discuss the matter and consult each other.[92]

These (few) examples from the history of the Pious Caliphate period prove the importance, validity, and lawfulness of *Shura* (consultation) with the *Ummah* or their representatives in the affairs of the Islamic State. The caliphs really deserved to be titled *Khalifah* (Successor of the Prophet) because they followed the Islamic political principles laid by the Prophet (pbuh)—like consultation, justice, equality, and freedom—in the true and real sense.

On this aspect of Islamic history, Basam Tibi (in his 'Major themes in the Arabic political literature of Islamic Revivalism' *ICMR*), comments as: 'The Prophet Muhammad [pbuh] consulted with his close contemporaries and followers, foremost of whom were Abu Bakr and 'Umar. The four righteous caliphs of early Islam maintained this tradition. The largest number of consultees with whom the *shura* was pursued was under 'Umar who increased the number of counsellors to six.'[93]

Discussing the procedure of the appointment of the *Khalifah* and the *Shura* under them, Obaidullah Fahad draws the following conclusions, viz.: (i) the *Shura* system during the Pious Caliphate period was implemented with due importance; (ii) the religious and worldly affairs were presented to the *Shura* for its discussion. Administrative as well as legal aspects were discussed and after reaching to a consensus, the final verdicts were given. In case the consensus was not possible, the opinion of the majority was followed; and (iii) the head of the state was either nominated as was done in the case of 'Umar; or proposed by *Majlis al-Shura* as was practiced in the selection of 'Uthman, or selected by the eminent *Sahabah* and was presented, later, to the general public for approval as was followed in the election of Abu Bakr, or was elected by the people directly as was in the case of 'Ali.[94] Similarly, regarding the governmental system of Pious Caliphs, Syed Ameer 'Ali argues that nothing was decided without consultation:

> The Caliph, who was the supreme head of the Government, was assisted by a Council of Elders composed of the principal Companions of the Prophet [pbuh], who held their sittings in the principal Mosque [*Masji-i-Nabwi*], often assisted by the city notables and Bedouin chiefs present in Medina. Several of the Companions were entrusted with special duties.... Every detail of the administration was thus looked after, but nothing was decided without consultation.[95]

While as, for M. Y. Faruqi, the examples of deciding matters through mutual consultation by the Pious Caliphs and the Companions of the Prophet (pbuh) have achieved the status of *Ijma'* (Consensus) in the modern times; he argues:

> The practice of mutual consultation initiated by the *Rashidun Khulafa'* infused in the *fuqaha* [jurisprudents] the spirit of developing deep into the knowledge of traditions and thus institutionalized the principle of *Shura* in order to deal with the social, political, judicial and administrative affairs of the Muslim community.... The example left behind by the *Rashidun Khulafa'* and the Companions of the Holy Prophet [pbuh] to decide matters through mutual consultation have, in the course of time, achieved the status of Ijma'.[96]

Thus, the above discussion of *Shura* in practice under the Prophet (pbuh) and the *Khulfa'-i-Rashidun* reveals that the system was democratic in spirit; its political technique was common consultation and election of representatives; and that in form it was representative government. These constitute the essential and integral features of an Islamic government. It also reveals that the Caliphs were, in Goran Larsson's maxim, 'in favor of democracy (derived from the Arabic concept of *Shura*), and in line with this argument it is held, that these Caliphs did not call for a government based on religion alone.'[97]

## The Practice of Shura in the Post-Pious Caliphate Era (660–1924 CE)

With the assassination of Caliph 'Ali, the era of the Pious Caliphate came to an end, and was followed by what is generally known as the *Malukiyah* (Monarchy/dynastic rule). Muawiyya of *Banu Ummayya* (r. 661–750) assumed the caliphate and thereafter, the caliphate became hereditary, passing from one king to another within the same family. The idea of *Shura*—as a means of selecting caliphs and other great men in the state, i.e. the principle of election—seems to have been especially attractive during the reign of the Umayyad period or for zealots, rebels, and dissidents. But, in the pages of history, there are no records of the practice of *Shura* as a means of consultation, conference, and counselling, until the reign of 'Umar bin 'Abd al-'Aziz, commonly known as 'Umar-II (r. 717–720 CE). Crone puts it as: 'The calls for *shura* came to an abrupt end in 750 [CE].'[98] Since the entire Umayyad period witnessed incessant rebellions that entailed the necessity of politico-military consolidation, so their rule altered the very character of the early Caliphate. The Umayyads imposed their own political logic where *Shura*—far from facilitating the participation by the community at large—became restricted to those who supported the regime. As noted by Bosworth, in his entry on 'Shura: In Early Islamic History' in the *Encyclopedia of Islam (EI²)*: 'Hence 'Umar b. Abd al-Aziz may have contemplated its use for his own successor; ... ; and the ephemeral Umayyad Caliph Yazid III b. al-Walid in 126[AH]/744 [CE] endeavored to rally support for his claim to the throne by appealing to the Book of God, the *Sunna[h]* of Prophet [pbuh] and succession to the rule by a Shura.'[99]

In fact, *Shura* vanished into that very cliquing which had been condemned by the Qur'an only; this cliquing was the work of the successful group—the rulers. It was the development of an administrative structure, argues Fazlur Rahman (Pakistani-born Muslim modernist thinker), which now supplied the link between the rulers and the ruled, only this link worked essentially from the top downward as opposed to *Shura*, which worked in the reverse.[100] The institution of *ba'yah*, or the oath of allegiance, for the validation of a new caliph, however, continued to operate during the Umayyad rule. Khurshid Ahmad also claims that after the Pious Caliphs when hereditary rule crept in, *bay'ah*, *Shura*, *nasiha* (advice), *ikhtilaf* (disagreement), and other concepts continued to play important roles at all times and in a variety of ways:

> Even when this principle of the community's choice was abandoned and heredity rule crept in, the function of *bay'a[h]* (people's acceptance of the rulers) continued. The institutions of *nasiha* (advice), *Shura* (consultation), *Ikhtilaf* (disagreement/differences of opinion), *al-amr bil maruf* (commanding right and virtue), *al-nahi an al-munkar* (forbidding wrong and vice), and *hisba* (public accountability and ombudsman-ship) continued to play important roles at all times and in a variety of ways.[101]

It was 'Umar II, who tried to revive and regenerate the institution of *Shura* even before he became *Khalifah*. During his governance of al-Hijaz, he established a council and consulted it on all important affairs of the province; and about this council, al-Khaduri writes:

> He ['Umar II] sent for ten of the Jurists of al-Medina ... who were the leading Jurists of the [then Muslim] world. When they appeared before him, ... he said to them: 'Verily I have summoned you for a business [responsibility] in consideration of which you shall be rewarded (by God) and on account of which you will become the upholders of the right (*al-Haqq*: [Truth]). I do not desire to decide any matter except by your counsel or the counsel of such of you as may be present.[102]

When 'Umar-II succeeded to the throne of *Khilafah*, he assembled the citizens of Damascus and addressed them. It was an assembly, convened to hear the new ruler who was 'a staunch advocate of *Shura*'; and he 'endeavored to get around him as many of the best men among scholars and divines as possible, but his reign was so short that he could not accomplish anything definite in this direction'.[103] All along, it was recognized in theory that the caliph should consult his subjects through a selected few in all matters of administration. But nothing definite could be done under the Umayyad rule. With some exceptions like 'Umar-II and Yazid-III, as Syed Ameer Ali argues, 'the government of the [Umayyad] Caliphs was a pure autocracy'.[104] The Umayyad dynasty was dethroned, in 750 CE, by the 'Abbasids, who ruled up to 1258 CE.

'Under the first five Caliphs of the Abbaside dynasty, the government continued to be more or less same autocratic, although the departmental ministers and prominent members of the family formed a body of unauthorized counselors'.[105] The increasingly authoritarian character of government under the Abbasids is vividly expressed in a passage quoted by many authors. Sudayf, a *mawla* of the Hashimites, is quoted as complaining of the charges resulting from the Abbasid accession: 'By God, our booty, which was shared, has become a perquisite of the rich; our leadership, which was consultation (*mashwara*), has become arbitrary; our succession, which was by the choice of the community, is now by inheritance'.[106]

Later, Al-Mamun (r. 813–833 CE) was the first to think of constituting a central body. On the consultative councils during Ummayads and Abbasids, Mishal Fahm al-Sulami is of this opinion: 'From the time of the Bani Umayyads up to the collapse of the 'Abbasid caliphate, the *shura* council was definitely not developed; nor was it as it had been in the reign of the preceding Rightly Guided Caliphs. The *shura* council was replaced by a consultative council, whose role was limited to presenting opinions or advice to the Caliph in making decisions on state matters'.[107] As noted by Ameer Ali, during the reign of Abbasid Caliph Mamun and in later dynasties—like the Buwayids, the Samanids, the Seljukids/Seljuqs, and the Ayyubids—all had their councils in which the people were more or less represented, showing, to some extent, the republican and democratic nature. He writes:

> A regular council of state, representing every community owning allegiance to the Caliph, was for the first time established in his reign. The representatives of the people enjoyed perfect freedom in the expression of the opinions, and do not seem even to have been hampered in their discussions. The Caliph's council in later times, when they had lost their temporal authority, and their influence rested on their spiritual prestige,

turned into a synod of divines and doctors of law. But the Buyides [or Buwayids, r. 934–1055 AD in Iran and Iraq], the Samanids [r. 819–999 AD in Central Asia and Khorasan], the Seljukides [Seljuqs, r. 11th–14th century in Central Asia and Middle East], and the Ayubides [or Ayyubid dynasty, r. 1171–1341 in Cairo and Damascus], all had their councils in which the people were more or less represented. Saladin's [Salahuddin Ayyubi, c. 1138–93 of Ayyubid dynasty] council met regularly, either under his presidency or that of the vizier (al-Kazi al-Fazil), for the transaction of business, and seem to have followed the Sultan in his campaigns.[108]

The political system during the Prophet (pbuh) and Rightly Guided Caliphate, as mentioned earlier, was based on two main principles: the rule of law and equality of all before the law; and supremacy of the Qur'an and Sunnah and resort to *Ijtihad* in matters not covered by these sources. The entire corpus of Muslim law has been developed through a 'rational, democratic and popular process' in which the learned and the concerned 'participate through debate, dialogue and discussion'. This was the voluntary acceptance of and submission to the law so developed by the *Ummah* that gave legitimacy to different schools of law. It is one of the major marvels of history that law in the Muslim society was never derived from the will of the rulers, as was the case in other contemporaneous societies and cultures. The entire legal system evolved outside the corridors of political power and, once established, the rulers were as much subject to this law as were commoners. This has worked as a great check on arbitrary power and has entrenched the true credentials of the concept of 'participatory democracy' in Muslim society.[109] In this regard, John Esposito and John Voll, argue:

> In the long-standing concept of 'oriental despotism,' there is no sense of a separation of powers or structures limiting the power of the ruler. However, such unlimited power was not available to leaders in classical Muslim societies, and this situation is visible both in Islamic law of political structures and in actual historical practice.... It was the consensus of these scholars, and not the commands and rules of the caliphs, that provided the basis for formal Islamic law. No ruler was

recognized as being above the law and all rulers would be judged by that law.[110]

The separation of the judiciary from the executive and its total independence at all levels has been a cardinal feature of the Muslim experience. This is why the rule of law and access to justice for all remained unchallengeable aspects of Muslim society. This, by and large, protected Muslim lands from the tyranny of arbitrary rule. This principle of the separation of powers, established as it was during the period of the Rightly Guided Caliphs, continued in later periods despite certain degeneration in the system. The supremacy of the constitution, i.e. Islam, remained an integral part of the Muslim experience.

According to an Ottoman historical tradition, the very foundation of the Ottoman dynasty and state (r. 1299–1924) was due to a consultative act. The Ottoman authors, like other Islamic authors, urged the importance of consultation by the ruler, and in the Ottoman Empire, such was indeed in practice. The term *mashwara* (Ottoman *meshweret*) is used commonly by the Ottoman historians to denote ad hoc meetings and councils of military and other dignitaries to consider problems as they arose. References to such meetings are common in the Ottoman chronicles of the sixteenth to the eighteenth centuries.[111] In its later centuries, the Ottoman Empire was an Islamic empire and its head, the Sultan, was subject to Islamic law. Recording a certain aspect of it, Esposito and Voll argue that in the Ottoman Empire, the

> Ulama [*'Ulama*] of the imperial system had the accepted right—which was not often exercised, because of political reasons—to invalidate any regulation issued by the Sultan if they judged it not to be in accord with Islamic Law.[112] Even more, the head of the hierarchy of the official Ulama in the empire, the Shaykh-al-Islam, could issue judgments deposing the Sultan for violating the basic Islamic Law. Although this power was exercised infrequently, it actually was exercised in the depositions of Sultans Ibrahim (1648), Mehmed IV (1687), Ahmed III (1730), and Selim III (1807). In these formal actions, the historic check on the power of the ruler formed by the fact that the Ulama were the representatives of the 'constitution,' that is, the Islamic law, is fully reflected. It shows the potential dimension of the separation of powers in the Islamic heritage.[113]

The Umayyad, 'Abbasid, Ottoman, and other ruling dynasties ruled in multifaceted forms of administrations. At times, multiple Caliphates were running parallel to each other. Internal conflicts, rebellions, and rivalries leading to oppression, and bloodshed were not exceptional. Thus, the institution of Caliphate, slowly and gradually, lost much of its legitimacy in the eyes of the Muslim *Ummah*. Clearly, these so-called caliphs were far-removed from the norms set by the Prophet (pbuh) and the early *Khulafa* to be serious contenders for the leadership of Muslims. None of them could claim to be the spiritual and religious leader of the entire Muslim *Ummah*.[114]

## Shura in the Modern Arab (post-1924 era)

The idea and practice of consultation in government had an intermittent history in Islam prior to the nineteenth century. In that century, as the Ottoman Empire's encounter with Europe accelerated, the old principle was revived in a series of institutions established in the empire's centre and its Arab provinces, as part of the effort to modernize the political order. Bodies with deliberative and advisory authority bearing the name *Shura* (or *mashwara*, its interchangeable derivative) were set up by Muhammad 'Ali in Egypt, in the 1820s; by his son Ibrahim in Egyptian-occupied Syria and Palestine, in the 1830s; and by his grandson, the Khedive Isma'il, in Egypt again. The latter assembled a 'Consultative Council of Delegates' (*Majlis Shura al-Nuwwab*) in 1866, featuring the novel quality of being elective, though indirectly, which operated until the 1882 British occupation. These councils represented a dual phenomenon: an embodiment of the Islamic ideal of consultation in government, and an attempted emulation of European-type parliaments.[115]

From the early nineteenth century, the word *Shura* or *mashwara* was applied to every type of western governmental body, including elective and representative parliaments. At the same time, applied in a local context, *Shura* connoted the newly revived traditional idea of a ruler consulting with his chosen group of advisers, and as noted by A. Aylon (in *EI²*): 'Such a two-fold application of the word [*Shura/Mashwara*] made it possible, and convenient, for thinkers such as Muhammad 'Abduh and Rashid Rida to justify the borrowing of parliaments—an alien idea—by associating them with the Islamic notion of consultation'.[116]

Within the context of modern period, Fazlur Rahman puts it as:

> Since about the mid-nineteenth century, prominent leaders of reformist thought in Islam have argued that in order to implement Islam in the public sector, rule must be established in accordance with the will of the people. One consideration that weighed particularly heavy with reformers like Jamal al-Din al-Afghani was that without the participation of the people in the government, Muslim states cannot become strong enough to withstand the pressures of the expanding West. Rulers without public support and confidence gave in easily to the demands of the Western powers. Secondly, for purposes of internal progress and development, without which Muslim states must also remain weak, the willing participation of the people was equally required. Namik Kemal, in his discussion of *shura*, raises more theoretical questions about the legitimacy of rule without the approval of the people: if a person sets himself up as a judge merely on the strength of his own declaration without appointment by a competent authority, his claim is regarded as invalid, but how about a person who declares himself to be a ruler, wages war and peace on behalf of people and levies taxes on them, yet all without their consent?[117]

## Mandatory and Legally Binding Nature of the Institution of Shura

The two Qur'anic verses (3: 159 and 42: 38) and the *Ahadith*, cited above, leave no doubt about the significance, and place of, the institution of *Shura* (or *Shura'iyat*) as a fundamental part of the political system of Islam. Hence, it is a legal and mandatory decree of the Qur'an that the rulers must obey under all circumstances, if they really believe in *Tawhid* (Monotheism) and the teachings of Islam. The entire teachings of Islam and the practice of the Prophet (pbuh) and the Rightly Guided Caliphs indicate the mandatory nature of the institution of *Shura*. A profound study of the rationale and purpose of Islam and its teachings also substantiates and supports the view that the institution of *Shura* is legally binding on the people, including the rulers. Caliph 'Umar stressed that 'there was no caliphate (vicegerency) without consultation (*Shura*)'. *Shurai'yat* (or the institution of *Shura*) and *Mashwara* (consultation, conference, and counsel), in the words of Afzalur Rehman, are essential to the foundation of an Islamic government.[118]

Numerous scholars, of past and present, have suggested about the mandatory and binding nature of the institution of *Shura*. For example, according to Ibn 'Atiyya al-Hayan, *Shurai'yat* is 'one of the fundamental and basic principles of the *Shari'ah* and *al-Din*. And if any *Amir* (ruler) does not consult *ahl al-'Ilm* (people of knowledge) and *ahl al-Din* (experts in Religion), his removal and dismissal becomes obligatory, and this is a matter on which there is no disagreement'.[119] Abu Hamid al-Ghazzali (1058–1111) in his *Tibrul Masbuk* makes *Shura* (or taking counsel) a requisite for successful kingship. Throughout his book, he asserts on the importance and necessity of rulers taking counsel. He says that 'the ruler should take advice from those who are *ahl al-'Ilm* (learned) or are experts in any branch of administration (*ahl al-hall wa al-'aqd*)'. According to him, the 'rulers/kings who take counsel from the learned and the experts are considered the best of rulers'. In support of his view, he mentions that the Prophet (pbuh) used to 'take advice of his Companions according to definite orders of God as enjoined in the Qur'an'.[120]

For Abd al-Rahman Azzam, Q. 3: 159 makes 'consultation a general principle, whose application is mandatory and whose observance is to be respected by all Islamic states and communities [as an imperative verdict from the Sovereign] at all times. Human experience has demonstrated the continuous character of this principle and its uses.'[121] For Egyptian Muhammad Saleem El-'Awa, *Shura* is a basic principle in Islamic constitutional theory which is established by the Qur'an (Q. 3: 159 and 42: 38) and was practised firmly by the Prophet (pbuh) and his Companions. The Islamic rules on *Shura* are very flexible, allowing the Muslim community to choose the best means to suit its requirements according to the circumstances of time and place.[122]

In his *Fann al-Hukm fi al-Islam* (*The Art of Government in Islam*), Mustafa Abu Zayd Fahmi has devoted a lengthy chapter on *Shura*, which is exclusively based on Q. 3: 159 and 42: 38.[123] 'The significance of the chapter does not derive from the value of its statements', comments Tibi, 'but from its exemplary characterization of the argumentation with regard to projecting modernity into Islam'.[124] In this book, Fahmi writes about the nature and significance of *Shura* in these words: 'Most significant is the operative value of the *shura* as a major principle of government, in as much as it advances the will of the people to make it the major source of conduct of public affairs'. He further states that 'Islam, being the final divine revelation, is by definition par excellence intellectual progress itself in all realms, in devotion to God, the conduct of public affairs and in politics alike'.[125] He also refers to the practical aspects of transforming values into realities as he raises the question of how to institute this system: 'The answer is very simple and clear. Islam knows only one system of government which is the system of *shura*. If we want to know how to implement the *shura* then we have to refer to the *shura* itself'.[126] On the legally binding nature of *Shura*, Fahmi states that legislation has to be made in accordance with the Islamic principle of *Shura*:

> The Shari'a[h] has admitted the *shura* as a major pillar in this field [system of government] which means that the legislative power must be set in accordance with the *shura* provision. The people can practice the *shura* as they want: either directly, if their number is small to the extent that a direct democracy in the sense of modern constitutional theory is feasible, or indirectly through elected deputies as in parliamentary democracy.... In the revelation, Islam has instituted the *shura* as a major principle of government: Muslims 'conduct their public affairs in mutual consent'. Thus, legislative power has to be organized along the lines of the *shura*.[127]

In Fahmi's understanding, 'Islamic *Shura*-democracy' is the only true democracy in the world: 'The Islamic system of government is the most advanced pattern humanity has ever known. Islam established democracy and instituted *shura* as its major element ... In this act Islam's achievement is unprecedented in the history of mankind'.[128]

Furthermore, referring to the Q. 3: 159, Muhammad Asad in his *The Principles of State and Government in Islam*, maintains:

> This *nass* or Injunction must be regarded as the fundamental, operative clause of all Islamic thought relating to statecraft.... The word *amr* in this injunction refers to all affairs of a communal nature and therefore also to the manner in which the government of an Islamic State is to be established: that is, to the elective [representative]

principle underlying all governmental authority. Beyond that, the phrase *amrhum shura baynahum*—literally 'their communal business *is* consultative among themselves' [Q. 42: 38]—makes the transaction of all political business not only consequent upon, but synonymous with, consultation: which means that the legislative powers of the state must be vested in an assembly chosen by the community specially for this purpose.[129]

Yusuf al-Qaradawi, one of the prominent moderate Muslim voices in the present times, in his *State in Islam*[130] refers to *Shura* under the subheading '*Shura*—an obligation, not an option' which clearly indicates his stance on this issue. On this point, he refers to Q. 3: 159 and 16: 91, gives evidence of the Prophetic Tradition that '*Muslims should abide by their conditions*', and asserts that 'Islam has made *Shura* as obligatory from both sides, on the ruler or governor to consult his nation and on the nation to give advice to the ruler.'[131]

The mandatory nature of the principle is very evident from the Qur'anic text, according to which it is obligatory and imperative for the ruler to seek the advice of a consultative council on all state matters. The mandatory status of *Shura* acts as a check on the power of the ruler and also to make the decisions of the government as near as possible to the aspirations and needs of the people as well as choose to the spirit and wisdom of the universal principles of Islam.

## Modern Theories Regarding Shura

Based on the Qur'anic injunctions (mainly 3: 159 and 42: 38), modern scholars consider *Shura* to be the basis for the implementation of democracy. That is, in the contemporary period, Muslim scholars and theorists have sought to compare the Qur'anic concept of *Shura* with the modern Western notion of democracy. Modernist/reformist scholars argue that *Shura*, along with the concepts of *Ijma* (literally consensus) and *Ijtihad* (literally 'effort'/personal reasoning) are the operational key concepts of democracy in Islam. Many contemporary Muslims have compared the concept of *Shura* to the principles of western parliamentary democracy.[132] In the words of Halim Rane,

> Islamic principles such as *shura* (consultation), *ijma'* (consensus), *ijtihad* (independent reasoning), and *bay'ah* (allegiance or elect oral endorsement) ... have been identified by scholars within the field of Islamic studies as an indication of the potential for democracy to develop in Islam. However, the utility of these principles to generate a genuine democratic tradition within Islam has been undermined by a lack of constitutional provision.... Potentially democratic concepts such as *shura* (consultation) and *ijma'* (consensus) are left as mere principles not developed into processes, procedures, or institutions of government.[133]

Numerous modern Muslim scholars, writing mostly on Islamic sociopolitical theory, emphasize on the vital role that *Shura* plays (and can play), and explain that the process of *Shura* is a means for allowing the Islamic Law (*Shari'ah*) to sensibly evolve, offering solutions to new issues which Islam has not previously encountered. For example, Asad states that *Shura* caters to the continuous temporal legislation of our social existence,[134] and when describing the institution of *Shura* in general terms, Tariq Ramadan describes it as 'the space which allows Islam the management of pluralism', or in other words, *Shura* echoes the 'principle of managing pluralism';[135] and refutes the view of some *Ulama* and thinkers from the 'traditionalist and literalist schools of thought' who argue that the 'democratic system (not a Qur'anic concept) does not respect Islamic criteria (the criteria of *shura*)'.[136]

Over a couple of centuries, Muslim scholars have tried to broaden the conceptualizations of *Shura* and in the contemporary scenario, it is of direct concern for the advocates of 'Islamic democracy'. From the studies of Sadek Jawad Sulaiman (an Omani diplomat and intellectual), for example, it can be established that the principles of justice, equality, and human dignity—which constitute Islam's moral core—are best realized, in personal as well as public life, under *Shura* governance.[137] He accepts the compatibility of democracy and *Shura* on the grounds that *Shura*, as a concept and a principle, does not differ from democracy; and in his *Democracy and Shura*, he writes:

> Both *Shura* and democracy arise from the central consideration that collective deliberation is more likely to lead to a fair and sound result for

the social good than individual preference. Both concepts also assume that majority judgment tends to be more comprehensive and accurate than minority judgment. As principles, *Shura* and democracy proceed from the core idea that all people are equal in rights and responsibilities. Both thereby commit to the rule of the people through application of the law rather than the rule of individuals or a family through autocratic decree. Both affirm that a more comprehensive fulfillment of the principles and values by which humanity prospers cannot be achieved in a non-democratic, non-*Shura* environment.[138]

Although democracy and *Shura* differ in specifics of application to challenge the social customs, Sulaiman regards both of them as identical in conception and principle, on the basis that they reject any government lacking the legitimacy of free elections, accountability, and the people's power; does not accept hereditary rule; reject government by force; and both forbid privileges—political, social, and economic—claimed on the basis of tribal lineage or social prestige. On these grounds, therefore, '*Shura* and democracy are thus one and the same concept. They prod us [i.e. Muslims] to find better and better realizations of the principles of justice, equality, and human dignity in our collective socio-political experience'.[139]

Similarly, many modernists derive more examples from the pious caliphate period in order to further support and strengthen their argument that consultation is a mandated practice in all matters, and practically in the political realm. They highlight the inaugural speech of Abu Bakr, which emphasized governance based on consultation (and which from the 'liberal' perspective is understood as being 'supportive of and requiring consultative, democratic forms of government in Islamic societies today'),[140] 'Umar's setting up of the six-man electoral council, to deliberate upon the choice of his successors, is a 'powerful arrow in the quiver of the modernists.'[141] Afsaruddin, in the light of views and writings of various modernists, has made the following observations regarding the modern theories concerning *Shura*:

> This *Shura* is sometimes understood by them [i.e., modernists/reformists] to be the precursor of the modern parliament or legislative assembly, setting a normative example for the translation of

broad guidelines of proper governance into administrative reality. Modernists point to these historical instances to make their case that a representative and accountable government that upholds justice and equitable treatment for all its citizens is the only kind permissible within Islam regardless of what its actual structure and mode may be.[142]

Thus, *Shura* is regarded as a basic principle in all the spheres of Islamic political and social systems. It is also 'essential for the proper functioning of the organs of the state, its overall activity and Islamic identity'.[143] Placing consultation in a generally accepted framework, Muhammad Hamidullah argues, by referring to a number of Quranic verses (like 3: 159; 27: 32; 42: 38; and 47: 21), that the 'importance and utility of consultation' cannot be too greatly emphasized. For him, the Qur'an commands the Muslims again and again to take their decisions after consultation, whether in a public matter or a private one.[144]

Some non-Muslim scholars also argue the same views. For example, John L. Esposito, regarding the importance of *Shura*, writes:

> The necessity of consultation is a political consequence of the principle of the caliphate of human beings. Popular vicegerency in an Islamic state is reflected especially in the doctrine of mutual consultation (*Shura*). The importance of consultation as a part of Islamic systems of rule is widely recognized.[145]

Thus, consultation is an important operational concept and element with regard to the relation of Islam with democracy. Particularly, during the nineteenth and twentieth centuries 'there have been significant efforts to broaden the conceptualization of consultation, and this are associated with *advocates of Islamic democracy.... Shurah* thus becomes [in this perspective] *a key operational element in the relationship between Islam and democracy*'. (Italics added)[146]

The importance of *Shura* is best understood only when we look back to the political system of the Prophetic era and of *Khulfa'-i-Rashidun* period (i.e. 610–660 CE). A thorough study of the political system of these two periods (phases), as discussed above, reveals that the system was truly democratic in spirit because its political technique was common consultation and election of representatives and that in form it was representative. These constitute the essential and integral features of an Islamic State.

Tariq Ramadan[147] argues that the Arabic word *Shura* signifies not only 'consultation' or 'deliberation', but is, as mentioned above as well, the space which allows Islam the management of pluralism. For him, taking into consideration 'the diversity of practices of consultation in the history of Islamic civilization and the reflections produced by the *"ulama"*',[148] seven principles can be extracted which are inherent in the notion of *Shura*. These are summarized below:

1. The political head must offer to the community the means of deliberation and, hence, of participation in running its affairs, either by direct elections, or under the model of representation.
2. The creation of a 'Council of *Shura* (deliberation)', i.e. *Majlis al-Shura*, imposes itself and necessitates structuring the modes of people's consultation, which allows for the election of members to this Council. Whether it is direct elections, the formation of regional councils, or something else, all these forms are acceptable so long as they allow participation and consultation of the grassroots according to the Qur'anic expression.
3. Members of this Council are chosen with regard to their competence, and according to the specific role devolved upon the Council; and it seems evident that there must exist two types of competence in this Council: on the one hand, those related to the knowledge of the acknowledged principles of Islamic orientation, to which must be added mastery of economic, political and social affairs according to the domains whereby reflection is engaged. Suitably appointed commissions, as nowadays found in all parliaments, can legitimately do this job. It is inside this authority or another which is appointed to it that the practice of *Ijtihad* must be elaborated, and which links the sources with concrete realities. This is the role of those who are known in Islamic jurisprudence by the name of 'the people who tie and untie' (*Ahl al-Hall wa al-'Aqd*). It is impossible nowadays to leave this function to theologians alone. Social, political, economic, and even medical and experimental sciences have reached such a level of complexity that it is not possible to deal with

related juridical and ethical questions without consultation with experts in these various domains.
4. Selection of the person responsible for the nation (the President or *Imam*—the one who is placed ahead) can be delegated to the *Shura* Council, but it can also be the doing of the population. Once again, the principle of choosing people is inalienable in Islam. The form which its realization takes depends on a great number of historical, geographical, and even cultural factors. The idea of a mandate of a determined period does not contravene Islamic teachings.
5. The President of the nation is, thus, chosen by the community (men and women equally). As any other President bound by the constitution of his country, he must respect the principles of the Islamic reference. He must also be its guarantor before the *Shura* Council (as also before the people) to whom he must give an account of his general politics as that of his ministers. This is exactly what Caliphs Abu Bakr and 'Umar did, and it is in this sense that, in modern societies, the executive and legislative powers are articulated.
6. The separation of power is one of the fundamental principles of the organization of the city, and this was respected from the moment Abu Bakr succeeded to the Caliphate. The judges (*qudat*, sing. *qadi*) had to exercise their function in an autonomous fashion and according to the principle of equality of all before the law.
7. The people, as long as the principles of election have been respected, make an act of allegiance (*bay'ah*) to the one whom the majority has chosen. This allegiance presupposes conditions and cannot be one of blind submission. It requires a critical conscience from the people towards the one who has the responsibility of running their affairs. This critical participation, for Islam, is one of the fundamental duties of the citizen. A president or king who spreads injustice, corruption, and denies citizens their rights cannot receive allegiance.[149]

Omar Ashour (a political scientist at *University of Exeter*, UK) considers *Shura* as 'an Islamic basis for participatory governance'[150] on the grounds that as the mechanisms and the details of the *Shura* have never been static, most contemporary Islamic studies scholars, Islamist thinkers, and Muslim jurists have provided 'firm theoretical grounds that can be used as tools to transform *Shura* into a broader form of modern participatory government'.[151] He further argues that several bases for democracy do exist in Islamic concepts such as *Shura* and *Bay'ah*, although the strength of these foundations is dependent on *Ijtihad*, or human agency. However, for him, if

> Islam's ultimate aims are understood to include the promotion of social and political justice and equality, and if democracy is a system of rule that guarantees a fairer socio-political system relative to other systems of governance, then interpretations of Islam that strengthen its democratic bases are justifiable. These bases could be emphasized and developed to promote the compatibility between Islam and democracy.[152]

It is pertinent to mention here that in his influential *Political Islam*, Nazih Ayubi (*University of Exeter*, UK), who has written extensively on Middle East politics—building on the statements of Egyptian thinker Khalid M. Khalid—is of the opinion that 'the Islamic principle of *shura* is exactly equivalent to the term 'democracy' in its modern connotations'.[153] He quotes Khalid, who is of the opinion that '*Shura* in Islam is the democracy that gives people the right to choose their rulers and their deputies and representatives, as well as the right to practice freedom of thought, opinion and opposition'.[154]

Asma Afsaruddin, in her *Contemporary Issues in Islam*, puts it as: 'the principle of *shura* or consultation, endorsed in the Qur'an as the basis for collective decision-making and administration of public affairs' is generally understood, in the present times, 'to provide the conceptual grounding for consultative governance and collective decision-making'.[155] Ziauddin Sardar, one of the present-day influential scholar-critic, is of the opinion that 'the only term with any specific political connotation that appears in the Sacred Text is *shura* or consultation'—'consultation in running the affairs of the community'—which is so important that even Prophet (pbuh) is required to consult (Q. 3: 159). A 'paramount principle in all affairs of the state', it is this *Shura* process that gives, as Sardar puts it, 'legitimacy to political authority'.[156]

According to Muhammad Shahroor, a leading Syrian Islamic intellectual, 'democracy, as a mechanism, is the best achievement of humanity for practicing consultation' (*Shura*); and it 'is the best relative mechanism for organizing opposition'. Seeing the concept of opposition as a means by which to attain the Qur'anic precept of 'urging the good and forbidding the evil', Shahroor points out that 'democracy, as a form for governing and as a framework for organizing human relations, has negative as well as positive characteristics. Whatever the negative side is, there is no justification for abolishing democracy and replacing it with the absolute rule of one person, one party or one elite'.[157]

The re-interpretation of the Islamic political key concepts and institutions (especially *Shura*) is regarded as a key operational element in Islam–democracy relationship. In his *Reading the Qur'an in the Twenty-First Century*, Abdullah Saeed is of the opinion that the modern interpretations of '*Shura* as democracy' demonstrate that since the twentieth century, the general trend is to interpret *Shura* in the light of new socio-political and cultural contexts. Muslim exegetes and intellectuals 'have been slowly but surely reinterpreting the concept of *Shura as being [not only] akin to democracy and democratic institutions*' but is '*very closely connected to the kind of ideas, values, and institutions of democracy and participatory systems of governance*' as well (italics added).[158]

The whole discussion has shown that the practice of *Shura*, an explicit Qur'anic injunction mandated in the Qur'an and in the Sunnah of the Prophet (pbuh), plays an important role in the socio-political system as it discusses the most important issues of human life. For Muslims, *Shura* is the preferred and desirable method of resolving matters of all walks of life—whether social or political, communal or collective. What also becomes clear is the fact that Prophet (pbuh) used to consult Companions constantly, and in a way, he himself laid the foundations of the institution of Shura (*Shurai'yat*).[159]

From the above discussion, it can be easily inferred that the Muslim exegetes, especially of the modern period, have explored the concept of *Shura* in detail; and thus, since the twentieth century, Muslims have been slowly but surely reinterpreting the concept of Shura as being akin to democracy and democratic values and ideas. Likewise, what also becomes evident, and to put in the terminology of Afsaruddin, is that in the contemporary period, 'liberal and reformist Muslims tend to conflate [compare] *shura* with modern notions of democracy (constitutional and/or liberal).[160] *Shura*, thus, becomes first and foremost key operational concept in the relationship between Islam and democracy and/or the very basis of Islamic democracy.

## Khilafah (Caliphate/Vicegerency)

*Khilafah*, translated as Caliphate/Vicegerency/Representativeness/Stewardship,[161] is an Islamic concept that determines both the actual status of humans as well as shapes the socio-political order of the society. It is the second important concept (after *Shura*) related to contemporary negotiations on Isla and democracy. The Qur'an (Q. 2: 30) introduces Prophet Adam (AS) as the embodiment of the *Fitrah*, or primordial norm, and as the caliph, representative, or vicegerent of God on earth.[162] *Khilafah* is the other name of the God's trust/*Amanah* (Q. 5: 4) bestowed by Allah to humans and is one among the fundamental principles of Islamic political order; and in the study of Islamic political thought, the concept of *Khilafah*, 'has been primarily related to the issue of defining political leadership for the community'.[163] It is considered as the second 'operational' key concept, and a basic stimulator, of the democratic concept in Islam, because in addition to the connotations of being a 'successor', the Arabic term *Khalifah* also involves a sense of a 'deputy, representative, or agent'. And Q. 2: 30 is interpreted in this very sense so as to identify the 'human beings in general as God's agents (*khalifahs*) on earth, and human stewardship over God's creation as the broader cosmic meaning of *khilafah*'.[164] It is on the basis of this broad context and connotation of the term '*Khalifah*' that Abu'l Ala Mawdudi (d. 1979)—one of the prominent South Asian Muslim thinkers and the founder of *Jama'at-i-Islami*—utilized it as a basis for his interpretation of democracy in Islam. Therefore, extensive references have been made of the works, and/or the views, of Mawdudi for the reason that he is the only scholar, among his contemporaries, who utilized the concept of *Khilafah* as a basis for the interpretation of, as well as basis of, democracy in Islam. This concept amplifies and expounds, for Mawdudi, democracy in the following several ways:[165]

Firstly, *Khilafah* is bestowed on the entire group of people, the *Ummah* (universal community of the Muslims) as a whole and is not specified for a few individuals. To put in other words, it is a kind of popular vicegerency, not limited to any particular person, family, tribe, or race, as every Muslim is a *Khalifah* and everyone is accountable to Allah for his services/actions as a vicegerent on the earth. The Qur'an designates all humans as caliph (*Khalifah*), identifying them as the deputies or agents of God on earth. As such, it provides a possible foundation for an Islamic democratic perspective.

Secondly, there is no discrimination of race, colour, and language in sharing the responsibility of the state, everyone is equal in participating in it affairs, for, there is no superiority of one individual over another (except on the basis of *Taqwa* or good deeds) and as Prophet Muhammad (pbuh) has explained in clear terms:

> No one is superior to another except in point of faith and piety. All men are descendants of Adam and Adam was made of clay. An Arab has no superiority over a non-Arab nor a non-Arab over an Arab; neither does a white man possess any superiority over a black nor a black man over a white man, except in point of piety.[166]

In Islamic society, thus, there is no place for dictatorship or authoritarianism of any person or group (as everyone is *Khalifah*). Nobody can deprive the people of their rights to popular vicegerency and declare himself as the absolute ruler. For the purpose of ruling the state, by their will and choice, people concentrate their power or entrust *Khilafah* in a person—on whom *Khilafah* is centred by virtue of his merits—who on the one hand is accountable to Allah whose commands he enforces and on the other to the people who entrust (their) *Khilafah* on him. He has to abide, in all respects, by the divine principles and keep away from any despotic, arbitrary, and totalitarian acts. In this regard, Mawdudi opines that Islam seeks to set up on the one hand, this *superlative democracy* and on the other, it has put an end to that individualism that militates against the health of the body politics. The relations between the individual and the society have been regulated in such a manner that neither the personality of the individual suffers any diminution, nor is the individual allowed to exceed his bounds to such an extent as to become harmful to the community: namely, the execution and enforcement of Divine Law and the attainment of God's pleasure.[167]

Thus, for Mawdudi, the caliphate, when discussed in its proper sense and perspective, is not the point where democracy begins in Islam, but goes further to describe 'the political system of Islam as a *'perfect form of democracy*—as perfect as a democracy can ever be'. He also proclaimed that *Khilafah* as popular vicegerency is the *'real foundation of democracy in Islam'* (Italics added).[168]

Regarding these views of Mawdudi, Esposito and Voll argue that this 'perception of "caliph" becomes' not only 'a foundation for concepts of human responsibility and of opposition to systems of domination', but 'also provides a basis for distinguishing between democracy in Western and in Islamic terms'.[169]

Similarly, for Sadek J. Sulaiman, the concept of *Khilafah*, i.e. God's delegation of authority to the *Ummah* to maintain peace, justice, and prosperity on earth, is universal in the sense that every individual member of the *Ummah* is legally obligated to ensure the proper execution of the delegated authority. Representative governance, through which alone this collective obligation can be properly fulfilled, thus becomes constitutionally binding in Islam. Absolute, cosmic Sovereignty belongs to God, but He has delegated the sovereignty on earth to the people (*Ummah*) through the mandate of *Istikhlaf* (succession). By collectively enjoining the right and forbidding the wrong *(Amr bi al-Ma'ruf wa Nahi 'an al-Munkar)*, the *Ummah* would move ahead, achieving unprecedented heights in human development.[170] Esposito and Voll, basing their views on the arguments and analysis of scholars like Mawdudi, Ayatollah Khomeini, Khurshid Ahmad, thus argue:

> The absolute sovereignty and oneness of God as expressed in the concept of *tawhid* and the role of human beings as defined in the concept of *khilafah* thus provide a framework within which both Sunni and Shi'i scholars have in recent years developed distinctive political theories that are self-described and conceived as being democratic. They involve special definitions and recognitions of popular sovereignty, and an important emphasis on equality of human beings and the obligations of the people in being the bearers of the trust of government. Although these perspectives may not fit into the limits of a Western-based definition of democracy, they represent important perspectives in the contemporary global con-text of democratization.[171]

In presentations of democracy within a broad Islamic conceptual framework, much attention is given to some specific aspects of social and political operation. In particular, 'Islamic democracy' is seen as affirming longstanding Islamic concepts of mutual consultation, consensus, and independent interpretive judgment (*Shura, Ijma', and Ijtihad*). Though these terms/concepts, like many concepts in Western political tradition, 'have not always been identified with democratic institutions and have a variety of usages in contemporary Muslim discourse', however, 'these terms are central to the debates and discussions regarding democratizations in Muslim societies'.[172]

## *Ijma'* (Consensus)

*Ijma'* (literally 'Assembly' or 'consensus')[173]—regarded as the third fundamental source of Islamic *Shari'ah*, after the Qur'an and *Sunnah*—is an Arabic term referring ideally to the consensus of the scholars of Islam (on a particular issue at a particular period of time). It is another 'important operational concept' regarding Islam-democracy compatibility,[174] for ideally speaking, it is the 'consultative process and collective decision-making'.[175] The foundation for the validity of *Ijma'* is the often-cited hadith that the Prophet (pbuh) stated: 'Never will Allah make my Ummah (Community) agree on a wrong course' or 'My Community will never agree upon an error'.[176] *Ijma'* is a consensus, expressed or tacit, on a question of law. Along with the Qur'an, Hadith, and Sunnah, it is the basis that legitimizes law.[177]

*Shura* and *Ijma'* (consultation and consensus), along with other concepts and values, are frequently seen as the basis for Islamic democracy in modern times. Many Muslim writers have claimed that the use of *Ijma'* makes Islamic law compatible with democracy. For John Esposito, 'Consensus played a pivotal role in the development of Islamic law and contributed significantly to the corpus of law or legal interpretation'.[178] Muhammad Hashim Kamali, who defines *Ijma'* as 'the unanimous consensus of the qualified scholars of the Muslim community on a particular issue',[179] is of the opinion that in the pre-modern era of Islamic history, '*Ijtihad* and *ijma'* were the nearest equivalent to parliamentary legislation'; for him:

Two of the most important principles of Islamic law, personal reasoning (*ijtihad*) and consensus (*ijmaʿ*), were put into practice by the jurists without the participation of the government in power. *Ijtihad* and *ijmaʿ* were the nearest equivalent to parliamentary legislation in pre-modern Islam.[180]

In the modern times, Muslim thinkers have imbued the concept of consensus with new possibilities. Louay M. Safi (*Hamad bin Khalifah University*, Doha, Qatar), in this regard, comments that the 'legitimacy of the state depends upon the extent to which state organization and power reflect the will of the *Ummah*', for as classical jurists have insisted, the legitimacy of the state institutions is not derived from textual sources but is based primarily on the principle of *Ijmaʿ*'.[181] Similarly, Mohammed Abu-Nimer (*American University*, Washington, USA) puts it as: 'In addition to *shura, ijma*' (consensus building) is an important mechanism of Islamic decision-making because, with *shura*, it supports collaborative and consensus building processes rather than authoritative, competitive, or confrontational procedures for dealing with differences'.[182]

On this basis, *Ijmaʿ* can become both 'the legitimation and the procedure of an Islamic democracy', or in other words, *Ijmaʿ* (consensus) offers both the 'legitimation of Islamic democracy and a procedure to carry it out'.[183] *Ijmaʿ* needs not to be static as it offers 'great possibilities of developing the Islamic Laws and adapting it to changing circumstances'.[184] *Ijmaʿ*, thus, represents the democratic idealism in Islam.

## *Ijtihad* (Independent Interpretive Reasoning)

*Ijtihad* (literally effort, striving, exerting),[185] is generally translated as independent interpretive judgment or independent legal reasoning, and technically refers to the use of independent judgment to arrive at legal ruling in matters that are not explicit in the Islamic foundational sources. *Ijtihad* is considered, after *Shura and Khilafah,* and *Ijmaʿ*, another operational concept of major importance and basis of the concept of democracy in Islam.[186]

The modernists have adopted and implemented the term ijtihad as a rallying cry, transforming its meaning into the more general task of rational interpretation that helped it adapt to change and new issues arising in the present. It is also regarded as the calling on the believers to draw independent conclusions and judgments on legal and other issues. For Kamrava, the reformists embraced, in a general way, a 'dynamic and context-driven' approach to *Ijtihad*, calling for interpreting the text based on changing and evolving circumstances.[187] The Qur'an repeatedly asks Muslims to change themselves and to constantly strive to change the world so that it could become a more just, equitable, and peaceful abode for humanity (as in *Surah An-Najm*, 53: 39–41). That is why, in Ziauddin Sardar's terminology, at the core of *Shari'ah*, we find the 'principle of *Ijtihad* (sustained and reasoned struggle)'—'a renewed struggle for independence'—which is concerned primarily 'with change and with shaping and reshaping the future'.[188]

In the words of Fazlur Rahman, the formulation of an adequate hermeneutical method is 'imperative' to a proper understanding of Islam.[189] He characterized the intellectual element, both in fundamentalism and modernism movements, as *Ijtihad*, which he defined as 'the effort to understand the meaning of a relevant text or precedent in the past, containing a rule, and to alter that rule by extending, restricting or otherwise modifying it in such a manner that a new situation can be subsumed under it by a new solution'.[190]

Moreover, many Muslim thinkers view it as the key to the implementation of God's will in any given time or place. The position of Khurshid Ahmad is typical of the overall reformist approach to *Ijtihad*:

> God has revealed only broad principles and has endowed man with the freedom to apply them in every age in the way suited to the spirit and conditions of that age. It is through the *Ijtihad* that people of every age try to implement and apply divine guidance to the problems of their times. Thus the basic guidance is of a permanent nature, while the method of its application can change in accordance with the peculiar needs of every age. That is why Islam always remains as fresh and modern as tomorrow's morn.[191]

Virtually all the Muslim intellectuals of the twentieth century and of the contemporary era show much fervour for the concept of *Ijtihad*. Allama Iqbal, Khurshid Ahmad, Taha Jabir al-'Alwani, and Muqtedar Khan being few of them. The advocacy of *Ijtihad* in the context of modernity is explained by Altaf Gauhar with his following insights:

> The present represents a great opportunity to reconstruct our society.... We have to break out of our present state of intellectual stagnation.... It is possible for a secular leader to suggest that power flows out of the barrel of a gun. In Islam power flows out of the framework of the Qur'an and from no other source. It is for Muslim scholars to initiate universal *Ijtihad* at all levels. The faith is fresh; it is the Muslim mind which is befogged. The principles of Islam are dynamic; it is our approach which has become static. Let there be fundamental rethinking to open avenues of exploration, innovation and creativity.[192]

Calling *Ijtihad* as the 'principle of movement in the structure of Islam', and rejecting the so-called closing of the doors of *Ijtihad*, Muhammad Iqbal (d. 1938), the great twentieth-century South Asian Muslim poet-philosopher and intellectual reformer, called for an end to obscurantism, rigidity, and intellectual stasis. In his *Reconstruction of Religious Thought in Islam*, Iqbal argued for the necessity of innovation in Islamic thought through the hermeneutic tool of *Ijtihad*. And in specifically political terms, he notes the relationships between *Ijma'*, democratization, and *Ijtihad* in these words:

> The growth of republican spirit and the gradual formation of legislative assemblies in Muslim lands constitute a great step in advance. The transfer of the power of *Ijtihad* from individual representatives of schools [i.e., classical schools of law] to a Muslim legislative assembly which, in view of the growth of opposing sects, is the only form *Ijma'* can take place in modern times will secure contributions to legal discussion from laymen who happen to possess a keen insight into affairs. In this way alone can we stir into activity the dormant spirit of life in our legal system outlook, and give it an evolutionary outlook.[193]

Challenging the notion that the gates of *Ijtihad* were closed,[194] he asked: 'Did the founders of our schools [of juristic thought] ever claim finality for their reasoning and interpretations?' and answered this question with an emphatic 'Never!' His oft-quoted concluding statement reads:

The claim of the present generation of Muslim liberals to reinterpret the foundational legal principles in the light of their own experience and altered conditions of modern life is, in my opinion, perfectly justified. The teaching of the Qur'an that life is a process of progressive creation necessitates that each generation, guided but unhampered by the work of its predecessors, should be permitted to solve its own problems.[195]

*Ijtihad* is, at the same time, one of the several fundamental Islamic concepts that have been misunderstood or misappropriated by the Muslims; and in this context, al-'Alwani observes that 'the reality, the essence, the rules, the conditions, the premises, the means, and the scope of *ijtihad* have remained a source of debate engaging some of the Islamic world's greatest theologians, scholars of *al-usul*, and *fuqaha'*, from the very beginning to the present day.[196] Because of the 'danger of its misuse', and vulnerability of its misapplication, *Ijtihad* has 'always been controversial concept',[197] and the need of the hour is, as al-'Alwani emphasizes, to 'interpret *Ijtihad* in such a way that it can be used to justify the results, regardless of whether the rulings were based on traditional *fiqhi* [Islamic jurisprudential] criteria or not'.[198]

Thus, many Muslim thinkers, around the globe, today support the idea of using *Ijtihad* to adapt the *Shari'ah* to modern life, even if it means turning away from rulings preserved in the traditional legal schools. Thus, *Ijtihad* is one of the several fundamental Islamic concepts and the need of the hour is to interpret the principle of *Ijtihad* in the right way, for it has a great significance and relevance in the present prevailing conditions in the Muslim world. Al-'Alwani, for instance, advocates the use of *Ijtihad*, especially in cases where modern Western knowledge had to have been taken into consideration. Emphasizing the importance of *Ijtihad*, he expresses the hope that appropriate *Ijtihad* will make it possible for

> Muslim social scientists [need] to study social phenomenon ... with [in] an Islamic framework and epistemological paradigm and then begin the process of rebuilding Islamic civilization on the basis of its own understanding of the social sciences. This deconstruction and subsequent reconstruction is what is needed if the Muslim *ummah* [community] is ever to assume its divinely ordained position as a witness to other nations.[199]

## *Bayʻah* (Oath of Allegiance)

*Bayʻah* (literally 'a pact' or 'an oath of fealty or allegiance' or 'Consent') means, in a very broad sense, the act by which 'a certain number of persons, acting individually or collectively, recognize the authority of another person'—a ruler, a king, or an *Amir*.[200] It also indicates 'a contract between someone who makes an offer and another who accepts it, the latter being the one engaged in *bayʻah*'; and in the political context, means the 'act of accepting and declaring allegiance to a potential ruler'.[201] An important principle of the constitution of Madina was that the Prophet (pbuh) governed the city-state of Medina by virtue of the consent of its citizens. This constitution 'established the importance of consent and cooperation for governance' and the principles of 'equality, consensual governance, and pluralism' are beautifully enmeshed in it.[202] *Bayʻah* was an important institution during the classical/formative period of Islamic history. The early Caliphs adopted *Bayʻah* in order to legitimize the authority of Caliph.

The *Bayʻah*, speaking etymologically, has two principal aims which differ both in their scope and nature: the first is essentially that of adherence to a doctrine and recognition of the pre-established authority of the person who takes it. It is in this sense that the *Bayʻah* was practiced in the relations between the Prophet (pbuh) and his freshly received followers (Q. 43: 10, 18; 60: 13). In the same sense, but with a more restricted purpose, the *bayʻah* served simply to recognize the pre-established authority of a person and to promise him obedience. Such was the case with the *Bayʻah* effected in favour of a new caliph whose title to succeed has been established by the testamentary designation (*ʻAhd*) of his predecessor. In the second sense, the principal aim of the *Bayʻah* is the election of a person to a post of command and, in particular, the election of a Caliph, when a promise of obedience is implied. It was thus that the first Caliph, Abu Bakr (r. 632–634 CE), who was designated through *Bayʻah* of the assembly of S*aqifah* (8 June 632 CE); and the same invariably applied on all subsequent occasions that the seat of the Caliphate fell vacant and no successor designated by other means existed.[203]

In the legal nature, the *Bayʻah* is like a 'contractual agreement': on the one side, there is the will of the electors, expressed in the designation of the candidate, which constitutes the 'offer', and on the other side, the will of the elected person which constitutes the 'acceptance'.[204] Thus, the *Bay'ah* is an act perfected solely by agreement; and its form remains the same in both its roles—that of election and that of simple offer of homage.

In the modern times, the 'process of nomination' followed by elections can serve as a necessary 'modernization of the process of *bayah [Bay'ah]*'; and replacing it with ballots makes the process of pledging allegiance 'simple and universal'. Therefore, in the present times, the elections are 'neither a departure from Islamic principles and traditions nor inherently un-Islamic in any form'.[205] The Qur'anic verses, 4: 59, 3: 159, and 42: 38, also recognize the authority of those who have been chosen as leaders (through consensus or *Bay'ah*) and in a sense deputizes these consensual rulers.

Many modernists[206] tend to interpret the early form of *Bay'ah* as the equivalent of the modern ballot, whereby individuals are allowed to register their opinion regarding the eligibility of specific political candidates. For them, since the rationale behind the *Bay'ah* in the Pious Caliphate period was the soliciting of individual opinion in the election of the leader and such a rationale can best be realized in the contemporary period through the modern voting system—for voting, a right, is now considered to be enshrined in the modern concept of political enfranchisement.

## *Maslaha* (Public Interest)

*Maslaha* (or sometimes as *Maslahah*)—generally speaking, denotes 'welfare'—is used by the jurists to mean 'general good' or 'public interest'. *Maslaha*, a concept in traditional Islamic Law, is invoked to prohibit or permit something on the basis of whether or not it serves the public's benefit or welfare. The concept is related to that of *Istislah*: while the meaning of *Maslaha* is 'public interest', the meaning of *istislah* is 'to seek the best public interest'. According to necessity and particular circumstances, it consists of prohibiting or permitting a thing on the basis of whether or not it serves a 'useful purpose' or *Maslaha*. It can be defined as the establishment of a legal principle recommended by reason of being advantageous.[207]

The famous medieval Muslim scholar and expert, al-Ghazali (d. 1111)—in whose writings *Maslaha* appeared as a mature concept—stated that, in a wider context, *Maslaha* represents 'the preservation of the objective [*maqsud*] of the law [*Shari'ah*] which consists in five things: the protection of religion, life, intellect, lineage, and property. Whatever ensures the protection of these five principles [*usul*] is *maslaha*; whatever goes against their protection is *mafsada* [injury] and to avoid it is *maslaha*'.[208]

Moreover, *Maslaha* was used in one sense by the Maliki jurist Abu Ishaq al-Shatibi (d. 1388), who focused on the motives behind the Islamic Law. Regarding questions related to the obedience to God, i.e. *'ibadat*, humans should look to the Qur'an or the Sunnah for answers, but regarding the relationship between humans, i.e. *mu'amalat*, humans should look for the solutions that suit the public best. Since societies change, al-Shatibi thought that the *mu'amalat* part of the Islamic Law also needed to change.[209]

Historically,[210] this tool of Islamic law—though ably defended by some of its adherents, like al-Shatibi, and others—did not find support in the era when *Ijtihad* was discouraged and *taqlid* prevailed. However, in the modern age, the concept of *Maslaha* has become the subject of an increasing interest among jurists who have sought legal reforms in order to meet the requirements of the modern-day Muslim society. *Maslaha* has also been used by several Muslim reformers in recent centuries, and is more known to Islamic modernists. Among them, Muhammad 'Abduh is especially recognized for using the concept of *Maslaha* as the basis for reconciling modern cultural values with the traditional moral code of Islamic law in the late nineteenth century. But Rashid Rida (d. 1935) might be regarded as the most effective protagonist of the use of *Maslaha* as a source for legal and political reform. In his treatise *al Khilafah, wa al-Imamah al-'Uzma* ('The Caliphate or the Supreme Authority'), Rida tried to re-interpret the *Shari'ah* on the basis of *Maslaha* and *darurah* (necessity) as the expression of the public interest. He made a distinction between *'Ibadat* and *Mu'amalat*, and sought to reform the *Shari'ah* by an 'elected assembly in which the ulema would be represented on the principle of *Maslaha* and *darurah*, presumably by the method of *Ijtihad*, guided by reason'. This approach to legal reform, partly based on *maslaha*, and other legal devices, encouraged modern jurists such as Abd al-Razzaq al-Sanhuri (d. 1968) and others to provide 'modern civil codes' based partly on *Shari'ah* but mainly on Western law. Richard C. Martin highlights the contemporary relevance of *Maslaha* in these words: 'the principle of *maslaha* remains of vital interest and discussion among Muslim jurists, theologians, and social theorists in contemporary Islamic thought'.[211] Among the contemporary reformist thinkers, Tariq Ramadan has dealt with and discussed the concept of *Maslaha* to a great extent. For him, for example, it is a very 'specific concept—in its scope, its levels, its types and its conditions—and requires' a new orientation, direction, and interpretation; and he regards it, along with Ijtihad, as sources and 'foundations of governance' in Islam.[212]

## *Ahl al-Hall wa al-'Aqd* (the 'Wise Ones')

*Ahl al-Hall wa al-'Aqd* is translated variedly as: "Men with the power to loosen and bind' that is, representatives of the community with the power to offer the caliphate to the most qualified person and to depose a sinful ruler'; 'those who are qualified to unbind and to bind'; 'the people who tie and untie'; or those representatives of the Muslim community 'who act on their behalf in appointing and deposing a caliph or another ruler'[213] Azizah al-Hibri translates it as 'those who can enter into a contract or dissolve it', or simply as the 'Wise Ones'; while Hasan al-Turabi renders it as 'those who resolve public affairs'.[214] Having introduced in the classic Islamic political literature, this concept has been interpreted diversely by scholars and is increasingly referred to in the recent times. It is a 'title given to the religious scholars, political leaders and intellectuals who have the authority and influence in the society and the government'.[215] This concept is interpreted diversely by scholars. Such groups of notables in the Muslim society are obliged to carry on several roles, the most important of which is to choose the Muslim ruler. Al-Mawardi and Ibn Taymiyah, along with other classical scholars of Islamic political theory, admit the importance of the notables and their role in choosing the ruler. In medieval political theory, their main function was to offer the office of the caliphate to the most qualified person and, upon his acceptance, to administer to him an oath of allegiance (*bay'ah*) and, in modern political thought, according to Wael B. Hallaq:

> [The title] *ahl al-hall wa-al-'aqd* has gained particular significance. The title is now intimately connected with an expanded meaning of the

concept of *shura*, a term ... [meaning consultation] on political matters, including the appointment of a caliph. In nineteenth- and particularly in twentieth-century political thought, the *ahl al hall*, through the medium of *shura*, speak[s] for the full community.[216]

The Tunisian reformist, Khayr al-Din al-Tunisi (d. 1889) equates this title with a European-style parliament, while as the Egyptian Rashid Rida (d. 1935) entrusts them powers to elect and depose rulers by virtue of their influential status on the community and of their mutual consultation. For Rida, the ruler becomes subservient to *ahl al-Hall*, who expresses through their consultation the will of the community on matters of public law and policy.[217]

Moreover, an investigation of the arguments of several Islamic scholars about the nature of the group of notables and their duties makes it clear that elections of the Muslim ruler through *Ahl al-Halll wa al-'Aqd* is a system that abides by the conditions and guidelines laid down in Qur'an and Sunnah and overcomes several of the flaws that will be presented to be found in the traditional democratic mechanism. Calling them the 'Wise Ones', Azizah al-Hibri, on the selection mechanism (both in past and present) is of the opinion that

> Historically, however, there was no general election of the Wise Ones to their preferred position. Indeed, there was no specific mechanism for selecting them or removing them. They were simply recognized in their society as the Wise Ones. Originally, in the small community of the *Sahaba* and the early Muslims, such recognition was easily achieved. However, as Islam grew and Muslim communities proliferated, it became necessary to develop new ways for choosing the Wise Ones which could cope with the sheer size of the Muslim state, as well as its diverse communities. This was not done. Instead, Islamic government took a different direction.[218]

Thus, all these concepts/notions are not only the basic concepts for understanding the relationship between Islam and democracy, but they provide an 'effective foundation' to build an Islamic basis for democracy as well.[219] The meanings of these terms are contested and their definitions shape Muslim perceptions of what represents legitimate and authentic democracy in an Islamic framework. In a nutshell, these are the concepts for the articulation of Islamic democracy. Presently there are various scholars who are greatly devoted to the Islamic political issues. Sincerely engaged in the resurgence of the Muslim world, they have been engaged in a lively debate on 'Islam and modernity' (e.g. the outlook of Islam on democracy, equality, human rights, minority, gender issues, and women's rights).

Thus, the efforts to utilize these longstanding traditions, ideas, tools, and concepts reflect concern to create more effective forms of participatory democracy. In this regard, Esposito and Voll argue that with the development of 'democratic institutions and practices across significant cultural boundaries over the millennia, it seems at least possible that the forces of globalization will not eliminate wars but will make it possible for different experiences of democratization to assist and influence each other'.[220]

Besides these concepts, the Constitution of Medina is also interpreted not only as a source of constitutionalism and democratizing reform but also of pluralism as well. This represents an important episode in the history of Islam and serves as the bedrock of the Islamic system of governance. Therefore, it is pertinent here to provide a brief explanatory note on it.

## *Mithaq al-Medina* (The Constitution of Medina)

The Constitution/Charter/Covenant of Medina—the principles of which were based on the Qur'an and Sunnah—constitutes the cardinal foundation on which the society and state of Medina were founded. Various modern scholars consider it as a source of constitutionalism, democratizing reform, and of pluralism in Islam as well.[221] It is considered not only as the 'First Written Constitution of the World',[222] but as the 'first Constitution of democracy in the history of constitutional rule',[223] as well as 'the first effort at crafting a political framework for Islamic governance based on the idea of a social contract'.[224] In other words, for modern Muslim scholars, the constitution of Medina is hailed as a predecessor to modern constitutionalism and the rule of law equivalent to the Magna Carta and is often cited as 'key precedent for constitutionalism, rule of law, collective leadership, and democratizing reform'.[225]

With the formulation of the Constitution of Medina (on the basis of Qur'an and Sunnah), the Prophet (pbuh) managed to establish the first Islamic state. This state included people with multi-religious and multi-cultural backgrounds 'into a single community' or *Ummah al-wahidah*, based on universal principles that constituted the Charter or as it is commonly known the 'Constitution of Medina', completed on 24 September 622 CE. In the preamble, the initiator of the Constitution was the Prophet (pbuh) himself and he determined their rights as well as their duties and their position in the society, as one *Ummah*. This Constitution begins as follows:

> In the name of God, the Beneficent and the Merciful. This is a prescript of Muhammad (pbuh) the Prophet and the Messenger of God (to operate) between the faithful and the followers of Islam from among the *Quraish* and the people of *Medina* and those who may be under them, may join then and take part in wars in their company. They shall constitute a separate political unit (*Ummat*) as distinguished from all the people (of the world)'.[226]

The Charter consists of 47 clauses, and according to Muhammad Hamidullah, of 53 clauses/articles.[227] Clauses 1, 2, and 39 state the formation of a sovereign nation-state with a common citizenship, consisting of various communities, principally Muslim Arabs from Makkah (the *Muhajirun* or Immigrants), Muslim Arabs from Yathrib—later on Medina—(the *Ansar* or Helpers), and other monotheists from Yathrib (i.e. the Jews) and others who must be at that time still pagans. They all constituted a unified citizenry (Arabic term, *Ummah*), having equal rights and responsibilities, as distinct from other peoples. 'The Charter provided a federal structure with a centralized authority, with the various tribes in various districts constituting a unit and enjoying autonomy in certain matters of a social, cultural, and religious character.'[228] For Hamidullah, this new constitution of Medina city-state

> brought with it very important and—to Arabia at least—very revolutionary change and improvement, by providing the people with a

central public institution for seeking justice in the place of everyone seeking it with the power of his own hand or at best of that of his family. This epoch-making innovation ... brought an end for all times, to the chaos of tribalism and which laid the basis for a wider institution, viz., state.[229]

The Constitution considered humanity itself as the basis of freedom, justice, and equality (i.e. articles 15 and 17). Montgomery Watt states that the Jews and Christians are with Muslims in constituting a political unit of a new type, an Ummah or 'community';[230] or in Khalid Ahmad Blankinship's words, as a collectivity, the members of the Medina polity are all referred to as believers (*mu'minun*) and one community, whether Muslims or Jews, reflecting the situation shown in the Qur'an 2: 62; 3: 64; and 5: 69, among other verses; and, in this way, providing an 'ideological basis for the Polity'. For him, the Constitution depicts a 'federation of tribes more akin to a republic than an autocracy'.[231]

For Kassim Ahmad, in the constitution of Medina, all the major principles, governing an Islamic society are present: principles like justice, brotherhood and unity of believers, unity and cooperation among citizens of the state, freedom of religion, strict adherence to pacts entered into between parties, cooperation to do good and to prevent evil, encouragement for high moral conduct, and consultation as a method of government. This important constitutional document of Islam 'does not anywhere use the term "Islamic state" of "Islamic society"'.[232]

This Constitution offered the normative establishment of a 'pluralistic community' by granting certain rights and guarantees for both Muslims and non-Muslims living in Medina.[233] On this Constitution, L. Ali Khan argues:

> Conceptually, the Constitution establishes the concept of the community of believers (*ummat-al mumunin*). The community of believers treats all Muslims with equal respect and dignity. It dissolves the distinction between natives and immigrants, offering principles of equality and justice to all Muslims, regardless of their origin of birth, nationality, tribe, or any other ethnic or racial background. It does not allow natives to have superiority over immigrants or vice versa.[234]

Ali Bülac (b. 1951), a prominent Turkish theorist, understood the early Islamic political experience (including the Medina constitution) as democratic and constitutional.[235] Kassim Ahmad considers the Medina Charter as a truly 'remarkable political-constitutional document'[236] and is important not only in the sense that it was the first written constitution but also that it was promulgated for a plural society, giving equal rights to every citizen as well as giving them a say in administrative matters.

Muqtedar Khan believes that the Constitution/Charter of Medina, which established the importance of consent and cooperation for governance, is a 'particular precedent set by the Prophet Muhammad (pbuh) that not only supports the democratic theories of Islamic state but also provides a very important occasion for the development of political theory itself'.[237] According to this Charter, Muslims and non-Muslims were equal citizens of the Islamic state, with identical rights and duties. Communities with different religious orientations enjoyed religious autonomy. The constitution of Madina established a 'pluralistic state—a community of communities'. The principles of equality, consensual governance, and pluralism were central to the Charter of Medina. It is amazing, Khan argues, to see how the Prophet (pbuh) interpretation of the Qur'an was so 'democratic, so tolerant, and compassionate', while some contemporary interpretations of the same are 'so harsh, so authoritarian, and so intolerant.[238] For Khan, the first Islamic state established in Medina was 'based on a social contract, was constitutional in character and the ruler ruled with the explicit written consent of all the citizens of the state'. The Charter of Medina indeed considered all those who were party to it as people who constituted one nation.[239]

Khan, who regards the Constitution of Medina as a 'Social Contract', argues that if we bypass the legalist tradition and return to the original sources of Islam, we will find in the Prophet's example 'an excellent model for an Islamic democracy'; or in other words, as he puts it, the constitution of Medina is an 'excellent manifestation of the Prophet's affinity to democracy and governance by consent'.[240]

Khan even goes further to argue that this Charter 'provides an excellent historical example of two theoretical constructs that have shaped contemporary democratic theory—constitutions and social contracts—and should therefore be of great value to theoretical reflection on the Islamic state'. On the basis of the Compact of Medina, Prophet Muhammad (pbuh) 'ruled Medina by the consent of its citizens and in consultation with them'. The Charter of Medina, which served the dual function of a social contract and a constitution, legitimized his authority over Medina. The Prophet (pbuh), with his prophetic in wisdom, demonstrated a democratic spirit quite unlike the authoritarian tendencies of many of those who claim to imitate him today. He chose to construct and implement a historically specific constitution based on the eternal and transcendent principles revealed to him and sought the consent of all who would be affected by its implementation.[241]

The Constitution introduced a number of political rights and facilities to be provided by the state to all its members, Muslims and non-Muslims alike, in return for the duties. For example, the Constitution promulgated: (i) standing laws defining the rights and duties of all members, (ii) arrangements for impartial decisions on matters of right, and (iii) unfailing protection of the members of the community in the enjoyment of their rights. Indeed, the forty-eight articles of the Constitution of Medina provided these and other facilities and political rights, including: the freedom of belief; the freedom of movement from and to Medina; the assurance that if there is an external threat to non-Muslims, the Muslims would help them and vice versa; the assurance that both Muslims and non-Muslims are believers and would stand together to defend Medina against any attack; and others.[242]

In 'Islamic Constitutionalism and the Concept of Democracy', Azizah al-Hibri, while discussing the role of democracy in the Muslim world, concludes that Islamic *Shari'ah* is compatible with democratic governance and is in structure and form quite similar to the American constitution.[243] She imagines an Islamic polity whose form is democratic and whose content is Islamic. In her own words:

> Islamic law rests on the consent of the Muslim people same way the American Constitution rests on the consent of the American people....
> Regardless of the form of government chosen, the Qur'an requires that the Muslim government be based on the principle of *shura* (consultation). This requirement, combined with the supremacy of Islamic law

and the fact that the interpretation of such law rests with the *mujtahids* points to a *de facto* if not *de jure* separation of powers.

For this reason, the ... attempts by Muslim to improve the democratic character of their various Muslim states, if properly undertaken, need not run afoul of the rule of Islamic law, but may in fact enhance it (italics in original).[244]

The above discussion reveals that there are numerous concepts—ideas and ideals—which are regarded, and (re)interpreted as the basis and foundations of democracy in Islam. Especially, the concept of *Shura* is viewed not only the source of democratic ethics in Islam but is also considered, by many intellectuals and scholars, as the synonymous and similar to western democracy in its spirit and procedure. It also reveals that the ideas pertaining to democracy have their origins in the foundational texts of Islam and scholars, in the modern times, have attempted to show their resemblance with the (modern) democracy and democratic procedures. How these notions—ideas and ideals—are conceptualized, envisioned, and projected as the basis of democracy in Islam, is further elaborated in the next chapters, which focus on the views and observations of modernist/reformist thinkers' of the nineteenth to twenty-first centuries, whether of South Asia, or Arab world, or the Muslim scholars of (or based in) the West.

## Notes

1. *Tawhid*, the acknowledging of the Unity of Allah, the Indivisible, Absolute, and the sole Real, is the co-ordinal, basic and fundamental principle of Islamic life meaning that Absolute Sovereignty and Ultimate Authority belong to Him, as in the Qur'an, Q. 25: 2: *It is He who has control over the heavens and earth and has no offspring—no one shares control with Him—and who created all things and made them to an exact measure.* For details see, Cyrill Glasse, *Concise Encyclopedia of Islam* (London: Stacey International, 1989), p. 400.
2. Fazlur Rahman, *Major Themes of the Qur'an* (Minneapolis: Bibliotheca Islamica, 1980), p. 58.
3. Isma'il Raji' al-Faruqi, *Al-Tawhid: Its Implications for Thought and Life*, 2nd ed. (Herndon, Virginia: IIIT, 1992 [1982]), p. 1.
4. Khurshid Ahmad, *The Religion of Islam* (Lahore: Islamic Publications, 1967), pp. 6–7; Idem., (ed.), *Islam: Its Meaning and Message* (London: The Islamic Foundation, 1999 [1975]), pp. 29–31 [hereinafter abbreviated as *IIMM*].

5. Khurshid Ahmad, 'Islam and Democracy: Some Conceptual and Contemporary Dimensions', *The Muslim World*, 90: 1&2, Spring 2000, p. 2 [hereafter Ahmad in *MW*].
6. John L. Esposito and John O. Voll, *Islam and Democracy* (New York: Oxford University Press, 1996), pp. 23, 27.
7. Ahrar Ahmad, 'Islam and Democracy: Text, Tradition, and History', *AJISS*, 20, 1 (2003): 20–45, pp. 35–36.
8. Ibid., p. 36.
9. For this section, the main works consulted are: Ibn Manzur, *al-Lisan al-Arab* (Beirut: Dar Sadir, 1968), IV: p. 434–437; Abdul Mannan Omar, *Dictionary of the Holy Qur'an: Arabic Words-English Meanings (with Notes)*, Rep. 2010 (Hockessin, New Castle: Noor Foundation International, Inc., 2010 [2003]), p. 301; Elsaid M. Badawi and Muhammad Abdel Haleem, *Arabic-English Dictionary of Qur'anic Usage* (Leiden and Boston: Brill, 2008), p. 502; Zahoor Ahmad Azhar, 'Shura', in Mahmudul Hasan Arif (Editor-in-Chief), *Urdu Dai'rah Ma'arif-i-Islamiya*, 24 Vols. (Lahore: Danishgah Punjab, 1975), XI: 810–812, p. 810; Bernard Lewis, 'Shura', in C. E. Bosworth, et al., (eds.), *The Encyclopedia of Islam* [*EI²*], New Edition (Leiden: E. J. Brill, 1997), IX: p. 504; Ahmad Mubarak al-Baghdadi, 'Consultation', (trans.) Brannon M. Wheeler, in Jane Dammen McAuliffe (ed.), *The Encyclopedia of Qur'an* [*EQ*] (Leiden: E. J. Brill, 2001), I: p. 406; Afzalur Rehman (ed.), *Muhammad: Encyclopedia of Seerah* [*MES*] (London: Seerah Foundation, 1998), VI: 395; Patricia Crone, ' "Shura" as an Elective Institution', *Quaderni di Studi Arabi* [*QSA*], 19 (2001): 3–39; Csaba Okvath and Muzaffar Iqbal, 'Consultation (Shura)', in Muzaffar Iqbal (General Editor), *The Integrated Encyclopedia of Qur'an* [*IEQ*], Vol. 1 (Sherwood Park, Canada: Centre for Islamic Sciences, 2013), retrieved from https://online.iequran.com/articles/C/85 (last accessed on 15 July 2021); Tauseef Ahmad Parray, *Towards Understanding Some Qur'anic Terms, Concepts, and Themes* (Karachi: Qirtas Books, 2017), pp. 249–261; Idem., *Exploring the Qur'an: Concepts and Themes* (Srinagar, J&K: Kitab Mahal Publishers, 2019), pp. 207–226; Idem., *Recent Trends in Qur'anic Scholarship* (New Delhi: Viva Books Pvt. Ltd., in association with K. A. Nizami Centre for Quranic Studies, AMU, Aligarh, 2020), esp. ch. 2, 'The Qur'anic Concept of *Shura*: Text, Tradition, and Modern (Varied) Interpretations': 26–47.
10. Parray, *Recent Trends in Qur'anic Scholarship*, p. 26.
11. Crone, in *QSA*, *op. cit.*, p. 3.
12. Mufti Muhammad Shafi, *Ma'ariful Qur'an* (trans.) Muhammad Shamim (New Delhi: Farid Book Depot, 2008), II: p. 227 [hereafter abbreviated as *MQ*].
13. Amin Ahsan Islahi, *Tadabbur al-Qur'an* (Delhi: Taj Company, 1989), II: p. 178 [hereafter abbreviated as Islahi, *Td.Q*].
14. Asma Afsaruddin, 'The "Islamic State": Genealogy, Facts, and Myths', *Journal of Church and State* [*JCS*], 48, 1 (2006): 153–173, p. 159; Idem., 'Consultation, or *Shura*', in Josef W. Meri (ed.), *Medieval Islamic Civilization: An Encyclopedia* [*MICE*] (New York: Routledge, 2006), I: p. 171; Idem., *The First Muslims: History*

*and Memory* (Oxford: Oneworld Publications, 2008), pp. 169–170 [hereafter cited as Afsaruddin, *The First Muslims*].
15. Afsaruddin, in *MICE*, I: 171; Idem., *The First Muslims*, p. 170.
16. These verses read as: 'and if they decide on weaning, by mutual consent, and after due consultation (*tashawur*), there is no sin on them'. (2: 233); 'and consult with them (*shawirhum*) in the affairs. Then when you have taken a decision, put your trust in Allah' (3: 159); and 'and who conduct their affairs by mutual consultation (*Shura*)' (42: 38).
17. Al-Baghdadi, *loc. cit.*
18. Okvath and Iqbal, in *IEQ, loc. cit.*
19. S. A. Q. Husaini, 'The Shura', *Journal of the Pakistan Historical Society*, III, II (April 1955): 151–165, p. 151 [hereafter cited as Husaini, *JPHS*]. *Journal of the Pakistan Historical Society* is now known as *Historicus*.
20. Afsaruddin in *MICE*, I: 171; Idem., in *JCS*, p. 168. *Mala'* literally means a 'group (of people)', or a 'host', or a 'crowd'. The word denotes decisions taken as a result of collective consultation. Since collective decisions are taken usually by the leaders of the group, al-Mala' very often denotes the notables and leaders of the community. For details, see, U. Rubin, 'Mala', in *EI²*, XII: 573–574.
21. Husaini, *op. cit.*, p. 152.
22. Ana Belén Soage, '*Shurà* and Democracy: Two Sides of the Same Coin?', *Religion Compass*, 8, 3 (2014): 90–103, p. 90.
23. Al-Sulami, *The West and Islam*, p. 38.
24. Ibid.
25. Qussay (or Kusayy), an ancestor of the Prophet (pbuh) in the 5th generation, was the restorer of the pre-Islamic cult of the Ka'bah in Makkah—built a house quite close to the Ka'bah was henceforth the centre of the civil and religious functions of the Quraysh under the name of Dar al-Nadwah. For details, see, G. Levi Della Vida, 'Kusayy', in *EI²*, V: 519–20; R. Paret, 'Dar al-Nadwah', in *EI²*, II: 128.
26. Paret, *op. cit.*, II: 128; Syed Ameer Ali, *A Short History of Saracens*, 4th ed. (New Delhi: Adam Publishers and Distributors, 2010 [1898]), p. 6; Ibn Hisham, *Al-Seerah al-Nabwiyya* (Cairo: Dar al-Fikr, 1996), I: pp. 141–142; al-Sulami, *op. cit.*, pp. 38–39.
27. al-Baghdadi, *op. cit.*, I: 407; Obaidullah Fahad, *Islamic Shura: State, Religion and Government* (New Delhi: Serials Publications, 2007), p. 22.
28. Ibn Hisham, *op. cit.*, II: 508.
29. Husaini, *op. cit.*, p. 154.
30. al-Baghdadi, in *EQ*, 1: 407.
31. Ibid. *cf.* Okvath and Iqbal, in *IEQ, loc. cit.*
32. al-Baghdadi, 'Consultation', *loc. cit.*
33. Ahmad al-Raysuni, *Al-Shura: The Qur'anic Principle of Consultation* (trans.) Nancy Roberts, and abridged by Alison Lake (Herndon, VA: The International Institute of Islamic Thought [IIIT], [2011] 2012), p. 3.

34. *Surah al-Baqarah* (2: 233) reads as: '... No mother shall be treated unfairly on account of her child, or father on account of his child. And on the (father's) heir is incumbent the like of that (which was incumbent on the father). If they both decide on weaning, by mutual consent, and after due consultation, there is no sin on them. And if you decide on a foster suckling-mother for your children, there is no sin on you, provided you pay (the mother) what you agreed (to give her) on reasonable basis. And fear Allah and know that Allah is All-Seer of what you do'.
35. Yusuf Ali, *op. cit.*, fn. no. 266, p. 93.
36. *Surah Al-i-'Imran* (3: 159) reads as: 'And by the Mercy of Allah, you dealt with them gently. And had you been severe and harsh-hearted, they would have broken away from about you; so pass over (their faults), and ask (Allah's) Forgiveness for them; and consult them in the affairs. Then when you have taken a decision, put your trust in Allah, certainly, Allah loves those who put their trust (in Him)'.
37. Regarding the commentary (*tafsir*) of these two verses (3: 159 and 42: 38), references have been made to the commentaries of those exegetes (*Mufassirun*) whose views are to be discussed in the coming chapters of this work, like Mufti Muhammad Shafi, Mufti Shabbir Ahmad 'Uthmani, Abul Kalam Azad, Syed Abu'l 'Ala Mawdudi, Amin Ahsan Islahi, etc.
38. Shafi, *MQ*, II: 226; also cited in Parray, *Recent Trends in Qur'anic Scholarship*, p. 30.
39. Islahi, *Td.Q*, II: 208–209; also cited in Parray, *Recent Trends in Qur'anic Scholarship*, p. 30.
40. Jalal al-Din al-Suyuti, *Al-Durr al-Manthur fi Tafsir bi al-Mathur* (Beirut: Dar al-Thaqafah, n.d.), II: p. 90; also cited in Parray, *Recent Trends in Qur'anic Scholarship*, p. 30.
41. Shafi, *MQ*, II: 227; also cited in Parray, *Recent Trends in Qur'anic Scholarship*, p. 30.
42. Muhammad Yusuf Faruqi, 'The Institution of *Shura*: Views of Early *Fuqaha*' and the Practices of the *Rashidun Khulafa*", *Jihat al-Islam*, 1, 2 (2008): 9–30, p. 12 [hereafter cited as Faruqi in *JI*].
43. Mawlana Abul Kalam Azad, *Tarjaman al-Qur'an* (New Delhi: Sahitya Academy, 1966), V: p. 334 [hereafter abbreviated as *Tj.Q*]; Mawlana Abu'l 'Ala Mawdudi, *Tafhim al-Qur'an* (New Delhi: Markazi Maktaba Islami Publishers, 2003), IV: p. 508 [hereafter abbreviated as *Tf.Q*], as cited in Parray, *Recent Trends in Qur'anic Scholarship*, p. 30.
44. *Surah al-Shura* (42: 38) reads as: 'Those who hearken to their Lord, and establish regular Prayer; who (conduct) their affairs by mutual Consultation; who spend out of what We bestow on them for Sustenance'.
45. Shafi, *MQ*, II: 228; also cited in Parray, *Recent Trends in Qur'anic Scholarship*, p. 30.
46. Azad, *Tj.Q*, V: 334–335.
47. Mufti Shabbir Ahmad 'Uthmani, *Qur'an Majeed* (New Delhi: Taj Company, n.d.), p. 632.
48. Parray, *Recent Trends in Qur'anic Scholarship*, p. 31.
49. Afsaruddin, 'Consultation', in *MIC-E*, I: 171–172.
50. Parray, *Recent Trends in Qur'anic Scholarship*, p. 32.

51. Abdullah Saeed, *Reading the Qur'an in the Twenty-First Century: A Contextualist Approach* (London: Routledge, 2013), pp. 148, 157.
52. Asma Afsaruddin, *Contemporary Issues in Islam* (Edinburgh: Edinburgh University Press, 2015), p. 77.
53. This hadith is cited in Shafi, *MQ*, II: 219 and VII: 698 and Mawlana Gauhar Rahman, *Islami Siyasat* [*Islamic Politics*] (Rampur, U.P., India: Maktaba Zikra, 1982), p. 284.
54. *Baihaqi*, as quoted in Shafi, *MQ*, II: 228 and VII: 698.
55. Ibn Majah, *al-Sunnan* (ed.) M. Fuad Abdul Baqi (Cairo, n.p.; n.d.), II: 1233, *Hadith* no. 374.
56. See, for example, Husaini, *op. cit.*, p.155; Rehman, *MES*, VI: 395; Al-Sulami, *op. cit.*, pp. 43–45; Fahad, *op. cit.*, p. 24; Soage in *RC*, pp. 91–92.
57. See, for example, Ibn Hisham, *op. cit.*, I: 620; Rehman, *loc. cit.*; Fahad, *op. cit.*, pp. 24, 25; Mohammad Muslehuddin, *Islam and Its Political System* (Islamabad, Pakistan: Dr Muslehuddin Islamic Trust, IIUI, 1988), pp. 137–138. See also, Q. 2: 217.
58. See, for example, Muslehuddin, *op. cit.*, p. 139; Rehman, *loc. cit.*; Fahad, *op. cit.*, p. 27; al-Sulami, *op. cit.*, pp. 43–44; Rahman, *Islami Siyasat*, p. 270; see also, Q. 3: 159.
59. See, for example, Al-Waqidi, *Kitab al-Maghazi* (Oxford: Oxford University Press, 1966), II: pp. 444–445, also cited in Fahad, *op. cit.*, p. 29.
60. For details, see, Waqidi, *op. cit.*, 2: 643–644; Fahad, *op. cit.*, pp. 30–31.
61. See, Ismail al-Bukhari, *al-Jame al-Sahih*, 'Kitab al-Maghazi', III: 31–32, as quoted in Fahad, *op. cit.*, p. 34; Rehman, *MES*, VI: 395; Rahman, *Islami Siyasat*, p. 282.
62. Al-Sulami, *op. cit.*, p. 43.
63. Ibn Hisham, *op. cit.*, II: 128–129.
64. Bukhari, *op. cit.*, 'Bab al-Masjid', as quoted in Fahad, *op. cit.*, p. 37.
65. Ibn Hisham, *op. cit.*, I: 234, as cited by Fahad, *loc. cit.*
66. Suyuti, *loc. cit.*; also cited in Fahad, *op. cit.*, p. 21; Soage in *RC*, pp. 91–92. Afsaruddin, *JCS*, p. 159, mentions this Tradition as: '*I did not see anyone more [predisposed] to consultation with his Companions than the Prophet.*'
67. Soage in *RC*, p. 92.
68. Abdul Rashid Moten, *Political Science: An Islamic Perspective* (London: Macmillan Press Ltd., 1996), pp. 91–92.
69. S. Waqar Ahmed Husaini, *Islamic Environmental Engineering Systems* (USA: American Trust Publications; and UK: Macmillan, 1980), p. 96, as cited in Moten, *op. cit.*, pp. 92–93.
70. Muhammad b. Abdullah al-Darmi, *Al-Sunnan* (India: al-Matba al-Nizami), I: pp. 32–33, no. 161; al-Baihaqi, *al-Sunnan al-Kubra*, 10: 114–15, as cited by Fahad, *op. cit.*, pp. 42–43; Faruqi in *JI*, *op. cit.*, p. 20; Rahman, *Islami Siyasat*, p. 288.
71. Allama Shibli Nu'mani, *Al-Farooq* (Azamgarh: Ma'arif Press, 1376/1956).
72. Ibid., Part II, p. 13.

73. Ibn al Sa'ad, *al-Tabaqat al-Kubra* (Beirut: Dar Sader, 1957), III: p. 134, as cited in Nu'mani, *op. cit.*, II: 14.
74. Nu'mani, *op. cit.*, pp. 14, 15.
75. Ibid., p. 16.
76. Tabari, *op. cit.*, III: 480–483, as cited by Faruqi in *JI*, p. 21.
77. Faruqi, *loc. cit.*
78. For details, see Abu 'Ubayd, *Kitab al-Amwal* (Cairo: Maktabba al-Kulliyya al-Azhariyyah, 1395/1975), pp. 60–61; Abu Yusuf, *Kitab al-Kharaj* (Cairo: Maktabba al-Salaffiyyah, 1976), p. 27, as cited by Faruqi, *JI*, p. 22.
79. For details, see al-Tabari, *op. cit.*, III: 586–588; also cited in Faruqi, *JI*, pp. 22–23; Muslehuddin, *op. cit.*, pp. 140–141.
80. See, Ahmad b. Yahya al-Baladhuri, *Futuh al-Buldan* (Cairo: Dar al-Nashr li al-Jamein, 1957), pp. 635–636, as cited by Fahad, *op. cit.*, p. 70.
81. See, Abu Yusuf, *op. cit.*, p. 64; Fahad, *op. cit.*, p. 71.
82. See, Tabari, *op. cit.*, IV: 100.
83. Ibid., IV: 38, 39.
84. Nu'mani, *op. cit.*, II: 123 ff.
85. In this regard, Shibli Nu'mani has cited many examples; e.g. the case of bath of *Janabah* (sexual purification); differences of opinion with regard to the number of *Takbirs* in the funeral Prayer (*Nimaz al-Janazah*). For details, see, Nu'mani, *op. cit.*, II: 123.
86. Shah Wali Ullah, *Hujjatullah al-Balighah*, 1st ed. (Lahore: Maktabah al-Salafiyyah, 1975), I: p. 132; as cited by Nu'mani, *op. cit.*, II: 216; see also Amin Ahsan Islahi, *Islami Riyasat*, 'The Islamic State' (trans.) Tariq Mahmood Hashmi (Germany: Lambert Academic Publishing, 2012), p. 20.
87. Tabari, *op. cit.*, IV: 229, as cited in Faruqi, *op. cit.*, p. 24.
88. Majid Khan, *The Pious Caliphate* (Kuwait: Karamatullah Sheikh, 1982), p. 101.
89. Crone, in *QSA*, *op. cit.*, p. 14.
90. Waki, *Akhbar al-Qudat* (Cairo: 'Alam al-Kutub, n.d.), 1: 110.
91. Urooj Sadeq Ibrahim, *'Uthman b. 'Affan* (Cairo, 1947), p. 99, as cited in Fahad, *op. cit.*, p. 78.
92. Tabari, *op. cit.*, IV: 433, as cited in Faruqi, *op. cit.*, p. 26.
93. Tibi, 'Major Themes in the Arabic Political Literature of Islamic Revivalism' (II), *ICMR* (1993), p. 87.
94. Fahad, *op. cit.*, pp. 78–79.
95. Ali, *op. cit.*, pp. 56–57.
96. Faruqi, *loc. cit.*
97. Goran Larsson, 'Yusuf al-Qaradawi and Tariq Ramadan on Secularization: Differences and Similarities', in Gabriele Marranci (ed.), *Muslim Societies and the Challenge of Secularization: An Interdisciplinary Approach* (London: Springer, 2010), ch. 4, pp. 47–63, p. 50.
98. Crone, in *QSA*, *op. cit.*, p. 26.
99. C. E. Bosworth, 'Shura: In Early Islamic History', in *EI$^2$*, IX: 505.

100. Fazlur Rahman, 'The Principle of *Shura* and the Role of the Umma in Islam', *American Journal of Islamic Studies (AJIS)* [later renamed as *American Journal of Islamic Social Sciences* (AJISS) and again as *American Journal of Islam and Society* (AJIS)] 1, 1 (Spring 1984): 1–9.
101. Ahmad in *MW*, p. 12.
102. Al-Khaduri, *Tarikh Umam al-Islamiyah*, II: 292, as cited in Husaini, *op. cit.*, p. 162.
103. Husaini, *loc. cit.*
104. Ali, *op. cit.*, p. 405.
105. Ibid.
106. See, among others, Lewis, '*Mashwara*', in *EI²*, VI: 725.
107. Al-Sulami, *op. cit.*, p. 53.
108. Ali, *op. cit.*, p. 406.
109. Ahmad, *MW*, p. 11.
110. Esposito and Voll, *Islam and Democracy*, p. 47.
111. Lewis, *op. cit.*, VI: 725.
112. Here Esposito and Voll, *op. cit.*, p. 48, refers to Stanford J. Shaw, *History of the Ottoman Empire and Modern Turkey* (Cambridge: Cambridge University Press, 1976), I: pp. 134–138.
113. Esposito and Voll, *op. cit.*, pp. 48–49.
114. Mubasher Ahmad, *Khilafat and Caliphate*: 1–13, p. 7, available online at https://www.alislam.org/topics/khilafat-and-caliphate/ (last accessed 20 May 2010)
115. A. Ayalon, 'Shura: In the Modern Arab World', in *EI²*, IX: 506.
116. Ibid.
117. Rahman, *AJIS*, pp. 6–7.
118. Rahman, *MES*, VI: 402.
119. Ibn 'Atiyya al-Hayan, *Al-Bahr al-Muhit*, as quoted in Rahman, *loc. cit.*
120. *Tibrul Masbuk*, p. 71, as cited by H. K. Sherwani, *Studies in Muslim Political Thought and Administration*, 2nd and Rev. ed. (Lahore: Sheikh Mohd. Ashraf, 1945), pp. 177–178.
121. Abd al-Rehman Azzam, 'The Islamic State', in *Concept of Islamic State* (London: Islamic Council of Europe, 1979), pp. 11–18, p. 12, as cited by Rehman, *MES*, VI: 403.
122. Muhammad Saleem El-Awa, *On the Political System of Islamic State* (Indianapolis: American Trust Publications, 1980), p. 97.
123. Mustafa Abu Zayd Fahmi, *Fann al-Hukm fi al-Islam* [The Art of Government in Islam] (Cairo: Al-Maktab al-Misri al-Hadith, 1981), pp. 195–255, as cited in Tibi, *op. cit.*, p. 87.
124. Tibi, *op. cit.*, p. 87.
125. Fahmi, *Fann al-Hukm fi al-Islam*, pp. 200–201, as cited in Tibi, *op. cit.*, p. 88.
126. Fahmi, *op. cit.*, p. 204, as cited in Tibi, *loc. cit.*
127. Fahmi, *op. cit.*, p. 212, as cited in Tibi, *op. cit.*, p. 89.
128. Fahmi, *op. cit.*, p. 248, as cited in Tibi, *loc. cit.*

129. Asad, *The Principles of State and Government in Islam,* pp. 44–45. *Cf.* Idem., *The Message of the Qur'an* (Gibraltar: Dar al Andalus, 1980), Q. 3: p. 159, fn. 122, p. 145; Q. 42: 38, fn. 38, p. 1013.
130. Yusuf al-Qaradawi, *State in Islam,* 3rd Ed. (Cairo: Al-Falah Foundation for Translation, Publication and Distribution, 2004), pp. 218–220. The book is originally in Arabic: *Min Fiqh al-Dawla fi al-Islam* (Cairo: Dar al-Shurouk, 2001 [1997]).
131. Hafijur Rahman, 'Toward a Wise Political Fiqh: The Perception of State in the Political Thought of Yusuf al-Qaradawi', *ASBIDER—Akademi Sosyal Bilimler Dergisi,* 7, 21 (2020): 6–22, p. 19.
132. Parray, *Recent Trends in Qur'anic Scholarship,* p. 35.
133. Rane, in Lukens-Bull and Woodward (Eds.), *Handbook of Contemporary Islam and Muslim Lives,* p. 1071.
134. Asad, *The Principles of State and Government in Islam,* p. 43.
135. Tariq Ramadan, *Islam, the West and the Challenges of Modernity* (Leicester, UK: The Islamic Foundation, 2004), pp. 81, 92.
136. Tariq Ramadan, *Western Muslims and the Future of Islam* (New York: Oxford University Press, 2004), pp. 158–159 [hereafter cited as Ramadan, *Western Muslims*].
137. Sadek J. Sulaiman, 'Shura Principle in Islam', http://www.alhewar.com/SadekShura.htm (last accessed on 25 December 2021).
138. Sadek J. Sulaiman, 'Democracy and Shura', in Kurzman (ed.), *Liberal Islam, op. cit.*: 96–98, p. 97 [hereafter cited as Sulaiman, in Kurzman, *Liberal Islam*].
139. Ibid., p. 98.
140. Afsaruddin, *The First Muslims,* p. 198.
141. Ibid., p. 170; Idem., in *JCS,* p. 159.
142. Afsaruddin, *The First Muslims, loc. cit.*
143. Sayed Khattab and Gary D. Bouma, *Democracy in Islam* (New York: Routledge, 2007), pp. 91–92.
144. Muhammad Hamidullah, *Introduction to Islam,* new and enlarged edition (Gary, Ind.: International Islamic Federation of Student Organizations, 1969), p. 100.
145. John L. Esposito, *Islam and Politics,* 3rd ed. (Syracuse: Syracuse University Press, 1991), p. 149.
146. Esposito and Voll, *op. cit.,* p. 28.
147. Ramadan, *Islam, the West and the Challenges of Modernity,* pp. 84–86. This section is reproduced, in excerpts, online as 'Notion of Shura: Shura and Democracy', on *The American Muslim (TAM),* dated 1 September 2002, http://www.theamericanmuslim.org/tam.php/features/articles/notion_of_shr_shr_or_democracy/
148. Ramadan, *Islam, the West and the Challenges of Modernity,* p. 84.
149. Ibid.

150. Omar Ashour, 'Democratic Islam? Assessing the Bases of Democracy in Islamic Political Thought', *McGill Journal of Middle East Studies* [*MJMES*], 9, 1 (2008): 7–27, p. 14.
151. Ibid., p. 16.
152. Ibid., p. 19.
153. Nazih N. Ayubi, *Political Islam: Religion and Politics in the Arab World* (London and New York: Routledge, 1993 [1991]), p. 49.
154. Khalid M. Khalid's interview in *Mayu*, 8 March 1982, as cited in Ayubi, *loc. cit.*
155. Asma Afsaruddin, *Contemporary Issues in Islam* (Edinburgh: Edinburgh University Press, 2015), p. 77.
156. Ziauddin Sardar, *Reading the Qur'an: The Contemporary Relevance of the Sacred Text of Islam* (Gurgaon, India: Hachette Book Publishing India Pvt. Ltd., 2011), pp. 295–296.
157. Muhammad Shahroor, 'A Proposed Charter for Muslim Activists', August 1999, as cited in Graham E. Fuller, *The Future of Political Islam* (New York: Palgrave Macmillan, 2003), p. 61 and Saeed, *Reading the Quran in the Twenty-First Century*, p. 155.
158. Saeed, *Reading the Quran in the Twenty-First Century*, p. 157 [ch. 13, '*Shura* and democracy', pp. 148–159].
159. Parray, *Recent Trends in Qur'anic Scholarship*, p. 42.
160. Afsaruddin in *JCS*, p. 160.
161. Caliphate/Caliph (Arabic: *Khilafah/Khalifah*): Caliph is the title of the ruler of the Islamic community after the demise of Prophet (pbuh) in 632 CE. The term *Khalifa*—which is used in the Qur'an with reference to Adam (*Q.* 2: 30) and David (*Q.* 38: 26)—is understood in Sunni juristic theory as the successor of the Prophet (pbuh). The Arabic term *Khilafah*, 'caliphate', denotes the political headship of the Muslim community, which remained in vogue, though nominally, from 632 to 1924 CE.
162. Glasse, *op. cit.*, p. 84.
163. Esposito and Voll, *Islam and Democracy*, p. 25.
164. Ibid., p. 26.
165. For details, see Syed Abu Ala Mawdudi, *Islamic Way of Life* (trans.) Khurshid Ahmad (Delhi: Markazi Maktaba Islami, 1967); Idem., *Islami Riyasat* [Islamic State] (New Delhi: Islamic Book Foundation, 1991).
166. Baihaqi Vide, Mawdudi, *Islami Riyasat*, p. 141.
167. Mawdudi, *op. cit.*, p. 143.
168. Ibid., p. 140; Idem., *Islamic Way of Life* (trans.) Khurshid Ahmad (Delhi: Markazi Maktaba Islami, 1967), p. 44.
169. Esposito and Voll, *Islam and Democracy*, p. 26.
170. Sulaiman, *loc. cit.*
171. Esposito and Voll, *Islam and Democracy*, p. 27.
172. Ibid.

173. *Ijma'* (literally 'Assembly') is a consensus (of scholars), expressed or tacit, on a question of law. It is one of the principles of Islamic law, based on the *Hadith* (Prophetic saying), '*my community shall never be in agreement in error*' (Al-Tirmidhi). Along with Qur'an and Hadith, it is the basis that legitimizes the law.
174. Esposito and Voll, *Islam and Democracy*, p. 28.
175. Afsaruddin, *op. cit.*, p. 171.
176. *Al-Tirmidhi*, on the authority of 'Abd Allah Ibn 'Umar (RA), vide Asad, *op. cit.*, p. 38.
177. Glasse, *op. cit.*, p. 182.
178. John L. Esposito, *Islam: The Straight Path*, 5th ed. (New York: Oxford University Press, 2016 [1988]), p. 107.
179. Mohammad Hashim Kamali, 'The *Shari'a*: Law as the Way of God', in Vincent J. Cornell (ed.), *Voices of Islam*, 5 vols.; Vol. I: Voices of Tradition (Westport, CT: Praeger Publishers, 2007) [ch. 12: 149–181], p. 171.
180. Ibid.
181. Louay M. Safi, 'The Islamic State: A Conceptual Framework', *AJISS*, 8, 2 (Sep 1991): 221–34, p. 233 [hereafter cited as Safi in *AJISS*].
182. Mohammed Abu-Nimer, 'Framework for Nonviolence and Peacebuilding in Islam', in Abdul Aziz Said, Mohammed Abu-Nimer and Meena Sharify-Funk (eds.), *Contemporary Islam: Dynamic, Not Static* (Oxon and New York: Routledge, 2006), ch. 9, pp. 131–172, p. 160.
183. Esposito and Voll, *Islam and Democracy*, p. 29.
184. Hamidullah, *Introduction to Islam*, p. 130.
185. *Ijtihad* (literally 'effort') means, in general usage, the utmost effort, physical or mental, expended in a particular activity. In its technical and legal connotations, it denotes the thorough exertion of a jurist's mental faculty in finding out a solution to a legal question. For history, development, trends, and controversies in *Ijtihad*, see Wael B. Hallaq, *A History of Islamic Legal Theories* (Cambridge: Cambridge University Press, 1997); Idem., 'Was the Gate of Ijtihad Closed?', *International Journal of Middle East Studies* [*IJMES*] 16 (1984): 3–41; Joseph Schacht, *An Introduction to Islamic Law* (Oxford: Clarendon Press, 1964).
186. Some of my previous writings related to *Ijtihad* are: Tauseef Ahmad Parray, 'The Legal Methodology of '*Fiqh al-Aqalliyyat*' and Its Critics: An Analytical Study' *Journal of Muslim Minority Affairs* [*JMMA*], 32, 1 (March 2012): 88–107; Idem., 'Importance of *Ijtihad* for Muslims in 21st Century', *Kashmir Reader*, 13 March 2015, p. 7; Idem., '*Ijtihad*: Connotation and Implication', *Pakistan Observer*, 27 March 2015, p. 5; Idem., 'Tools for Reformation in Islam', *The Islamic Quarterly* [*IQ*], 60, 2 (2016): 231–245; Idem., *Towards Understanding the Qur'anic Terms, Concepts, and Themes* (Karachi, Pakistan: Qirtas Publishers, 2017), esp. ch. 20, '*Ijtihad*: Implications and Importance', pp. 240–248.
187. Kamrava, *New Voices of Islam*, p. 10.
188. Ziauddin Sardar, 'What Do We Mean by Islamic Future?' in Ibrahim Abu Rabi' (ed.), *The Blackwell Companion to Contemporary Islamic Thought* (UK, USA, Australia: Blackwell Publishing Ltd., 2006), pp. 562, 572.

189. Fazlur Rahman, *Islam and Modernity: Transformation of an Intellectual Tradition* (Chicago: University of Chicago Press, 1982), p. 4; see also, Abdullah Saeed, 'Fazlur Rehman: A Framework for Interpreting the Ethico-legal Content of the Qur'an', in Suha Taji-Farouki (Ed.), *Modern Muslim Intellectuals and the Qur'an* (New York: Oxford University Press; in association with London: The Ismaili Institute, 2004), pp. 37–66, p. 43.
190. Rahman, *Islam and Modernity*, p. 8.
191. Khurshid Ahmad, 'Islam: Basic Principles and Characteristics', in *IIMM*, pp. 42–43, (ch. 2, pp. 27–30).
192. Altaf Gauhar, 'Islam and Secularism', in Altaf Gauhar (ed.), *The Challenge of Islam* (London: Islamic Council of Europe, 1978), pp. 298–310, p. 307.
193. Sir Muhammad Iqbal, *The Reconstruction of Religious Thought in Islam* (London: Oxford University Press, 1934), p. 165.
194. For this see, Hallaq, in *IJMES, op. cit.*
195. Iqbal, *The Reconstruction*, p. 168.
196. Taha J. al-'Alwani, 'Taqlid and Ijtihad', *AJISS*, 8, 1 (Mar 1991): 129–142, p. 129.
197. Esposito and Voll, *Islam and Democracy*, p. 30.
198. Al-'Alwani, *AJISS*, p. 141.
199. Ibid., p. 142.
200. Glasee, *op. cit.*, p. 69; E. Tyan, 'Bay'a', in *EI²*, I: 1113. See also, Emile A. Nakhleh, 'Bay'ah', in John L. Esposito (ed.), *The Oxford Encyclopedia of the Modern Islamic World* [*OEMIW*] (New York: Oxford University Press, 1995), I: pp. 205–206.
201. Azizah Y. al-Hibri, 'Islamic Constitutionalism and the Concept of Democracy', *Case Western Reserve Journal of International Law*, 24, 1 (1992): 1–27, p. 11.
202. Khan, in Hua *op. cit.*, p. 22.
203. Tyan, *loc. cit.*
204. Ibid.
205. Khan, *loc. cit.*
206. This passage is taken from Afsaruddin, *op. cit.*, p. 171.
207. Madjid Khadduri, 'Maslaha', *EI²*, vi: 738–39; Abdul Rehman I. Doi, 'Maslaha', in *OEMIW*, III: 63–65, p. 63.
208. Al-Ghazali, *al-Mustaf min 'Ilm al-Usul* (Baghdad, Muthana, 1970), I: pp. 286–287; as cited by Tariq Ramadan, 'Ijtihad and Maslaha: The Foundations of Governance', in Khan, *Islamic Democratic Discourse*, p. 5 (ch. 1, pp. 3–20). English translation is of Ramadan.
209. Al-Ghazali, *al-Mustaf* (Cairo: 1356/1937), pp. 139–140; Abu Ishaq al-Shatibi, *al-I'tisam* (Cairo: 1331 AH), as cited by Khadduri, *loc. cit.*
210. The source of this whole passage is Khadduri, *op. cit.*, p. 739.
211. Richard C. Martin, 'Maslaha', in Richard C. Martin (ed.), *Encyclopedia of Islam and Modern World*, 2nd ed. 2 vols. (New York: Macmillan, 2016 [2004]), II: p. 440.
212. See, for example, Ramadan, *loc. cit.* This essay is actually extracted from ch. 2, pp. 31–61 of his *Western Muslims*.

213. Ludwig W. Adamec, *Historical Dictionary of Islam*, 2nd ed. (Lanham, MD: The Scarecrow Press, Inc., 2009), p. 21; H. A. R. Gibb, 'Ahl al-Hall w'al-'Akd', in *EI²*, I: 263–4, p. 263; Wael B. Hallaq, 'Ahl al-Hall wa al-'Aqd', in *OEMIW*, I: pp. 53–54, p. 53; Ramadan, *Islam, the West and the Challenges of Modernity*, p. 85.
214. Al-Hibri, *op. cit.*, p. 12; Hasan al-Turabi, 'Islamic State', in Esposito, *Voices, op. cit.*, pp. 241–251, p. 243.
215. Obaidullah Fahad, *Redefining Islamic Political Thought: A Critique in Methodological Perspective* (New Delhi: Serials Publications, 2006), p. 228.
216. Hallaq, *loc. cit.*
217. Vide, Hallaq, *op. cit.*, pp. 53–54.
218. al-Hibri, *op. cit.*, p. 13.
219. Esposito and Voll in *MEQ*.
220. Esposito and Voll, *Islam and Democracy*, p. 32.
221. For details, see M. Dawood Sofi and Tauseef Ahmad Parray, 'Reinterpreting *Mithaq al-Medina*: A Study of Some Contemporary Scholars', *The Journal of Rotterdam Islamic & Social Sciences* [JRISS], 7, 1 (2016): 75–90.
222. Muhammad Hamidullah, *The First Written Constitution in the World* (Lahore: Sheikh Muhammad Ashraf, 1968 [England, 1941]). Also available online, in pdf format, at, https://muqith.files.wordpress.com/2016/01/dr-hamidullah-the-first-written-constitution-of-the-world.pdf (last accessed on 10 August 2015) [hereafter cited as Hamidullah, *First Written Constitution*].
223. Khattab and Bouma, *op. cit.*, p. 32.
224. Joseph J. Kaminski, *The Contemporary Islamic Governed State: A Reconceptualization* (London: Palgrave Macmillan, 2017), p. 81.
225. Khalid Ahmad Blankinship, 'The Constitution of Medina', in Meri, *op. cit.*, I: 171.
226. Another version read as: 'In the name of God, the Compassionate, the Merciful. This is a document from Muhammad the prophet (governing the relations) between the believers and Muslims of Quraysh and Yathrib, and those who followed them and joined them and labored with them. They are one community (*umma*) to the exclusion of all men'. See, Hamidullah, *The First Written Constitution*, pp. 31–32. For the complete Arabic version of Constitution of Medina, see Abd al-Malik Ibn Hisham, *al-Sirah al-Nabawiyyah* (The Prophetic History), 1st ed., 4 vols (Beirut: Dar Ihya' al-Turath, 1995), vol. 2, pp. 115–116. For English translations see, A. Guillaume, *The Life of Muhammad: A Translation of Ishaq's Sirat Rasul Allah*, introduction and notes by A. Guillaume (Oxford and Delhi: Oxford University Press, 1955), I: pp. 231–232; Muhammad Husayn Haykal, *Hayat-i-Muhammad (The Life of Muhammad)*, English trans by Ismail Raji al-Faruqi, 8th ed. (Indianapolis: American Trust Publications, 1976), pp. 182–83; W. Montgomery Watt, *Muhammad, Prophet and Statesman*, (London: Oxford University Press, 1961), pp. 94–96.
227. Hamidullah, *First Written Constitution*, pp. 12–13.

228. Kassim Ahmad, 'A Short Note on the Medina Charter'. Available online at https://www.dinmerican.wordpress.com/2015/12/09/kassim-ahmad-on-the-medina-charter/ (last accessed on 18 January 2011).
229. Hamidullah, *First Written Constitution*, p. 11.
230. Watt, *op. cit.*, p. 94.
231. Blankinship, *op. cit.*, p. 170.
232. Kassim, *loc. cit.*
233. Kaminski, *The Contemporary Islamic Governed State*, p. 81.
234. L. Ali Khan, 'Commentary on the constitution of Medina', in Hisham Ramadan (ed.), *Understanding Islamic Law: From Classical to Contemporary* (New York: Alta Mira Press, 2006), p. 206, as cited in Kaminski, *loc. cit.*
235. For details, see, Ali Bulac, 'The Madina Document', in Kurzman (ed.), *Liberal Islam*, pp. 169–178; Ozlem Denli, 'An Islamic Quest for a Pluralistic Political Model: A Turkish Perspective', in Khan (ed.), *Islamic Democratic Discourse* (ch. 5, pp. 85–103).
236. Kassim, *loc. cit.*
237. M. A. Muqtedar Khan, *American Muslims: Bridging Faith and Freedom* (Beltsville, MD: Amana Publications, 2002), p. 99 [hereafter, Khan, *American Muslims*].
238. Ibid., p. 102; See also M. A. Muqtedar Khan, 'The Compact of Medina: A Constitutional Theory of the Islamic State', *The Mirror International*, 30 May 2001. Also available online at http://www.Ijtihad.org/compact.htm (last accessed on 25 May 2010).
239. Ibid; see also M. A. Muqtedar Khan, 'Islamic Governance and Democracy', in Hua, *op. cit.*, pp. 21–22 (ch. 1, pp. 13–27).
240. M. A. Muqtedar Khan, 'The Priority of Politics—A response to *"Islam and the Challenge of Democracy"'*, *Boston Review* (April–May 2003), available online at https://bostonreview.net/forum_response/ma-muqtedar-khan-priority-politics/ (last accessed on 25 May 2010); M. A. Muqtedar Khan, 'The Primacy of Political Philosophy", in Khaled Abou El Fadl, *Islam and the Challenge of Democracy: A Boston Review Book*, Joshua Cohen and Deborah Chasman (eds.) (Princeton, NJ: Princeton University Press, 2004), pp. 63–68; see also Khan, *American Muslims*, p. 102.
241. Khan, 'The Priority of Politics', *loc. cit.*
242. Haykal, *op. cit.*, pp. 181–182; Guillaume, *op. cit.*, pp. 231–233.
243. Al-Hibri, *op. cit.*
244. Ibid., pp. 26–27.

# 3
# Nineteenth- and Twentieth-Century Muslim Intellectuals on Islam–Democracy Compatibility
## Voices from Arab World

The relationship between Islamic political notions and democracy or democratic notions (and democratization) is of crucial significance in the contemporary political dynamics of the Muslim world. The way this aspiration is defined reveals the great diversity within this vast region, as well as the many ways of working towards democratizing its polities. From the Middle East and North Africa (MENA) to Asia (South/Southeast/Central Asia), Muslims pursue this effort by cooperating with the existing governing authorities—ranging from republics to authoritarian regimes, and from monarchies to democracies (of various sorts/degrees).

The Muslim world today, undoubtedly, contains the most diverse ruling political systems: old-fashioned and constitutional monarchies, dictatorships, secular and (at least some) liberal democracies, and Islamic republics as well. Such diversity, of course, shows that Islam has sufficient intellectual and ideological resources to substantiate a wide range of governing models. History itself confirms Islam's dynamic force, as its principles are dynamic and were—and still tend to be—able to support the society's political life. This is not due to change, but as per its norms and directions. Moreover, at certain times it even reformed existing political systems and transformed, for example, the city-state of Medina (and others) into numerous empires and sultanates.

This dynamic character, on the one hand, reveals that Muslims have failed to produce a viable and considerable model of governance and in the contemporary times, the Muslim world boasts of a diversity of regime types—dictatorships and sham democracies, secular democracy in Turkey, monarchies in the Gulf, pluralistic democracies in Bangladesh and Malaysia and an Islamic state (a sort of *Theo-democracy*) in Iran. And due to the 2010-2011 uprisings and revolutions in the Middle East, i.e. the 'Arab Spring'/'Arab Uprisings'—which still continues to unravel so many uncertainties in the Middle East and, thus, was described as a revolution *still in the making*[1]—some of them are even in a changing condition.

On the other hand, it is important to note that neither the Qur'an nor the Prophetic tradition/practice (*Sunnah*) prescribes any particular form of government nor elaborates a constitutional theory; it is for the Muslims of every period to discover and realize the most suitable form of government to address their needs—on the condition that the form and the institutions they choose are in full agreement with the explicit, unequivocal Islamic laws (*Shari'ah*).

In response to the contention that Islam provides no viable governing model, Muqtedar Khan (*University of Delaware*, USA) argues that the Muslim world boasts of a diversity of regime types: dictatorships/monarchies in the Gulf; sham, secular, and pluralistic democracies in South and Southeast Asia; and an Islamic state in Iran (a sort of *theo-democracy*).[2] As regards the contention that Muslims are free to devise and formulate the most suitable form of government, Abdul Rashid Moten (formerly professor of Political Science, *International Islamic University Malaysia*), Sayed Khatab (*Monash University*, Australia) and Muhammad Asad, Hasan Yousefi Eshkevari (Iranian cleric and reformist thinker), Khaled Abou El-Fadl (*UCLA*, USA), and many others share similar views. For example, Asad argues that 'the political ordinances of the Qur'an and Sunnah... do not lay down any *specific* form of state', that is,

> [T]he *Shari'ah* does not prescribe any definite pattern [of governing model] to which an Islamic state must conform, nor does it elaborate in detail a constitutional theory. The political law emerging from the context of the Qur'an and Sunnah is, nevertheless, not an illusion. It is very vivid and concrete inasmuch as it gives us the clear outline of a political scheme capable of realization at all times and under all conditions of human life.... [T]here is not only one form of the Islamic state, but many; and it is for the Muslims of every period to discover the form most suitable to their needs—on the condition, of course, that the form

and the institutions they choose are in full agreement with the explicit, unequivocal *shar'i* laws relating to communal life.[3]

While as Eshkevari argues that 'never in Islam has the act of governing been mandated as a function of religion'; form or model of government, instead, is a 'purely human endeavor', and it is not possible to have one form and one type of government at all times, and is contextually dependent on the times and conditions.[4]

For Egyptian-American legal-theologian, Khaled Abou El-Fadl (*UCLA*, USA)[5]—one of the leading authorities in Islamic law in the United States and the world—the Qur'an 'does not specify a particular form of government' but identifies 'a set of social and political values that are central to a Muslim polity', which chiefly include 'pursuing justice through social cooperation and mutual assistance' (as in Q. 49: 13 and 11: 119), establishing 'a nonautocratic, consultative method of governance; and institutionalizing mercy and compassion in social interactions' (as in Q. 6: 12; 6: 54; 21: 107; 27: 77; 29: 51; and 45: 20).[6]

Although the Muslim scholarly debates over democracy, as well as its definitions and fundamentals, has spanned for a long time, it has acquired an edge in recent decades. Over the past two decades or so, in fact, it has emerged as a significant, fiercely debated issue among some prominent Muslim scholars all over the world. These intellectuals represent a vision of Islam and its role in the human polity, a vision that has attained so much certainty and loudness that it has recently come to dominate the face of Islam. Vigorous discussions continue within the Muslim intelligentsia regarding various Islamic concepts of political nature: their essence and nature, role and significance, relevance and importance, and compatibility, but the most burning issue is the process of democratization itself.

While some scholars chalk out historically important concepts from within the Islamic tradition together with the basic concepts of democracy as understood in the modern world, many others view democracy as an 'appropriate way to fulfill certain obligations of faith in the contemporary world'; and others see democracy as their main hope and medium of 'effective political participation'.[7]

Throughout the Muslim world, as will become evident from the discussion that follows, scholars are making rigorous efforts for defining, describing, and developing an authentic and viable Islamic democracy taking the help of utilizing long-standing traditions and conceptualization of *Shura, Khilafah, Ijma', Ijtihad*, etc.

Numerous Muslim thinkers have been actively engaged in defining, discussing, debating Islam, its institutions, systems, and concepts vis-à-vis the modern challenges (and 'Islam and democracy' being one of them); and writing prolifically on Islamic doctrines, law, politics, science, and economics. The Islamic modernist movements and their legacy have produced 'generations of reformers', throughout the Muslim world, especially from MENA to Asia: Jamal al-Din Afghani and Muhammad 'Abduh in the Middle East to Sir Syed Ahmad Khan, Muhammad Iqbal, and Abul Kalam Azad in South Asia.[8] The major 'founders of neo-revivalist movements from the pioneers (Hasan al-Banna, Mawlana Abul Ala Mawduudi, and Sayyid Qutb) to present-day movements' constituting the 'backbone [and moral fiber] of the second and third generation of Muslim intellectuals and activists across the Muslim world'; among them: Sudan's Hassan al-Turabi and Sadiq al-Mehdi; Tunisia's Rachid al-Ghannouchi; Iran's 'Ali Shari'ati and Abdulkarim Soroush; Algeria's Dr. Ali Abbassi al-Madni; Pakistan's Professor Khurshid Ahmad; Egypt's Hasan Hanafi, M. Saleem al-'Awwa; Malaysia's Mohammad Kamal Hasan, Osman Bakar, and Anwar Ibrahim; Indonesia's Dr Nurcolish Madjid, and Abdurrahman Wahid, etc.[9]

This broad spectrum does provide important insights into understanding the 'complex relationship' between Islam and democracy in the contemporary world. Despite the great dynamism and diversity, and multiplicity in contemporary Muslim political thought, certain concepts are central to the political positions of nearly all Muslims. In other words, contemporary Muslim scholars present certain concepts from within the Islamic tradition as the 'operational key concepts of democracy' in Islam.[10]

## Pioneering Muslim Modernists (of Arab World) on Islam–Democracy Compatibility

Although there are various operational key concepts that are regarded as the basis and foundations of democracy in Islam, but it is the concept of

*Shura* that is regarded not only the source of democratic ethics in Islam, but is considered, by many intellectuals and scholars, as the synonymous and similar to western democracy in its spirit and procedure.

In this context, this chapter deliberates on Islam and democracy reconciliation by providing an assessment of the views of some prominent pioneering Muslim modernists of the Arab world, of the nineteenth and some twentieth century, on Islam–democracy compatibility. Pioneering the modernist visions and agendas in the Middle East and South Asia, numerous Muslim thinkers of this period have tackled with, among others, the question of the relationship between religion and democracy—one of the important issues in the grand narrative of 'Islam and modernity' discourse. Providing a valuable contribution and some important insights to this hotly debated discourse, the prominent Arab thinkers included in this chapter are: Rifa'a al-Tahtawi (1801–1873), Jamal al-Din al-Afghani (1838–1897), Muhammad 'Abduh (1849–1905), and some later twentieth-century thinkers like Rashid Rida (1865–1935) and Malek Bennabi (1905–1973).

Before going into these details, it is pertinent to mention here that the first Islamic state and the practice of the earlier governments which succeeded the Prophet (pbuh) left a few methods that have been described as democratic models;[11] also the 'positive' features and values of democracy were extensively practiced through the prism of the consultation or the institution of *Shura*.[12] But it were these pioneers of reform and democratic thinking, from Tahtawi to Rida, who emphasized that the regeneration of Islam and the acceptance of the positive features of West were not at all incompatible. Approaching, and (re)interpreting, Islamic traditions rationally in a way that does not constitute a general break with the Islamic cultural past, their approach facilitated Islam's development and renewal.[13] They provided an obvious egalitarian and liberal discourse that emphasized openness and tolerance and advocated a rational and critical reading of the works of classical Muslims.

While reformists were, and continue even today, to be outnumbered by their traditionalist counterparts, they have exerted a profound, insightful, and far-reaching influence on modern Islamic thought and contemporary Muslim societies. Several influential and widely respected jurists and theologians within traditionalist circles of our time are on record as supporting democracy, parliamentary government, and other ideas that could not have been addressed, just a century earlier. Recent scholars have advanced a more open and tolerant vision of modern Islam, and have emphasized the values of democracy, freedom, pluralism, and equal protection of the law. The modern history of democracy in Islam begins with the Egyptian reformer Muhammad 'Abduh, who sought to strengthen the moral roots of Islamic society by returning to the past while recognizing and accepting the need for change and linking it to the teachings of Islam. He asserted Islam as the moral basis of modern, progressive society, but as this intellectual revolution would certainly have not been possible without the pioneers of constitutionalism, whose generation begins with al Tahtawi,[14] it is necessary to throw light on the thought of Tahtawi and Afghani as well.

## Rifa'a al-Tahtawi (1801–1873) on Reconciling Islam with Freedom and Democracy

Rifa'a Badawi Rafi' al-Tahtawi (1801–1873) was one of the pioneering figures of Islamic reformist/modernist thought, who graduated from the *Al-Azhar University* (Cairo). He is discussed by Albert Hourani, and is included in the 'first generation' of reformers, in his *Arabic Thought in the Liberal Age*;[15] Daniel Newman has described him as 'one of the driving forces of the nineteenth-century Egyptian Nahda ("Awakening" or "Renaissance")';[16] 'Egyptian Enlightener';[17] and is described as an 'Egyptian modernist and reformer' who studied 'the French language, literature, and political philosophy' and advocated, in his writings, 'educational reforms, modern development, and parliamentary democracy'.[18]

He was sent, by Muhammad 'Ali (the then Egyptian ruler), to Paris (as an *Imam*/religious cleric), where he learned and closely observed the enlightenments of the French Revolution for five years (1826–1831).[19] In Paris, he not only acquired knowledge of the French language but studied books on different subjects, ranging from 'ancient history, Greek philosophy and mythology, geography, arithmetic, and logic; ... ; and, most important, something of the French thought of the eighteenth century—Voltaire, Condillac, Rousseau's *Social Contract*, and the main works of Montesquieu'.[20] Or as Antony Black puts it: 'Tahtawi (1801–73), writing in Egypt in the late 1860s, owed his intellectual formation to his stay in

Paris (1826–31), where he had drunk at the well of Montesquieu and Rousseau; he combined the Middle Eastern tradition of strong central authority and the four social orders with an urgent plea for education, civic virtue and patriotism.[21]

On his return, Tahtawi brought some leading ideas from European liberal thought that had influenced him and through him on the Islamic political thought of the age. The most dominant of these ideas were freedom, law, and rationality as a source independent from religion for true human knowledge. He diagnosed that the backwardness of the Muslim community was due to the lack of freedom, justice, and equality; and he suggested 'multi-party democracy as a remedy'.[22] Speaking of society, he says: 'The society is a university where all students, Muslims and non-Muslims, get together under its roof; all are equal and brothers with no distinction between them on any basis of religions or colors'.[23] In his writings, Tahtawi expounded the theme of 'reform of Islamic law based on the needs of the modern age' that enthralled 'later modernist thinkers'.[24]

Tahtawi's political discourse implements the notion that the nature of society and the function of government were different from what they had been in the past. Shortly after his return to Egypt from Paris in 1831 (after spending five years, from 1826 to 1831), Tahtawi chronicled a description of his journey and stayed in Paris in his seminal work, *Takhlis al Ibriz fi [ila] Talkhis Bariz* ('Liberation of the Pure Gold in the Summary of Paris' or 'The Extraction of Pure Gold in the Abridgment of Paris'). About this book, Daniel Newman writes: 'He chronicled his journey in a book titled *Takhlis* ... . Rather than a mere travelogue (*rihla*), the book ... was the first of its kind and introduced Arab readers to all aspects of European culture and society'.[25] Regarding the selection of the words in this book, Khattab and Bouma state that 'Tahtawi selected those four Arabic words, in this poetical title, to suggest that the 'pure gold' (*al-Ibriz*) of Islam is in captivity and that the 'liberation' (*Takhlis*) of this pure gold is in his book or the 'summary' (*Talkhis*) of 'Paris' (*Bariz*). This theme provides the framework of his book'.[26] This book achieved great fame and was translated into Turkish. It contains many interesting and accurate observations of the manners and customs of modern France, and praised the values of democracy as he observed it in France and as he witnessed its defence and reassertion through the 1830 Revolution of the republicans against King Charles X (1757–1836). Tahtawi tried to show that the democratic attitude towards the individual and groups is compatible with the law of Islam. He compared political pluralism with forms of ideological and jurisprudential pluralism that existed in the Islamic experience:[27]

> Religious freedom is the freedom of belief, of opinion and of a sect, provided it does not contradict the fundamentals of religion. An example would be the theological opinions of the *Al-Asha'irah* and the *Al-Maturidiyah*;.... The same would apply to the freedom of political practice and opinion by leading administrators, who endeavor to interpret and apply rules and provisions in accordance with the laws of their own countries. Kings and ministers are licensed in the realm of politics to pursue various routes that in the end serve one purpose: good administration and justice.[28]

In translating the French Constitution, Tahtawi focused on those particular items which declare, and deal with, freedom, justice, and equality. Speaking of freedom, Tahtawi outlined five specific interrelated types of freedom:

> All French are equal before the Shariah [*Shari'ah*: Islamic law].... The French's glorification of Freedom as a comprehensive expression indicates the higher level of justice... There is natural freedom, freedom of behavior, religious freedom, civil freedom, and political freedom... Freedom of this type is a great means of development and prosperity.[29]

Tahtawi's advocacy for democracy continued in various capacities in his publications and activities. He postulated that a regeneration of Islam and an acceptance of the 'positive' features of Western civilization were not incompatible. He campaigned for interaction with the European civilization with the objective of borrowing from it that does not conflict with the established values and principles of the *Shari'ah*.[30]

From his experience in France, Tahtawi emphasized that the power of the ruler is not absolute. The ruler should be 'tempered by respect for the law and those who preserve it', arguing that 'the government should be in the hands of "the people"'.[31] Moreover, he tried to show that the democratic concept he was explaining to his readers was compatible with

Islam.[32] In his words, 'what is called freedom in Europe is exactly what is defined in our religion [Islam] as justice ['*Adl*], right [*Haqq*], consultation [*Shura*], and equality [*Musawat*] ... This is because the rule of freedom and democracy consists of imparting justice and right to the people, and the nation's participation in determining its destiny'.[33]

## Jamal al-Din al-Afghani (1838–1897) on *Shura* and 'Despotic Government'

Jamal al-Din al-Afghani (1838–1897), an outstanding ideologist, political activist, and most influential Muslim reformer of the late nineteenth-century Muslim world—whose influence has continued strongly in many Muslim countries, particularly in the Middle East, South Asia, and Europe—was one of the founders of Islamic modernism and an advocate of pan-Islamic unity. Afghani's anti-imperialism and his stress on certain virtues in the early periods of Islam with appropriate interpretations of the Qur'an and hadith entered the mainstream of Islamic modernism, reformism, nationalism, movements for self-strengthening, and anti-imperialism.[34]

Afghani's reform endeavours made him travel to Europe and the Muslim world, from India to Constantinople.[35] His influential character and ideas helped him in winning, towards his cause, the people of every country he visited. In Egypt, he lived for seven years and won over such powerful thinkers as Muhammad 'Abduh (later Rector of *al-Azhar*), Sa'd Zaghlul (leader of the Egyptian nation), and the leading Syrian scholar and journalist Rashid Rida and many others like Abdullah al-Nadim, Qasim Amin, Waliyy al-Din Yakan, and Mustafa al-Manfaluti who played a significant role in Islamic reform in modern history.[36]

One of the objectives of Afghani was to establish religion–polity relationship. He felt that the processes of reform and democracy should emerge out of the society itself. The people must be educated about their rights (political or others), and their application to bring reform and freedom. People should be allowed to assume their political and social roles by participating in governing through *Shura* and elections. He was addressing these and other issues of interest in forms of theology, jurisprudence, mysticism, and philosophy.[37]

In 1884 (Paris), Afghani joined Muhammad 'Abduh and together they established *al-'Urwah al-Wuthqa* ('The Firm Bond', referring to the Qur'an, 2: 256), an Arabic periodical, well known for its political, social, and intellectual line of Islamic reform. In 1879, Afghani outlined through *al-Ḥukumat al-Istibdadiyyah* ('The Despotic Government'), published in the journal *Misr* (Egypt), that the decline of the Muslim world was the direct result of the dictatorship systems. It is because of those tyrannies that thinkers could not enlighten the Muslim public about the essence and virtues of the 'republican government'. He goes further to assert:

> For those governed by a republican government, it is a source of happiness and pride. Those governed by a republican form of government alone deserve to be called human; for a true human being is only subdued by a true law that is based on the foundations of justice and that is designed to govern man's moves, actions, transactions and relations with others in a manner that elevates him to the pinnacle of true happiness.[38]

In Afghani's estimation, the weakness and decline of Muslims were due to the corrupt state apparatus, and the absence of justice and consultation (*Shura*). In other words, he diagnosed 'the absence of '*adl* (justice) and *shura* (council), and non-adherence by the government to the constitution' as the main causes of decline in the Muslim world.[39]

Afghani and (his companion) 'Abduh opposed the monarchy and dictatorship prevailing in the then Muslim world, and wrote in support of *Shura*, republicanism, and representative/constitutional government in *al-'Urwah al-Wuthqa*. Afghani's usage of the word 'republican' does not mean that he advocated a fixed form of government or governance; it is only a matter of translation of his Arabic word *jumhuri* (i.e. publican and republican) by which he means an absolute government: a restricted form of government based on *Shura* in which the ruler consults the ruled for the welfare of the individual and the community as well as for the state. The government is responsible for the people and should consult them, relieve them of the burdens laid upon their shoulders, and lift them from the state of decadence to the highest level of perfection. Muhammad 'Abduh stated that Afghani was a thinker, philosopher, and writer with deep cognizance and connections with the world's ideological and intellectual movements. He appeared always with a modern mentality accepting many of the modern ideas of his age. It was also not difficult for him to verify all of that with his tongue and his pen; that Islam is not, and never, was a body without spirit; he sees Islam, if those mythical and alien papers brushed away, will remain a living power compatible with the ideas of Western civilization, and able to fulfil the needs of the people of any age. Focusing on the political and social spheres of Islam, Afghani argued that the essence of Islam is liberty and democracy is its component; it gives the people the right to involve in the administration of the state and instructs them to watch over the government.[40]

In Afghani's view, the government in Islam is limited; it is neither tyrannical nor hereditary; it is neither based on estate nor wealth nor privilege; 'it derives [its legitimacy] only from the ordinances of Shari'ah the activity to implement the law, and the community's satisfaction.'[41] Regarding *Ijtihad*, Afghani argued that the door of *Ijtihad* is not closed, and it is a duty as well as the right of Muslims to apply the principles of the Qur'an afresh to the problems of their time. Any refutation to do so is to be guilty of stagnation (*jumud*) or imitation (*taqlid*), and these are enemies of true Islam, just as materialism is an enemy.[42]

## Muhammad 'Abduh (1849–1905) on *Shura* and Parliamentary Democracy

Muhammad 'Abduh (1849–1905)—an Egyptian jurist, religious scholar, and liberal reformer—is regarded as the founder of 'Islamic Modernism' and is widely considered as one of the most important historical figures of the twentieth century. He led the late nineteenth-century movement in Egypt and other Muslim countries to modernize Muslim institutions. 'Abduh was greatly influenced by Afghani; and under his influence, he combined journalism, politics, and his own fascination in mystic spirituality. Afghani taught him about the problems of Egypt and the Islamic world and about the technological achievements of the West.[43]

As a thinker and intellectual, 'Abduh made 'invaluable contributions not only in the religious teaching but also to nationalist politics and the Egyptian intellect [intellectual life as well]. His *protégés* include Rashid Rida ('Abduh's official biographer); Qasim Amin (the backbone of the

[Muslim] women's movement); Mustafa 'Abd al-Raziq (Rector of al-Azhar, 1945–47); Taha Husayn (the prince of Arabic literature ... )'.[44]

'Abduh's intellectual legacy—which opposes despotism and champion's freedom, law, and rationality—was imprinted on the Muslim community and politics, on all spheres of Islamic thought, and on the hearts and the minds of many thinkers of Islam in the liberal age.[45] "Abduh made it clear that neither the achievement of the West nor the failure of the East was due to religions. He believed that Islam's relationship with the modern age was the most crucial issue that Islamic communities needed to deal with".[46] In an attempt to reconcile Islamic ideas with Western ones, he focused diligently on *Shura* (consultation) as an Islamic principle that limits the power of government.[47] 'Abduh emphasized that implementing *Shura* is an Islamic obligation rather than the imitation of foreigners. He noted that Islamic law does not stipulate exactly the *modus operandi* for *Shura*, and his writing hinted at satisfaction with the limited consultative roles reserved to the assemblies of his time.[48]

'Abduh focused more on two principles known in Islamic jurisprudence as S*add al-Dharai'* (blocking the means)—meaning to eradicate the means, causes, devices, and excuses[49]—and *al-Maslaha al-Mursalah* (public interest): referring to the benefit or public interest of a type about whose validity no specific or a direct authoritative text (*nass*) speaks of.[50] 'The scope of these two principles is wide and includes what fulfills the interests of society of any age and generation within the framework of Islam'.[51] The very idea and the methods by which the successors of the Prophet were elected to the office of the caliphate is one of the many examples of *Maslaha*.[52] The crux of the principle of *sadd al dharai'* (blocking the means) is that 'the means to something forbidden is itself forbidden, and the means of something obligatory is itself obligatory'.[53] Thus, 'while the basic principle with *masalih mursalah* is to look at the interest of the people, the basic principle with s*add al-zara'i* is to look at the outcomes of actions and their overall results. In either case, the aim and objective of these two principles are looking into the interest of the people and the welfare of the society'.[54] In this context, 'Abduh equated the Islamic concept of public interest (*al-Maslaha al-Mursalah*) with the concept of utility (*manfa'at*) in the Western thought.[55]

While reflecting on various versions of democracy, 'Abduh emphasizes that 'the essence of human *nature* and the *nature* of human society imply that men are well informed to apply their collective intelligence to the circumstances in which they find themselves, and this also can be discovered simply by examining the record of other nations'.[56] On this point, 'Abduh based his view on rational grounds, as he usually did, but within the confines of revelation and its spirit. He seeks to establish that laws should be based on the interests of the people and their collective reason. To him, collective intelligence corrects the errors of individual reasoning. He pointed out that the individual cannot rise above personal desires and self-interests, ambitions and personal inclinations with which he is surrounded. This facet of human nature is true for the ruler as well as for the subjects.[57]

'Focusing on the society—its interests, collective will, collective reason and collective intelligence, [as] all these are interrelated and communicated ideas—enabled 'Abduh to view *shurah* [*Shura*] (consultation) as a genuine restriction on the ruler's power. The government then is not absolute or autocratic, and it is not theocratic or any form of these word groups'.[58] 'Abduh insisted that

> the authority of the governor (*hakim*) or that of the judge (*qadi*) or that of the *mufti*, was civil ... Islam is a religion of sovereignty, of authority, and of unity between this world and the hereafter. Islam is a spiritual, social, political, civilian, and military system. Its military force is to protect the liberty of man, human equality, justice, and human rights and not to force others to embrace Islam.[59]

From this passage, it becomes evident that 'Abduh distinguishes between dictatorship and limited authority. Like other contemporary Muslim thinkers, Abduh believes that the Islamic institution of *Shura* is a principle of representative or constitutional government, which has its basis in the Islamic primary sources.[60] An ardent advocate of the parliamentary system, he defended pluralism and refuted the claims that it undermines the unity of the Muslim community. He argued that the European nations were not divided by the institution, and concluded that the 'reason is that their objective is the same. What varies is the method they pursue toward accomplishing it'.[61] Khatab and Bouma, on the authority of Abd al-Raziq, have summarized very beautifully the main insights of 'Abduh on these aspects as: 'He opened the gate very wide for *ijtihad* to address the emerging priorities and problems with the mind of the modern age; he turned the wheel back to democracy known to Islam; he liberated Islamic thought from the imitation of the customary paradigms of interpretation; he strongly believed in the close friendship between religion and sciences with no clash between them; he himself represented a good example of the harmonious relationships between the Islamic and Western civilizations'.[62]

Thus, Muhammad 'Abduh carried further the process of identifying certain traditional concepts of Islamic thought with the dominant ideas of Europe. Therefore, in this line of thought, *'Maslaha* gradually turns into *utility, Shura* into *parliamentary democracy, ijma* into *public opinion*; [and] Islam itself becomes identified with civilization and activity, [all constituting] the norms of nineteenth century of social thought'.[63]

## Rashid Rida (d. 1935) on *Shura, Maslaha,* and 'Positive' Features of Democracy

Muhammad Rashid Rida (1865–1935) is considered as one of the most influential scholars and jurists of his generation and the most prominent disciple of 'Abduh. Rida was attracted to 'Abduh's ideas during 1894 when the latter was in Syria; and in 1897, he moved to Cairo where he established himself as 'Abduh's closest disciple. Rida established his scholarly journal *Al-Manar* (light-stand or signpost), and al-Manar Publishing Press, and dedicated his career to collecting and interpreting 'Abduh's ideas and elaborating his teachings. This journal was, for him and his likes, the beacon of reform on the basis of 'Abduh's ideas.[64]

Like his predecessor, Rida confirmed the notions of democratic participation in Islam, and pointed out in some detail that Islam and democracy are not incompatible. The autocratic rulers, he contends, have encouraged such loss. True Islam, Rida argues, involves two things—*Tawhid* (the creed of monotheism) and *Shura* (council) in matters of governance. However, the autocratic rulers, he laments, tried to make Muslims forget the second by encouraging them to abandon the first.[65]

To those pioneers of constitutionalism and democratic thinking, 'democratic civility' is but a reproduction of Islamic institutions and conceptions, including *Shura* (consultation), *Ijma'* (consensus), *Ijtihad* (independent reasoning), *al-Maslaha al-Mursalah* (public interest), *Sadd al-Dharai'* (blocking the means), and *al-Amr bi al-Ma'ruf wa al-Nahi 'an al-Munkar* (commanding right and forbidding wrong) which is a comprehensive concept encompassing the activity of the state and its citizens and guaranteeing for the rulers and the ruled their 'Human Rights'.[66]

Rida also utilized *Shura* in rejecting the idea that religion is an enemy of democracy. He proclaimed that 'learning how government should operate and replacing tyranny with a *Shura* regime was the greatest benefit the people of the East gained from their interactions with Europeans, a benefit that might not had been achieved were it not for these interactions'.[67] He heavily emphasized on the Islamic roots and origins for *Shura*. He was of the opinion that political authority was reserved to a president while religious authority was reserved to a *Khalifah*; however, the president was to be nominated by the *Khalifah* from a shortlist submitted by an elected assembly.

In this sense, (i) the Qur'an laid down the principle of *Shura* to guide the community's decision-making process; (ii) the *ijma'* complements the *Shura* and adds another dimension by asserting that the principles of pluralism are compatible with divine guidance; (iii) the duty of commanding right and forbidding wrong is one among the important duties and sanctions for the practical implementation of 'Human Rights'; it is antithetical to all types and forms of corruptions and injustices, tyrants and despotism, violence and terrorism, autocracies, plutocracies, theocracies and the like; it is also a duty of political participations; that is if political participation is denied or ineffective, then revolution against the tyrannical rules becomes a duty; (iv) the different opinions which could come out of *Ijtihad* will not affect the eternal essence of the doctrine.[68]

These Constitutional and democratic views are based on the Qur'an (Q. 3: 104) and the Sunnah, and stand as a point of reference confirming that all 'good' things and 'positive' features found in the West, including democracy, are Islamic.

From the views and opinions of these early modernist/reformist thinkers, it becomes evident that the Western democracy has not necessarily been in conflict with Islamic ideals. These reformist thinkers argued that the reason for the underdevelopment of Muslim countries has been the absence of the practice of democratic ideals, such as tolerance, the rule of law, equality and justice, and people's participation in their social and political affairs. Instead of authoritarianism, which, according to them, contradicts Islam, Muslim countries should opt for establishing a participatory democratic order to attain prosperity in their societies.[69]

## Malek Bennabi (1905–1973) on developing 'Genuine Democracy'

Malek Bennabi (1905–1973)—a remarkable twentieth-century Algerian Muslim thinker—occupies a significant place in the history of modern Islamic religious thought. One of the most influential scholars, thinkers, writers, and social philosophers of the post-World War II period, his most important concern throughout his life was the adaptation of Islamic values to modernity. Bennabi emphasized in particular the compatibility of Islam and democracy, as much as the suitability of the modern sciences in Islam in the process of development and progression.[70]

Democracy, in his opinion, reflects perfection and has emerged as a result of rational and cultural development.[71] Bennabi's focus on democracy has three main points, or in other words, he looks at democracy from three perspectives: viz. 'as a feeling toward one's self, as a feeling towards others, and as a cluster of social and political conditions necessary for the formulation and the blossoming of similar feelings in the individual'.[72]

Dividing democracy into two concepts, secular and Islamic, he criticized the former. 'Secular democracy detects in man the presence of humanity and society, the Islamic democratic conception recognizes in man the presence of God'.[73] For him, secular democracy disrupts the link between God and humanity. But at the same time, he called attention to the 'social dimension of the democracy', believing that it can best be represented in Islam. In the Qur'an, one finds that Islam guarantees freedom of speech, the right to work, and travel, the privacy of the home, the rights of minorities, and so on.[74] As for the political dimension, the 'principle of consultation [*Shura*] provides the individual with responsibility in the constitution of power and all the guarantees against its abusive use'.[75]

According to Bennabi, Islam, which is a synthesis of political and social democracy, offers a 'genuine democracy'.[76] In accordance with democracy (a regime that offers equal rights to everyone), relations at the time of four Righty Guided Caliphs between ruler and ruled reflects the best example of 'democratic conscience' in Islam.[77] Perceiving democracy as the result of a humanistic cultural development, he insists that democracy is not merely the transmission of power to the masses or to a sovereign people by virtue of a constitution, but is the development of sentiments, reflexes, and criteria that make up the foundations of democracy in the consciousness of a people and its traditions.[78] In other words, before a democratic constitution is written, it must be preceded by a process of democratization. The process of democratization requires, according to Bennabi, that anti-democratic feelings and despotic tendencies be eliminated.[79]

The problem that he raises is to determine whether Islam can foster the three posited perspectives, i.e. whether

> Islam can augment the sentiment toward one's self and toward others, one that is compatible with the foundation of democracy within the individual's psychology and whether it can create social conditions that are favorable to the preservation and development of the democratic sentiment as well as its efficaciousness.[80]

Bennabi rejects every such democratic enterprise that consists of borrowing certain principles from foreign democratic constitutions without measures undertaken to instil them in the psychology of the people that borrow them.[81] The conclusion Bennabi draws from this remark is that 'if there exists a democratic tradition in Islam, it ought not to be sought in the letter of a constitutional text, but rather in the spirit of Islam in general'.[82] He also maintains that Islam must, therefore, be considered as the initiation of a process of democratization, that is, the advance of the individual and the society to which s/he belongs towards the democratic ideal.[83] What distinguishes Islam from any other democratic type (e.g. French, Russian, or Chinese), according to Bennabi, is that this religion confers upon man a value that transcends any political or social value. Whereas other democratic interpretations see in man the presence of humanity and society, the Islamic democratic conception recognizes in man the presence of God. In other words, the first explanation is of the secular type, whereas the second is of the sacred category.[84]

Bennabi argues that, in opposition to Islamic democracy, secular democracy confers upon humans' rights and guarantees, but does not save them from being crushed under the weight of cartels, trusts, or by the dictatorship of a class. Secular democracy, in other words, does not wash out from society the evils that produce slavery or despotism.[85]

Bennabi's conception of democracy is not limited to the political sphere, but extends to the social as well, because, in his view, 'an order which bestows upon man a ballot and allows him to starve is not a democratic order'.[86] Bennabi believed that the democratization process would only succeed when the Muslim world would give up to live in the past, depart from the historic process, and break through the life colonized and enslaved.[87] Thus, Islam, in his eyes, provides true democracy, for it constitutes a synthesis between political democracy and social democracy. Bennabi believes that the *Zakat* (the giving of mandatory alms) is a good example of Islam's social legislation posited by the Qur'an. The communication, that he believes prevailed between rulers and ruled in the time of the first Caliphs, is proof that there existed a 'democratic consciousness shaped by Islam'.[88]

Bennabi thought that Islamic democracy existed at its best during the era of first four Caliphs. Regression occurred when power became absolute, but also when Muslim democratic thinking disappeared from the moral order in the behaviour of the individual. Islamic democratization ended 'when it lost its foundation in the psychology of the individual, as soon as the latter lost definitively the appreciation of his own worth and the value of others'.[89] From this point onwards, Islamic civilization ceased to exist because it no longer rested on the excellence of the individual. Bennabi thought that the re-emergence of the democratic spirit had begun in some Islamic countries. However, he felt that the democratization process would only succeed when this new change has occurred within the individual's own conscience so that s/he was above both the despot and the slave. He was convinced that 'only Islam could undertake this re-evaluation in the countries where social tradition has been shaped by the Qur'anic notion'.[90]

## Notes

1. Irfan Ahmad, 'The Categorical Revolution: Democratic Uprising in the Middle East', *Economic and Political Weekly [EPW]*, xlvi, 44–45 (5 November 2011): 30–35, p. 34. Italics added for emphasis.

2. M. A. Muqtedar Khan, 'Introduction: The Emergence of an Islamic Democratic Discourse', in M. A. Muqtedar Khan (ed.), *Islamic Democratic Discourse: Theory, Debates and Philosophical Perspectives* (Lanham, MD: Lexington Books, 2006), p. xii.
3. Muhammad Asad, *The Principles of State and Government in Islam* (Berkeley and Los Angeles: University of California Press, 1961), pp. 22–23.
4. Hasan Yusofi Eshkevari, 'Hokumat-e Demokratik-e Eslami' [Democratic Islamic Government], in Ali Muhammad Izadi et al. (eds.), *Din va Hokumat* [Religion and Government] (Tehran: Rasa, 1377 AH/1998 CE), pp. 299, 300 as cited in Ziba Mir-Hosseini and Richard Tapper, *Islam and Democracy in Iran: Eshkevari and the Quest for Reform* (New York: I. B. Tauris, 2006), ch. 3, pp. 63–100; and Mehran Kamrava, 'Shi'ism at the Gates of Historic Change', in Mehran Kamrava (ed.), *Innovation in Islam: Traditions and Contributions* (Berkeley, Los Angeles, and London: University of California Press Ltd., 2011), ch. IV, pp. 58–81, p. 61.
5. Khaled Abou El Fadl, *Islam and the Challenge of Democracy: A Boston Review Book*, Joshua Cohen and Deborah Chasman (eds.) (Princeton and Oxford: Princeton University Press, 2004).
6. Ibid., p. 5.
7. John L. Esposito and John O. Voll, 'Islam and Democracy', *Humanities*, 22, 6 (November/December 2001), available online at www.artic.ua.es/biblioteca/u85/documentos/1808.pdf (last accessed 21 May 2022).
8. On the life and thought of later three, see Tauseef Ahmad Parray, *Mediating Islam and Modernity: Sir Sayyid, Iqbal, and Azad* (New Delhi: Viva Books Pvt. Ltd., 2019).
9. John L. Esposito, 'Contemporary Islam: Reformation or Revolution?', in John L. Esposito (ed.), *The Oxford History of Islam* (New York: Oxford University Press, 1999), pp. 680–681.
10. John L. Esposito and John O. Voll, *Islam and Democracy* (New York: Oxford University Press, 1996), p. 23.
11. Manzooruddin Ahmad, 'Classical Muslim State', *Islamic Studies*, 1, 3, (1962): 83–104, p. 95.
12. Abu al-Hasan al-Mawardi, *al-Ahkam al-Sultaniyyah* [The Rules of Islamic Governance] (Beirut: Dar al-Fikr, 1966), pp. 5–20.
13. Ibrahim M. Abu Rabi', *Intellectual Origins of Islamic Resurgence in the Modern Arab World* (New York: State University of New York Press, 1996), pp. 5–6.
14. Muhammad Hasanayn Haykal, *Kharif al-Ghadab* [The Autumn of Anger], 2nd ed., (Cairo: Sharikat al-Matbu'at, 1983), pp. 276–278, as cited in Sayed Khatab and Gary D. Bouma, *Democracy in Islam* (New York: Routledge, 2007), p. 42.
15. Albert Hourani, *Arabic Thought in the Liberal Age* (London, Oxford, and New York: Oxford University Press, 1970), pp. 68–102.
16. Daniel L. Newman, 'Rifa'a Rafi' al-Tahtawi (1801–1873)', in Richard C. Martin (ed.), *Encyclopedia of Islam and Modern World [EIMW]*, 2nd ed., 2 vols. (New York: Macmillan, 2016 [2004]), II: pp. 1178–1179, 1178. See also, Rifa'a

Rafi' al-Tahtawi, *An Imam in Paris: Account of a Stay in France by an Egyptian Cleric (1826–1831)*, Translated and Introduced by Daniel L. Newman, 2nd ed. (London: Saqi Books, 2011 [2004]).

17. Murman Kutelia, 'Egyptian Enlightener Rifa'a at-Tahtawi', *International Black Sea University Scientific Journal [IBSUSJ]*, 5, 1 (2011): 83–92.
18. Ludwig W. Adamec, *Historical Dictionary of Islam*, 2nd ed. (Lanham, MD: The Scarecrow Press, Inc., 2009), p. 300.
19. Hourani, *Arabic Thought in the Liberal Age*, p. 69.
20. Ibid.
21. Antony Black, *The History of Islamic Political Thought: From the Prophet to the Present* (New York: Oxford University Press, 2001; South Asian Edition, Karachi, Pakistan, Oxford University Press, 2004), p. 283.
22. Azam S. Tamimi, 'Islam and Democracy from Tahtawi to Ghannouchi', *Theory, Culture & Society* [*TCS*], 24, 2 (March 2007): 39–58, p. 43.
23. M. Muhammad Husayn, *Al-Islam wa al-Hadarah al-Gharbiyyah* [Islam and Western Civilization] (Beirut: Al-Risalah, 1985), p. 20; as cited by Khatab and Bouma, *op. cit.*, p. 42 [hereafter cited in its abbreviated form as Husayn, *IHG*].
24. Sohail H. Hashmi, 'Reform: Arab Middle East and North Africa', *EIMW*, II: pp. 574–77, p. 575.
25. Newman, in *EIMW*, II: 1178.
26. Khatab and Bouma, *op. cit.*, p. 42.
27. Ahmad Sudqi al-Dajani, 'Tatawur Mafahim al-Dimuqratiyah Fi al-Fikr al-'Arabi al-Hadith' [The Development of the Concepts of Democracy in the Modern Arab Thought], in *Azmat al-Dimuqratiyah Fi al-Watan al-'Arabi* [The Crisis of Democracy in the Arab Homeland] (Beirut: Arab Unity Studies Centre, 1984), p. 121 as cited in Tamimi in *TCS*, p. 43; see also, Hourani, *op. cit.*, pp. 69, 70–72; Khatab and Bouma, *op. cit.*, pp. 42–43.
28. Faruq Abd al-Salam, *Al-Ahzab al-Siyasiyah Fi al-Islam* [Political Parties in Islam] (Cairo: Qalyub Publishing House, 1978), p. 27, as cited in Tamimi in *TCS*, p. 43.
29. Husayn, *op. cit.*, p. 23; Khatab and Bouma, *op. cit.*, p. 43.
30. Ibid.
31. Hourani, *op. cit.*, p. 73.
32. Tamimi in *TCS*, pp. 42–44.
33. Cited in Shukri B. Abed, 'Islam and Democracy', in David Garnham and Mark Tessler (eds.), *Democracy, War, and Peace in the Middle East* (Bloomington: Indiana University Press, 1995), pp. 116–132, p. 119; Hamid Enayat, *Modern Islamic Political Thought* (Austin: University of Texas Press, 1988), p. 131; Md Nazrul Islam and Md Saidul Islam, 'Islam and Democracy: Conflicts and Congruence', *Religions*, 8, 6 (2017): 1–19, p. 5.
34. See Nikkie R. Keddie, 'Afghani, Jamal-al-Din', in *Encyclopedia Iranica (Online)*, 15 December 1983, available online at https://www.iranicaonline.org/articles/afgani-jamal-al-din (last accessed on 21 May 2022). Originally appearing in volume 1, pp. 481–486 of the print version.

35. Haykal, *op. cit.*, pp. 276–278.
36. For details see Muhammad Rashid Rida, *Tarikh al-Ustadh al-Imam al-Shaykh Muhammad 'Abduh*, 2 vols. (Cairo: al-Manar, 1931), II: p. 339; Khatab and Bouma, *op. cit.*, p. 45.
37. Ahmad Amin, *Zu'ama' al-Islah* [The Leaders of Reform] (Cairo: Lajnat al-Ta'lif wa al-Tarjamah, 1948), vide Khatab and Bouma, *op. cit.*, p. 45.
38. Jamal al-din al-Afghani, 'Al-Hukumah al-Istibdadiyah' [The Despotic Government], *Misr*, 14 February 1879, as cited in Abd al-Basit Hasan, *Jamal al-Din al-Afghani wa- atharuhu fi al-'alam al-Islami al-Hadit* (Cairo: Maktabat Wahbah, 1982), pp. 267–268; Khatab and Bouma, *op. cit.*, p. 46; Tamimi in *TCS*, p. 45.
39. al-Dajani, *op. cit*, p. 123, as cited in Tamimi in *TCS*, p. 44.
40. al-Afghani and 'Abduh *Al-'Urwa al-Wuthqa*, 23 July 1957, p. 25; Khatab and Bouma, *op. cit.*, p. 47.
41. al-Afghani and 'Abduh, *op. cit.*, pp. 9–12.
42. Hourani, *op. cit.*, p. 127.
43. For details, see Charles Adams, *Islam and Modernism in Egypt: A Study of the Modern Reform Movement Inaugurated by Muhammad 'Abduh* (New York: Russel and Russel, 1933; reissued 1968); Hourani, *Arabic Thought*; Malcolm H. Kerr, *Islamic Reform: The Political and Legal Theories of Muhammad Abduh and Rashid Rida* (Berkeley: University of California Press, 1966); and Mark Sedgwick, *Muhammad Abduh* ['Makers of Contemporary Islam' Series] (London: Oneworld Publications, 2014).
44. Khatab and Bouma, *loc. cit.*
45. Hourani, *op. cit.*, p. 135.
46. Khatab and Bouma, *loc. cit.*
47. Muhammad Abduh, 'Al-Shura wa al-Istibdad' [Consultation and Despotism] in Rida, *op. cit.*, II: 203–210.
48. Vide Shavit, *op. cit.*, p. 350. Shavit writes that Abduh articulated these ideas in the following articles published on 12, 24, and 25 December 1881, respectively: 'Fi al-Shura wal-Istibdad' [On *Shura* and Tyranny], 'Al-Shura' and 'Al-Shura wal-Qanun' [*Shura* and the Law], in Muhammad 'Imara, al-*A'mal al-Kamila lil-Imam Muhammad 'Abduh* (Beirut: al-Mu'assasa al-'Arabiyya lil Dirasat wal-Nashr, 1972), pp. 350–366.
49. See Ibn Manzur, *op. cit.*, 8: 96.
50. Ibid., 2: 517.
51. Khatab and Bouma, *op. cit.* p. 48.
52. Khatab and Bouma, *loc. cit.*
53. Zidan, *op. cit.*, pp. 203–204; Khatab and Bouma, *op. cit.*, pp. 48–49.
54. Khatab and Bouma, *op. cit.*, p. 49.
55. Azzam Tamimi, 'Democratic Synergies and Oppositions in the Muslim World: Arab Democracy and Islamic Democracy', paper presented at the PSA Conference, Leicester University, Wednesday, 16 April 2003, p. 4; see also al-Afghani and 'Abduh *Al-Urwa al-Wuthqa* (23 July 1957), p. 12.

56. Khatab and Bouma, *op. cit.*, p. 50.
57. Abduh, 'al-Shurah', 2: 210–213; vide Khatab and Bouma, *op. cit.*, p. 50.
58. Khatab and Bouma, *op. cit.*, p. 51.
59. Abduh, *Tafsir al-Manar*, 1: 11, as cited in Khatab and Bouma, *op. cit.*, p. 51.
60. Abduh, 'al-Shurah', 2: 203–210, as cited in Khatab and Bouma, *op. cit.*, p. 51.
61. Afghani and 'Abduh, *Al-'Urwa al-Wuthqa*, pp. 74–79, 135–140, as cited in Khatab and Bouma, *op. cit.*, p. 51.
62. Mustafa Abd al-Raziq, 'al-Shaykh Muhammad 'Abduh', in al-Afghani and 'Abduh (eds.), *Al-'Urwa al-Wuthqa wa al-Thawrah al-Tahririyyah al-Kubra*, 1st ed. (Cairo: Dar al-Arab, 23 July 1957), pp. 17–23, esp. 21, as cited in Khatab and Bouma, *op. cit.*, p. 51.
63. Hourani, *op. cit.*, p. 144; also quoted, variedly, by Tamimi in *TCS*, p. 46; Islam and Islam in *Religions*, p. 8.
64. Hourani, *op. cit.*, pp. 224–228.
65. Tamimi in *TCS*; Islam and Islam, *Religions*, p. 9.
66. Michael Cook, *Commanding Right and Forbidding Wrong in Islamic Thought* (Cambridge: Cambridge University Press, 2002), pp. 215–217, 470–474, 512, 524.
67. Vide Shavit in *MES*, p. 351; Islam and Islam, *Religions*, p. 9.
68. Muhammad Imarah, *Al-Islam wa Huquq al-Insan: Daruriyyat la Huquq* [Human Rights in Islam are Obligatory: Necessities, not Merely Rights], 1st ed. (Cairo: Dar al-Shuruq, 1989), pp. 82–84, 94, 116; Khatab and Bouma, *op. cit.*, p. 58.
69. Islam and Islam, *Religions*, p. 9.
70. Yahya H. Zoubir, 'Democracy and Islam in Malek Bennabi's Thought', *American Journal of Islamic Social Sciences*, 15, 1 (1998): 107–111; Harun Isik, 'Malek Bennabi's Approach to decadence and Democracy in Muslim World', *The Islamic Quarterly*, 53, 4 (2009): 343–354 [hereafter Isik, *IQ*]. See also Yahya H. Zoubir, 'State, Civil Society and the Question of Radical Fundamentalism in Algeria', in Ahmad S. Moussali (ed.), *Islamic Fundamentalism: Myths and Realities* (Reading, UK: Ithaca Press, 1998).
71. Zoubir, *AJISS*, pp. 107–112; Isik, *IQ*, p. 351.
72. Zoubir, *AJISS*, p.109; Bennabi, *op. cit.*, p. 10. The English translations are of Zoubir.
73. Bennabi, *op. cit.*, p. 19.
74. Zoubir, *AJISS*, pp. 109, 110–111; Isik, *IQ*, p. 351.
75. Zoubir, *AJISS*, pp. 110–111; Isik, *IQ*, p. 351
76. Zoubir, *AJISS*, p. 111; Isik, *IQ*, p. 352.
77. Zoubir, *AJISS*, p. 111.; Isik, *IQ*, p. 352.
78. Bennabi, *op. cit.*, pp. 16–17.
79. Bennabi, *op. cit.*, p. 12; see also Yahia H. Zoubir, 'Algerian Islamists' Conception of Democracy', 1996. Available online at http://www.thefreelibrary.com/Algerian+Islamists'+conception + of+democracy-a019129732 (last accessed on 20 January 2011).
80. Bennabi, *op. cit.*, p. 15.
81. Ibid. p. 17.

82. Ibid.
83. Ibid.
84. Ibid., p. 19.
85. Ibid., pp. 21–22.
86. Ibid., p. 24.
87. Zoubir, *AJISS,* pp. 107–112; Isik, *IQ,* p. 352.
88. Bennabi, *op. cit.,* p. 36.
89. Ibid., p. 42.
90. Ibid.

# 4
# Nineteenth- and Twentieth-Century Muslim Intellectuals on Islam–Democracy Compatibility

Voices from South Asia

In continuance with the previous chapter, this chapter reflects on Islam–democracy reconciliation by providing an assessment of the views of some prominent pioneering South Asian Muslim modernist intellectuals of the nineteenth and twentieth centuries. Providing a valuable contribution and some important insights into this crucial debate, the prominent thinkers included in this chapter are: Muhammad Iqbal (1877–1938), Abul Kalam Azad (1888–1958), Syed Abu'l 'Ala Mawdudi (1903–79), Fazlur Rahman (1919–1988), and Amin Ahsan Islahi (1904–1997). This is followed by a brief assessment of the views of scholars of 'Traditionalist' bent, especially belonging to 'Deoband' school of thought, including Mawlana Ashraf 'Ali Thanawi (1863–1943), Mufti Shabbir Ahmad 'Uthmani (1886—1949), Mufti Muhammad Shafi (1896–1976), Qari Muhammad Tayyib (1897–1983), and Abdul Majid Daryabadi (1892–1977).

## Muhammad Iqbal (d. 1938) on 'Spiritual Democracy'

Muhammad Iqbal (1877–1938: commonly known as 'Allama Iqbal')[1]— poet-philosopher, lawyer, Muslim reformer, great political ideologist and activist, outstanding man of letters—was one of the most distinguished and dominant figures of the twentieth century. Iqbal was an outstanding poet of Persian and Urdu, and in prose, he wrote in English and Urdu as well. For most of his life, he was professionally a lawyer, and his passion was writing prose and poetry. He has authored a number of works on religious reform and self-advancement. He was the man who was at the same time a philosopher in the line of al-Farabi, Ibn Sina, and al-Ghazali and a poet in the rank of Sa'adi and Hafiz. He studied both Islamic sciences and Western philosophy at Government College in Lahore; Trinity College at Cambridge (UK); and at *University of Munich*, Germany. Clinton Bennett (*State University of New York*, USA) has summarized his life and achievements, very strikingly, in these lines:

> Muhammad Iqbal's life and achievements can be critically discussed under various headings, such as his poetry, his philosophy, and his political life, although these overlap considerably. His life may also be subdivided into an early period from his birth until he went to Europe in 1905, his time in Europe (1905–1908), his career from 1908 until his official retirement in 1934, and his final years from 1934 to 1938.... He is honored in Pakistan by a national holiday, Iqbal Day (November 9), an unusual recognition for someone who never held a high political office. Popular designations include *Hakkeem-ul-Ummat* (Sage or doctor of the Ummah), *Shair-e-Mashriq* (Poet of the East), as well as the more official *Muffakir-e-Pakistan* (Thinker of Pakistan). Muslims representing diverse opinions continue to look to him for inspiration. He is widely regarded as one of the most important Muslim intellectuals of the twentieth century, though he is by no means an uncontroversial figure.[2]

Having studied in British-ruled India, at Cambridge (England), and at Munich (Germany), Iqbal took a more critical approach to the Western ideas and institutions. He neither rejected the positive aspects of Western civilization, nor supported their blind imitation by Muslims. Instead, he wanted to create a new intellectual framework for a more authentic Islamic modernity and searched for ways to regenerate Muslims and their civilization on the basis of their own religious and cultural heritage. In other words, Iqbal combined what he thought to be the best of the East and the West, and 'developed his own synthesis and interpretation of Islam in response to the socio-historical conditions and events of his time'.[3] It is this aspect of Iqbal's thinking, as Riffat Hassan asserts, which makes his discourse so relevant to those contemporary Muslim thinkers who are trying 'to balance the requirements of modernization with those of cultural authenticity'.[4] He judged the conditions of the Islamic community one of five centuries of 'dogmatic slumber' and stagnation as a result of *taqlid*—when it substituted inertia for its essential dynamism and adaptability—and called for the 'reconstruction' of religious thought to revitalize the Muslim *Ummah*.[5]

Iqbal's life was spent exclusively under British colonial rule, during which Muslims in the Indian subcontinent were profoundly and predominantly influenced by the religious thought of Shah Waliullah and Sir Sayyid, and Iqbal inherited the legacy of both these intellectuals.[6] Regarding these aspects of Iqbal, Esposito writes:

> Muhammad Iqbal's profession was the law; his passion, writing poetry and prose; his lifelong concern, Muslim religious and political survival and reform. From the time he returned from his doctoral studies in Europe, he devoted himself to the revival of Indian Islam. He did this both as a poet-philosopher and, more reluctantly, as a politician. He placed himself within the revivalist tradition of Ahmad Sirhindi, Shah Wali Allah, and Muhammad ibn Abd al-Wahhab while addressing the questions of Islamic modernism. Islam and the Muslim community were in danger; they remained in decay and decline, were politically powerless, morally corrupted, and culturally backward. All of this, for Iqbal, stood in sharp contrast with the inner nature of Islam, which was dynamic and creative. Drawing on his Islamic heritage and influenced by his study of Western philosophy (Hegel, Bergson, Fichte, Nietzsche), he developed his own synthesis and interpretation of Islam in response to the socio-historical conditions and events of his time.[7]

Between 1915 and 1938, Iqbal wrote twelve volumes of poetry (in Persian and Urdu), such as: *Asrar-i-Khudi* (Secrets of the Self); *Bal-i-Jabril* (Gabriel's Wing); *Javid Nama* (The Pilgrimage/Book of Eternity); *Payam-i-Mashriq* (Message of the East); *Rumuz-i-Bekhudi* (The Mysteries of Selflessness); *Zabur-i-Ajam* (Persian Psalms/Scripture of the East); *Zarb-i-Kalim* (The Rod of Moses), etc. Having been translated into various languages, these have been published collectively in two volumes of *Kulliyat-i-Iqbal*, Persian and Urdu.[8]

Iqbal's poetry is mainly philosophical and the questions relating to religion, race and civilization, government, progress of women, literature and arts, and world politics were of equal interest to him. Major themes of his poetry included the decline of Muslim creativity, influence, and authenticity. He sought to reverse this decline through the promotion of a dynamic and forward-looking sense of self.[9]

Iqbal studied both Islamic sciences and Western philosophy. His writings, in Esposito's evaluation, 'were indebted to two principal sources: his Islamic heritage and the Western philosophy he studied at Cambridge, Heidelberg, and Munich'.[10] That is to say, he combined modern western philosophy (of Hegel, Bergson, Fichte, Nietzsche, etc.) with his Islamic tradition and constructed a modern dynamic, Islam-based and Islam-informed worldview. To put in Esposito's words, Iqbal's writings reflect the influence of the Qur'an, hadith, and Muslim thinkers like the great jurist Ibn Taimmiyya (1263–1328), the Indian reformer Shah Waliullah (1703–1762), and the renowned Sufi sage Jalalud Din Rumi (1207–1273).[11]

Iqbal's philosophical and prose works are actually very few.[12] Most notable among them are: (i) *The Development of Metaphysics in Persia* (Cambridge, 1908), originally a dissertation submitted to Munich University (in 1907); (ii) *'Ilm al-Iqtisad* (1903; Reprinted from Karachi in 1962)—a book on economics; (iii) *Presidential Address to the Annual Meeting of All-India Muslim League*, 1930—wherein he argued that the predominantly Muslim regions of North-West India should be governed autonomously under an Islamic system—a very extensive review of the interaction among the British, the All-India National Congress, and the All-India Muslim League, from the perspective of a Muslim thinker who was anxious about the political and cultural future of Muslims in the Indian subcontinent; and (iv) *The Reconstruction of Religious Thought in Islam*:[13] a collection of seven lectures delivered in December 1928 at Madras, Hyderabad, and Aligarh. Iqbal took three years to compose these lectures and considered them reflective of his mature philosophical and rational approach to Islam. *The Reconstruction* made him the most important poet-philosopher of his time, not only in India but in the whole Muslim world.[14]

Throughout his life, Iqbal devoted himself 'to inciting activity, to insisting eloquently', as W. C. Smith puts it, 'that life is a movement, that action is good, that the universe is composed of processes and not of static things'; and bitterly criticized and attacked 'the attitudes of resignation and quiet contentment, the religious valuation of contemplation, passivity, and withdrawal from strife'.[15] His prime function was to lash men into furious activity, and (as he puts it in *Asrar-i-Khudi*), to 'imbue the idle looker-on with restless impatience'. 'This call to impatient initiative', Smith suggests, 'is the chief revolution wrought by Iqbal in Islamic thought'. It is a necessary, if Islam is to survive; and modern thinking must be dynamic, and modern ethics must be positive and creative.[16] Life is not to be contemplated, but to be passionately lived. The hub and heart of Iqbal's significance lies here:

> The pith of life is contained in action.
> To delight in creation is the law of Life
> Arise and create a new world!
> Wrap thyself in flames, be an Abraham!
> To comply with this world which does not favour thy purposes
> Is to fling away thy buckler on the field of battle.
> The man of strong character who is master of himself
> Will find Fortune complaisant.
> If the world does not comply with his humour,
> He will try the hazard of war with Heaven;
> He will dig up the foundations of the universe
> And cast its atoms into a new mould.
> He will subvert the course of Time
> And wreck the azure firmament.
> By his own strength he will produce
> A new world which will do his pleasure.[17]

Iqbal regards the doctrine of *Tawhid* and the Prophethood of Muhammad (pbuh) as the twin pillars of Islamic state and society. Regarding the concept of *Tawhid*, the doctrine of God's Oneness—that is, Allah as the Creator, Sustainer, and Judge of the Universe—Iqbal believed that God's Will or Law governed every aspect of life. For him, *Tawhid* is the principle that 'brings the community together, the source of its equality, solidarity, and freedom'.[18] In his *The Reconstruction*, Iqbal writes:

> The essence of *Tawhid*, as a working idea, is equality, solidarity, and freedom. The state, from the Islamic standpoint, is an endeavor to transform these ideal principles into space-time forces, an aspiration to realize them in a definite human organization. It is in this sense that the state in Islam is a theocracy, not in the sense that it is headed by a representative of God on earth who can always screen his despotic will behind his supposed infallibility. The critics of Islam have lost sight of this important consideration. The Ultimate Reality, according to the Qur'an, is spiritual, and its life consists in its temporal activity.... The State, according to Islam, is only an effort to realize the spiritual in a human organization. But in this sense all state, not based on mere domination and aiming at the realization of ideal principles, is theocratic.[19]

Although the views of Iqbal on democracy[20] cannot be studied in isolation with his broad and comprehensive perception of Islam, or his philosophy of 'dynamic self' or selfhood (*Khudi*), his concepts of man of belief (*mard-i-mu'min*), perfect man (*insan-i-kamil*), or divine vicegerent (*naib-i-ilahi*), and his views on *ijma'* and *ijtihad*, some of the important principles of democracy that are appreciated by Iqbal include 'freedom', 'equality' and 'election'. He finds these principles compatible with Islam to a certain extent.[21]

For instance, he points out that in Islam, although the interest of an individual is subordinated to the community but the individual is given sufficient liberty, which is necessary for the development of his personality. He contends that the Western theory of democracy also protects the interest of the community while providing a favourable environment to individuals for their own development in the same way as Islam does. In the article, *Islam as a Moral and Political Ideal*[22]—in which he argued for the 'progressive and egalitarian nature of Islam, in both the ethical and political realms'—Iqbal writes that the 'best form of government' for a Muslim community/society 'would be democracy, the ideal of which is to let man develop all the possibilities of his nature by allowing him as much freedom as practicable'.[23]

Iqbal believed that Islam provided its own religio-political alternative for Muslim societies, and thus he turned to the past to rediscover the principles and values that were deemed necessary for him in order to reconstruct an Islamic model for Muslim society with Islamic versions of democracy and parliamentary government.[24] Thus, for example, Iqbal argued that the centrality of such beliefs as the equality and brotherhood of believers made democracy a political ideal in Islam, which, although historically unrealized, remained a duty for Muslims in the twentieth century.[25]

Iqbal explored from 1910 to 1930s, to use Muqtedar Khan's lexis, 'the prospects of establishing an Islamic [form of] democracy'. Considering Islam as an egalitarian faith with no room either for a clergy or an aristocracy, Iqbal recognized the importance of *ijtihad* and 'argued for its democratization and institutionalization in a popular legislative assembly thereby bridging the theoretical gap between divine and popular sovereignty'.[26] A strong advocate of freedom, individuality, equality, and brotherhood—all of which are necessary ingredients of liberal democracy—he stressed equality and brotherhood and as a result asserted (as early as in 1909) that the best form of government for the Muslim community is 'democracy' because it is 'the most important aspect of Islam regarded as a political ideal'.[27] His recognition of democracy was Islamic, however, for he believed in the representation of God on Earth. Divine vicegerency is the representation of God on earth as revealed in the Quran and aims at the establishment of 'the Kingdom of God on earth' meaning the 'the democracy of ... unique individuals'.[28]

In other words, his recognition of democracy as an ideal form was not the same as it existed and functioned in the West. He strongly criticized the demerits of modern western democracy. Iqbal remained highly critical of states which considered themselves democratic but engaged in political, economic, social, and psychological exploitation of the deprived sections of the society within or outside of themselves.[29] To be precise, he was critical of it in the prevalent form and unflinchingly denounced and criticized it. Writing on 'Muslim Democracy' (in *The New Era*, 1916), Iqbal says:

> The Democracy of Europe—overshadowed by socialist agitation and anarchical fear—originated mainly in the economic regeneration of

European societies... The *Democracy of Islam* [on the other hand] did not grow out of the extension of economic opportunity; it is *a spiritual principle* based on the assumption that every human being is a centre of latent power, the possibilities of which can be developed by cultivating a certain type of character (Italics added).[30]

However, to him, real democracy was an integral part of his belief in the principle of *Tawhid* upon which he built his thought. To Iqbal, this principle implied the equality of all human beings created by the one God. He believed that the 'essence of *Tawhid*, as a working idea, is equality, solidarity and freedom.'[31] These are principles that many today would consider essential characteristics of a democratic society.

He also preferred the term, 'spiritual democracy', considering it the 'ultimate aim of Islam'. While discussing this topic in his *The Reconstruction*, Iqbal wrote that contemporary Muslims should be allowed to 'appreciate his [or her] position, reconstruct his [or her] social life in the light of ultimate principles, and evolve, out of the hitherto partially revealed purpose of Islam, that *spiritual democracy* which is the *ultimate aim of Islam*' (Italics added).[32]

About Iqbal's 'spiritual democracy', (Justice) Javed Iqbal in his 'Iqbal's Concept of *Ijtihad*' writes:

Some Iqbal scholars are of the view that the expression means tolerance and acceptance of different sects within Islam in his imaginary Islamic state. But in light of Iqbal's prose-writings the expression is not confined only to tolerating Muslim sects but is broad enough to include protection of the rights of non-Muslim minorities.[33] Although Iqbal did not explain what he meant by 'spiritual democracy', it is possible that he had the *Misaq-e-Medina* [*Mithaq al-Medina*: Constitution of Medina] in mind while evolving this idea, as it was a written constitutional document of federal democratic nature considering collectively the Muslim, Jewish, Christian and pagan citizens of the state of Medina as *Ummat-ul-Wahida* (a single community). It is also possible that foundations of his concept can be traced from Surah Al-Maida: Verse 48 [Q. 5: 48, which states '*We have assigned a law and a path to each of you. If God had so willed, He would have made you one community, but*

*He wanted to test you through that which He has given you, so race to do good*] ... Finally if Iqbal believes that the principle of *Tauhid* [*Tawhid*] is based on human solidarity, human equality and human freedom, when the obvious logical inference is that Islam must be understood as a democracy of a 'spiritual' nature.[34]

Thus, Iqbal raised the basis of democracy to spiritual elevation and better economic adjustment. He looked for Islamic democracy as a social order to materialize the concepts of equality, brotherhood, liberty, justice, and humanitarianism; and thus, his conception of Islamic democracy, 'cannot ignore the masses'; and it can 'neither be nationalism nor imperialism but a league of nations'.[35]

Accepting the fact that Iqbal considered the establishment of 'spiritual democracy' indispensable for Muslims and comprehending his views that this democracy should be established through an elected assembly and that the *'republican form of government is not only thoroughly consistent with the spirit of Islam*, but has become a necessity in view of the new forces that are set free in the world of Islam' (Italics added).[36] Iqbal, warning the West about the ephemerality of its civilization, says:

> O Western world's inhabitants, God's world is not a shop!
> What you are considering genuine, will be regarded counterfeit
> Your civilization will commit suicide with its own dagger
> The nest built on a frail branch will not be durable.[37]

This was, as Dr Waheed Ishrat interprets, due to the fact that the Western civilization was enamoured of the visible, had distanced itself from prophetic consciousness, had ignored the real purpose of the creation of the universe and life, and had accepted matter as its goal instead of keeping it at its proper place of being only a means for understanding the reality. In the same way, with regards to the social sphere, the West separated politics from religion (*deen*) and an unbridled democracy held sway everywhere which, while endowing man with unrestricted freedom estranged him from the real purpose of his existence.[38] According to Iqbal, the real reason for this was the separation of politics from *deen* (Religion/Islam); and thus, he clearly warned:

> Statecraft divorced from Faith to reign of terror leads,
> Though it be a monarch's rule or Commoners' Show (or)
> It may be the majesty of the royalty or the fanfare of democracy
> If deen is separated from politics the latter becomes mere tyranny.[39]

Considering *deen* essential for encompassing the entire life, Iqbal, in Ishrat's analysis, believed in keeping politics also subservient to it and wanted the shaping of political systems only under the guidance of deen. Iqbal's spiritual democracy is synonymous with the harmony between *deen* and politics, and sovereignty is the sixth pillar of *deen* and *deen* cannot be established without sovereignty and the state.[40]

Here it may be remarked that Iqbal borrowed from the West but was not uncritical of it. He levelled sharp criticism at European colonialism and imperialism. Though an admirer of the accomplishments of the West, its dynamic spirit, intellectual tradition, and technological advances, he denounced the excesses of colonialism and imperialism, the exploitation of capitalism, Marxist atheism, and the moral bankruptcy of secularism and Western democracy (at least the variant practiced at that time).[41] In Iqbal's view, democracy, which was not always guided by empirical considerations, 'has a tendency to foster the spirit of legality. This is not in itself bad; but unfortunately it tends to displace the purely moral standpoint, and to make the illegal and wrong identical in meaning'.[42]

Thus, Iqbal indeed wrote against democracy, but his criticism is not an outright rejection of the idea. As such, he was not against democracy itself, but against the demerits of modern western democracy. He was critical of it in the prevalent form and bold enough to denounce it publicly. The modern Western democracy, in his view, was a cover for many injustices. It was, for instance, a weapon in the hands of imperialism and capitalism; as he writes in *Bang-i-Dara*:

> In the West the people rule, they say:
> And what is this new reign?
> The same harp still, the same strings play
> The despots' old refrain;
> In Demos-dress let tyranny's
> Old demon-dance be seen,
> Your fancy calls up Liberty's
> Blue-mantled fairy queen![43]

And in the Poem, 'Democracy', in *Payam-i-Mashriq* (A Message from the East), he warns to refrain from it:

> Avoid the method of democracy;
> Become the bondman of someone of ripe intelligence;
> For a few hundred donkeys cannot have, combined,
> The brains of one man, of one homo sapiens.[44]

In the poem, *Iblees Ki Majlis-e-Shura* (The Parliament of Satan) in *Armaghan-i-Hijaz* (A Gift to the Hijaz), Iqbal asks the people of the East:

> Haven't you seen the democratic [popular] system of the West?
> Bright-faced with a heart darker than Changez.[45]

This poem is, in the assessment of Masood Raja (*University of North Texas*, USA), 'a scathing criticism of the major socio-political and economic systems offered by the West'; and this verse in particular refers to the 'rise of democracy in the west'.[46] Iqbal in *Bang-i-Dara* calls democracy 'a ghost of oppression' mistakenly considered as a 'beautiful fairy of independence'. It is evident from this poem that this particular form of democracy is 'another form of Kingship whose essence is darker than its appearance. Iqbal justifies this dark aspect of Western democracy under two registers: capitalism and lack of a religious spirit'.[47] Moreover, Iqbal's disbelief in democracy rests largely on his satirical view of democracy as enunciated in his *Zarb-i-Kalim* (The Rod of the Moses):

> A certain European [Stendhal[48]] revealed a secret,
> Although the wise do not reveal the core of the matter.
> Democracy is a certain form of government in which
> Men are counted but not weighed.[49]

Thus, Iqbal examined very critically the concept of modern secular democracy as preached and practiced by the West. In his various poems, he calls it with various forenames, as becomes evident from the above-quoted couplets. He observed *inter alia* that the sole function of the Western democracy is to exploit the poor in the interest of the rich. According to him, the institution and civilization built upon secular democracy can never be sound and best. Iqbal pointed out the defects of narrow concept of dialectical materialism and capitalistic Western democracy, and according to him, Class War is the result of Western Democracy whereas justice and unity are the results of Islamic democracy. He cautioned that democracy was a coat that several European countries discarded after trial and which a number of Asiatic countries have picked up to wear, however ill-fitting it may be.[50] In the words of Dr Ishrat, it was Iqbal's 'foresight which discerned the psychological problem constituting the background of his criticism of democracy and this was interconnected with the special political atmosphere of that time'.[51]

Judging both Iqbal's appreciation as well as criticism of the democracy, Dr Khalifa Abdul Hakim/Hakeem (d. 1959) is of the opinion that Iqbal considers democracy to be an ambiguous concept like many other social concepts: 'Democracy is also like those ambiguous concepts which have no meaning. In the present day world every nation desires for and strives to establish democracy, or claims to be the custodian of the correct democracy, and considers the claims to other forms of democracy baseless and imposturous'.[52] For Hakim, the 'true democracy' in Iqbal's view 'was represented' and 'experimented' during the early period of Islam: 'In this Islamic democracy there was no ruling class. Freedom reigned everywhere. The state was a welfare state. This kind of democracy exists neither in the East nor in the West'.[53]

Iqbal also argued that contrary to the Western caricature of Islam as 'a religion which implies a state of war and can thrive only in a state of war', the 'doctrine of aggressive war against unbelievers is wholly unauthorized by the Holy Book of Islam'. Thus, 'Islam is essentially a religion of peace'.[54] For Iqbal,

> All forms of political and social disturbance are condemned by the Qur'an in the most uncompromising terms ... [as stated in verses like Q. 2: 60; 7: 85; 28: 77, 83; 89: 11–13, which clearly show] how severely all forms of political and social disorder are denounced by the Qur'an. But the Qur'an is not satisfied with mere denunciation of the evil of *fasad* [corruption]. It goes to the very root of this evil [as proclaimed in Q. al-Mujadilah, 58: 9: '*O You who believe! When you hold secret counsel, do it not for sin and wrongdoing, and disobedience towards the Messenger*']....
> The ideal of Islam is to secure social peace at any cost. All methods of

violent change in society are condemned in the most unmistakable language.[55]

On these foundations, Iqbal stated that democracy is the 'most important aspect of Islam regarded as a political ideal'; and added that there is 'no aristocracy in Islam'.[56] Because, the only distinction Islam makes is, on the basis of piety or righteousness (*Taqwa*), as stated in Q. 49: 13. There is neither any privileged class and priesthood nor any caste system. Islam is a unity in which there is no distinction, and this unity is secured by making humankind believe in two prepositions: *Tawhid* and *Risalah*— the unity of God and the mission of the Prophet (pbuh); and it is this principle of the equality of all believers, which, for Iqbal, made 'early Musalmans ["*The First Muslims*"] the greatest political power in the world. Islam worked as a leveling force; it gave the individual a sense of his inward power; it elevated those who were socially low'.[57]

For Iqbal, just as there are two basic ideals underlying Muslim ethics, in the same way, there are two basic prepositions underlying the Muslim political constitution; these are: (i) 'The law of God is absolutely supreme. Authority, except as an interpreter of the law, has no place in the social structure of Islam. Islam has a horror of personal authority', which is regarded 'as inimical to the unfoldment of individuality'; and (b) the conviction in the 'absolute equality of all members of a community'.[58] In a letter to a colleague, Iqbal stated, 'For Islam the acceptance of social democracy in some suitable form and consistent with the legal principles of Islam is not a revolution but a return to the original unity of Islam'.[59]

From the above views of Iqbal, many scholars including Mazharuddin Siddiqui of Pakistan assert that 'Iqbal stresses the elective principle as the basis of Islamic democracy'. Besides, he believes in the supremacy of the law and the equality of all Muslims.[60]

Moreover, Iqbal wanted to resuscitate the Muslim community so that it could reclaim its political independence and rightful place in history. Iqbal attempted to develop alternative Islamic models for modern Muslim societies. Drawing on Islamic traditions, argues Esposito, Iqbal 'sought to "rediscover" Islamic principles and values that would provide the basis for Islamic versions of Western concepts and institutions such as democracy and parliamentary government'.[61]

In fact, according to Iqbal, it is Islam that has imported to the people their natural rights: equality, freedom, and justice. In Islam, from the times of the Prophet (pbuh) and the pious caliphs, the real meaning of liberty and equality was translated into practice. In other words, the principles of democracy, liberty, and equality are not new to Islam at all. In fact, Islam presents these concepts and is against the man-centred authoritarianism and dominations. That is, Islam is totally against hereditary monarchies, dynastic rule, empires, military dictatorships, and self-imposed rule over the people. Iqbal indeed wrote against (Western) democracy, but his criticism is not an outright rejection of the idea, and as the above views of Iqbal reveal, he also wrote much in support of democracy. Iqbal's criticism of Western democracy, to refer to Esposito's statement, 'followed from his belief that the Western capitalist system suppressed the individual and his growth and made true democracy [both a failure and an] impossibility'.[62] Likewise, Masood Raja puts it in these words:

> Iqbal, a product of the colonial system, does not only critique the West from the place of the native alone; his critique of the West comes from within the Western philosophies of self-representation. In such a critique Western liberal democracy's class hierarchies and wealth distribution is exposed.... In Iqbal's views a modern system must offer the best of all other systems, and to him Islam is that true system. The native is not just fighting for or appealing for inclusion in the colonial system; he is, rather, offering his own philosophical and political system as a solution to the problems of the colonial masters.[63]

Iqbal's position on democracy has been very beautifully summarized by Mustansir Mir (*Youngstown University*, USA) in these words: Though he criticized both the philosophical foundations and practical form of the western democracy, 'Iqbal was a strong supporter of the democratic principle and considered democracy an essential part of Islamic government'.[64] Thus, the above analysis of Iqbal's views on democracy clearly reveal that he accepted only some of the principles of democracy and, at the same time, rejected not only the secular foundations of democracy but those principles and core concepts of democracy as well which he found incompatible with Islamic philosophy and polity.[65]

## Abul Kalam Azad (d. 1958) on Reconciling Islamic Polity and Democratic Notions

Mawlana Abul Kalam Azad (1888—1958)[66]—Indian 'liberal theologian-philosopher',[67] Urdu journalist, educationist, an Islamic intellectual *par excellence*, and an influential politician of the first half of the twentieth century—was a scholar 'thoroughly trained in the traditional Islamic sciences', and in Islamic values and culture with an ardent openness of mind for modern Western thought and civilization.[68] In S. A. A. Rizvi's words, Azad utilized 'pan-Islamic feelings to whip up religious frenzy and arouse political consciousness among the Muslim masses'.[69]

In the terminology of Ian Douglas, 'Azad is, by any reckoning, a major figure in twentieth-century Indian history. He was a scholar thoroughly trained in the traditional Islamic sciences, with great intellectual abilities and eloquence of pen and speech. He had, in addition, a remarkable openness to modern western knowledge even as he opposed western rule over India. He made a lasting contribution to Urdu prose literature with his translation and interpretation of the Qur'an [*Tarjuman al-Qur'an*], his many other religious writings, and his introspective autobiographical and epistolary works', including his magazines like through *Al-Hilal* and *Al-Balagh*. Azad was, indeed, 'the man of religion, as a Muslim reformer and scholar of Islam'.[70]

Azad's views about democracy in Islam, *Shura* as an substitute for democracy, as well as the Prophetic and rightly guided caliphate period as the true basis of democracy in Islam, similarity between the basic principles of the French Revolution (of 1789) and the Qur'anic teachings about democracy and the parliamentary system, and many other such interrelated issues,[71] are spread in his commentary of the Qur'an, *Tarjuman al-Quran*;[72] throughout the volumes of his weekly magazine *al-Hilal* (first published in July 1912);[73] and in his other works/writings, like *Islami Jumhuriyya, Mas'ala Khilafat,* and *Qaul-i-Faisal*.[74]

Though in most writings on Azad, his thoughts on, and contribution to areas like, education, Qur'an exegesis, universalism, nationalism, and pluralism, have been highlighted to a great length, but, one of the important aspects of his thought is Islam–democracy reconciliation—which has been somewhat an overlooked aspect of his thought.

Azad translated Q. 3: 159, *nez is tarha ke ma'amlaat main (yeni Jung wa aman ke ma'amlaat main) unse mashwara kar liya karo* ('and consult them in matters of importance'), i.e. in matters related to war and peace'.[75] He renders Q. 42: 38 as: *'aur unko hukm diya ki mashwara kar ke tamaam amuur sar anjaam dein'* ('and who conduct their affairs by mutual consultation.')[76] Contextualizing Q. 3: 159 with the situation of battle of Uhud, Azad proclaims that here Qur'an addresses the Prophet (pbuh) to draw attention towards functioning of the leadership. Some of them include: (i) your procedure in matters of peace and war should be to take consult from those who are competent to advise; and (ii) the procedure may take this form: first, hold consultations and then make up your mind to decide on a definite thing. Once you have resolved, stick to it with firmness. Consultation, and then resolution, both are, at the proper moments, of equal importance. The question of resolution or decision does not arise till the consultation is over.[77] Regarding the obedience of the leader, he maintains that 'when the Prophet takes counsel of them before deciding on any line of action, it should behove them to obey him implicitly'.[78]

However, in the explanation of Q. 42: 38, wherein Azad identifies the compatibility between democracy and community deliberation and consultation (*Shura*), writes:

> To take consultation or deliberation from each other is one of the best characteristics of Muslims mentioned in this verse and Prophet (pbuh) is commanded to take consultation from the Companions in 3: 159 [*'and consult (shawirhum) with them in the affairs'*]. Except Obligatory Commandments, Prophet (pbuh) himself used to consult with his noble Companions on every matter related to state and administration. Later *Shura* was made into the very foundations of [the government system of the] Pious Caliphate period [r. 632–660 CE], and Abu Bakr [the first caliph, r. 632–632 CE] was nominated/selected under the same procedure. This proves that Islamic social order (*Nizam-i-Ijtima'yi*) is a pillar of Islamic way of life, having peculiar importance in it.[79]

The interpretations of Azad in these two verses (Q. 3: 159 and 42: 38) show that he has approached from a modernist perspective. He mentions that in this verse, Prophet (pbuh) is commanded to take deliberation with or consult his Companions in matters of importance.[80] Azad regards *Shura* as the real edifice of Islamic socio-political system and a crucial concept that has 'peculiar importance in Islam'.[81] He also speaks of *Shura* both in terms of 'war and peace', as becomes clear from his very translation of this verse as well as the basis of 'Islamic democracy', or what he calls as 'the real basis of democracy in Islam', and even goes further to argue that the 'Qur'an uses the term *Shura* for describing it [the real democracy] and what else term (other than *Shura*) can we use for describing it'.[82]

What also becomes clear is that Azad has not reflected on the issues related to the rules, structure, procedure, and form of *Shura*. He evades the issue on the pretext that it needs more discussion and deliberation;[83] thus, leaving behind, unaddressed, the central and serious issues ranging from the scope, significance, nature, application of *Shura*, to the procedure for the selection/election of counsellors, and other inter-related matters.

Besides *Tarjuman al-Qur'an*, Azad's views about democracy in Islam are spread, among others, throughout the volumes of his *Al-Hilal*—an 'influential religious and cultural weekly' magazine, first published in July 1912[84]—through which he 'persuaded the Muslims to have confidence in their faith, instead of numerical inferiority'.[85] Pranav Prakash (*University of Iowa*, USA) writes about *Al-Hilal* in these words:

> In July 1912, Azad inaugurated his illustrious weekly *al-Hilal*, for whose publication he introduced significant technical reforms in the Urdu press.... The readers liked the novel format of the weekly. It received more than 25,000 subscriptions in the first 3 months of its publication. More significantly, al-Hilal appeared at an opportune moment, when the Urdu press and readership were rapidly expanding.[86]

In the beginning volumes of *al-Hilal*, Azad was very much pre-occupied and immersed with 'dethroning false leadership based on hereditary religious status or on western education, and with proclaiming Islamic democracy which forbade autocratic personal rule'.[87] True leadership must be by the will of the entire community and in consultation with them. But his writings in *Al-Hilal* focused, all in all, mainly 'to definite contemporary events, provocations, challenges, or questions from correspondents', and the major reasons for Azad's success (through *al-Hilal*) involved 'timing, the choice of issues, and especially style'.[88]

Azad regards the Islamic system of governance established by the Prophet (pbuh) as an authentic picture of democratic system of government and calls it 'Islamic democracy' for which the Qur'an uses the term '*Shura*'. Islam is 'identical', he upholds, with the 'spirit of democracy and equality, and it cannot consider any government which is not parliamentary and constitutional as in accordance with God's will';[89] and that there are many evidences and proofs for the assertion that in Islam, the government is the possession of public (*jumhur*), neither hereditary nor personal; and the best attestation is the Qur'an itself: Q. 3: 159, and 42: 38.[90]

For Azad, 'Islam constitutes a perfected system of freedom and democracy',[91] and he considers 'every form of government which is non-constitutional and non-parliamentary as the greatest human sin'.[92] On the issue of 'democracy in Islam', Azad raised the question of whether Muslims were merely adopting ideas from the French Revolution (of 1789) and European thought, or whether the Qur'an itself taught democracy and the parliamentary system. He makes his views clear in various articles of *Al-Hilal*.

The Prophet (pbuh) came at a time, maintains Azad, when the rulers were virtually worshipped and he introduced a new system of democracy. Islam never accepted as legitimate 'a sovereignty which is personal or is constituted of a bureaucracy of a handful of paid executives', because Islam constitutes a 'perfected system of freedom and democracy. It has been sent down to get back for the human race the liberty which has been snatched away from it'.[93]

From its very beginning, Islam declared that the 'highest right is not might but right itself'.[94] Azad believes that liberty (freedom) is the 'natural and God-given gift to man' and neither an individual (human being) nor any human-made system (like bureaucracy) has the right 'to make the servants of God its own slaves' or 'to make serfs and slaves of God's creatures'.[95] All humans are equal, and their fundamental rights are on par and on the same level; he only is greater than others whose deeds are most righteous and virtuous, as the Qur'an states: *In God's eyes, the most honoured of you are the ones most mindful of Him* (Q. 49: 13). He lists five basic principles of the French Revolution (of 1789), also called the 'Revolution of 1789',[96] and proclaims that all of them had been present in Islam for centuries:

1) Sovereignty is vested in the people and is neither personal nor hereditary;
2) All human beings (citizens) are equal (in rights and in the eyes of the law);
3) The president of the country, known as *Imam* or *Khalifah* in the Islamic terminology, is appointed by the people, and has no essential superiority over others;
4) All decisions (of the president) must be made in consultation with able and worthy counsellors; and
5) The treasury (or *Bayt al-Mal*) is the property of the public, and the president may not spend it without authority.[97]

In the description and elucidation of these principles, Azad writes that there are many evidences for the claim that in Islam, government is the possession of public (*Jumhur*), and is neither hereditary nor personal/private; and the best attestation is the Qur'an itself, when it proclaims: *and consult with them in the affairs* (3: 159); and in the second place, in the admiration of Islamic government, it says: '*and who conduct their affairs by mutual consultation*' (42: 38). Besides this, the election of Caliphs, their counselling with the *Ahl al-Ra'y* (people of opinion) and with *Ahl al-Hall wa al-'Aqd* (the 'Wise Ones') are a few historical examples that support the argument that in Islam, government is not the power of any dictator or despotic ruler, but of the public (*Jumhur*).

In his *Tarjuman al-Qur'an*, Azad, in the interpretation of Q. 42: 38, mentions that '*Shura* was made into the very foundations of [the government of the] Pious Caliphate period' (r. 632–660 CE) and the first caliph, Abu Bakr (r. 632–634 CE) was also nominated under the same procedure, which proves that 'Islamic social order (*Nizam-i-Ijtimayi*') is a pillar of Islamic way of life, having peculiar importance in it'.[98] Similarly, in his *Islami Jumhurriya* ('Islamic Democracy'), he states very eloquently that Islamic democracy is the actual picture and authentic representation of democratic system of government; Islam is its very propagator; it was established by the Prophet (pbuh), and was carried on successfully by the rightly guided Caliphs. Islam is a democratic system of government first (in the history of humankind) to offer and guarantee human rights, and that too 1100 years before the French Revolution. It was established by opinion of Ummah (*Ra'y*), Vicegerency or succession (*Niyabah*) and by oath of allegiance (*Bay'ah*), and elections (*Intikhabat*). The Qur'an uses the term *Shura* for the system of governance (Q. 42: 38). What other term besides *Shura*, underscores Azad, can be used for describing a democratic system. The system of governance established by Islam was such, having no example anywhere. It affirmed (and guaranteed) rights to public, prescribed punishments (*hudud*) for crimes and penal ordinances, construed the laws—financial, indigenous, an administrative—expounded justice and benevolence, opposed nepotism and monarchy, and in the very first blow, eliminated absolute despotism and racial discrimination.[99] He also asserts that the political authority of the Prophet (pbuh) and of the caliphs was 'a perfected conception of democratic equality, and it could only take shape with the whole nation's will, unity, suffrage, and election'.[100]

Furthermore, Azad in his *Mas'la-i Khilafat* (The Issue of the Caliphate) defined caliphate as an essential Islamic institution that ensured the unity of the Muslim *Ummah* and guaranteed democratic governance against tyranny and absolutism. His political theory was essentially founded on the classical doctrine with some major revisions.[101]

Azad insisted that the theory and practice of Islam were both against kingship and the authority of the monarchy. He held that unity and sovereignty of God and the establishment of supremacy of a righteous order are the real elements of democracy; and that democracy, as a form of government, is based not on the force, but on the will of the people, characterized by tolerance, equality, and liberty. In a nutshell, Azad's thought was alleviated by his persuasion that Islam was essentially democratic in nature—thus making Islam and its principles relevant to the modern times.[102]

## Syed Abu'l 'Ala Mawdudi (d. 1979) on 'Theo-Democracy'

Syed Abu'l 'Ala Mawdudi (1903–1979)—a prominent and influential South Asian Muslim thinker-activist and founder of Islamic revivalist movement, *Jamaat-e-Islami*—was an Islamic ideologue, politician, journalist, prolific writer, most prominent revivalist thinker, and one of the leading Muslim polyglots of the twentieth century.[103] A major contributor to the promotion of Islam as *Din wa Dawla* (religion and state), he dispensed his energy resolutely into writings—which give strong expression and manifestation to the themes basic to present-day 'Islamic resurgence' or 'Islamic revivalism'—speeches, and religious and political activities. His bounteous academic output spans a wide range of areas/fields—tradition, law, philosophy, history, politics, economics, sociology, and theology.[104]

Mawlana Mawdudi advocated that Islam was both *Din wa Dawla* (religion and state) and resolutely rejected their separation. In numerous works, he expounded and explained his views on religion and its application and applicability in society, economy, and polity and deliberated on Islamic system of governance and its affinity with democracy—nevertheless within the bounds and limitations set by Islamic law. Rejecting religion-state separation, he proposed 'theo-democracy' as the basis of the 'Islamic state'. Thus, he was one of those modern voices who deliberated on Islamic system of governance and its affinity with democracy, though within bounds and limitations.[105]

For Mawdudi, the 'political system of Islam' is, and should be, 'based on three principles, viz., *Tawheed* (Oneness of God), *Risalat* (Prophethood), and *Khilafat* (Caliphate)'. In his estimation and assessment, it is challenging 'to appreciate the different aspects of Islamic policy without fully understanding these three principles'.[106] Though in his earlier writings, he criticized, especially from the political philosophy standpoint, the 'philosophical foundations of Western democracy' by declaring Islam as 'the very antithesis of secular Western democracy',[107] but he never rejected it wholly, as becomes evident from his various later writings. Relatively, he asserted that it should be outlined within the limits and boundaries of *Tawhid* on the grounds that if democracy was understood as a limited form of popular sovereignty—to be restricted and directed by God's law—then there is no incompatibility between the two. That is to say, for him, Islam constitutes its own form of democracy when conceived as a limited form of popular sovereignty directed by the Islamic Law (*Shari'ah*). Describing and pronouncing this alternate view by interpreting the concept of *Khilafah* (Vicegerency) as a basis for this interpretation, he used the term Theo-democracy (*Ilahi Jumhuri Hukumat*: a divine democratic government) for it.[108] He also maintains that Islamic polity is neither theocracy nor democracy, but contains elements of both of these systems;[109] thus, rightfully, contends:

> If I were permitted to coin a new term, I would describe this system of government as a *'theo-democracy,'* that is to say *a divine democratic government,* because under it the Muslims have been given a *limited popular sovereignty* under the suzerainty [paramount sovereignty] of God.... *In this sense, the Islamic polity is [a real] democracy.* (Italics added)[110]

Mawdudi designated the Islamic polity with the term 'theo-democracy' in order to distinguish it both from a theocracy, or a clergy-run state, and from the Western secular democracy. Many Muslim and non-Muslim scholars, including John L. Esposito, Dr Israr Ahmad, Munawar Haque, and many other Muslim and non-Muslim scholars endorse this viewpoint.[111]

Formulating and elucidating his views in light of the fundamental Islamic concepts, Mawdudi interpreted the concept of human vicegerency (*Khilafah*)—one of the basic principles of Islamic political philosophy as well as a significant 'Democratic notions' in Islam—for his interpretation of democracy in Islam. Describing the real significance and implication of *Khilafah,* he argues that the authority of caliphate is bestowed on the entire group of people, the community as a whole, which is ready to fulfil the conditions of representation after subscribing to the principle of *Tawhid* and *Risalah*. '*This is the point where democracy begins in Islam*' (Italics added).[112] Thus, for Mawdudi, the caliphate is, when discussed in its real sense and perspective, the point where democracy begins in Islam. Regarding his (these) views, Esposito and Voll, argue that Mawdudi's 'perception of "caliph" not only becomes a foundation for concepts of human responsibility and of opposition to systems of domination, but also provides a basis for distinguishing between democracy in Western and in Islamic terms'.[113]

While discussing the concept of *Khilafah* as one of the operational concepts of democracy in Islam, reference has been already made to the views of Mawdudi regarding it as a starting point of democracy in Islam (in Chapter 2). In order to stay away from repetition, suffice is to mention here that he called the political system of Islam as a 'perfect form of democracy—as perfect as a democracy can ever be', and proclaimed that *Khilafah* as popular vicegerency is the *real foundation of democracy in Islam* (Italics added).[114]

It is true that, in Islamic history, monarchy and dictatorship have often been accepted forms of government. However, the principle, the Qur'an spells and brings out is very clear. What this principle brings about in terms of its nature and foundation has been explained, while commenting on the verse 42: 38, very pertinently by Mawdudi.[115] He has made a detailed discussion on this verse and understood *Mashawarat* obligatory on the Muslim community due to three reasons, which are: (i) the decision of one person according to his/her own opinion is injustice when the interests of many are concerned; (ii) arbitrary action is morally detestable, as it is only the result of felt superiority or usurping of others' rights; and (iii) deciding in matters of common interest is a grave responsibility, so consultation is needed to share the burden.[116] 'A deep consideration of these three things', he further elaborates, 'can enable one to fully understand that consultation is a necessary demand of the morality that Islam has taught to man, and departure from it is a grave immorality'.[117] He also indicates that *Shura* extends beyond government and should permeate all aspects of Muslim life: ranging from the domestic affair, family, tribe/city, to nation. He criticizes, specifically, the act of obtaining power by force or deception as being un-Islamic.[118]

He further points out that the principle of consultation as enshrined in *Amruhum Shura Baynahum* by its very nature and structure demands five things, which are: (1) collective decision-making, that is, 'people whose interests and rights are directly affected by collective decisions should have the absolute right to express their opinions' (i.e., there should be freedom of opinion and freedom of information); (2) that the appointment of the persons 'responsible for the collective affairs [Representatives] of the Muslims should be with the free will of people'; (3) that representatives of people involved in consultation with the head of the state should be appointed on the basis of the 'genuine trust of people'; (4) that there should be freedom of expression for people's representatives to present their opinions correctly and honestly; and finally (5) the unanimous or majority verdict of the consultative body should be accepted.[119] Thus, for him, the implication of this verse is that Muslims can consult in order to come up with the most correct ruling in legal matters, but cannot give independent judgment in settled matters. Therefore, consultation and deliberation should be done in all collective matters of *Ummah*.

Thus, Mawdudi, like other exegetes of the noble Qur'an—for example, Azad, 'Uthmani, Shafi, Islahi, etc.—share the same view arguing that in verse 3: 159, the Prophet (pbuh) is commanded to take deliberation or consult Companions in matters of importance; and here (i.e. in 42: 38) Allah praises those Muslims who conduct their affairs through consultation, i.e. one of the best qualities and attributes of true believers is that they conduct their affairs by mutual consultation.[120]

Mawdudi believed that the renewal of Muslim society and its social transformation or modernization must be rooted in Islamic principles and values. Thus, instead of speaking of democracy as such, for Dr Munawar Haque, Mawdudi 'accepted the traditional concepts of consultation and community consensus, but noted that in Islamic democracy, the will of the people remained subordinate to the Divine will'.[121]

Moreover, it is pertinent to mention here that Mawdudi held that Islam constitutes its own form of democracy, i.e. 'theo-democracy'; but he concentrated on the relationship between divine and popular sovereignty. Arguing that democracy as commonly understood is based exclusively on the sovereignty of people, he concluded, from the standpoint of political philosophy, that Islamic state is 'the very antithesis of secular Western democracy'.[122] However, it is on the basis of the concept of sovereignty, law, and authority of the people that Mawdudi differentiates between Islamic and Western democracy. The major differences between the two, for him, are on these grounds: principle of Sovereignty of God (*hakimiyyah*) and Popular *Khilafah* in Islamic system vs. Popular Sovereignty in western conception; observing and obeying the laws (*Shari'ah*) given by God through His Book (Qur'an) to the Prophet vs. the laws made by the people; subservience to the Divine Law within the limits prescribed by *Shari'ah* vs. absolute authority. He thus asserts that 'Western democracy is a kind of absolute authority which exercises its powers in a free and uncontrolled manner whereas the Islamic democracy is subservient to the Divine Law and exercises its authority in conformity with the injunctions of God and within the limits prescribed by Him'.[123] For him:

> Of course, what distinguishes *Islamic democracy* from *Western democracy* is that while the latter is based on the concept of *Popular*

*Sovereignty* the former rests on the principle of *Popular Khilafah*. In Western democracy, the people are sovereign, in Islam *Sovereignty vests in God and the people are His Caliphs or representatives*. In the latter [Western] the people *make* their own laws (*Shari'ah*) in the former [Islamic] they have to *follow and obey the laws* (*Shari'ah*) given by God through His Prophet. In the one [Western] the government undertakes to fulfill the will of people; in the other [Islamic] the government and the people who form it have one and all to fulfill the purpose of God. In brief, *Western democracy* is a kind of *absolute authority* which exercises its powers in a free and uncontrolled manner whereas the *Islamic democracy* is subservient to the Divine Law and exercises its authority in conformity with the injunctions of God and within the limits prescribed by Him.[124]

In support of Mawdudi's above arguments, Khurshid Ahmad argues that the major difference between the two is on the basis of the concept of sovereignty. For him, the Islamic state is different from a secular democracy as it is 'diametrically opposed to the concept of Sovereignty of the people. Allah the Supreme Law-Giver and the *Shari'ah* is the law of the land. Within the framework of the *Shari'ah*, new problems are faced and their solutions worked out. This represents the co-ordinal difference [between the two]'.[125] Furthermore, Ahmad also makes a distinction between democracy 'as a philosophy' and as a 'form of organization'. For him, democracy as a philosophy is 'different from Islam, rather opposed to Islam'.[126] In other words, for Ahmad:

> The philosophical roots of democracy lie in the concept of 'popular sovereignty'. It consists ... of denial of the existence or at least the relevance of eternal religious guidance and absolute moral values in matters of political governance, and ... the affirmation that the people, their popular will be accepted as the real source of all authority and power.[127]

Allama Iqbal also makes a distinction between Islamic democracy and the democracy of the West on the basis of sovereignty. Iqbal, as quoted by A. Aleem Helal, also supports, to some extent Mawdudi's distinction between Islamic and Western democracy, when he says that what distinguishes the

Islamic democracy from the democracy of the West is that in an Islamic democracy, sovereignty is vested in a democratic Caliph or President, while in the Western democracy sovereignty is vested in the Parliament. Thus while Islam recommends a democratic Caliphate or a Presidential form of government, the political thinkers of West have recommended a parliamentary form of government.[128]

Similarly, while discussing 'Mawdudi on Democracy: A Critical Appreciation', Zeenat Kausar reaches the conclusion that the terminology used by Mawdudi for describing the Islamic political order was not the final, it was just for the sake of comparison that he used such terms/phrases like 'theo-democracy', 'democratic Khilafah', and 'Islamic democracy', while as in essence they are contradictory terms. She even goes further, by using new terminology for Islamic political order, to argue that

> Islam only accepts rule by Allah '*Allahcracy*' which should be established on the earth by the vicegerents of Allah, through the institution of (Shura) consultation method to keep the (Shari'ah) supreme. Such a form of government may be termed as '*Khilafacracy*' (rule by the vicegerents), or '*Shuracracy*' (rule by the vicegerents of Allah through consultation), or '*Shariahcracy*' (rule on the basis of Shari'ah). (Italics added)[129]

Additionally, it is pertinent to mention here that Mawdudi's concept of theo-democracy has received severe criticism from various corners amid its wide circulation and much appreciation. For example, Charles Adams stated that Mawdudi's *theo-democracy* cannot escape from the fault of tyranny, because 'While sovereignty may belong to God, God does not Himself intervene directly in the life of the Islamic state to give orders, decide policies, or render divisions'. There must be, he stressed, 'human agency to do those things on His behalf and in His name'; therefore, 'If the fault of theocratic governments lies in the fact that some human agency attains unrestricted power', then 'how the Islamic theo-democracy that Mawdudi proposed would escape this fault' is questionable.[130] How (and how much) 'Islamic' is Mawdudi's Theo-democracy? Afsaruddin raises this question in her analysis and asserts that theo-democracy is 'a-historical and unfaithful to, and even distorting of, the variegated pre-modern Islamic political tradition which evolved over time'.[131] Jackson echoes the same stance when he declares the concept of theo-democracy as 'a contradiction in terms', arguing that Mawdudi's claim that his Islamic society would be a 'theo-democracy' 'seems to beg the question: where is the democracy?'[132] Hartung, in his *A System of Life: Mawdudi and the Ideologisation of Islam*, remarks: 'In order to distinguish his envisioned political system and, at the same time, to further dissociate himself from Western concepts of democracy, Mawdudi coined the neologism 'theo-democracy' (*ilahi jumhuri hukumat*)'.[133]

Thus, it becomes evident that Mawdudi neither completely discarded western democracy nor proclaimed for its 'wholesale' acceptance and adoption, but rather embraced a convincing, reasonable, and 'reconciliatory' approach to the issue of Islam–democracy reconciliation.

## Fazlur Rahman (d. 1988) on *Shura* as 'People's Representation'

Fazlur Rahman Malik (1919–1988) of Pakistan—Professor of Islamic thought at the *University of Chicago* (USA) and *McGill University* (Canada), and an expert in Islamic philosophy—was a scholar of encyclopaedic extensiveness in the true tradition of classical Islamic scholarship. Rahman is unquestionably considered as 'one of the most important and influential Muslim modernist thinkers of the second half of the 20th century' in both the Western and Muslim worlds.[134] He is described by Abdullah Saeed as the 'most daring and original contributors to the discussion on the reform of Islamic thought in the twentieth century', who has made a 'major contribution to modern discussions of reform in Islamic thought'.[135] For Rozehnal, Rahman was 'a spokesman for liberal, reformist Islam, [who] championed Islam's relevance in the modern world [and] embraced an open, dynamic, and adaptive faith,' and for Ahad Ahmed, he was 'a noble scholar of Islamic philosophy and an important liberal Muslim thinker of the twentieth century' who wrote on a wide range of subjects.[136] His interests ranged from 'the classical period to modern times; from the Quran and Hadith to *fiqh* (Islamic jurisprudence) and ethics; from philosophy and science to theology and medicine; and from education and history to the contemporary sociopolitical and intellectual developments in the Muslim world'.[137]

In the context of Islam–democracy discourse, he mainly refers to the concept of *Shura*.[138] For example, referring to the case of the first caliph (Abu Bakr)—who was chosen by the elders from both the Emigrants and Helpers (*Muhajirun* and *Ansar*) and endorsed by the community—Rahman acknowledges that he had received his mandate from the people who asked him to implement the Qur'an and Sunnah.[139] In Rahman's opinion, this 'clearly establishes that the Islamic State derives its sanction from the Islamic community and that, therefore, *it is completely democratic*' in nature, but as democracy can take (and throughout history has taken) various forms and, thus, can be direct or indirect, parliamentary or presidential, liberal or constitutional, depending on the prevalent social and political conditions (Italics added).[140]

Given the underlying egalitarian ethos of Islam, he accepted the notion that governments must be based on 'popular will through some form of representation' and does not think that 'the adoption of modern democratic institutions' to be 'un-Islamic'.[141] However, drawing attention to the fact that the masses of Muslims are illiterate, he pointed out that it is not easy 'to implement democracy under such circumstances'.[142] Moreover, in view of the desire and need for 'rapid economic development, which is a common problem in the under-developed-countries, including all the Muslim countries', for Rahman, what is needed, is a strong government capable of a high degree of centralized planning and control of economic development.[143] Therefore, Rahman reaches the conclusion that from the Islamic viewpoint, 'there can be no harm in this [i.e., in having 'strong men' at the helm of affairs in underdeveloped countries], provided that, at the same time, the spirit of democracy is genuinely and gradually cultivated by the people'.[144]

For Rahman, *Shura*—the collective decision-making—prescribes that Muslims must decide 'their affairs by mutual consultation and discussion' (Q. 42: 38), which could only be done by the participation of the community in the affairs of the government. For him, although this could be achieved 'through the election of representatives', but this concept had been 'distorted into consultation by the ruler of such people who he thought worthy'. 'This distortion', he continues, 'occurred at the advent of

Khawarij, and as a reaction to their ultra-democratic stand'.[145] Looking at the concept of *Shura* in a historical development, he argues:

> The institution of *shura*, the collective decision-making council through which the elders of a tribe arrived at decisions concerning momentous issues of peace and war in pre-Islamic Arabia, was stifled [and subdued] instead of being developed in later Islamic political theory. This was despite the Quran's clear injunction: 'Their [i.e., the Muslim community's] affairs shall be decided through their collective or mutual discussion' (Q 42: 38). Indeed, *shura* came to mean that one man, the ruler, would 'consult' such persons as he thought appropriate and then execute his will. No wonder, then, that it required real heroic courage to speak out the truth before an autocratic ruler! For the *shura* and the role of the community in the decision-making process explicitly enjoined by the Qur'an vanished into thin air.[146]

In his *Major Themes of the Qur'an*, he recalls that *Shura* is instituted by the Qur'an for the Muslim community to carry on their collective business (government). For him, Qur'an asks Muslims to institute the institution of *Shura*, because

> *Shura* (a consultative council or assembly), [is the institution/system] where the will of the people can be expressed by representation. *Shura* was a pre-Islamic democratic institution which the Qur'an (42: 38) confirmed. The Qur'an commanded the Prophet himself (3: 159) to decide matters only after consulting the leaders of the people. But in the absence of the Prophet, the Qur'an (42: 38) seems to require some kind of collective leadership and responsibility.[147]

## Amin Ahsan Islahi (d. 1997) on *Shuracracy*

Amin Ahsan Islahi (1904–1997) was an exegete of the Qur'an from the Indo-Pak subcontinent, who is famous for his Urdu exegeses, *Tadabbur al-Qur'an* (*Reflections on the Qur'an*)—an exegesis that he based on Hamiduddin Farahi's (1863–1930) idea of thematic and structural coherence of the Qur'an. He is prominent and well known for his contribution to Qur'anic studies, especially for his approach, based and evolved around the concept of order and coherence (*Nazm, Rabt*) in the contents of the Divine Book. His political views about Islamic state, *Shura* and its democratic nature, and other inter-related aspects can be found in his explanations of Qur'anic verses 3: 159 and 42: 38 and in his book *Islami Riyasat* (translated into English as *The Islamic State* by Tariq Mahmood Hashmi of Pakistan).[148] In this book, Islahi discusses the basics of an Islamic state, rights and duties of its citizens, conditions for compliance, and responsibilities of the authority. The book is helpful in deriving Islahi's thoughts related to state and society.

According to Islahi, *Shura* means 'taking deliberation from each other'.[149] For him, in Q. 3:159 along the guidelines of seeking Allah's forgiveness, Prophet (pbuh) was advised to consult *Sahabah* (Companions) in matters of deliberation. Regarding religious matters, Prophet (pbuh) was not in need of consultation as he was guided by revelation. But in political and administrative matters, Prophet (pbuh) used to consult Companions constantly, and in this way, he himself laid the foundations of the institution of *Shura* (*Shurai'yat*) that has been an important characteristic of the Islamic political system.[150]

For Islahi, the principle of consultation assumed the 'central position in the political system', evolved by the rightly guided caliphs. 'Public opinion' was, therefore, 'not only considered necessary in the formation of the political system but also in running the state affairs'. Abu Bakr (r. 632–634 CE), the first caliph of Islam, was elected with the active will of the Muslims after due consultation. After assuming the chair of *Khilafah*, he discharged his political responsibilities and decided collective affairs, which were not dealt within the Qur'an and the Sunnah, through consultation with the major Companions who enjoyed the confidence of the majority Muslims and who were considered best among their peers in knowledge and piety.[151]

For Islahi, an Islamic state (*Khilafah*) does not differ much from an ordinary state in its formal and material structure (population, territory, internal independence, political institution); it differs in principles and objectives. *Khilafah* means complete equality; it is not limited to any specific class or person. He, however, regards both parliamentary and presidential systems, as currently in vogue, against Islam. Muslims have a limited right to legislate, in such matters which are not clearly given in the

Qur'an and Sunnah. Islahi differentiates between an Islamic state and the (modern) secular democracies, as:

> What differentiates between the Islamic state, ... , and the irreligious [secular] democracies, which attach the rights with loyalty to their country, nation and the national constitution? Nature of the demand by both sides is the same. Though both attach loyalty to a different entity—one demands that the citizens remain loyal to the Almighty Allah and the other wants this right reserved for the national constitution—yet there is no difference in the nature of both the views; both hinge the rights upon fulfillment of the condition of loyalty to some entity which ties the citizens in a common bond and thus works as a centre and reference point for all collective affairs. This principle is shared by both systems.... In short, the Islamic State, which is an ideological state by nature and is founded on the principle guidance of Islam, does not give rights to the individuals who do not believe in Islam and are rebellious to it. However, those rejecters of Islam, who are ready to submit before the political dominion of the faith and who intend to live in the Islamic State while being loyal to it are awarded some distinct rights.[152]

Although he regards the principle of *Shura* (consultation, or what he translates as 'taking deliberation from each other') as far better than the western model of democracy, but at the same time, he is of the opinion that in the present-day society, any setup of the institution of *Shura* can be introduced which not only matches the needs of the time but also facilitates the accomplishment of the ideals of *Shura* in an effective manner: 'Modern methods of election can be adopted and new reforms can be introduced into the system.... Legislation in this process would be perfectly in line with the intent of the shari'ah'.[153]

## 'Traditionalist' Approach to *Shura*-Democracy Nexus: A Brief Overview

A number of scholars, mainly exegetes, of the subcontinent, following in the category of 'Traditionalists'—one of the three broad categories, from an intellectual viewpoint, of contemporary understanding of

Islam: Traditionalists, Modernists, and Revivalists/Islamists[154]—have contributed to the discourse of 'Islam and modernity' in general and to *Shura*-democracy nexus in particular. Some of the South Asian figures falling in this category are: Mawlana Ashraf 'Ali Thanawi (1863—1943), Mufti Shabbir Ahmad 'Uthmani (1886—1949), Mufti Muhammad Shafi (1896—1976), and Qari Muhammad Tayyib (1897–1983)—all of them belonging to the 'Deoband school of thought'—as well as the Abdul Majid Daryabadi (1892–1977)—one of the prominent figures of the twentieth-century subcontinent whose Quranic scholarship is the 'representative of *Ahl Al-Sunnah wa Al-Jama'ah* (the mainstream Muslim stance on things Quranic)'.[155] Some of them have deliberated on the concept of *Shura*, both in the traditional as well as modern perspective, and below is provided a brief assessment of their interpretations and views so that to know the 'traditionalist' approach of twentieth-century Muslims to the concept of *Shura* and democracy.[156]

Mawlana Thanawi,[157] is unquestionably considered not only as one of the most prominent Deobandi scholars of his time, but is regarded as one of the most eminent traditional Islamic scholars of all time. 'Few figures from modern South Asia', as Muhammad Qasim Zaman puts it, 'better illuminate the culture of the traditionally educated Muslim religious scholars, the 'ulama, and their efforts to defend their scholarly tradition and articulate their authority in conditions of momentous religious and political change than Ashraf 'Ali Thanawi (1863–1943)'.[158] Mawlana Thanawi's thought was shaped 'during a time of great intellectual, religious, and political ferment in the history of modern South Asia',[159] and it had a great 'impact on the Deobandi scholarly tradition in modern South Asia' especially in three distinct facets,[160] and about these, Zaman writes:

> Three facets of Thanawi's impact on the Deoband scholarly tradition are especially noteworthy. First, some of the most prolific of the Deobandi 'ulama in postcolonial South Asia reflect his influence more than that of any other scholar [including Zafar Ahmad Uthmani, Mufti Muhammad Shafi, Justice Mufti Taqi Uthmani, etc.] ... Second, the work of Shafi' and Taqi 'Uthmani, but also that of many Deobandi 'ulama in India, has continued Thanawi's self-conscious effort to address his discourses to varied and multiple audiences. [ ... ] Thanawi's work illustrates, finally, a tension between a conservative outlook and substantial receptivity to

change. Together with many other tensions, this too has continued to shape the Deobandi scholarly tradition.[161]

Mawlana Thanawi was 'the first among the modern *'ulama* clearly to warn against such extremist efforts to reduce religious norms to political goals'.[162] Among the religious scholars affiliated with the Deoband, both Thanawi and Uthmani, in the opinion of Rizwan Malik, have not only made 'rich contributions ... in the struggle for Pakistan', but have 'responded to the concerns of the emerging nationalist consciousness of the Muslim community'.[163] Moreover, it is noteworthy to add here that in a recently edited volume, *Quran Interpretation in Urdu: A Critical Study*, two chapters are devoted to the exegesis of Mawlana Thanawi and Mufti Muhammad Shafi, respectively.[164]

Mawlana Thanawi translates Q. 3: 159 as 'and take deliberations in important matters', and Q. 42: 38 as 'and their every act (wherein there is no clear guidance [*nass*]) is solved through mutual consultation'. He adds a short note to Q. 42: 38, saying that 'deliberation is neither in ordinary matters nor in clearly prescribed acts' but in matters that need serious deliberation but are not mentioned clearly.[165]

Mufti Shabbir Ahmad 'Uthmani, was the 'founder of the Jamiatul Ulama-i-Islam and later acclaimed as Pakistan's Shaikhul Islam'.[166] He was the disciple of Maulana Mahmudul Hasan (d. 1920) and is credited for completing the Urdu exegesis started by his teacher. Writing about it precisely, Venkat Dhulipala (*University of North Carolina*, USA) states: 'When his teacher Maulana Mahmudul Hasan died in 1921, Usmani completed his translation of the Quran which became very famous under the title *Tafsir-i-Usmani*'.[167] It is also important to add here that this tafsir has been published in its revised form and has been translated into English now by Muhammad Ashfaq Ahmad (2008).[168] Moreover, it is interesting to add here that in *Creating a New Madina*, Dhulipala has devoted a complete chapter to Uthmani, entitled as 'Fusing Islam and State Power: Shabbir Ahmad Usmani and Pakistan as the New Madina'.[169]

In the interpretation of Q. 42: 38, Mufti 'Uthmani emphasizes that 'Allah likes working through deliberations, whether in worldly affairs or in religious ones', and the 'very foundation of Pious Caliphate [era: 632–660 CE] was laid on the notion of *Shura*'. However, in line with Thanawi, he stresses that deliberation and consultation are valid only for those matters 'about which there are no clear injunctions in the Qur'an and *Sunnah*'.[170]

However, it was Mufti Muhammad Shafi', who deliberated on the *Shura*-democracy nexus in a great detail—both from the linguistic as well as in the modern context—in his eight-volume Urdu exegesis, *Ma'ariful-Qur'an*.[171]

From the linguistic point of view, he stresses on the words *Amr* and *Shura* in Q. 3: 159—translated by him as '*and consult them in the matter*'— and deliberates on it linguistically and by following the 'contextualist' approach. He writes: the word *Amr* has several meanings, ranging from its reference to 'any saying or doing which is of great importance' and 'a particular attribute of Allah Almighty' to 'an injunction, order, command, rule or authority', as in Q. 7: 54; 11: 23; 3:154; 4: 59; 17: 85, etc.[172] In addition to this, in the context of Q. 3: 159 and 42: 38, *Amr*, for him, refers to 'every matter or affair which is particularly important irrespective of whether it belongs to the area of authority or mutual dealings'.[173]

Furthermore, for him, the Arabic words, *Shura, Mashwarah,* and *Mashawarat* (counsel, consultation, and/or mutual consultation), all connote the meaning of 'soliciting of advice and counsel in something that needs deliberation'.[174] On this basis, he argues that the expression '*and consult them in the matter*' (Q. 3: 159) means that 'the Holy Prophet (pbuh) is to seek their [i.e., of his Companions] advice in matters of concern' and those demanding 'deliberation, which include those of authority and government'. The intent is that they will feel 'satisfied and emotionally at peace' and thus 'will become an act of mollifying grace' on Prophet's side.[175] He further adds that Q. 3: 159 and 42: 38 collectively 'not only highlight the need for consultation very clearly; they also point out to some basic principles of Islam's system of government, and its constitution. The Islamic government is a government by consultation [*Shurai'yat: Shuracracy*] in which the *Amir* or chief executive is chosen by consultation and definitely not as a matter of family inheritance'.[176]

Referring to the then two superpowers, Persian/Sassanian Empire and Roman/Byzantine Empire—which were both monarchies headed by hereditary emperors on the basis of their power and supremacy and not on merit or ability—Shafi asserts that through *Shura*, 'Islam demolished the unnatural principle of government through hereditary and gave the choice of appointing and dismissing the chief executive to the people'. *Shura* is 'a just and natural system', which later became the 'spirit of a system of government' known as democracy.[177]

In the verse Q. 42: 38, *and whose affairs are (settled) with consultation between them*, he adds that 'important affairs include affairs of the state as well as important affairs in general'; and further writes:

> The selection of the head of the state through consultation, ordained by Islam, brought to an end the autocratic rule of kings of the days of ignorance who used to take the state as an inherited estate. As such, *Islam laid the foundation of real democracy by ending autocracy*. But Islam, unlike western democracies, has not given total authority to the public. There are certain restrictions on the members of the advisory body. So the *system of government in Islam* is a very moderate one, *quite apart from* autocracy and *western democracy*. (Italics added)[178]

Thus, from his interpretations and explanations of these verses, it is evident that his approach to the concept of *Shura* is both linguistic as well as modern, showing that, although a scholar of traditional bent (and his exegesis being commonly referred as a 'juridical exegesis'), he tackles with the modern issues as well. This is substantiated by Khursheed Ahmad Nadeem when he writes:

> Mufti Shafi belongs to the Deobandi school of thought and he follows the footsteps of his predecessors in his commentary. He does not say something new and prefers to remain unflinchingly committed to the Qur'anic interpretation of the earlier exegetes ... [like] Tafseer Qurtubi, Tafseer Ibn Katheer, Tafseer Bahr al-Muheet and Tafseer-e Mazhari. He also discusses some burning issues of his time ... and tries to make readers understand the current issues in the light of the Qur'an, reports of Prophet Muhammad (SAAS) and the interpretations of the Qur'an by the righteous predecessors.[179]

Furthermore, in his book, *Fitri Hukumat*[180]—loosely translated as Natural/Divine State—Tayyib states that the government on earth is *Khilafah* (deputy of God), which establishes a system of government on the pattern of the Divine natural state. Islamic caliphate is distinct from all other systems because in these systems, humans assume the vicegerency of Divine authority. Islamic system of government also differs from others in the following aspects:

> *Imaret* (leadership/government), without *Shura* [mutual consultation] is tyranny (*istibdad*) and dictatorship; and *Shura* without *Amir* is anarchy (*fawdawiyyat*) and de-centrism (*la markaziyyat*). In its most excellent form of a comprehensive and moderate religion, Islam combines autocracy and democracy.... Consequently, an Islamic government combines autocracy and democracy, neither is autocracy independent of democracy, nor is democracy independent of autocracy.[181]

Another prominent voice of the traditional bent is Abdul Majid Daryabadi (d. 1977)—an illustrious Qur'anic scholar and exegete of the twentieth century who made excellent contributions to Islamic learning and Urdu literature.[182] For Abdur Raheem Kidwai (*Aligarh Muslim University*), Maulana Daryabadi 'holds the unique distinction of having authored two independent *tafasir* of the Quran, one in Urdu and the other in English. So doing, he kept in mind the needs and intellectual level of his reading public'.[183]

In his *tafsir*,[184] he interprets Q. 3: 159 both as taking counsel 'in the important affairs of the community, such as peace and war' as well as denoting the 'essentially democratic character of the commonwealth of Islam'.[185] For him, this verse makes it clear that the Islamic political system—one of the fundamental basis of which is being consultative—is different both from despotic as well as (secular) democratic system.[186] With reference to Q. 42: 3, he highlights that by mentioning *Shura* in between the two fundamentals of Islam—*Salah* and *Zakah*—demonstrate its significance, and at the collective level, it stands for the 'consultative government—same as was during the *Khulafa-i-Rashidun* period'.[187] Nevertheless, it does not mean (e.g. as pointed out M. Y. Faruqi) that the *Shura* is one of the pillars of Islam; however, the style of its description provides ample evidence of its special importance in the Islamic polity.[188]

These interpretations and explanations, though varied, demonstrate that since the late nineteenth century, and in twentieth century as well, the general trend has been 'to interpret *Shura* in the light of new social, political and cultural contexts'.[189] Muslim exegetes and intellectuals have been, slowly but surely, reinterpreting the concept of *Shura* not only as being '*akin to democracy* and democratic institutions' but 'very closely connected to the kind of ideas, values, and *institutions of democracy and participatory systems of governance*' as well (italics added).[190] This will be further elaborated in the next two chapters with a focus on the views and visions of some globally reputed twenty-first-century Muslim scholars, activists/leaders, and analysts.

## Notes

1. For life, legacy, and thought of Iqbal, see, Abdullah Anwar Beg, *Poet of the East* (Lahore: Qaumi Kutub Khana, 1939); Annemarie Schimmel, *Gabriel's Wing: A Study of the Religious Ideas of Sir Muhammad Iqbal* (Leiden: E. J. Brill, 1963); Hafeez Malik (ed.), *Iqbal, Poet-Philosopher of Pakistan* (New York: Columbia University Press, 1971); Syed Abdul Vahid, *Iqbal: His Art and Thought* (New Delhi: Deep and Deep Publications, 1988); Idem. (ed.), *Thoughts and Reflections of Iqbal* (Lahore: Sheikh Muhammad Ashraf, 1992); Abdul Aleem Helal, *Social Philosophy of Sir Muhammad Iqbal* (New Delhi: Adam Publishers and Distributors, 1995); Muhammad Khalid Masud, *Iqbal's Reconstruction of Ijtihad* (Lahore: Iqbal Academy, 2003); Mustansir Mir, *Iqbal: Makers of Islamic Civilization* (London: I. B. Tauris, 2007); Clinton Bennett, 'Iqbal, Allamah Sir Muhammad', in Zayn R. Kassam, Yudit Kornberg Greenberg, and Jehan Bagli (eds.), *Islam, Judaism, and Zoroastrianism* (Dordrecht, The Netherlands: Springer, 2018), pp. 312–321.
2. Bennett, in Kassam, et al., *op. cit.*, p. 312.
3. John L. Esposito, *Islam: The Straight Path*, 5th ed. (New York: Oxford University Press, 2016 [1988]), p. 171.
4. Riffat Hassan, 'Islamic Modernist and Reformist Discourse in South Asia', in Shireen T. Hunter (ed.), *Reformist Voices of Islam—Mediating Islam and Modernity* (New Delhi: Pentagon Press, 2009), pp. 159–186, p. 162.
5. Tauseef Ahmad Parray, 'A Survey of Four Indo-Pakistani Scholars' Perspectives on the Islam-Democracy Discourse', *American Journal of Islamic Social Sciences* [*AJISS*], 29, 1 (2012): 146–159, p. 143; Idem., 'Allama Iqbal on Islam-Democracy Discourse: A Study of his Views on Compatibility and Incompatibility', *Islam and Muslim Societies—A Social Science Journal* [*IMS*], 4, 2 (2011): 9 pp.; Idem., 'Modern Muslim Scholars' on Islam-Democracy Discourse: Views of Azad, Iqbal, and Maududi', *Journal of the Institute of Islamic Studies* [*JIIS*], 40 (2011): 27–50, pp. 36–43; Idem., *Mediating Islam and Modernity: Sir Sayyid, Iqbal and Azad* (New Delhi: Viva Books Pvt. Ltd., 2019), especially 3rd chapter, 'Islamic Modernist and Reformist Thought in Colonial India: A Comparative Study of Sir Sayyid and Muhammad Iqbal': 44–80, esp. pp. 59–79.

6. Parray, *Mediating Islam and Modernity*, p. 60.
7. Esposito, *Islam: The Straight Path*, p. 171.
8. Iqbal's Urdu poetry was published in various forms, but was first collected in four major works: *Bang-i-Dara* (1922), *Bal-i-Jibra'il* (1936), *Armaghan-i-Hijaz* (1936), and *Zarb-i-Kalim* (1936). All these works are collected in Muhammad Iqbal, *Kulliyat-i-Iqbal* (Lahore: Shaykh Ghulam 'Ali & Sons, 1973). A selection from all these works is also available in the Urdu original with an English translation: D. J. Matthews (ed. and trans.), *Iqbal: A Selection of Urdu Verse* (New Delhi: Heritage Publishers, 1993).
9. Beg, *Poet of the East*, p. 350.
10. John L. Esposito, 'Muhammad Iqbal and the Islamic State', in John L. Esposito (ed.), *Voices of Resurgent Islam* (New York: Oxford University Press, 1983), ch. 8, pp. 175–190, p. 176.
11. Ibid., p. 176. cf. Esposito, *Islam: The Straight Path*, p. 171.
12. See, for example, Tauseef Ahmad Parray, 'Introducing Iqbal's "less-explored" Prose Works', *Pakistan Observer*, 21 April 2018, p. 5, also available online at https://pakobserver.net/introducing-iqbals-less-explored-prose-works; Idem., 'The Less Studied Iqbal: Allama Iqbal's Prose Works on Islam/Muslims vis-à-vis Socio-Politico-Economic Issues', *Greater Kashmir*, 21 April 2019, p. 9.
13. Muhammad Iqbal, *The Reconstruction of Religious Thought in Islam*, Edited and Annotated by M. Saeed Sheikh, 2nd ed. (Lahore: Iqbal Academy Pakistan and the Institute of Islamic Culture, 1986 [1930; 1934; 1962] London: Oxford University Press, 1934; Lahore: Shaikh Muhammad Ashraf, 1962). This book was first published in 1930 (Lahore: Institute of Islamic Culture) and later in 1934 (London: Oxford University Press) and in 1962 as well. *The Reconstruction* has been republished with a new Introduction by Javed Majeed (King's College, London). For detail, see, Muhammad Iqbal, *The Reconstruction of Religious Thought in Islam*, Edited and Annotated by M. Saeed Sheikh, with a new Introduction by Javed Majeed (Stanford, California: Stanford University Press, in collaboration with Iqbal Academy Pakistan, Lahore, 2012). For detail, see, Tauseef Ahmad Parray, 'Iqbal's *Reconstruction*: Reception, Responses, & Reactions', *Greater Kashmir*, 9 November 2017, p. 9; Idem., 'On the Reception & Responses to Allama Iqbal's Masterpiece: *Reconstruction*', *Kashmir Reader*, 9 November 2017, p. 7; Idem., 'Iqbal's *Reconstruction* vis-à-vis "Religion-Modernity Encounter"', *Greater Kashmir*, 23 April 2020, p. 5.
14. Hafeez Malik and Sohail Hashemi, 'Iqbal, Muhammad', in John L. Esposito (ed.), *The Oxford Encyclopedia of Modern Islamic World* (New York: Oxford University Press, 1999), I: 509–512, pp. 510–511.
15. Wilfred Cantwell Smith, *Modern Islam in India: A Social Analysis* (Lahore: Minerva Book Shop, 1943), p. 115.
16. Ibid., p. 116.
17. Muhammad Iqbal, *Asrar-i-Khudi*, English Trans. & Introduction, R. A. Nicholson, *Secrets of the Self*, p. 21, available online at http://disna.us/files/SECR

ETS_OF_THE_SELF.pdf, also quoted in Smith, *Modern Islam in India*, pp. 115–116; Parray, *Mediating Islam and Modernity*, pp. 63–64.
18. Esposito, 'Muhammad Iqbal and the Islamic State', *op. cit.*, p. 179.
19. Iqbal, *The Reconstruction*, pp. 122–123.
20. Some important writings on Iqbal's thoughts on Islam–Democracy Discourse, published in the *Iqbal Review: Journal of the Iqbal Academy Pakistan*, are: Professor Muhammad Munawwar, 'Iqbal's Idea of Democracy', *Iqbal Review*, 26, 1 (1985): 120–139; Abdul Haq, 'Iqbal: Concept of Spiritual Democracy', *Iqbal Review*, 27, 3 (1986): 67–73; Waheed Ishrat 'Iqbal and Democracy' (trans.), M. A. K. Khalil (Parts I & II), *Iqbal Review*, 34, 3 (1993): 51–77 and 35, 1 (1994): 16–47 [hereafter cited as 'Ishrat, in *Iqbal Review* 1993/1994', respectively]; Zeenath Kausar 'Iqbal on Democracy: Acceptance or Rejection?' *Iqbal Review*, 42, 4 (2001): 33–60.
21. Parray, *Mediating Islam and Modernity*, p. 69.
22. Shaikh Muhammad Iqbal, 'Islam as a Moral and Political Ideal' (Parts I & II), *Hindustan Review*, Allahabad, India, 20 (119), July 1909: 29–38 and 20 (120), August 1909: 166–171, pp. 169, 170 [hereafter cited as Iqbal in *Hindustan Review*]. It has been reprinted in Kurzman, *Modernist Islam*, ch. 41, pp. 304–313. Hereinafter references of this essay have been provided both from the original as well as from Kurzman.
23. Iqbal, in *Hindustan Review*, p. 169; Iqbal in Kurzman, *Modernist Islam*, p. 311.
24. Taken from John L. Esposito, 'Contemporary Islam: Reformation or Revolution?', in John L. Esposito (ed.), *The Oxford History of Islam* (New York: Oxford University Press, 1999), pp. 643–690, p. 649.
25. Parray, *Mediating Islam and Modernity*, p. 70.
26. M. A. Muqtedar Khan, 'Introduction: The Emergence of an Islamic Democratic Discourse', in Khan (ed.), *Islamic Democratic Discourse*, pp. xiii–xiv.
27. Iqbal, in *Hindustan Review*, pp. 169–170; Iqbal, in Kurzman, *Modernist Islam*, p. 312.
28. Iqbal, 'Introductory Note' in *Secrets of the Self* [3–5], p. 3; see also Beg, *Poet of the East*, p. 298.
29. Riffat Hassan, 'Iqbal's View of Democracy', *Dawn*, 11 June 2010.
30. Muhammad Iqbal, 'Muslim Democracy', in *The New Era*, Lucknow, 1916, p. 251, as cited by Nicholson in Iqbal's *Secrets of Self*, pp. 5–6 and Vahid, *Iqbal: His Art and Thought*, p. 131.
31. Iqbal, *The Reconstruction*, p. 122.
32. Ibid., p. 142.
33. A. R. Tariq (Compiler), *Speeches and Statements of Iqbal* (Lahore: Sheikh Ghulam Ali & Sons, 1973), p. 10.
34. Javed Iqbal, 'Iqbal's Concept of *Ijtihad*', *QLCian*, 2009: 16–21, p. 19.
35. See, Helal, *op. cit.*, pp. 263–286.
36. Iqbal, *The Reconstruction*, p. 125.

37. Iqbal, *Bang-i-Dara, The Call of the Caravan Bell*, Preface by Sir Abd Al-Qadir (translated by M. A. K. Khalil), p. 172, available online at http://disna.us/files/ The_Call_of_The_Caravan_Bell.pdf. Also cited (though with a minor varied translation) in Ishrat, in *Iqbal Review*, 1994.
38. Ishrat, in *Iqbal Review*, 1994, p. 22.
39. Iqbal, *Bal-i-Jabriel*, p. 262; also cited in Ishrat, *op. cit.*
40. Ishrat, *op. cit.*
41. See, for example, Beg, *Poet of the East*, p. 375; Esposito in *Voices*, p. 188.
42. *Shamloo, Speeches and Statements of Iqbal*, as cited in Hassan, in *Dawn*.
43. Iqbal, *Bang-i-Dara* (Poem: 'The State', translated by V. G. Kiernan), pp. 216–217; also quoted in *Kulliyat-i-Iqbal*, 1st ed. (New Delhi: Markazi Maktaba Islami, 1993), pp. 212–213. The same is also quoted, though with varied translations, in Beg, *Poet of the East*, p. 339; Helal, *Social Philosophy*, p. 222; and Esposito in *Voices*, pp. 184–185. For example, in another version, it reads as:

> The Democratic system of the West is the same old instrument,
> In its strings there are no tunes but those of imperialism.
> The Demon of despotism/autocracy dances in democratic garb,
> Yet you consider it to be the fairy Queen of Liberty.

44. Iqbal, *Payam-i-Mashriq* (trans.) M. Hadi Husain, *A Message from the East*, p. 96; available online at http://disna.us/files/A_MESSAGE_FROM_THE_EAST.pdf
45. Iqbal, *Armaghan-i-Hijaz*, as cited/translated in Masood A. Raja, 'Muhammad Iqbal: Islam, the West, and the Quest for a Modern Muslim Identity', *The International Journal of the Asian Philosophical Association* [IJAPA], 1, 1 (2008): 37–49, pp. 43–44; Helal, *Social Philosophy*, p. 222.
46. Raja, in *IJAPA*, p. 41.
47. Ibid., p. 44.
48. Stendhal (d. 1842) was a French writer; his full/real name was Marie-Hneri Beyle.
49. Iqbal, *Zarb-i-Kalim, The Rod of the Moses* (This verse is translated by Jan Marek), available online at http://disna.us/files/THE_ROD_OF_MOSES.pdf (last accessed on 25 May 2011).
50. For more details on Iqbal's criticism, see, Mujibur Rahman, 'Iqbal's Critique of Democracy', *DISNA*, 15 October 2010, available online at http://disna.us/alla maiqbal/2010/10/15/iqbal%E2%80%99s-critique-of-democracy/#more-119; Muhammad Mumtaz Ali, 'Political Thought of Iqbal and Contemporary Islamic Resurgence', *DISNA*, 18 March 2011, available online at http://disna.us/allamaiq bal/2011/03/18/political-thought-of-iqbal-and-contemporary-islamic-resurge nce (last accessed on 28 May 2011).
51. Ishrat, in *Iqbal Review*, 1993, p. 68.
52. Khalifa Abdul Hakeem (Hakim), *Fikr-i-lqbal* [The Thoughts of Iqbal], 4th ed. (Lahore: Bazm-i-Iqbal, 1968), p. 281; also cited in Ishrat, in *Iqbal Review*, 1993, p. 56.

53. Hakeem, *Fikr-i-Iqbal*, p. 258, vide Siddiqi, *Modern Reformist Thought*, p. 128; see also Khalifa Abdul Hakim, *Islam and Communism* (Lahore: Institute of Islamic Culture, 1969), p. 287, as cited in Raja, in *IJAPA*, p. 44.
54. Iqbal, in *Hindustan Review*, pp. 166–167; Iqbal, in Kurzman, *Modernist Islam*, p. 310.
55. Iqbal, in Kurzman, *Modernist Islam*, pp. 310–311. The verses quoted in this passage read as: *Eat and drink the sustenance God has provided and do not cause corruption in the land* (2: 60); *do not cause corruption in the land after it has been set in order: this is better for you, if you are believers* (7: 85); *Do not seek to spread corruption in the land, for God does not love those who do this; We grant the Home in the Hereafter to those who do not seek superiority on earth or spread corruption* (28: 77, 83); *On that Day 'where they will hear no idle talk, with a flowing spring, raised couches'* (89: 11–13).
56. Iqbal, in *Hindustan Review*, pp. 169, 170; Iqbal, in Kurzman, *Modernist Islam*, p. 312.
57. Iqbal, *Hindustan Review*, p. 170; Kurzman, *Modernist Islam*, p. 312.
58. Iqbal, *Hindustan Review*, p. 170; Kurzman, *Modernist Islam*, p. 312.
59. Schimmel, *Gabriel's Wing*, p. 235.
60. Mazharuddin Siddiqi, *Concept of Muslim Culture in Iqbal* (Islamabad: Islamic Research Institute, 1983), p. 82.
61. John L. Esposito, *The Islamic Threat: Myth or Reality?* (New York: Oxford University Press, 1988), p. 60.
62. Esposito in *Voices*, p. 184.
63. Raja, in *IJAPA*, p. 49.
64. Mustansir Mir, 'Iqbal, Muhammad', in Gerhard Bowering et al. (eds.), *The Princeton Encyclopedia of Islamic Political Thought* (Princeton and Oxford: Princeton University Press, 2013): 259–260, p. 259.
65. Parray, *IMS*, June 2011, p. 7; Idem., *JIIS*, 2011, p. 43.
66. His full name was Abul Kalam Muhiyuddin Ahmed Azad, and he is commonly remembered as 'Maulana Azad'. For the penetrating study of his life and works, see, Ian Henderson Douglas, *Abul Kalam Azad—An Intellectual and Religious Biography*, Gail Minault and Christian W. Troll (eds.) (Delhi: Oxford University Press, 1988); Imadulhasan Azad [I. H. A.] Faruqi, *The Tarjuman al-Quran: A Critical Analysis of Maulana Abul Kalam Azad's Approach to the Understanding of the Quran* (New Delhi: Vikas, 1982; [1991]); Kenneth Cragg, *The Pen and the Faith: Eight Modern Muslim Writers and the Quran* (London: George Allen & Unwin, 1985), pp. 14–32; Pranav Prakash, 'Abu'l Kalam Azad', in Zayn R. Kassam et al. (eds.), *Islam, Judaism, and Zoroastrianism* (Dordrecht, The Netherlands: Springer, 2018), pp. 7–15.
67. 'Liberal theologian' and 'Indian theologian-philosopher' are used, respectively by Aziz Ahmad, 'India and Pakistan', in P. M. Holt, A. K. S. Lambton, and Bernard Lewis (eds.), *The Cambridge History of Islam* (Cambridge: Cambridge University Press, 1970), vol. 2A: pp. 97–119, p. 98; Ahmad in *PSC*, p. 467.

68. Douglas, *Abul Kalam Azad*, pp. 1–2, 282.
69. S. A. A. Rizvi, 'The Breakdown of Traditional Society', in Holt et al. (eds.), *The Cambridge History of Islam* (Cambridge: Cambridge University Press, 1970), vol. 2A: pp. 67–97, p. 94.
70. Douglas, *Abul Kalam Azad*, pp. 1–2, 282.
71. Parray, *JIIS*, 2011, 34–36. Idem., *Mediating Islam and Modernity*, especially ch. 4, '"Islamic Democracy" or "Democratic Islam": Re-Reading Abul Kalam Azad on Shura-Democracy Nexus', pp. 81–104, esp. pp. 83–91.
72. Maulana Abul Kalam Azad, *Tarjuman al-Qur'an*, 3 vols. (Lahore: Islami Academy, n.d.); Idem., *The Tarjuman al-Quran*, Edited and Translated by Syed Abdul Latif, 5 Vols. (Hyderabad: Dr Syed Abdul Latif Trust for Quranic Cultural Research, 1962–1978; New Delhi: Sahita Academy, 1966). In this work, references are given both from the original Urdu as well as from the English version, and are mentioned in abbreviated forms, as *Tj.Q* and *TTQ*, respectively.
73. Abul Kalam Azad, *Al-Hilal* (Calcutta). Here I have referred to the volumes published in September and December 1912 and July 1918.
74. Abul Kalam Azad, *Islami Jamhurriyah* [*Islamic Democracy*] (Lahore: Al Hilal Book Agency, 1956); Idem., *Mas'la Khilafat* [The Issue of Caliphate] (Lahore: Maktaba Ahbab, n.d.); Idem., 'The Last Word' [*Qaul-i-Faisal*], in Kurzman, *Modernist Islam*, 325–33. The last is originally a Statement delivered in Calcutta, India on 11 January 1922, and published the same year under the title *Qaul-i-Faisal* (The Last Word); also republished as 'Statement of Maulana Azad before the Presidency Magistrate', translated from Urdu by Durlab Singh, in *Famous Trials of Mahatma Gandhi, Jawaharlal Nehru, Maulana Abul Kalam Azad* (Lahore, Pakistan: Hero Publications, 1944), pp. 41–67. In this work, its references are given from Kurzman.
75. Azad, *Tj.Q*, 1: 317; *TTQ*, II: 195.
76. Azad, *Tj.Q*, III: 331; *TTQ*, II: 195; Idem., 'Al-Hilal ke Maqsad aur Political Taleem ki Nisbat Eik Khat aur iska Jawab [Answer to a Letter regarding the Mission of Al-Hilal and Its Political Teachings]', *Al-Hilal*, 9, 1 (8 September 1912): 4–8, p. 8.
77. Azad, *Tj.Q* I: 317, fn. 15; *TTQ*, II: 194–195.
78. Azad, *Tj.Q*, I: 317–18, fn. 16; *TTQ*, II: 195.
79. Azad, *Tj.Q*, V: 334–35 (English translation is mine).
80. Azad, *Tj.Q*, III: 330–1; *TTQ*, V: 334.
81. Azad, *Tj.Q*, III: 331; *TTQ*, V: 334–335.
82. Azad, 'Al-Hilal ke Maqsad aur Political Taleem ki Nisbat Eik Khat aur iska Jawab [Answer to a Letter Regarding the Mission of Al-Hilal and Its Political Teachings]', *Al-Hilal*, 9, 1 (8 September 1912): 4–8, p. 8; Idem., *Islamic Jumhuriyya*, pp. 1–3.
83. Azad, *Tj.Q*, III: 331.
84. Ahmad, 'India and Pakistan', in Holt et al., *Cambridge History of Islam*, 2A: 98.
85. Azad, 'The Last Word', in Kurzman, *Modernist Islam*, p. 332.
86. Prakash, in Kassam et al., *op. cit.*, p. 11.
87. Douglas, *Abul Kalam Azad*, p. 133.

88. Ibid., pp. 98, 284.
89. Azad, 'Al-Hilal ki Political Taleem [Political Teachings of Al-Hilal Magazine]', *Al-Hilal*, 1, 8 (1 September 1912), p. 9; Douglas, *op. cit.*, p. 137.
90. Mazherrudin Siddiqi, *Modern Reformist Thought in the Muslim World* (New Delhi: Adam Publishers and Distributors, 2014 [1982]), pp. 129–132.
91. Azad, 'The Last Word', in Kurzman, *Modernist Islam*, pp. 328–329.
92. Azad, 'Wa'az-e Yusufi [Prophet Joseph's Preaching]', *Al-Hilal*, 23, 1 (18 December 1912): 5–11, p. 6.
93. Azad, 'The Last Word', in Kurzman, *Modernist Islam*, pp. 328–329.
94. Ibid., p. 329. Also quoted in Sushila Nayar, 'Mawlana Abul Kalam Azad and National Integration', in Subhash C. Kashyap (ed.), *Mawlana Abul Kalam Azad—A Centenary Volume* (New Delhi: National Publication House, 1989), pp. 67–77, p.71; Moin Shakir, 'Political Ideas of Mawlana Azad', in *Azad, Islam and Nationalism*, Essays by Moin Shakir and others (New Delhi: Kalamkar Prakashan, n.d.), ch. 1, pp. 9–39, pp. 25–26.
95. Azad, 'The Last Word', in Kurzman, *Modernist Islam*, pp. 328–329.
96. French Revolution (of 1789), also known as the 'Revolution of 1789', led to the 'Declaration of the Rights of man and of the citizen', which is regarded as one of the basic charters of human liberties, and its 17 articles (adopted during August 20–26, 1789, by France's National Assembly) served as the preamble to the constitutions of 1791, 1793, and 1795. For details, see, 'Declaration of the Rights of man and of the citizen [1789]', in *EB*[15], X: 7; 'Rights of man and of the citizen, Declaration of the', in *EB*[15], X: 69.
97. Azad, *Islami Jumhuriyya*, pp. 18–19; also quoted in Douglas, *Abul Kalam Azad*, pp. 132–133; Shakir, *op. cit.*, p. 28.
98. Azad, *TQ*, III: 331; *TTQ*, V: 334–335.
99. Azad, *Islami Jumhuriyya*, pp. 1–3, 18 (English translations are my own). See also, Siddiqi, *Modern Reformist Thought*, p. 130.
100. Azad, 'The Last Word', in Kurzman, *Modernist Islam*, p. 329.
101. Azad, *Mas'ala Khilafat*, 'Shara'it Immamaah wa Khilafah (Conditions for Imamate and Caliphate)', pp. 68–81; also quoted in Muhammad Khalid Masud, 'Islamic Modernism', in Muhammad Khalid Masud et al. (eds.), *Islam and Modernity: Key Issues and Debates* (Edinburgh: Edinburgh University Press, 2009), pp. 237–260, p. 245.
102. Parray, *JIIS*, 2011, p. 36. Idem., *Mediating Islam and Modernity*, p. 91.
103. On his life, works, thought, and impact, see Charles J. Adams, 'Mawdudi and the Islamic State', in *Voices of Resurgent Islam*, ed., John L. Esposito (New York: Oxford University Press, 1983), pp. 99–133; Masudul Hasan, *Sayyid Abul A'ala Maududi and His Thought*, 2 vols. (Lahore: Islamic Publications, 1984); Khurshid Ahmad (ed.), *Islamic Perspectives: Studies in Honour of Sayyid Abdul A'la Mawdudi* (Leicestershire: Islamic Foundation, 1979); Idem., (ed.), *Mawdudi: An Introduction to His Life and Thought* (Leicestershire: Islamic Foundation, 1979); Seyyed Vali Raza Nasr, *The Vanguard*

of *Islamic Revolution: The Jama'at-i Islami of Pakistan* (Berkeley: University of California Press, 1994); Idem., *Mawdudi and the Making of Islamic Revivalism* (Oxford: Oxford University Press, 1996); Idem., 'Mawdudi, Sayyid Abu Al-Ala', in Emad El-Din Shahin (ed.), *The Oxford Encyclopaedia of Islam and Politics* [*OEIP*], 2 vols. (New York: Oxford University Press, 2014): II: pp. 43–47; Roy Jackson, *Fifty Key Figures in Islam* (London: Routledge, 2006); Idem., *Mawlana Mawdudi and Political Islam: Authority and the Islamic State* (Oxon, New York, and Canada: Routledge, 2011); Joshua T. White and Niloufer Siddiqui, 'Mawlana Mawdudi', in John L. Esposito and Emad El-Din Shahin (eds.), *The Oxford Handbook of Islam and Politics* (New York: Oxford University Press, 2013), pp. 144–155.

104. Parray, *AJISS*, 2010, pp. 143–144; Idem., *JHI*, 2011, pp. 15–22; Idem., *JIIS*, 2011, 43–46.

105. On this aspect, see, for example, Adams, 'Mawdudi and the Islamic State', pp. 99–133; Nasr, *The Vanguard of Islamic Revolution*; Idem., *Mawdudi and the Making of Islamic Revivalism*; Zeenat Kausar, 'Mawdudi on Democracy: A Critical Appreciation', *The Islamic Quarterly* 47, no. 4 (2003): 301–33; Jackson, *Fifty key Figures in Islam*; Idem., *Mawlana Mawdudi and Political Islam*; Asma Afsaruddin, 'Mawdudi's "Theo-Democracy": How Islamic Is It Really?', *Oriente Moderno* 87, 2 (2007): 301–325; Idem., 'Theologizing about Democracy: A Critical Appraisal of Mawdudi's Thought', in Asma Afsaruddin (ed.), *Islam, the State, and the Political Authority: Medieval Issues and Modern Concerns* (New York: Palgrave Macmillan, 2011), pp. 131–154; Irfan Ahmad, *Islamism and Democracy in India: The Transformation of the Jamaat-e-Islami in India* (Princeton, NJ: Princeton University Press, 2009); Idem., 'Islam and Politics in South Asia', in John L. Esposito and Emad El-Din Shahin (eds.), *The Oxford Handbook of Islam and Politics* (New York: Oxford University Press, 2013), pp. 324–339; White and Siddiqui, 'Mawlana Mawdudi', 144–155; Jan-Peter Hartung, *A System of Life: Mawdudi and the Ideologisation of Islam* (London: Hurst and Co. 2020 [2013]).

106. Mawdudi, *Islamic Way of Life*, p. 40.

107. Abu Ala Mawdudi, 'Political Theory of Islam', in *IIMM*: 141–171, pp. 159–160. Also reproduced in John L. Esposito and John Donohue (eds.), *Islam in Transition: Muslim Perspectives*, 2nd ed. (New York: Oxford University Press, 2007), pp. 262–270.

108. Syed Abu Ala Mawdudi, *Islamic Law and Constitution*, Khurshid Ahmad (trans. and ed.,) (Lahore: Islamic Publications Pvt. Ltd., 1960); Idem., *Islami Riyasat* [Islamic State] (New Delhi: Islamic Book Foundation, 1991).

109. Mawdudi, 'Political Theory in Islam', in *IIMM*. Cf. Idem., *Islami Riyasat*.

110. Ibid., pp. 160–161; Idem., *Islamic Way of Life*, pp. 139–140; see also Mawdudi, *Islami Riyasat*, pp. 129–130.

111. For details, see, Esposito, *The Islamic Threat*, p. 156; Israr Ahmed, *Khilafah in Pakistan: What, Why and How?* A collection of two articles written by Israr

Ahmad, compiled by Shoba Samo Basr (Lahore, Pakistan: Markazi Anjuman Khuddam-ul-Qur'an, 2006 [2001]), pp. 7-17; and Munawar Haque, 'Sayyid Abul Ala Mawdudi's Views on Ijtihad and Their Relevance to the Contemporary Muslim Society', *Journal of Islam in Asia [JIA]*, 6, 2 (2010): 123-151.
112. Mawdudi, *Islamic Way of Life*, pp. 42-43.
113. John L. Esposito and John O. Voll, *Islam and Democracy* (New York: Oxford University Press, 1996), p. 26.
114. Mawdudi, *Islami Riyasat*, p. 140; Mawdudi, *Islamic Way of Life*, p. 44; Mawdudi, *Islamic Law and Constitution*, p. 149.
115. For details, see, Mawlana Abul Ala Mawdudi, *Tafhim al-Qur'an/'Towards Understanding the Qur'an'* [English translation Zafar Ishaq Ansari, assisted by A. R. Kidwai] (Markfield, Leices, London: Islamic Foundation, 1989); also published and reprinted in New Delhi by Markazi Maktaba Islami Publishers, 1999). Its English version (S. A. A. Mawdudi, *Tafhim al-Qur'an—The Meaning of the Qur'an*) is also available online at www.englishtafsir.com
116. Mawdudi, *Tafhim*, IV: 508-509.
117. Ibid., p. 509.
118. Ibid.
119. Ibid., pp. 509-510 (English Version, pp. 549-50).
120. Ibid., p. 508.
121. Haque in *JIA*, p. 145.
122. Mawdudi, 'Political Theory of Islam', in *IIMM, op. cit.*, p. 159.
123. Ibid., pp. 44-45.
124. Mawdudi, *Islamic Way of Life*, pp. 44-45.
125. Ahmad, *MW*, p. 14.
126. Ahmad, *Islam, op. cit.*, fn. 24, p. 160.
127. Ahmad, *MW*, pp. 3-4.
128. Helal, *op. cit.*, p. 285.
129. Kausar, 'Mawdudi on Democracy', pp. 301-333, p. 324.
130. Adams, 'Mawdudi and the Islamic State', p. 118.
131. Afsaruddin, 'Mawdudi's "Theo-Democracy"', p. 302.
132. Jackson, *Fifty Key Figures*, p. 195; Idem., *Mawlana Mawdudi and Political Islam*, p. 4.
133. Hartung, *A System of Life*, p. 109.
134. Hassan, 'Islamic Modernist and Reformist Discourse in South Asia', in Hunter (ed.), *Reformist Voices of Islam*, p. 170; Ahad M. Ahmed, *The Theological Thought of Fazlur Rahman: A Modern Mutakkalim* (Kuala Lumpur, Malaysia: Islamic Book Trust, 2017), p. xv.
135. Abdullah Saeed, 'Fazlur Rahman: A Framework for Interpreting the Ethico-Legal Content of the Qur'an', in Suha Taji-Farouki (ed.), *Modern Muslim Intellectuals and the Qur'an* (New York: Oxford University Press, in association with Institute of Ismaili Studies, London, 2004): pp. 37-66, p. 37; Idem., *The Qur'an: An Introduction* (London: Routledge, 2008), p. 222.

136. Robert Rozehnal, 'Debating Orthodoxy, Contesting Tradition: Islam in Contemporary South Asia', in R. M. Feener (ed.), *Islam in World Cultures— Comparative Perspectives* (Santa Barbara, CA: ABC-CLIO, Inc. 2004), pp. 103– 131, p. 113; Ahmed, *The Theological Thought of Fazlur Rahman*, p. 1.
137. Mumtaz Ahmad, 'In Memoriam: Prof. Fazlur Rahman 1919–1988', *The American Muslim* (*TAM*), 1 October 2005, available online at http://www.theamericanmuslim.org/tam.php/features/articles/rahman_prof_fazlur_in_memorium_1919_1988 (last accessed on 25 December 2021).
138. Parray, 'Islamic Democracy', *WJIHC*, 2012, pp. 77–78.
139. Fazlur Rahman, 'Implementation of the Islamic Concept of State in the Pakistani Milieu', *Islamic Studies*, vi, 3 (1967): 205–223, p. 207.
140. Ibid.
141. Fazlur Rahman, 'Revival and Reform in Islam', in John P. Holt et al. (ed.), *Cambridge History of Islam* (Cambridge: Cambridge University Press, 1970), II: pp. 632–656, p. 654.
142. Ibid.
143. Ibid.
144. Ibid.
145. Fazlur Rahman, *Revival and Reform in Islam: A Study of Islamic Fundamentalism*, Edited and with an Introduction by Ebrahim Moosa (Oxford: Oneworld Publications, 2000), p. 162.
146. Ibid., p. 75.
147. Fazlur Rahman, *Major Themes of the Qur'an*, 2nd ed. (Kuala Lumpur: Islamic Book Trust, 1999), p. 43.
148. Amin Ahsan Islahi, *Islami Riyasat* (Lahore: Anjuman Khuddamul Qur'an, 1977). This book has been translated into English as '*The Islamic State*' by Tariq Mahmood Hashmi (Germany: Lambert Academic Publishing, 2012). References are given, as otherwise mentioned, of the English version.
149. Islahi, *Td.Q*, 2: 178.
150. Ibid., 2: 208–209.
151. Islahi, *The Islamic State*, p. 19. An excerpted (as an article) of the same book has been translated as 'The Institution of Consultation during the Reign of Rightly Guided Caliphs' (trans. Jhangeer Hanif), available online at http://www.amin-ahsan-islahi.com/?=136 (last accessed on 20 May 2011).
152. Islahi, *The Islamic State*, pp. 68–69.
153. Ibid., p. 25.
154. This interpretation is based on Rozehnal, 'Debating Orthodoxy, Contesting Tradition', pp. 107–113.
155. Abdur Raheem Kidwai, 'Foreword', in Gowhar Quadir Wani and Abdul Kader Choughley (eds.), *Abdul Majid Daryabadi's Tafsir-ul-Qur'an: A Critical Study* (Aligarh: Brown Books, in association with KAN-CQS, AMU and Ahsan Academy of Research, Springs, South Africa, 2021), pp. ix–xi, p. ix.
156. Parray, *Mediating Islam and Modernity*, pp. 91–97.

VOICES FROM SOUTH ASIA 181

157. For his life, legacy, and thought, see Muhammad Qasim Zaman, *The Ulama in Contemporary Islam: Custodians of Change* (Princeton and Oxford: Princeton University Press, 2002); Idem., *Ashraf Ali Thanawi: Islam in Modern South Asia* (Oxford: Oneworld Publications, 2007); Brannon Ingram, 'Ashraf Ali Thanawi', in Kassam, et al. (eds.), *Islam, Judaism, and Zoroastrianism*, pp. 82–84.
158. Zaman, *Ashraf Ali Thanawi*, p. 1.
159. Ibid., p. 2.
160. Ibid., p. 121.
161. Ibid., pp. 122, 123, 125.
162. Muhammad Taqi 'Uthmani, 'Hakim al-Ummat ke Siyasi Afkar', *al-Balagh* (Karachi), March 1990, pp. 23–53, reprinted in Muhammad Ishaq Multani, *Islam awr Siyasat* [Islam and Politics] (Multan: Idara-yi ta'li-fat-i ashrafiyya, 1998): 21–76, p. 27, as cited in Zaman, *Ashraf Ali Thanawi*, p. 118.
163. Rizwan Malik, 'Muslim Nationalism in India: Ashraf Ali Thanawi, Shabbir Ahmad Usmani and the Pakistan Movement', *Pakistan Journal of History and Culture*, XVIII, 2 (1997): 73–82, p. 73.
164. Muhammad Mubeen Saleem, '*Bayan al-Qur'an* by Ashraf Ali Thanwi' and '*Ma'arif-ul-Qur'an* by Muhammad Shafi', (both) in Nazeer Ahmad Ab. Majeed (ed.), *Quran Interpretation in Urdu: A Critical Study* (New Delhi: Viva Books, in association with K. A. Nizami Center for Quranic Studies, AMU, 2019), pp. 64–82 and pp. 152–164.
165. Mawlana Muhammad Ashraf Ali Thanawi, *Tafsir Bayan al-Quran*, 3 vols. (Lahore: Maktaba Rahmaniya, 1934), I: p. 294; III: pp. 353, 354; also cited in Parray, *Mediating Islam and Modernity*, p. 92.
166. Venkat Dhulipala, *Creating a New Madina: State Power, Islam, and the Quest for Pakistan in Late Colonial North India* (New Delhi: Cambridge University Press, 2015), p. 5.
167. Ibid., pp. 358–359. Commonly known as *Tafsir-e-Usmani*, this Urdu Commentary was initially written by 'Shaykh al-Hind' Mawlana Mahmudul Hasan (d. 1920), but he could not complete it, and it was his disciple, Allama/Mufi Shabbir Ahmad Uthmani, also known as 'Shaikh-ul-Islam of Pakistan', who later completed it; hence, known by latter's name. It has been translated now into English by Muhammad Ashfaq Ahmad in three volumes (2008). Moreover, a revised version of the original Urdu has been published by Maktaba Bushra in two volumes; however, in this work, the original one has been consulted and cited.
168. Mohammad Ashfaq Ahmad (trans.), *The Noble Qur'an: Tafsir-e-Usmani*, 3 vols. (New Delhi: Idara Impex, 2008).
169. Ibid., pp. 353–388.
170. Mufti Shabbir Ahmad, 'Uthmani, *Qur'an Majeed* (New Delhi: Taj Company, n.d.), p. 632; also cited in Parray, *Mediating Islam and Modernity*, p. 93.
171. Saleem, '*Ma'arif-ul-Qur'an* by Muhammad Shafi', in Majeed (ed.), *Quran Interpretation in Urdu*, pp. 152–164.

172. Ibid., II: 227.
173. Ibid.
174. Ibid., II: 227.
175. Ibid., II: 226, 227.
176. Ibid., II: 233.
177. Ibid., II: 233–234.
178. Ibid., VII: 697; also cited in Parray, *Mediating Islam and Modernity*, p. 93.
179. Khursheed Ahmad Nadeem, 'Barr-e Sagheer ki Chand Aham Tafaseer: Ek Taqabuli Jayezah [Some Prominent Quran Exegesis of the Subcontinent: A Comparative Study]', *Fikr-o-Nazr*, 32, 3 and 4 (1999): 323–351, p. 329, also cited in Saleem, 'Ma'arif-ul-Qur'an by Muhammad Shafi', in Majeed (ed.), *Quran Interpretation in Urdu*, pp. 160–161.
180. Qari Muhammad Tayyib, *Fitri Hukumat* [The Natural State] (Lahore: Idara Islamiyyat, 1963).
181. Ibid., p. 220.
182. For life and works of Daryabadi, see Abdur Raheem Kidwai, *From Darkness into Light: Life and Works of Mawlana Abdul Majid Daryabadi* (Springs, South Africa: Ahsan Publication, 2013); Akhtarul Wasey and Abdur Raheem Kidwai (eds.), *Journey of Faith: Maulana Abdul Majid Daryabadi* (New Delhi: Shipra Publications, 2016); Wani and Choughley (eds.), *Abdul Majid Daryabadi's Tafsir-ul-Qur'an*, op. cit. For the details of his *tafsir*, see, Abdul Majid Daryabadi, *Tafsir-i-Qur'an: Translation and Commentary of the Holy Qur'an*, 4 vols. (Karachi: Darul Ishaat, 1991); Idem., *Tafsir-i-Qur'an: Tafsir-i-Majidi*, 2nd ed. (Urdu) (Lucknow, India: Academy of Islamic Research and Publications, 2003); Idem., *The Glorious Qur'an: Text, Translation, and Commentary* (Leicester, Mark.: The Islamic Foundation, 2001).
183. Kidwai, in Wani and Choughley (eds.), *Abdul Majid Daryabadi's Tafsir-ul-Qur'an*, p. ix.
184. For the details of his *tafsir*, see, Daryabadi, *Tafsir-i-Qur'an*; Idem., *Tafsir-i-Qur'an: Tafsir-i-Majidi*, 2nd ed. (Urdu) (Lucknow, India: Academy of Islamic Research and Publications, 2003); Idem., *The Glorious Qur'an*.
185. Daryabadi, *The Glorious Quran*, fn. 239, p. 146.
186. Daryabadi, *Tafsir-i-Qur'an*, fns. 325, 326, I: 196.
187. Ibid., fn. 43, p. 974; also cited in Parray, *Mediating Islam and Modernity*, p. 92.
188. For this viewpoint, see, for example, Muhammad Yusuf Faruqi, 'The Institution of Shura: Views of Early Fuqaha' and the Practices of the Rashidun Khulafa', *Jihat al-Islam*, 1, 2 (June–July 2008): 9–30, p. 12.
189. Parray, *Mediating Islam and Modernity*, p. 97.
190. Saeed, *Reading the Quran*, p. 157.

# 5
# Twenty-First Century Muslim Thinkers on Islam–Democracy Compatibility—I

The relationship between Islam, democracy, and democratization—as was highlighted in the previous chapters as well—is of crucial importance in the contemporary political dynamics of the Muslim world. Though this debate has gone for a long time, it has acquired an edge in recent decades. In fact, over the past three decades or so, it has emerged as a highly influential and debated discourse among some prominent Muslim scholars all over the world; and in the twenty-first century, especially in the wake of post-9/11 scenario, and again during the 2010–2011 'Arab uprisings', the discourse gained momentum. In the contemporary Islamic political thought, the issue of compatibility and convergence of Islam with democracy and the process of democratization is the most burning issue.

## Twenty-First Century Muslim Thinkers on Islam–Democracy Compatibility

Elaborating further on the discussion made in previous chapters, the focus of this chapter is to present the discourse on Islam–democracy compatibility in the light of the views and observations of some of the globally reputed twenty-first-century intellectuals—including academicians, political leaders/activists, and analysts. The objective is to unfold the issue of democratization and its compatibility and consistency with Islam's key political notions/norms—like *Shura, Khilafah, Ijma', Ijtihad,* etc. They unanimously agree that Islam and democracy are compatible on many grounds; and thus, their contribution to this discourse represents a significant contribution to this ongoing debate.

Some of the twenty-first-century Muslim thinkers—religious/political leaders, academicians, analysts, etc.—who have written on this theme extensively and expansively, and have been selected for this chapter, include: Mohamed Fathi Osman (1928–2010), Dr Israr Ahmed (1932–2010), Asghar Ali Engineer (b. 1939–2013), Mawlana Wahiduddin Khan (d. 2021), Sadek J. Sulaiman (d. 2021), Yusuf al-Qaradawi (b. 1926), Khurshid Ahmad (b. 1932), Muhammad Khalid Masud (b. 1939), Rachid al-Ghannoushi (b. 1941), Abdulaziz Sachedina (b. 1942), and Abdolkarim Soroush (b. 1945). In the next chapter, other selected figures of the twenty-first century include Javed Ahmad Ghamidi (b. 1951), Abdelwahab el-Affendi (1955), Louay M. Safi (b. 1955), Khaled Abou El Fadl (b. 1963), Radwan Masmoudi (b. 1963), M. A. Muqtedar Khan (b. 1966), and Kamran Bokhari (b. 1968).

## Mohamed Fathi Osman (d. 2010) on Democracy as the Best Application of *Shura*

Mohamed Fathi Osman (1928–2010)—an Egyptian author and scholar—was one of those contemporary Islamic scholars and intellectuals who meticulously worked to move both the Muslim world and the West towards better mutual understanding with regard to Islam–democracy relationship. He was recognized, throughout the world, as a pioneer of contemporary Islamic thinker amongst scholars of his era. His writings, including 40 books written in English and Arabic, were aimed at making Islamic civilization and culture more understandable to non-Muslims and at showing followers of Islam that the religion provided the flexibility to adapt to modern times. Dr Osman wrote and lectured widely, offering an expansive, liberal interpretation of the Qur'anic teaching on topics like *Shari'ah* in contemporary society, human rights, women in Islam, pluralism, the 'other', the permanent and transitional in the sacred sources, *Shura* and democracy, democratic pluralism, and the obligation of Muslims in the West to embrace Western civic values or applicability of Western ideas by Muslims and on other contemporary issues of the time.[1] According to Dafer M. Dakhil (Co-Founding Director, Center for Muslim-Jewish Engagement, *University of Southern California*, USA), Dr Osman believed that Islam is a 'dynamic and flexible religion ... [capable] to engage modernity and the issues of human rights and women's issues'.[2]

Translating *Shura* as the 'participation with others in making a decision that concerns them', Osman argues that the Qur'an makes *Shura* a consequence of faith in God and an obligation second in importance only to performing prayers to Allah (Q. 42: 38).[3] It is not limited to the political field only, but extends into different aspects of life. Consent must be based on mutual consultation and given careful consideration, and consultation must be based on mutual consent and not exercised in the manner of a superficial formality.[4] Explaining further this statement, he states that the initiative of involving others in making a decision of common interest has to come from those who are responsible for leadership and making such decisions. However, those concerned people take the initiative to offer their *nasihah* (advice) to the leadership in a suitable way when they find this necessary, since giving advice is an obligation of every individual towards leaders and the public as well *a'imah al Muslimin wa 'ammatihim*, according to a tradition of the Prophet (pbuh) reported by *Sahih Muslim*. Enjoining the doing of right/good and forbidding the doing of wrong/evil (*amr bil ma'ruf wa nahi' an al-munkar*) is the responsibility of the state authorities as well as the people and any group of them (Q. 3: 104, 110; 22: 41).[5]

From the Qur'anic instruction to Prophet (pbuh) to rely on *Shura* (Q. 3: 159), when making decisions about common matters, Dr Osman infers that 'all believers a *fortiori* must follow this teaching'.[6] He also stresses that 'Shura means a serious and effective participation in decision making, and the example of the Prophet [pbuh] proves that it cannot be merely a formal or ceremonial exercise'.[7]

Similarly, while discussing '*Shura* in the Political Life', he contends that everyone has the right and obligation to participate in deciding who will be their leaders and representatives by *Shura*, and the elected public bodies must reach their decisions by *Shura*. The primary area for *Shura* is in choosing the head of the state, and in contemporary times, the state leader may be directly chosen by the people or by their elected representatives.[8]

The verse Q. 4: 59, for him, offers a clear indication that those in authority should be 'from among you who are entrusted with authority by you' (*ulil-amr minkum*). This reminds us, in his opinion, of the characterization of democracy as establishing, 'the government of the people by the people for the people'—the definition provided by Abraham Lincoln.[9]

While a democratic decision has to comply with 'imagined' natural human rights or a social contact as a safeguard against any possible majority injustice, Muslims and those who are entrusted with authority *from among them, by them* are bound by the goals and general principles of *Shari'ah* that secure human dignity, and guard and develop for all human beings: their life, families and children, minds, freedom of faith and ownership of private or public property.[10]

Constructing his arguments on the views of Rashid Rida's *Tafsir al-Manar*, Osman maintains that the head of the state can be elected directly by the people, or by the parliamentary representatives of the people, or can be nominated by these representatives and introduced to the public vote. Any procedure can be followed according to its own merits and to the given circumstances, and Islam accepts that which is in the interest of the people. Early Caliphs were chosen primarily from a narrow circle and vested by *bay'ah* (oath of allegiance), and then the chosen Caliphs would go to the public to get their acceptance through the public *bay'ah*. As previously indicated, *bay'ah* is a mutual pledge: from the ruler to follow the Islamic Law and satisfy the public, and from the people to support the ruler and advise him.[11]

For him, *Shura* is not limited to the political arena only, but there are 'Other Areas for *Shura*', as well, which are seven (7) in number, viz.:

1. *Shura* has a role in the election of the people's representatives in the parliamentary body/ies and its practice of legislation, guarding the public interest through checking the executive exercise of power, and pursuing the people's concerns.
2. Discussions, hearings, and reaching decisions by the representative body and its committees also represent a vital area for the practice of *Shura*.
3. A significant practice of *Shura* may occur if the public referendum is found appropriate in certain matters of special importance, which may be decided by the legislature.
4. In the executive branch and its departments, *Shura* naturally has its place in the discussions and decisions.

5. *Shura* has also to be practiced in the elections of leaders and boards in workers', professionals', etc., and in the discussions and decisions of these elected bodies.
6. Technical and professional *Shura* ought to be conducted in schools, hospitals, factories, companies, or any other business.
7. In the courts, *Shura* is followed when there is more than one judge ruling over the case, or when the jury system is applied.[12]

Osman, thus, advances the argument that democracy acknowledges that natural human rights supersede any legislation, and in a parallel way, Muslims can always stress the supremacy of God's guidance ideologically, legally, and practically. Setting democracy in opposition to Islam, he argues, is unfair for both; and thus, we should deal with a concrete, political democratic process and not talk about theories and hypotheses. Moreover, he emphasizes that Muslims should not develop hypothetical and unrealistic fears about a democratic process to implement *Shura* in a contemporary Islamic state. For him, while the means of implementing *Shura* may have been relatively informal in the past, in today's world *Shura* should be implemented through democracy.[13] Lastly, he sees Islam and democracy compatible in one more aspect, that Islam is a religion of peace (not of violence) and in a democracy also, there is no place for violence.[14] In a nutshell, he understands and recognizes that 'democracy is the best application of Shura'.[15]

## Dr Israr Ahmed (d. 2010) on *Shura* and Limited Democracy

Dr Israr Ahmed (b. 1932, India–d. 2010, Lahore, Pakistan) was an Islamic theologian, preacher, and the founder of the *Tanzeem-e-Islami* (1975)—an off-shoot of the *Jama'at-i-Islami*—and has been very influential in both in South Asia and in the South Asian diasporas, and had his 'followers in Pakistan, India and gulf countries, especially in Saudi Arabia'.[16] His supporters describe him as having spent the last four decades of his life in 'reviving the Qur'an-centered Islamic perennial philosophy and world-view' with the ultimate objective of establishing 'a true Islamic State, or the System of Khilafah'. Unconvinced with the efficacy and efficiency of 'parliamentary politics of give-and-take' in establishing an 'Islamic politico-socio-economic system', he considers its implementation as a 'revolutionary process'.[17] Though he is best known as a scholar of the Qur'an, Dr Israr was the Founder of the Islamic revolutionary movement *Tanzeem-e-Islami* (the Islamic Organization), the research, instructional, and outreach institute *Anjuman Khuddam-ul-Qur'an Lahore* (Society of the Servants of the Qur'an), and the populist *Tehreek-e-Khilafat* (Caliphate movement).[18]

His views on *Shura, Khilafah,* democracy, and his support for Mawdudi's '*Theo-democracy*' and Iqbal's position on *Ijtihad*, etc., are found in some of his lectures—which were later published in the form of booklets and pamphlets. For example, in 'The Constitutional and Legislative Framework of the System of Khilafah in Modern Times',[19] he discusses 'the practical issues relating to the constitutional and legislative framework of a modern Islamic State, or the structure of the system of *Khilafah* in modern times'.[20] Dr Ahmed, though, relies on the views of Iqbal and Mawdudi, and appreciates them, but at the same time, he shows certain reservations with Mawdudi's concept of 'popular vicegerency'.

Citing Iqbal's observations, mentioned in latter's *The Reconstruction*, regarding the establishment of Islamic State as well as the relationship between *Ijtihad* and republican form of government,[21] Dr Ahmed upholds: 'I have given these two quotes because I myself *fully agree with both of these observations*' (italics added).[22] That is to say, he believes in the dynamic character of *Ijtihad* as well as believes in the republican form of government—on the condition that it, and the procedures and methods it adopts, are in full agreement with the *Shari'ah* (Islamic Law).

Regarding the views of Mawdudi, who coined two key terms in connection with Islamic political policy: *theo-democracy* and *popular vicegerency*, Dr Ahmed says: by coining the term *theo-democracy*, 'Mawdudi has emphasized the point that the Islamic political system is neither a pure theocracy nor a full-fledged Western style democracy, but that it has elements of both'.[23] Moreover, he is not convinced with Mawdudi's description of the concept of *popular vicegerency* that he coined 'to delineate the fact that Islam rejects the idea of "popular sovereignty"'.[24] Showing disagreement with Mawdudi, Dr Ahmed argues that although 'Popular vicegerency' is a 'satisfactory term', and thus suggests 'improvement to prevent any misunderstanding'; and thus, he suggests the phrase 'collective vicegerency of the Muslims'; he explains it as: 'In the Islamic political system, the *Khilafah* or vicegerency actually belongs to the Muslims rather than to all the citizens of a given nation-state irrespective of their beliefs'; and that is why Ahmed prefers to use the term '*collective vicegerency of the Muslims*' instead of *popular vicegerency* (italics in original).[25]

Thus, for Dr Ahmed, 'although we are free within the limits of the *Shari'ah*, we cannot—under any circumstances whatsoever—transgress' the limits prescribed in *Shari'ah*—as 'these constitute *hudud Allah*, the limits set by the Creator Lord ... which can neither be amended nor abrogated. No one has the authority to change these limits, not even the entire body of a legislative assembly!'[26] Accordingly, in this perspective, for him:

> The restriction of staying within the limits of the *Shari'ah* constitutes the *theo* element in the Islamic political system. There is no special or privileged class of priests or infallible religious divines in Islam. The inclusion of the word *theo*, therefore, does not imply the rule of any particular ecclesiastic class or group. Instead, it refers to the fact that, just like an individual Muslim, the Islamic State must remain within the limits of the *Shari'ah* and must not transgress the *hudud Allah*.[27]

While referring to the verse Q. 42: 38, he maintains that it does not mean that any 'legislative assembly in an Islamic State can change in any way the injunctions of Qur'an and *Sunnah*, even by full consensus';[28] because, for him:

> The 'mutual consultation', therefore, is meant only for those affairs in which the choice is between two or more lawful [permissible or legitimate: *mubah*] alternatives [and not between lawful and unlawful, or good and bad that are mentioned in clear-cut injunctions of Islam]. In the Islamic scheme of things, if all the available options in a particular case are *mubah*, the matter should be decided by discussion, deliberation, and mutual consultation. In this regard, there is absolutely nothing wrong if the final decision is reached by a counting of votes. Under the system of *Khilafah*, all the *higher values of democracy* can be incorporated [and integrated] within the circle of the lawful or *mubah*.[29]

Furthermore, in the interpretation of this verse in his exegesis, *Bayan al-Qur'an*, he states: 'For establishing the Religion, organizational/collective effort is necessary; and for collective effort, mutual consultation is a necessity in different matters' and this 'process of consultation strengths the process of resolving collective affairs'.[30]

Dr Ahmad shows strong reservations against 'democracy in Islam' on the grounds that it is based on the concept of 'sovereignty of people', which is 'totally incompatible with the Islamic spirit, as it challenges the basic Islamic principle of 'Divine Sovereignty' which necessitates the supremacy of the Qur'an and *Sunnah*'.[31] For him, there is neither any place for theocracy nor for pope or his group of hierarchy in Islam. Moreover, in a video lecture on 'Democracy, Theocracy, and Voting', Ahmed articulates very clearly that:

> Republican government is the one established by Prophet Muhammad (pbuh) in the form of *Khulafa-i-Rashidun*, which was based on consultation and deliberation, not of any single individual but on the principle of '*amrhum Shura baynahum*'. *Shura* in those matters which are not discussed in the Qur'an and *Sunnah*; and this is *real form of democracy in Islam*. (Italics added)[32]

However, within the parameters of *hudud Allah*, there is democracy in Islam, which he terms as 'limited democracy'. He is of the opinion that if in any country it is accepted that Sovereignty belongs to Allah, Qur'an and Sunnah are superior and that no legislation will be repugnant to them and after (these two) is accepted *amruhum shura baynahum* (mutual consultation and deliberation on issues about which there are no clear/direct guidelines in the Qur'an and Sunnah), then there is no problem (with regard to Islam and democracy relation), it is but natural that they have to make or establish some governmental system. In other words, he says that under the System of *Khilafah*, all the 'higher values of democracy can be incorporated within the circle of lawful or *mubah*'.[33]

In the interpretation of Q. 3: 159 in his *Bayan al-Qur'an*, he writes that the Prophet (pbuh) always consulted his Companions (RA) for advice in different matters as he did before the Battle of *Uhud* (634 CE) when he asked his Companions (RA), whether to stay in *Medina* or go out and meet the enemy in the open. This verse also states that *Then when you have taken a decision, put your trust in Allah (SWT)*, i.e. whatever the decision is made after the consultation, then stick to it and put your trust in Allah (SWT). *Certainly, Allah (SWT) loves those who put their trust in Him*.[34] For him, this verse is also important regarding the leadership of an Islamic movement, for it provides some important clues as to what qualities should a leader (*Ameer*) of an Islamic party possess. It also describes the characteristics of Prophet (pbuh) as a leader, a perfect example for all to follow.[35]

Regarding the form of democracy, Dr Israr preferred 'the modern presidential form of government' as being 'closer in spirit' to the governmental system of Pious Caliphate era than any other systems of government, including parliamentary form, because the caliph would be elected by direct vote.[36] He provides a detailed explanation on this point:

> As far as the details of the workings of state and government is concerned, there is no definite and binding framework provided to us by the Qur'an and Sunnah. As a matter of fact, all the various forms of government that are in vogue today are essentially permissible in Islam. From an Islamic point of view, it does not make any difference if the government is unitary, confederal, or federal, and whether it is presidential or parliamentary, etc. However, we do need to recognize that the system of the *Al-Khilafah Al-Rashidah* was a unitary system and closer in spirit to the modern presidential form of government as compared to the parliamentary form. We also need to realize that this is not binding for us.[37]

In his comparative study of the discourses of Mawdudi, Ghamidi, and Israr related to the 'Discussions on Democracy and Islamic States',[38] Faisal Awan (*University of Karachi*) states that the important point to note here is that Dr Israr 'does not deny the efficacy of democracy as a system for running affairs. Democracy along with its institutional framework is viable and essential, but not enough to bring about Islamic revolution'.[39] However, it is interesting to add here that Dr Israr emphasizes that *there is no definite form or structure of government in Islam*, but only 'certain basic principles and ideals' that must be 'uphold and implement[ed] ... according to the changing social and political conditions' (italics added).[40] He further elucidates that in this context,

we believe that *there are three basic principles* that, if incorporated in any form of government, will lead to the establishment of the System of *Khilafah*. These three principles are as follows:
(1) Sovereignty belongs to Almighty Allah (SWT) alone;
(2) No legislation can be done at any level that is totally or partially repugnant to Qur'an and *Sunnah*; and
(3) Full citizenship of the state is for the Muslims only, while non-Muslims are a protected minority.

If these three principles are incorporated in their true spirit in any form of government, it will become an Islamic State or embodiment of the System of *Khilafah*, irrespective of the specific details of governance. (Italics added)[41]


## Asghar Ali Engineer (d. 2013) on Harmonizing *Shura*—Democracy Spirit

Asghar Ali Engineer (b. 1939–d. 2013) was an Indian (Shia) Muslim reformist-writer and activist who 'holds liberal, rational views on Islam' and is 'known internationally for his work on liberation theology in Islam'. Most of his works and activities mainly focused on (and action against) communalism and communal and ethnic violence in India and South Asia and he was an ardent advocate of a culture of peace, non-violence, and communal harmony.[42] Riffat Hassan describes him as 'India's Reformist Scholar-Activist',[43] and Imtiyaz Yusuf describes him as 'an Indian Muslim reformer of the modern age' who 'engaged in Muslim social reform activism combining the theological and axiological dimensions of the Islamic worldview' by upholding, all through is life, 'the values of equality, justice, and freedom'.[44] Besides these aspects of his multifaceted personality, Engineer is remembered, as described by Hilal Ahmed (*Centre for the Study of Developing Societies*, New Delhi), for his abiding legacy of 'establishing an emancipatory form of intellectual politics'.[45] He was Founding Chairman of the *Asian Muslim Action Network* (AMAN)—an organization that promotes human rights and inter-faith understanding Asia-wide; Director of the *'Institute of Islamic Studies'* (IIS); and Head of the *Center for Study of Society and Secularism*

(CSSS)—a civil society organization located in Mumbai (India).[46] He has authored (and edited) more than 50 books and many articles in various national and international journals, and has contributed to the theme of Islam and democracy compatibility as well. Some of his writings on Islam–democracy themes are: 'Is Islam compatible with democracy and modernity?'; 'On absence of democracy in the Muslim World'; 'What I Believe'; 'Islam is for Democracy', etc.[47]

In Yusuf's assessment, 'Engineer developed an Islamic theology of liberation and social reconstruction based on the core Qur'anic values of *rahmah*, compassion; *ihsan*, benevolence; '*adl*, justice; and *hikmah*, wisdom for building equality, justice, and freedom', and thus, he saw Islam not only as 'mere rituals and priesthood; [but as]... a value system that lays stress on love, practicing nonviolence, compassion, equality, justice, human dignity, and truth'. Moreover, Engineer stressed that 'all religions emerge in particular geographic contexts', and thus, 'carry within them the cultural and linguistic specificities of their origin'; i.e. he distinguished between 'normative' and 'contextual' Islam—the latter being culturally mediated versions of Islam practiced around the world.[48] In the observation of Yoginder Sikand, 'Engineer [has] developed his own understanding of Islam as a means and a resource for social revolution. One can discern in his thought and writings a multiplicity of influences: Mu'tazilite and Isma'ili rationalism, Marxism, Western liberalism, Gandhism, and Christian liberation theology, and the impact of the Iranian 'Ali Shariati as well as Indian Muslim modernists such as Sayyid Ahmad Khan and Muhammad Iqbal'.[49] It is within this context that one needs to understand his rationale for Islam–democracy compatibility theme.

In response to the question 'Whether Islam and democracy are compatible?' Engineer writes that it is true that *Shura* (mutual consultation) and modern-day representative democracy—a Qur'anic concept and a merely human concept, respectively—may not be 'exactly similar'. However, 'the spirit of modern democracy and the Qur'anic injunction to consult people is the same in spirit'. As new institutions keep on developing and human beings, depending on their worldly experiences, keep on changing and refining these institutions, so, in the contemporary world, for Engineer, the concept of *Shura* means democratic process and constitution of proper democratic institutions, of which elections are a necessary requirement.⁵⁰ The Qur'anic text not only gives the concept of *Shura* (democratic consultation) but 'does not support even remotely any concept of dictatorship or authoritarianism'. For him, some people try to use the Qur'anic verse 4: 59 to justify obedience to any kind of authority including 'a monarch or a caliph or a military dictator'. It is certainly not the spirit of the Qur'anic verse, he claims boldly, and one has to see it in historical background. And, if this verse is read in conjunction with the verses 3: 159 and 42: 38, it would mean one has to submit to a 'properly and democratically constituted authority'.⁵¹

For him, the Prophet (pbuh), who was the founder of Islamic state and society at Medina, enjoyed an enormous moral authority but he never converted it into formal political power. He was succeeded by four Caliphs referred to as rightly guided Caliphs (r. 632–660 CE) as they, in spite of tremendous problems, tried to follow the vision of Islam and always consulted Muslims before taking any important policy decision. Though formally it was 'not a democratic society' in the sense modern societies are, it was, for Engineer, 'democratic in spirit' during the first thirty years of rightly guided caliphs, as Umayyads (r. 660–750 CE), who became rulers after the first four caliphs, managed to capture the power and converted 'a proto-democratic society into a feudal hierarchical one'.⁵² He further argues that the 'Islamic democracy' as prevailed in the days of the Prophet (pbuh) and the four caliphs could not be 'revived' and revitalized again, as all succeeding regimes in the Arab as well as non-Arab world (from Umayyads, 'Abbasids, to Ṣaffavids, Ottomans, and Mughals) were 'dynastic and had nothing to do with elective principle', and thus 'Islamic political culture became more and more feudalized'.⁵³

Commenting on this further, Engineer, in his 'Islam and Secularism', argues that the 'primitive Islamic state was democratic in spirit' and the Caliphs often consulted their colleagues and companions of the Prophet (pbuh) while making any decision so as to conform to the Islamic values; and thus, regards the Pious Caliphate period as the 'golden period of Islamic democracy'. But the 'conquests, internal strife among the Muslims, struggle for power among different tribes, groups and personalities', and many other factors, he continues, created strong pressures so much so that the 'institution of Caliphate itself did not survive', and was ultimately 'replaced [with the establishment of Umayyad rule in 660 CE] by monarchy and dynastic rule', that continued, due to failure of re-establishment of Caliphate, until the Western colonial rule took over the major Muslim world.[54] On this change in government structure, he further asserts that

> The Islamic state which came into existence after the death of the Prophet [pbuh] ... also became a model for the subsequent generation though this model was hardly followed even in the early period of the Islamic history. The Umayyad and the Abbasid empires which came into existence after what is called khilafat-e-rashidah (i.e., the rightly guided period of khilafat, Islamic state) never followed this religious model. Both the empires were based on personal and authoritarian rule and were Islamic only in name.[55]

Furthermore, in his 'What I believe', he reveals his beliefs, or what his ideology and his views are. For example, regarding democracy and pluralism, he writes:

> I strongly believe in pluralism and diversity. I believe that uniformity ... result only in suppressing human creativity. Human creativity can thrive only in situation of freedom and diversity. Democratic freedom has meaning only if diversity is allowed to flower. Strict uniformity can, and often does, lead to fascism. A truly democratic society can be promoted only, and only if diversity is allowed to flower. I, therefore, *believe in three 'ds' i.e. democracy, diversity and dialogue.*
>
> I believe that democracy, diversity and dialogue sustain and strengthen each other. *If there is no diversity, there can be no democracy* and if there is no dialogue, diversity cannot be strengthened. Dialogue is the very spirit of religious and cultural diversity. A genuine dialogue can be conducted only in the *spirit of democracy.* (Italics added)[56]

There are, at present, different political systems in different Islamic countries from monarchy to military dictatorship, and from limited democracy to democracy. But it would be naïve, claims Engineer, to blame Islam for this. One has to look into the political history of the country rather than search for its causes into Islamic doctrines. Islamic doctrines do not cultivate any concept of absolutism as perhaps no other religion does. In fact, the emphasis of Qur'an on consultation (*Shura*), and even the Prophet (pbuh) used to consult his companions in secular (worldly) matters.[57]

Lastly, in his 'Islam, Democracy and Violence',[58] he argues that it is not at all correct to say that Islam is incompatible to democracy, because Islam does not come in the way of democracy; it is dictators and monarchs who come in its way. The authoritarian societies negate all these and hence monarchy and dictatorship are un-Islamic, not democracy. As the modern society is emphatic about human equality without any distinction and human rights and gender equality are of great significance and hence democracy is the only way out for the Qur'anic concept of just society to be realized. Thus we must properly educate the Muslim masses and prepare them for acceptance of democracy in the Islamic world. They should be made aware that those who oppose democracy in the name of Islam are really serving certain vested interests rather than Islam. Islam is quite compatible with democracy. It is rather the interests of rulers of Muslim countries which are not compatible with democracy. Elsewhere he echoes almost similar views and further states: 'There is a great deal of emphasis on freedom of conscience and human rights in the modern civil society' as they are 'quite integral to each other'; however, it is 'highly regrettable [to see] that most of the Muslim countries do not have a good record in this field'. But the fact is, the 'lack of democracy and human rights' in most of the Muslim countries is 'not because of Islam or Islamic teachings but due to authoritarian and corrupt regimes which totally lack transparency in governance'.[59]

It is on these grounds and evidences, and on the basis of the norms laid down by the Qur'an (as in Q. 5: 48, 2: 148, 60: 7–8, 22: 40, 17: 70. 49: 13, 2: 213, and 29: 46) and their interpretations that Engineer discovers connections between Islam and (liberal) secularism as well.[60] He asserts that 'Islam upholds pluralism, freedom of conscience and human rights and thus does not clash with the concept of secularism.... Islam and secularism can and should go together in the modern world'.[61]

Thus, Engineer reaches the conclusion that the absence of democracy in Muslim countries is not by means 'on account of Islamic teachings or incompatibility of democracy with Islam but due to host of factors': political, historical, social, economic, and cultural; and it is these conditions which are more 'responsible for lack of democracy in the Islamic world and not the Islamic teachings'.[62] However, Engineer is not unique in arguing the same. Shirin Ebadi (2003 Noble Prize winner of Iran), also stresses on this viewpoint that there is no inherent contradiction between Islam and democracy or human rights, and says:

> The lack of democratization in the Islamic world does not emanate from the essence of Islam. Rather, it is due to the unwillingness for numerous of Islamic states to embrace an interpretation of Islam that is compatible with human rights, preserves individual and social freedoms, and advocates democratic statecraft.[63]

## Mawlana Wahiduddin Khan (d. 2021) on Democracy as a 'Blessing for Muslims'

Mawlana Wahiduddin Khan (b. January 1925, Azamgarh–d. April 2021, New Delhi, India)—a leading scholar of Islamic thought among contemporary Indian Muslims—was an Islamic spiritual scholar well versed in both classical Islamic learning and modern sciences. His mission was the establishment of worldwide peace, to which end he devoted much time and effort and developed a complete ideology of peace and non-violence based on the teachings of the Qur'an. He was a peace activist and authored over 200 books on Islam and its diverse aspects—ranging from the Quran, the Sirah/Prophet's Biography, theology, morality, spirituality, non-violence, peace/peace-building, to gender studies and Islam and science. Though he wrote mostly in Urdu, but many of his works have been translated into Arabic, Hindi, English, and various European languages as well (a full list of his books can be accessed from the website of *Centre for Peace and Spirituality* [CPS], www.cpsglobal.org).[64]

Khan—who combines knowledge of traditional religious sciences with the cultural, socio-political, and ethical discourse of his times—draws on his knowledge of contemporary events to highlight the 'moral plight of our [i.e. Modern] times'; and in the words of Irfan A. Omar, his writings display 'an eagerness to apply the lessons learned from his explorations to critical issues facing Muslim societies [today] both in India and elsewhere'.[65]

Khan—who argues for the temporal separation of religious and political action—maintains that the 'establishment of an Islamic state is nowhere required either in the Qur'an or in the Sunnah of Prophet Muhammad [pbuh].... By confusing a political agenda with our spiritual goals we not only misunderstand *din* or faith as enunciated in the Qur'an, we also endanger our social causes by being labeled as divisive and sectarian in an increasingly pluralist world'.[66]

With reference to the Indian Muslim community (especially), he argues that what is lacking in it at large, is a 'coherent vision of the reapplication (by way of *ijtihad*) of the Islamic ideals', such as 'pluralism, tolerance of differences, utilizing peaceful means to activism and becoming progressive within the scope of the teaching of Islam'.[67] He has not written much about the Islam and democracy theme, as he deals least with the political aspect of Islam. But, his views on democracy, *Ijtihad*, etc. are scattered in his various writings—books and articles alike.

In his *God Arises*, Mawlana Khan argues that democracy is 'a system of government by the people, directly or by representation, and a country may be said to be truly democratic only when its political organization abides by this criterion'. For him, when we approach democracy practically, as it is practiced in various countries like 'the democracies of Britain, America, China and Egypt', or the 'democracy of India' and 'the democracy of Pakistan', there seems rarely 'anything common' between them, and the 'image' that emerges, rather than being crystal clear, is like 'muddied water', because, when put within an 'evolutionary framework', the term democracy not only becomes 'more confusing', but becomes 'meaningless' as well.[68]

For Khan, although democracy has 'wide popular support, it has also been subjected to sharp criticism on a theoretical plane', especially on the grounds that (a) it is impossible (in practice) to establish 'rule by the people'—the literal meaning of democracy. How can all the people govern and be governed at the same time? Khan questions; and (b) the entire basis of democracy is the belief that people are born equal; with equal rights and that they are free. But the problem afflicting democracy is alluded to in the very first lines of the French philosopher Jean-Jacques Rousseau's (1712–1778) *The Social Contract*: 'Man was born free and everywhere he is in the chains'.[69] He further adds that Rousseau was 'one of the founders of modern democracy', but the 'sentiment' he expresses by the 'lamentation over human bondage—is not in actual fact Rousseau's gift to humanity. It is rather an echo of a more splendid utterance of the Islamic Caliph, 'Umar Ibn Khattab (586–644), which he made to his governor of Egypt: 'O Amr, since when have you enslaved people whose mothers gave birth to them in freedom?' The occasion for this rebuke was the flogging by 'Amr's son of a young Egyptian who had beaten him in a horse race as recounted above'.[70]

'The concept of democracy in Islam', for Khan, 'is best understood that Islam is practiced at two levels—the *Infaradi*, the individual level, and the *Islamayee* [sic. *Ijtima'yee*], the collective level. At the individual level, a person is free to adopt the manner of worship he likes etc. But at the collective level, it is the voice of the people, which is to be given preference. In the social context, it is the *Islamayee* Islam, which is to be practiced, and democracy is a social concept'.[71]

Furthermore, Khan asserts that the 'the revolution brought about by the Prophet Muhammad [pbuh] and his companions caused the barriers of discrimination to be swept away, all over the world. It saw the birth of a new age of human equality, which ultimately developed into modern democracy'.[72] He further states: 'The revolution to bring freedom and democracy to the people which began in Europe, later spreading to the rest of the world in modern times, is but the second stage of that revolutionary process which was set in motion in the seventh century by Islam'.[73] Khan summarizes it as: 'The scientific and democratic revolution of Europe might be termed the 'secular edition' of the monotheistic revolution of Islam'.[74] In the elaboration of the above statements, and in the context of social revolution brought by Islam, Khan further writes:

> While, on the one hand, Islam changed the human mind, on the other, it brought about a practical revolution on such a vast scale that it ushered in a whole new era of human freedom and human respect. Across the centuries, this revolution went from strength to strength, ultimately bringing Europe under its benign influence. There it culminated in the modern freedom and democracy, which nowadays people tend to imagine, has existed for all time. But this democratic revolution of modem Europe is but the secular version of the Islamic revolution which was given its first impetus in seventh century Arabia by God's final Prophet [pbuh].[75]

In support of these statements of Khan, Rajat Malhotra (a member of Khan's *CPS*) writes that 'Islam was a key contributor to the history of thought that removed persecution and ushered in the age of enlightenment'.[76] Malhotra concludes his study—which is based on the writings of various scholars, including Khan—with these remarks: 'Seen in the light of the original sources ... Islam is completely compatible with democracy and with the key concepts related to it such as equality, ..., mutual consultation, secularism and peace. While Islam may not have used these terms, the Prophet Muhammad [pbuh] and his Companions followed the same principles'.[77]

In his *Din-o-Shari'at*,[78] Khan argues that the corpus of *fiqh* had been developed in an age of monarchy, and that is why it had no conception of modern democracy. Consequently, Muslims who thought in terms of the established corpus of *fiqh* could not appreciate or understand the importance of democracy. That is why some of them branded it as irreligious (*la-dini*) and considered it prohibited (*haram*). Others denounced it as a system of counting heads, where numbers are given the importance that quality deserves.[79] But, the fact is that

> Democracy has the potential of being a blessing for Muslims. In contrast to the old monarchical system, democracy is based on the principle of power-sharing. It offers Muslims the opportunity to gain political importance if they act wisely. But because of the lack of *ijtihadi* insight Muslims failed to do so.... [They] also failed to see how by participating in democratic governance and getting involved in democratic processes they might be able to make a place for themselves in democratic countries. The reason for this terrible backwardness of present-day Muslim thought is the refusal to engage in *ijtihad*, to come out of the boundaries of the established corpus of fiqh and to gain guidance directly from the Quran and Hadith.[80]

Regarding the significance of *Ijtihad* and the need to reconstruct Islamic thought in the light of new challenges, Khan, in his *Fikr-e-Islami* (Islamic Thought), has devoted two chapters each to 'Significance of Ijtihad' and the 'Reconstruction of Islamic Thought',[81] and has argued passionately for the need to continuously undertake *ijtihad* to 'respond to the intellectual and practical problems of the modern age in a way that one can take full account of the spirit of Islam while addressing the new needs [of the time]'.[82]

In his *Din-o-Shari'at*, as an evidence in support of his argument to come out of the boundaries of the established corpus of *fiqh* and to gain guidance directly from the Qur'an and Hadith[83] he also cites the example of Prophet Yusuf (Joseph), who was appointed 'to a high political position' by the Egyptian king (a non-Muslim). In other words, Prophet Yusuf's (AS) position in the political system was that of the highest official, as he was 'made in-charge of food and agriculture, but he had more powers than this, acting, in a sense, as the deputy of the king, because in the ancient agricultural age the economy of countries was based essentially on agriculture'. From this, he deduces that if 'modern-day Muslims did not bind themselves to taqlid but, instead, approached the Quran in a spirit of ijtihad and pondered on it carefully, they would have realized that this incident about the Prophet Yusuf [AS] is a prophetic example for them to seek to emulate. They should understand that they can use the principle of power-sharing of modern democracy for their benefit, being confident that doing so is in accordance with a prophetic practice'.[84]

Thus, Khan stresses on understanding the real context, and importance, of *ijtihad* as well as the spirit of democracy and democratic procedures, which he finds as a 'blessing for Muslims'.

## Sadek Jawad Sulaiman (d. 2021) on Promoting '*Shura*-as-Democracy'

Sadek Jawad Sulaiman, sometimes written as Sadiq Jawad Suleiman (b. 1933, Oman–d. 2021, India) was an Omani writer, thinker, and diplomat, who had served as ambassador to Iran and the USA. After his retirement from the diplomatic services, he devoted himself to expanding his knowledge and completed a Master's degree in International Public Policy from *Johns Hopkins University* (USA).[85] Sulaiman was one of the founders of the 'Omani Society for Writers and Literates'[86] and *Al-Hewar (Dialogue) Centre*, Washington (1994)—The Centre for Arab Culture and Dialogue: 'an independent forum for dialogue among the various members of the Arab community with the goals of finding common ground within the community as well as bringing about greater mutual understanding between the Arab community and American society at large'.[87] He is one of those few voices from the contemporary Muslim world featuring in Charles Kurzman's anthology on *Liberal Islam* on the theme of 'Democracy',[88] as he is one of the few voices from Oman who has contributed significantly to the theme of Islam–democracy compatibility by highlighting the similarities between Shura and democracy[89] and has contributed to 'The Islamic Democratic Tradition' of Oman.[90]

He assents the compatibility of democracy and *Shura* on the grounds that *Shura*, as a concept and a principle, does not differ from democracy. In his *Democracy and Shura*,[91] he very rationally argues that 'equality'— the affirmation that all people are equal—is democracy's core principle. In other words, any discrimination among people on any basis (e.g. race, gender, religion, or lineage) is inherently invalid. Democracy is based on certain characteristics, among them, freedom of speech, press, and assembly; the free exercise of religion; free elections; majority rule and minority rights; separation of the power into legislature, executive, and judicial branches; constitutional authority (i.e. supremacy of the rule of law); and freedom of action for individuals and groups. These democratic principles, although recognized as universal human principles since ancient times, continue to demand a more complete fulfilment in the experience of all nations.[92]

He argues that both democracy and *Shura* arise from the central belief that collective deliberation, rather than individual preference, is more likely to lead to a fair and sound results for the social good. As principles, both of them proceed from the core idea that all people are equal, in terms of their rights and responsibilities, and affirm that a more comprehensive fulfilment of the principles and values by which humanity prospers cannot be achieved in a non-democratic, non-*Shura* environment.[93] Sulaiman views the Qur'anic term *Shura* as neither rejecting nor being incompatible with the basic elements of a democratic system, nor as being a specifically ordained system of governance. Instead, he sees it as a principle governing the Muslims' public life and holds that the more any system can constitutionally, institutionally, and practically fulfil the principle of *Shura* or, for that matter, the democratic principle, the more Islamic it becomes.[94] Leaving aside the differences in how they are applied, he regards both terms as synonymous in conception and principle on the basis that the logic underlying *Shura*, like that underlying democracy, rejects hereditary rule because wisdom and competence are never the monopoly of any one individual or family. Both reject government by force (any rule sustained by coercion is illegitimate), as well as any political, social, or economic privileges claimed on the basis of tribal lineage or social prestige.[95]

Furthermore, he also finds Islam's compatibility with democracy by distinguishing between God's 'absolute sovereignty' and human sovereignty of running state affairs and through the 'liberal interpretation' of *Shura* as put forth in his 'Religion, Democracy, and the Arabs' View of America'.[96] For him,

> absolute sovereignty rests in God, but sovereignty in terms of running our lives on this planet rests in us. Islam does not mandate a religious state; it rather requires all states and societies to abide by the principles and values that benefit humankind. This view is not inconsistent with democracy. [ ... ] In the liberal interpretation *Shura* is broad and binding mutual consultation through which a decision is democratically arrived at. It implies equality of status among citizens, male and female, in the consultative process. In this view, Islam is compatible with democracy.[97]

In his 'The Shura Principle in Islam',[98] Sulaiman begins by this strong argument in which he links *Shura* with three other cardinal Islamic principles: *Shura* constitutes one of the *four cardinal principles* in Islamic perspective on socio-political organization. The other three are *justice, equality,* and *human dignity*. (Italics in original)[99] Besides *Shura*, he refers to 'some fundamental Islamic percepts that rarely receive due consideration in discussions about political Islam' and he considers the understanding of these principles as necessary so that 'to grasp the fullness and coherence of the Islamic perspective on governance'.[100] These are: *Rida al-'awam* (popular consent); *Khilafah* (God's delegation of authority to the Ummah); *Bay'ah* (a form of electing or confirming the *Khalifah*); *Shura* (mutual consultation and deliberation); and *Wikalah* (representation, or legal construct of appointing a deputy). Among these, he provides the following explanation regarding the first and fifth principles:

Islam stipulates '*rida al-'awam*', that is *popular consent*, as a prerequisite to the establishment of legitimate political authority, and *ijtihad jama'i*, that is *collective deliberation* as a requisite to the proper administration of public affairs. Beyond that, Islam stipulates '*mas'uliyah jama'iyyah*', that is *collective responsibility*, for maintaining the public good of society. And by affirming all humans as equal before God, Islam stipulates *equality before the law*; for to claim parity before God and disparity among ourselves is plain hypocrisy. Finally, by rejecting man's subservience to anyone but God, Islam stipulates *freedom as the natural state of man*, hence liberty within the limits of law is an Islamic stipulation. [ ... ]

A fifth precept is that of *wikalah*, which means representation, [and is] basically a legal construct according to which one may appoint a deputy for acting on one's behalf concerning matters in which representation is valid. In the constitutional context, it can mean electing deputies to represent the electorate in the affairs of the governance (Italics in original).[101]

On the basis of interpretation and explanation provided for these principles and precepts, Sulaiman, therefore, states that

> the ideas of constitutionalism and representative governance are well rooted within the Islamic socio-political perspective. They have their basis not only in Islam's ethical imperatives of *justice, equality, and the dignity of the human being*, but also in its well-established legal precepts. Granted that these precepts have traditionally been narrowly defined, and historically hardly ever applied after the first four *khalifas* [Pious Caliphate Era], they have never been openly challenged or denied by either the ruling regimes or the traditional schools [of juristic thought] (Italics in original).[102]

He substantiates his claims with the argument that recent Islamic scholarship 'has tended toward a broader understanding of these precepts and in some cases has in fact offered broader constructions'. Here he refers to the impact of the reformist legacy of Arab modernists like Muhammad 'Abduh and Rashid Rida and states that 'not only has the authenticity of *Shura* come to be more widely recognized, but the scope of its application has come to be viewed as essentially at par with that of modern democratic systems, incorporating all the main elements thereof, such as people's sovereignty, popular elections, separation of powers with built-in checks and balances, political pluralism, legal opposition, and freedom of speech'.[103]

Thus, '*popular consent, collective deliberation, shared responsibility, personal freedom, justice, equality, and dignity of the human individual*, all conceived within the *Shura* framework of governance' are the authentic Islamic positions; and thus, reveal clearly that 'Islam rejects all kinds of autocratic authority or privilege; that it rejects hereditary rule, for no particular lineage has monopoly over competence and integrity'. (Italics in original)[104]

Democracy and Islam are consistent because *Shura* and democracy are one and the same concept, a concept that prods us to find better and better realizations of the principles of justice, equality, and human dignity in a collective sociopolitical experience. Thus, it seems that Sulaiman is one of the primary proponents of '*Shura*-as-democracy'.[105]

## Yusuf al-Qaradawi (b. 1926) on Muslim World's Need for 'Real Democracy'

Allama (Dr) Shaykh Yusuf al-Qaradawi (b. 1926, Egypt) is an eminent scholar of the present era, preacher, and moderate and well-balanced mufti and orator. This Egyptian-born and (since 1961) Qatar-based most influential jurist, has spoken in favour of democracy in the Muslim world, and need for reform of political climates in the Middle East specifically.[106] An acclaimed author of over hundreds of books and having a number of awards for his significant contribution to the Islamic scholarship to his credit, Qaradawi is considered one of the most influential living scholars and is included in the list of 'Top 50' scholars in *The Muslim500—The World's 500 Most Influential Muslims* and in the *Foreign Affair's The World's Top 20 Public Intellectuals*. He is described as 'one of best known and more important contemporary Muslim clerics', a 'Moderate Voice from the Muslim World', and is considered 'the vital theorist of Islamic movements and Islamist political parties'.[107] His writings cover a vast range of subjects—including Qur'an, Seerah, theology, legal aspects, and contemporary issues—which 'are inundated with modern concepts such as democracy and feminism' as well[108] and his 'perception of the Islamic state positively approaches modern state terms, i.e., democracy, pluralism, women participation in the legislative council, etc.'[109] With reference to the major arguments put forth by al-Qaradawi in his *State in Islam*,[110] Rahman further states:

> By several proofs from text, history, and the nature of Islam, he intended to prove the existence of Islamic state during the 7th century to the 20th century [in his masterpiece, *State in Islam*]. Al-Qaradawi intended to develop a positive and wise political Fiqh considering the present time, environment, and circumstances. He was concerned to consider overall text toward an objective of flexible Islamic Shari'ah. He featured of Islamic state as a civilian state with Islamic norms, values, and morals. He argued that the Islamic state is a global state within the Ummah's concept, but nothing prohibited it to start within a nation state. He approached the modern state with a positive view of accepting good things, ideas and concepts that do not oppose the trends of Islamic values. Within this viewpoint, he responded democracy, pluralism, participation of Women and non-Muslim in the parliament in a positive way.[111]

Qaradawi asserts that an 'Islamic state is founded on the best principles of democracy' but at the same time warns that 'it is not a copy of western democracy'. He even argues that in the Muslim system, as is the case in the Western one, 'a nation should be given the right to choose its ruler and that he should not be forced upon his will'.[112] This is explained and expressed by Rahman as: 'Islamic state is founded based on the consultative feature (*Shura*), which is an essential principle of democracy [,] but not the same or a copy of Western democracy. In Islam, it is agreed that a nation should be given the right to choose its ruler without any type of force'.[113]

In his *Priorities of the Islamic Movement in the Coming Phase*,[114] he states that Islam does not allow any kind of autocracy or monarchy; that democracy is consistent with Islam and the fundamental rights prescribed in Islam can be ensured through democracy—on the condition that it must be within the limits of Islamic law. He considers it a duty incumbent on Islamic movements to oppose not only all the political systems that are against Islam, like 'totalitarian and dictatorial rule, political despotism and usurpation of people's rights' but to 'stand by political freedom, as represented by true, not false, democracy'.[115]

He emphasizes that as 'Islam is not democracy and democracy is not Islam'; therefore, Islam should not be attributed to any 'principle or system', because 'Islam is unique in its means, ends and methodologies'. He does not wish that 'Western democracy be carried over' to any Muslim country 'with its bad ideologies and values', and in order to integrate it into the Islamic comprehensive system, Muslims should add some values and ideologies.[116] Nevertheless, he sees the tools and guarantees created by democracy as being very close to the political principles of Islam, as he argues:

> [T]he tools and guaranties created by democracy are as close as can ever be to the realization of the political principles brought to this earth by Islam to put a leash on the ambitions and whims of rulers. These principles are: *Shura* [consultation], *good advice* [*nasiha*], enjoining what is proper and forbidding what is evil, disobeying illegal orders, resisting unbelief and changing wrong by force whenever possible. It is only in democracy and political freedom that the power of Parliament is evident and ... that the strength of free Press, free Parliament, opposition and the masses is most felt.[117]

As reported by *The Muslim News,* Qaradawi (in a 2006 conference in Istanbul, Turkey) said: 'The Muslim world needs democracy. It wants democracy. But it should be real democracy and not just democracy by name only'. For him, democracy has done some good things: democracy has 'saved humanity from despots and dictators who act like gods. The details should be left to the people. Let them decide for themselves'. He, however, argues that democracy in the Muslim world would be different from that of Western countries, because of the reason that 'in Islam there are some fixed principles that cannot be changed. But there are some things where the people can call for change, depending on the time and place'.[118]

Qaradawi also suggests that 'there is no legal objection to adopting a theory or an idea initiated by non-Muslims (as long as it promotes the public interest of the Muslims)', as illustrated by the Prophet's adoption of the idea of digging a trench, which was originally a Persian technique, in the battle of Trench (627 CE) or the teaching project by non-Muslim captives for Muslim youth after the battle of Badr.[119] In this regard, he refers to the Prophetic tradition that *Wisdom, after all, is the lost property of a believe; he has the most rightful claim to it, wherever he finds it* and, thus, asserts: 'we have the right to borrow what is of benefit to us of the ideas, disciplines and systems so long as they do not run counter to the essence of a text or a firm juristic ruling'.[120]

Certainly, there are varied views among Islamists about both the substance of democracy and its compatibility with Islamic socio-religious and political ideas and notions, however, for Qaradawi, the real meaning and essence of democracy is that

> people choose their ruler by themselves. No ruler or regime is to be forced upon them without their full consent. They must have the right to bring him to account if he commits a mistake. Moreover, they must have the right to depose him and choose a new ruler if he goes astray. People must not be led against their will to advocate economic, social, cultural or political trends and programs that they are not satisfied with.... This is the typical meaning of democracy which is embodied in elections, public opinion poll, preference of the majority rule, multi-party system, ..., etc.[121]

Moreover, Qaradawi argues that 'Islam has the precedence over democracy in setting the bases on which it [the essence of democracy] flourishes rests' and has left the details to be worked out by Muslims through their independent juristic reasoning (*Ijtihad*) and in accordance with the principles of their religion, their worldly interests, the evolving circumstances of their lives in terms of time and place, and changing human conditions.[122]

Calling it an unacceptable view to assert that 'democracy signifies the rule of the people by the people, and that this entails a rejection of the principle that sovereignty belongs to God', he states that democracy is based on the principle of the people's rule [or popular rule], but does not contradict the principle that says that the rule is only for Allah on which Islamic jurisprudence is based. It rather runs counter to the principle of the individual's rule on which dictatorship is based.

Upholding democracy does not necessarily mean the rejection of the Rule of Allah that is conducted and embraced by human beings.[123]

He bases this analysis on the argument that the principle of God's sovereignty (*al-hakimiyya li'llah*), which is undisputable—*Judgment is for God alone* and *Authority belongs to God alone* (as in Q. 6: 57 and 12: 40, respectively)—is a 'typical Islamic principle which scholars ascertained by consensus in their quest for the legitimate rule and ruler'.[124] However, this sovereignty is of two kinds: the first is 'universal' and 'determinative' (*hakimiyya kawniyya qadariyya*), as becomes evident from Q. 13: 41, which means that 'Allah is the Sole Conductor of the universe', which evidently means a determinative sovereignty over the cosmos rather than a legislative sovereignty. The second kind of sovereignty relates to legislation and commands (*hakimiyya tashri'yya amriyya*), that is, the authority 'of assignment of duties, enjoining, forbidding, obligation and choice'—or to impose legal obligations, to command and to forbid, to make things binding or a matter of choice.[125] Thus,

> The Muslim who call for democracy seeks it as a form of governance that embodies the political principles of Islam regarding the choice of the ruler, consultation and advice, commanding right and forbidding wrong, resisting oppression and rejecting sinfulness, especially when the latter reaches the point of 'open unbelief' (or 'flagrant disbelief').[126]

Moreover, Qaradawi has been quoted in the *ash-Sharq* Newspaper as: 'He who says that democracy is disbelief; neither understands Islam, nor democracy';[127] or, as he writes in his *Priorities*: 'We have seen some people who regard *shura* [consultation] as mere informative, not a compulsory duty, ... , and we have seen still others *who consider democracy as a form of unbelief* (italics added).[128] The following passage from his 'Islam and Democracy' section in his *State in Islam* clearly reveals his vision about democracy and his position on Islam–democracy relationship:

I am one of those who call for democracy [not simply as a slogan, but] because it is feasible and disciplined means to an honorable life, one in which we can call others to God and to Islam according to our beliefs and without being thrown into dungeons or executed. This democracy would also be the means to a free and honorable life for our people, in which they enjoy the right to choose their rulers, to hold them accountable, and to change them if they go astray without having to resort to revolutions or assassins.[129]

He ends his discussion on the issue of 'Islam and Democracy' with this statement: 'Islamic *Shura* conforms to the essence of democracy' or 'the essence of democracy comes to accord with the spirit of Islamic consultation'.[130] Thus, it is on these grounds that Qaradawi finds the content of democracy as congruous with democracy.

## Khurshid Ahmad (b. 1932) on Harmonizing *Shura* and 'Democratic Governance'

Professor Khurshid Ahmad (b. 1932)—a prominent Pakistani Islamic scholar, a revivalist thinker, and spokesman of the Islamic movements around the world—is one of the prominent ideologues of the Islamic revival in the contemporary world, who has been 'increasingly involved internationally in the Islamic revivalist tide' and thus has been included 'among the dominant figures', and is described as 'Muslim activist-Economist', in *Makers of Contemporary Islam*.[131] He has very persuasively written on the Islam–democracy theme as well.[132]

Like his mentor (Mawdudi), Ahmad believes that 'Islam is the religion of truth', and is 'the embodiment of the code of life', revealed by God for the guidance of the humankind. He believes that the comprehensive guidance of Islam and its integral relationship to all aspects of life are rooted in the doctrine of *Tawhid*, the Unity or Oneness of God that 'points to the supremacy of the law in the cosmos, the all-pervading unity behind the manifest diversity'. Presenting 'a unified view of the world' and offering 'the vision of an integrated universe', *Tawhid* is, 'not merely a metaphysical concept', but a 'dynamic belief' and a 'revolutionary concept'; it 'constitutes the essence of the teachings of Islam'.[133]

For Ahmad, the vocation of humanity is to serve as God's vicegerent, representative (*Khilafah*), on the earth (Q. 2: 30–39), and to fulfil God's will by establishing a new order of equity and justice, peace and prosperity. This duty is incumbent on both the individual and the Muslim community. The concept of *Khilafah*, for him, is the unique Islamic concept of man's trusteeship in moral, political, and economic terms. It is the source of the Muslim vocation and mission:

> This [concept] exalts man to the noble and dignified position of being God's deputy on earth and endows his life with a lofty purpose; to fulfill the Will of God on earth. This will solve the perplexing problems of human society and establish a new order wherein equity and justice and peace and prosperity will reign supreme.[134]

Furthermore, while delineating on the 'Basic Characteristics of Islamic Ideology', Ahmad asserts that Islamic basic 'teachings are simple and intelligible ... free from superstitions and irrational beliefs.... They are based on reason and sound logic ... and are simple and straightforward. There is no hierarchy of priests, no far-fetched abstractions, [and there are] no complicated rites and rituals'.[135]

Other unique features of Islam, as highlighted powerfully by Ahmad are: that Islam 'does not divide life into water-tight compartments of matter and spirit'; that it 'does not admit any separation between 'material' and 'moral', 'mundane' and 'spiritual' life and enjoins man to devote all his energies to the reconstruction of life on healthy foundations'; and 'it establishes a balance between individualism and collectivism'.[136] He, thus, concludes that Islam is a simple, rational, and 'practical religion'; and a 'complete way of life' which provides 'guidance for all walks of life—individual and social, material and moral, economic and political, legal and cultural, national and international'.[137]

Regarding the principles of permanence and change, he is of the belief that 'Islam presents an ideology which satisfies the demands of stability as well as change'.[138] For him, the 'Qur'an and the *Sunnah* contain the eternal guidance', which are 'free from the limitations of "space" and "time" [constrains] and as such the principles of individual and social behavior revealed by Him [God] are based on reality and are eternal'; but

God has revealed only broad principles and has *endowed man with the freedom to apply them in every age in the way suited to the spirit and conditions of that age*. It is through the *Ijtihad* that people of every age try to implement and apply divine guidance to the problems of their times. Thus the basic guidance is of a permanent nature, while the *method of its application can change* in accordance with the peculiar needs of every age. That is why Islam always remains as fresh and modern as tomorrow's morn. (Italics added)[139]

These unique features of Islam, in his perception, 'establish its credentials as the religion of man—the religion of today and the religion of tomorrow'.[140]

It is within this context of his understanding of Islam, its beliefs, and its principles of permanence and change that one needs to evaluate and appreciate his ideas and thoughts on the issues of Islam and democracy, put forth in his various writings.

Regarding democracy, he is of the opinion that the term 'democracy' is both a philosophy and a form of organization. The term indicates a set of ideals and principles and a political system, a mechanism for governance, and a politico-legal culture. He argues that democracy as a 'philosophy' and democracy as a 'form of organization' is not one and the same thing. In the form of organization, Islam has its own system of democracy, but as a philosophy, 'the two, i.e. Islam and western democracy, are basically different, rather opposed to each other'.[141]

The political system during the Prophet (pbuh) and rightly guided Caliphate period was based on two main principles: (a) the rule of law and equality of all before the law and (b) supremacy of the Qur'an and Sunnah, and resort to *Ijtihad* in matters not covered by these sources. Consequently, Ahmad argues that Islam and Muslim *Ummah* brook no sympathy for arbitrary and authoritarian rule. Whatever arbitrary power reigns is more a product of colonialization and westernization, not of Muslim ideals, history, and contemporary aspirations. Muslims have their own concept and tradition of democracy and people's participation that ensures just rule, consultative processes at all levels, respect for rights and dissent, the independence of judiciary, and political co-cultural pluralism. He very rationally argues that there is 'no contradiction between Islam and the [real] essence of democracy'; Islam and true democratization are two sides of the same coin; and, as such, 'democratic processes and Islam would go hand in hand'. This is because democratization is bound to be 'a stepping stone of Islamization'; and the fulfilment of Islamic aspirations would become possible only through 'promotion of democratic process'.[142]

While describing the present striving of Muslims for the achievement of democratization, Ahmad claims that despite freedom from the colonial oppression, the Muslim *Ummah* is still striving for its right—its democratic right to freely develop its polity, society, and economy in light of its own ideas, values and aspirations:

> It [Muslim *Ummah*] refuses to live under the dictate of concepts and models in conflict with its faith, opposed to its values, distasteful to its history and repugnant to its traditions. If democracy means rights of a people to self-determination and self-fulfillment, that is what Islam and Muslims have been striving for, nothing more and nothing less.[143]

For Ahmad, the following seven principles are an 'illustrative example of the unique Muslim tradition of governance' and constitute significant pointers towards the development of 'a distinctly *Islamic model of democratic governance*'. For him, these can be the source of inspiration and guidance for 'developing *Islamic democratic* models in the contemporary world'. (Italics added)[144] These principles are:

(i) The rule of law and equality of all before the law;
(ii) The supremacy of the Qur'an and Sunnah, and resort to *Ijtihad* in matters not covered by these sources;
(iii) *Shura* as the mechanism of decision-making as much as for the selection of the political leadership at all levels;
(iv) Respect for human rights (including those of minorities);
(v) The separation of the judiciary from the executive and its independence at all levels;
(vi) System of social security based on *Zakat* (compulsory transfer payments from the rich to the poor), *sadaqat* (voluntarily charitable contributions), *waqf* (trust foundation), *infaq* (spending in the path of Allah), *wassiya* (will), *wiratha* (distribution of wealth through inheritance), and *hiba* (bequest/donations), (and/or)

establishment of an egalitarian socio-economic system on these concepts and values; and

(vii) Acceptance of dissent and opposition—individual as well as collective.[145]

Ahmad further maintains that Islam is a spiritual experience, dynamic tradition, and an historical movement that has existed for over 1400 years, while as modern democracy is a political idea and movement that has existed for only 400 years. While arguing that 'Muslims want democracy, but not an imposed democracy', he makes it clear that 'Western ideas must not be "explored" but rather discussed and voluntarily adopted by those who accept them. People should be free to express themselves and choose their future'. He also revealed that on an 'operational level', there is little dividing democracy from Islam, but some secular conceptions of democracy are antithetical and hostile to a Muslim's faith.[146]

How does contemporary Islam view democracy?[147] In answering this question, Ahmad provides many more insights and ideas on Islam–democracy compatibility, when he says that from the Islamic viewpoint, the concept of democracy has two different dimensions: (a) *Ultimate Source*: In Islam, 'as far as the ultimate source of values and guidance is concerned, it is God, Who is the Source of guidance that is not changeable by the human vote'; (b) *Khilafah*: 'instead of *sovereignty* of man' in Islam, there is the concept of '*vicegerency* of man; and our [Islamic] system is popular, which means that all members of the society have to be consulted and it is they who should be deciding who should rule, how and what policies should be formulated. Then there is accountability to people'. Therefore, for him, there are two pillars of legitimacy in Islam: (i) 'belief in God and the supremacy of the Divine Law'; and (ii) 'reference to the people, and their authority to conduct their affairs by mutual consultation' on the Qur'anic principle of *Amruhum Shura Baynahum* (Q. 42: 38): 'This is not just a choice, it is an *amr* (commandment); it is not recommendatory, but mandatory'.

He further deliberates on the connotation and scope of *Shura* and asserts that '*Shura*, or consultation, is possible only when there is freedom. If there is no freedom, there can be no discussion, no dissent, and no variety of opinions. *Shura*, for him, also means that 'those who have to run the affairs should be elected by *Shura*, not imposed on people [forcibly]. Then, they should run the affairs by *Shura*. So, rule of law, fundamental rights of freedom, right to differ, change through people, all this is integral' to Islamic political system.[148]

With reference to the similarities and differences between Islamic political system and democracy and its principles and values, Ahmad is of the opinion that 'the Islamic concept of democracy has a vast area of commonality with the contemporary human experience at the operational, institutional level. At the level of principles too, there are common points, like the rule of law, right to dissent, and freedom—even separation of powers—between the judiciary, legislature, and the executive'. With reference to the differences, he mentions that Islam does not 'grant to the people ... the right to change the Divine Law'; and thus, concludes: 'there is democracy [in Islam], it is not merely compatible, it is mandatory' and considers the 'period of the Righteous Caliphs' as 'democratic' in the real sense.[149]

Democracy has been described as a 'contested concept', and there is no universally accepted model of democracy; so it remains a multi-faced phenomenon, both at the conceptual as well as operational level—i.e. both in theory as well as in practice. Within the context of Islamic faith, culture, history, and contemporary experience, Ahmad finds clear guidelines that suggest a unique and distinct political framework—one that can be described as truly participatory, both in substance and spirit; and one that can establish a political order committed to the twin goals of '*Adl* (justice) and *Shura*, the real substance of operational democracy.[150]

## Muhammad Khalid Masud (b. 1939) on 'Defining Democracy in Islamic Polity'

Muhammad Khalid Masud (b. 15 April 1939) is a Pakistani scholar and legal expert whose methodology, 'notably in its emphasis on context', in many respects, is similar to that of Fazlur Rahman (d. 1988). He has served as Director General, *Islamic Research Institute*, Islamabad; Chairman, *Council of Islamic Ideology*, Islamabad; Professor at the *International Islamic University*, Kuala Lumpur, Malaysia; and Academic Director of the *Institute for the Study of Islam in the Modern World* (ISIM), Leiden (the Netherlands).[151] Since 2012, he has been serving as the 'Ad hoc Judge' and 'Member Shariat Appellate Bench', Supreme Court of Pakistan. Having completed his doctoral thesis on Shatibi's philosophy of Islamic law with a special focus on his contribution to *maslaha*,[152] Masud has taught Islamic Law at various universities in Pakistan, Nigeria, France, Malaysia, and the Netherlands. He has published extensively on Islamic law and contemporary (legal and socio-political) issues and trends in Muslim societies, including pluralism, Muslim minorities, and other related subjects.

Described as a 'Keeper of the Reformist Tradition (in Pakistan)', he is indeed one of the 'pioneering examples of 21st-century Muslim Reformist thinkers' not only in the Sub-continent but in the whole Muslim world.[153] His views on democracy can be found in his various essays and articles like 'Defining Democracy in Islamic Polity',[154] 'Islam and Democracy in Pakistan',[155] 'Religion and State are Twin Brothers',[156] etc.

Masud considers the Qur'an not just 'a book of laws but acknowledges its normative character'. Besides, the contextualist approach, he also 'stresses [on the application of] the importance of linguistic analysis', which, in his opinion, requires 'a thorough understanding of the Arabic of the time of revelation, and a holistic rather than piecemeal approach to the study of the Qur'an'.[157]

Having contributed significantly to the reformist and modernist thought and its trends, the discourses on reform,[158] for Masud, have 'varied in their perception of modernity and tradition' and he identifies three Reform discourses, viz. Revivalist, Modernist, and Islamic Modernist.[159] 'Islamic Modernism', for him, means 'an interactive discourse that revisited the notions of compatibility, modernity and tradition during its debate with others', contrasting the two other discourses of Revivalism and Reform discourse, and Western Modernist discourse, that 'aims to root 'modernism' in Islamic tradition'.[160] He further adds that this pushes 'to reform Muslim society' by affirming that 'modernity is compatible with Islam, and a new Islamic theology is required in order to justify this compatibility'.[161]

Similarly, on Islam–democracy discourse, Masud is of the opinion that the discourse of Islam–democracy compatibility 'has been under discussion for more than a century' and has 'again come into focus in the wake of the war on terror' (unleashed in the wake of 9/11). In his opinion, three broad views/perspectives have emerged in this regard:

> One view, often favored by the Western media, holds that Muslim societies are unable to develop a liberal culture and hence Muslim countries have not been able to achieve democracy. Another, although a majority view among Muslim intellectuals, ..., claims that democracy is not only compatible with Islamic teachings but also that Islamic polities in history have been more democratic than any other system in the world. The third view maintains that democracy is a foreign Western concept and does not go along with Islamic teachings.[162]

He is of the opinion that 'Islamic democracy, i.e., democracy defined from the [Islamic] perspective, differs from 'Western' democracy in form as well as objectives. Whatever the perspective, studies on Islam and democracy never fail to stress the point that building democracy in Muslim countries is a formidable task.'[163]

In this essay, Masud analyses the four texts (articles and books)[164] that illustrate these three broad views, viz.: Martin Kramer's *Islam vs. Democracy* (1996);[165] Khalifa Abdul Hakim's *The Prophet and his Message* (1987);[166] Amin Ahsan Islahi's *Islami Riyasat/Islamic State* (1977);[167] and Qari Tayyib's *Fitri Hukumat* [Natural State] (1963).[168]

Masud has aptly reviewed three contrasting scholars' views on Islam and democracy: Hakim's modernist approach, Tayyib's traditional (Deobandi) standpoint, and Islahi's Islamist standing.[169] After making this analysis, he explores the question: why is building democracy such a formidable task? Basing his viewpoint on the views and visions of these four scholars, Masud is of the opinion that in defining democracy within the framework of Islamic polity, the scholars focus on the concepts and issues of 'Rule of law, equality, freedom, liberty, right to vote, elections, party system, parliamentary system, legislative authority, a state's right to legislate, forms of government, and sovereignty'. But, 'the real problem', for Masud, 'is the recognition of the role, place and right of a common man in government'.[170]

In his assessment and understanding, 'the real issue in defining democracy rests in the value and place assigned to the common man as an individual', which is something not yet fully developed in the present political systems.[171] He concludes that 'in spite of emergence of democracy in the Western systems, the concept is still in the making [in the Muslim world]. [Therefore, the] main problem is the fundamental paradigm shift in political thinking. The emphasis on the role of masses in the present political systems is not yet fully developed'.[172]

For Masud, one of the many reasons that democracy was not accepted in most of the Muslim societies was the notion widely held by the elite that the masses were not qualified to govern themselves. He says that the notion and such thinking that in Islam, 'Sovereignty belongs to God alone' and 'how is this sovereignty exercised?' He answers this question through a twofold formula: Sovereignty of God is expressed through Shari'a[h] because it is revealed by God. Since only the experts in Islamic tradition can properly interpret Shari'a[h], they alone can represent the sovereignty of God'.[173] This kind of misconception and misunderstanding regarding the concept of sovereignty gives rise to the rejection of popular participation in politics in predominantly Muslim countries, argued Masud in a conference (in Jakarta, Indonesia 2004) and also blamed western countries for persuading Muslim nations that democracy was simply incompatible with Islam.[174] However, in its clarification, he takes the support of Abdul Hakim's views who argues that sovereignty indeed belongs to God but since Islam does not allow any priesthood or monarchy and the *Khalifah* exercises a delegated authority, in fact, sovereignty is delegated to the Muslim community, or *Ummah* as a whole.[175] The same viewpoint is also shared by Yusuf al-Qaradawi.

In the context of Pakistan, Masud argues that it is not the religion (Islam), but 'religious arguments' and religious interpretations, along with a multitude of factors, ranging from historical, political, and economic, etc., which not only dominate the obstruction to democracy,[176] but create interruptions, interferences, and disturbances in establishing firmly, and in stabilizing and solidifying, the democratic governance in Muslim countries. To this Touqir Hussain adds:

> The fact is that it is not the 'idea', but 'practice' of democracy, that has failed; however, the majority of people do not realize that. Islam is indeed incompatible, on some grounds, with a Western liberal democracy that rests on individualism and secularism, but it is not incompatible with democratic ideals such as basic human rights, respect for human dignity, and social justice.[177]

## Rachid al-Ghannoushi (b. 1941) on Implementing Democracy via *Shura*

Rachid al-Ghannoushi, sometimes written as Rached Ghannocuhi (b. June 1941, Tunisia)—the Islamic leader of Tunisian Islamic Tendency Movement now called the Renaissance Party (*Hizb an-Nahdah*)—is another prominent voice among the present-day thinker-activists of political pluralism and democracy,[178] whose thought has been conditioned and transformed by multiple influences: 'Islamic traditions, the experience of the failures of Arab nationalism and socialism, life under an authoritarian government, the influences of leaders, movements, and events in other Muslim countries, and the experience of exile in the West'.[179] Named by the *Time* as one of '100 Most Influential People in the World' (2012), included in the *Foreign Policy's* 'Top 100 Global Thinkers' (2011), and included in the list of '100 Most Influential Arabs in the World' in *Global Influence List* 2018, he is described, among others, as a 'Democrat within Islamism',[180] a 'Key Muslim Thinker of the 21st Century',[181] and 'one of the leading Muslim intellectuals in contemporary time'.[182]

His thought reflects a masterly understanding of Western and Islamic philosophies and a genuine concern for 'reconciling the basic tenets of Islam with modernity'. Holding a 'non-traditional' view on a number of issues,[183] his intellectual contribution and political activism have gained him prominence within the Islamic movements of the twentieth and twenty-first centuries. In the twenty-first century, he has emerged as 'one of the dominant entities who cogently express Islam-Democracy compatibility', has been active contributor in 'championing the trend of democratization', and thus, has been rightly described as 'one of the leading Muslim figures heavily engaged in blending Islam with democracy'.[184] Hafijur Rahman counts Ghannoushi, Hasan al-Turabi, and Yusuf al-Qaradawi among those contemporary Arab voices, after Malek Bennabi, who 'strongly argued for democracy in Islamic political thought'.[185]

Ghannoushi, who leads a school in modern Islamic political thought that advocates democracy and pluralism, believes democracy to be a set of mechanisms for guaranteeing the sovereignty of the people and for supplying safety valves against corruption and the hegemonic monopoly of power.[186] He acknowledges democracy as among the positive contributions or accomplishments of the West.[187] He puts it in his book on *Civil*

*Liberties in Islamic State* (1993)—which is described by Rahman as his 'masterpiece to understand the political thought'[188]—in these words:[189]

> Democracy is an authority practiced [by the people] through a set of constitutional techniques that may differ in their particulars in any system but agree in terms of equity, selection, separation of authorities, political pluralism, freedom of expression, freedom of gathering, setting up of associations, acknowledgement for the majority to decide and rule, and for the minority to oppose for the sake of reciprocation. This ends up in allowing the citizen a set of social securities.[190]

Like other Muslim supporters of Islam–democracy compatibility, Ghannoushi finds 'no necessary contradiction between democracy and the traditional Islamic tenets such as *ijtihad* [independent interpretive reasoning], *ijma* (consensus), *baya* [*Ba'yah*] (oath of allegiance), and *shura* (consultation), which governs the relationship between the political authority and the people'.[191] He has been in agreement with the view that the system of democracy is a direct consequence of a particular western experience. Perceiving democracy as not merely a method of government but also as a philosophy, to him, Muslims don't have any problem with democratic institution, but with the secular and nationalistic values behind democracy. Islamic democracy is distinguished from other systems by its moral content as derived from the *Shari'ah*.[192]

In an attempt to find a historical link between the development of Western democracy and Islam, Ghannoushi maintains that democratic notions and liberal democratic values were derived from medieval Europe, which in turn was influenced by Islamic civilizations. Democracy offers the means to implement the Islamic ideal today: 'Islam, which enjoins the recourse to Shura (consultation)... finds in democracy the appropriate instruments (elections, parliamentary system, separation of powers, etc.) to implement the Shura'.[193] Highlighting the significance of *Shura*, Ghannoushi says:

> *Shura* is the second source of Islamic system, next only to the scriptural text. *Shura* is in itself a statement acknowledging the deputized community's right to participate in ruling matters. It is one of the legal duties because it is a special feature of Islamic state and the Muslim

community. It is, therefore, absolutely right to say that it is the state of *Shura* and the community of *Shura* Islam is unique in this regard because it has adopted the principle of *Shura* as a general practice and as a method of public administration.[194]

*Ijma'* (consensus), for him, provides the basis for participatory government or democracy in Islam. He believes that democracy in the Muslim world as in the West can take many forms. In an interview with Professor(s) Esposito and Voll (1993), he revealed that he (himself) favours a 'multiparty system of government'.[195]

In his *Civil Liberties in Islamic State*, Ghannoushi emphasizes that the democratic values of political pluralism and tolerance are perfectly compatible with Islam. His Islamic system accommodates majority rule, free election, multiple political parties, religious or secular alike, freedom of expression, equality of all citizens and women's rights and gender equality. And in Dr Bustami Khir's observation, this line of thinking is the same as that of Muhammad 'Abduh.[196]

Ghannoushi categorically rejects theocracy or 'the rule of mullahs', arguing that 'government in Islam embodies a civilian authority whose political behavior is answerable to public opinion'.[197] Regarding the Islam–democracy relationship, he maintains that

> If by democracy is meant the liberal model of government prevailing in the West, a system under which the people freely choose their representatives and leaders, and in which there is an alternation of power, as well as all freedoms and human rights for the public, then the Muslims will find nothing in their religion to oppose democracy; and it is not in their interest to do so.[198]

He believes that once the 'Islamists are given a chance to comprehend the values of Western modernity, such as democracy and human rights, they will search within Islam for a place for these values where they will implant them, nurse them, and cherish them'.[199] He advocates an Islamic system that features majority rule, free elections, a free press, protection of minorities, equality of all secular and religious parties, and full women's rights in everything. Islam's rule is to provide the system with moral values.[200] Furthermore, in his 'Self-Criticism and Reconsideration', he makes it clear that many Islamists associate democracy with foreign intervention and non-belief. Democracy, for him, is neither disbelief nor foreign intervention, but is a set of mechanisms to guarantee freedom of thought and assembly and peaceful competition for governmental authority through ballot boxes. For him:

> The negative attitude of Islamic movements towards democracy is holding it back. We have no modern experience in Islamic activity that can replace democracy. The *Islamization of democracy is the closest thing to implementing* [the Islamic concept of] *shura* (consultation). Those who reject this thought have not produced anything different than the one-party system of rule. (Italics added)[201]

Writing on the legality of participating in non-Muslim regimes, Ghannoushi points to a Muslim's duty to advance whatever Muslim goals are within his power to advance;[202] and as Shavit puts it: 'Independence, development, compatriot solidarity, public and individual political freedoms, human rights, political pluralism, independence of the judicial system, freedom of the press, freedom for mosques and for *da'wah* activities—a prospect of promoting these obliges Muslims to participate in the establishment of a secular democratic regime, in case the establishment of a Muslim one is not possible'.[203]

In his recent work on Ghannoushi, M. Dawood Sofi,[204] summarizes his thoughts on Islam–democracy compatibility as:

> In case of Islam-democracy compatibility, Ghannushi is well known for his pro-democratic character.... He has highlighted, in case of democracy, the importance and application of *Shura* that forms one of the very significant traditions of Islam. He tries to convey to the Muslim population that several Islamic practices and traditions like *Shura, Ijma', and Ijtihad* are attuned with democracy and thus, in a way persuades them to look for common objectives and goals between Islam and the West.... It signifies that his style and approach regarding Islam-Democracy compatibility or incompatibility is quite different from that of other Muslim thinkers, particularly when viewed in the context of his emphasis and acceptance of Western form of multi-party system.[205]

All these views and interpretations, collectively, lead one to the assumption that Ghannoushi frequently tries to convey that several Islamic practices and traditions like *Shura, Ijma*, and *Ijtihad* are in harmony with democracy. Moreover, it is 'one of the best tools that can guarantee the sovereignty of the people and can also help to end corruption and hegemonic monopoly of power in the Muslim world'.[206]

In his latest study on the 'Perception of Muslim Democracy in the Political Thought of Rachid Ghannouchi', Rahman states that he considers 'democracy as a government system that works to ensure the rights and freedom of the people. It is combining of some mechanism as election, parliament, majority role, pluralism, etc. Within the present context of the World, it is the best system of government where another system is not found, which may become an alternative of this'.[207] Furthermore, Azzam Tamimi sums up Ghannoushi's position on this discourse as:

> The central theme in Ghannouchi's thought is that democracy is compatible with Islam, and that Muslims need to incorporate it into their political thought in order to institutionalize the concept of *shura*. His theme is based on the belief that civilizational products and achievements are universal.[208]

Thus, Ghannoushi is indeed one of those prominent voices in the contemporary Arab world, both in pre- and post-Arab Spring era, who has been arguing for democracy as the best means of politics and government and considers democracy not only as the best product of contemporary civilization but also the better means to establish Islamic values and norms.

## Abdulaziz Sachedina (b. 1942) on 'Islamic Roots of Democratic Pluralism'

Abdulaziz Sachedina (b. 1942, Tanzania)—Professor of, and IIIT Chair in, Islamic Studies at the *George Mason University* (GMU, USA),[209] teaching mainly subjects like Islam in the modern age, Islam, democracy and human rights, etc.—is regarded not only one of today's major voices of pluralism in Islam, but is 'a keen proponent of democracy as an

Islamic value' as well.[210] In his *The Islamic Roots of Democratic Pluralism* (2001),[211] and even more emphatically since the events of 9/11, he has argued that Islam's essential pluralism demands democracy.[212] Using the Qur'an as a yardstick, and analysing critically Muslim teachings on issues of pluralism, civil society, war and peace, violence and self-sacrifice, etc., in this book Sachedina shows how the Qur'anic philosophy is not only democratic in its nature but also completely pluralistic and universal. The teachings in the Qur'an, which Sachedina explains in this book, are essential in establishing the basis for mutually respectful and democratic relationships among Muslims, and between Muslims and the non-Muslim world.[213] Democratic pluralism thrives on the ability of citizens to value each other and respect each other's dignity and human rights.

With reference to the specific and selected verses of the Qur'an that emphasize the dignity of the individual, freedom of conscience, etc., Sachedina argues that these are essential in reestablishing the basis for mutually respectful and democratic relationships among Muslims and between Muslims and non-Muslim world.

In this book, Sachedina (being a theologian), approaches the issue of Islam–democracy relationship (or democratic pluralism) in a comprehensive way, and shows how strongly Islam advocated pluralism. It also underscores the necessity for the full-blown development of Muslim/Islamic democratic theory. Sachedina argues that Muslims need to learn how to guide themselves and their community 'back to the sources' and lays emphasis, very seriously, 'on building nurturing, constructive relationships of justice and charity at all levels of human existence'.[214] He believes that, given that Islam provides comprehensive guidance, it is virtually unthinkable that it would not concern itself with governance.

Furthermore, by exploring the historical and the potential role that Islam has played and can play in governance, Sachedina—in his 'The Role of Islam in Public Square: Guidance or Governance?'[215]—demonstrates how theologians and students of theology can illuminate the role of religion in political sphere and contribute to the development of political theory and philosophy. He identifies Islamic sources that can refine that experience and allow Islam to play a central role in contemporary societies with particular sensitivity towards the need for inclusive and pluralistic political systems. For example, he argues:

The Shari'a[h] regulates religious practice with a view to maintaining the individual's well-being through his or her social well-being. Hence, its comprehensive system deals with the obligations that humans perform as part of their relationship to the Divine Being, and the duties they perform as part of their interpersonal responsibility.[216]

Thus, in the modern pluralistic society, Islam need not be marginalized. Instead, its heritage of respect for religious diversity and human initiative offers clear guidance, if not governance, for Muslims to participate fully in democratic governance.[217] Thus, for Sachedina:

> Fostering a positive understanding of *democratic ideals within an Islamic framework*... is not a matter of superficial 'Islamizing' verbiage, but rather a deep and comprehensive effort to show... that *democratic ideas* can and must be thought from within the authentic ethical culture of Islam and its teachings about the awesome accountability of human beings in this world and the next. (Italics added)[218]

Furthermore, he argues that there are sufficient grounds in Islamic tradition to vindicate democracy. For him, Muslims have developed, as a political community, into a social order that unifies its members on a religious basis. But Islamic tradition has not developed a concept of inclusive governance based on citizenship. Herein lies the challenge, in Sachedina's view, to Muslim intellectuals: to make a case for democratic politics without ignoring the political agenda of Islam to foster a unified community.[219]

At no other time in their history have the Muslims been required to evaluate their political heritage critically in the context of modern constitutional developments. Developments in contemporary political culture are challenging Muslim thinkers to find ways of engendering a more evolved political consciousness among Muslim peoples, one that is receptive to popular governance. Unless the community itself undertakes to define constitutional principles that are consistent with the rights of all citizens, regardless of their religious affiliation, there can be no democracy in the Muslim world.[220] While expressing his concerns about democracy and democratic ideals, he argues:

I do not wish to imply that the Muslim public is so religiously inclined that *democracy should be fictitiously 'Islamised'* [Islamized] to suit its taste. Rather, my major concern is to find ways of demonstrating to Muslim[s] ... that *democratic ideals are very much part of Islamic ethical culture*, which speaks about human responsibility and accountability in day-to-day existence. Instead of prescribing a shortcut to secularism as the guarantee of liberal democracy, Muslim intellectual endeavors should be to demonstrate that at the core of the Islamic belief system is an emphasis on interpersonal relationships at all levels of human existence. Since Islam values the nurturing and maintaining of relationships, Islamic civic education should undertake to grant citizens in a Muslim country their basic freedom in negotiating and maintaining all social relationships with a sense of equality, dignity, and freedom of conscience. (Italics added)[221]

Thus, Sachedina is one of the prominent American Muslim academicians/intellectuals who have contributed significantly to shape the theoretical understanding of 'Islamic democracy' and/or 'democratic pluralism' and thus have advanced this decades-old-discourse many steps further.

## Abdolkarim Soroush (b. 1945) on Inevitable Association of Islam and Democracy

Abdolkarim Soroush (b. 1945, Tehran; the pen name of Hossein Dabbagh) is an eminent reformist thinker and intellectual figure, a pharmacologist, philosopher, and one of the prominent speakers of Iran today. A distinguished voice on Islam–democracy compatibility,[222] he does not perceive contradictions between Islam and the freedoms inherent in democracy. Islam and democracy, for him, are 'not only compatible, [rather] their association is inevitable'. In a Muslim society, one without the other is not perfect.[223]

For Soroush, the only form of government that does not transform religion into an ideology or obstruct the growth of religious knowledge is a democratic one. He does not identify democracy with a particular Western culture as a foreign force to be resisted; rather, he considers it as a form of government that is compatible with multiple political cultures, including Islamic ones.[224]

He believes that the will of the majority must shape the ideal Islamic state, and that Islam itself is evolving as a religion, which leaves it open to reinterpretation: Sacred Texts do not change, but interpretation of them is always in change because the age and changing conditions in which believers live influence understanding. He philosophically offers the compatibility of Islamic rationality with freedom and democracy, laying more stress on the concept of *freedom*.[225]

In an interview with *Sharqh* Newspaper (December 2003), he said: 'What I have in mind when I speak about democracy is *democracy as the rejection of tyranny*'; or 'an anti-tyranny theory', because democracy also means 'freedom of choice'.[226] Regarding the question of the 'elections process', he is of the opinion that 'democracy is not summarized in the elections and democracy has its own constituents. Democracy is not realized merely with a high voter turnout. Democracy is made up of the legislature, judiciary and the executive powers. We need an efficient, neutral and powerful judiciary in order to have clean elections'.[227]

For Soroush, democracy is both 'a value system' and 'a method of governance': as a value system, it respects human rights, the public's right to elect its leaders and hold them accountable, and the defence of the public's notion of justice. And as a method of governance, democracy includes the traditional notions of separation of powers, free elections, free and independent press, and freedom of expression, freedom of political assembly, multiple political parties, and restrictions upon executive power. Soroush argues that no government official should stand above criticism, and that all must be accountable to the public. Accountability reduces the potential for corruption and allows the public to remove, or restrict the power of, incompetent officials. Democracy is, in effect, a method for 'rationalizing' politics.[228]

Propositioning the possibility of a 'religious democratic state' (*Hukumat-i Dimukratik-i Dini*),[229] Soroush believes that if democracy is irreconcilable with the normative legal reading of Islam, it can be compatible with another understanding that accords primacy to human values such as rationality, justice, freedom and human rights. Therefore, democracy can work in a religious society only if the respective theoretical foundations are harmonized.[230]

For him, a discussion of democracy is not a jurisprudential (*fiqhi*) issue in any sense. It is rather associated with the rule of reason and the rejection of absolutist authority, the latter being characteristic of a dogmatic understanding of Islam.[231] Soroush's view on religious government and the possibility of its taking on a democratic form are summarized by Jahanbakhsh in the following lines:

> The normative aspect of government deals with values of both a religious and a non-religious nature.... The right to govern originates either from God or from the people. If it is going to be exercised in the form of a *democratic government*, then this might cannot be entirely divine because the people's right to oversee, supervise, criticize and control the power of the political authority is their *a priori* human right, one that should be exercised without any restraint.... Also, that understanding of religion which assumes man's intellect to be incapable of administering his worldly affairs ... not only compromises the lofty goal of religion but is also certainly incompatible with democracy. The nature of a *true religious government* is, in principle, that of a *human government*, no more no less. Its business is to administer the nation's affairs and nothing else. In this respect it is like any other government. It is religious only because its whole governing machinery is at the service of the society of believers to fulfill their material needs, so that they can pursue their spiritual ends. In other words, a religious state differs from a non-religious only in aim, not in form. (Italics added)[232]

Soroush seeks to undermine the widely tensions between faith and freedom and reason and religion. For him, if Islam is compatible with freedom and reason—the constitutive principles of democracy—then Islam should be compatible with democracy.[233] He further argues that democracies are basically means to an end and as long as Islam is understood as a reasoned justification of God's rights over humanity, a religious society should have no problems in establishing a democracy as a means to good and just governance.

Soroush accepts that democracy as a 'sociological construct',[234] treating it as 'a combination of institutions' that increases 'public participation' and reduces 'the power of individuals in political decision making'. He also focuses on its religious concerns: 'A true democracy requires the highest moral standards. In those religions that demand the observance of God's strict imperatives, democracy is not achievable'. By this, Soroush seems to claim, for Mirsepassi, that a precondition for establishing a democratic politics is the existence of religious standards which are compatible with democracy, and that those religions which lack such standards cannot allow democracy to flourish'.[235]

Soroush accepts that 'Religious governments could be either democratic or undemocratic depending on the extent to which they benefit from collective reason and the respect they show toward human rights'.[236] This means, for Mirsipaasi, that 'what gives a government its democratic character is not the religiosity of the state but majority rule among the state's citizens, the collective rationality of the people, and, finally, respect for universal values such as human rights'.[237]

Similarly, Soroush's discussion about Islam and democracy, for Jahanbakhash, should take place not from within but from without formal religion. As long as the problem is not solved on a very deep theoretical plane, any demonstration of the compatibility or incompatibility of Islam and democracy on the basis of Islamic legal doctrines or through reworking certain of its older institutions is fatally flawed. Unlike other Muslim scholars, Soroush's arguments do not rely on the Qur'anic verses, the hadith, legal injunctions, or events from early Islamic history. Going beyond the contradictions and ambivalence that the normative legal version of Islam offers in a comparative analytical framework, Soroush argues that although democracy is irreconcilable with this reading of Islam, namely the Islam of *fiqh*, it cannot be incompatible with another understanding of it in which human values such as freedom, justice, rationality, and human rights are accorded a position of primacy.[238]

## Notes

1. William Grimes, 'Fathi Osman, Scholar of Islam, Dies at 82', *The New York Times*, 19 September 2010, available online at http://www.nytimes.com/2010/09/20/us/20osman.html?_r=1 (last accessed on 25 February 2011).
2. Elaine Woo, 'Fathi Osman Dies at 82; Voice for Modernism in Islam', *Los Angeles Times*, 15 September 2010, available online at http://articles.latimes.com/2010/sep/15/local/la-me-fathi-osman-20100915 (last accessed on 25 February 2011).
3. Fathi Osman, 'Islam in a Modern State: Democracy and the Concept of Shura', *Occasional Papers Series* (Washington: Center for Muslim-Christian

Understanding, Georgetown University, 2005 [2001]), pp. 1–22, p. 11 [hereafter cited as Osman, *Islam in a Modern State*'].
4. Ibid., p. 10; see also Fathi Osman, '*Shura* in Islamic Life', *Muslim Democrat* [*MD*], 1, 2 (September 1999): 6–7 (hereafter cited as Osman, *MD*).
5. Osman, '*Islam in a Modern State*', p. 10; Osman, *MD*, p. 6.
6. Osman, '*Islam in a Modern State*', pp. 10–11.
7. Fathi Osman, 'Shura and Democracy', in John J. Donohue and John L. Esposito (eds.), *Islam in Transition: Muslim Perspectives*, 2nd ed. (New York: Oxford University Press, 2007), pp. 288–295, p. 288; also cited in Tamara Sonn, 'Voices of Reformist Islam in the United States', in Shireen T. Hunter (ed.), *Reformist Voices of Islam—Mediating Islam and Modernity* (New Delhi: Pentagon Press, 2009) [ch. 9, pp. 267–286], p. 273.
8. Osman, '*Islam in a Modern State*', p. 12.
9. Ibid.
10. Ibid.
11. Muhammad Abduh and Rashid Rida, *Tafsir al-Qur'an al-Hakim* (*Tafsir al-Manar*), IV: 200–202; as cited in Osman, *loc. cit.*
12. See, Osman, '*Islam in a Modern State*', p. 13.
13. Sonn, in Hunter, *Reformist Voices*, p. 273.
14. Osman, '*Islam in a Modern State*', p. 19.
15. Fathi Osman, 'Islam Should be Recognized as Dynamic, Flexible Religion', *Al-Hewar Center* (Washington, DC), 6 May 1998, available online at http://www.alhewar.com/FathiOsman.html; also cited in Dr Mohammad Omar Farooq, 'Islam and Democracy: Perceptions and Misperceptions', 2002, available online at www.papers.ssrn.com/sol3/papers.cfm?abstract_id=1772541/ (last accessed on 20 August 2018).
16. For biography of Dr Israr Ahmed, see, 'Profile Introduction', available online at http://www.drisrarahmed.com/; 'Renowned Religious Scholar Dr Israr Ahmed Passes Away', *Daily Times* (Pakistan), 15 April 2010, http://www.dailytimes.com.pk/default.asp?page=2010%5C04%5C15%5Cstory_15-4-2010_pg13_7 (last accessed on 14 June 2011); 'Prominent Scholar Dr Israr Ahmed Dies', *Dawn*, 15 April, retrieved from http://www.dawn.com/news/857508/prominent-scholar-dr-israr-ahmed-dies (last accessed on 14 June 2021).
17. See, 'Profile Introduction', *op. cit.*
18. Mahan Mirza, 'Ahmad, Israr (1932–2010)', in Gerhard Bowering et al. (eds.), *The Princeton Encyclopedia of Islamic Political Thought* (Princeton and Oxford: Princeton University Press, 2013), pp. 23–24.
19. Israr Ahmed, *Khilafah in Pakistan: What, Why & How?* compiled by Shoba Samo Basr (Lahore: Markazi Anjuman Khuddam-Ul-Qur'an, 2006 [2001]), pp. 7–19.
20. Ibid., p. 7.
21. These passages, quoted by Dr Israr, read as: 'The republican form of government is not only thoroughly consistent with the spirit of Islam, but has also become a necessity in view of the new forces that are set free in the world of Islam'; 'The

transfer of the power of *Ijtihad* from individual representatives of schools to a Muslim legislative assembly which, in view of the growth of opposing sects, is the only possible form *Ijma'* can take in modern times'. See, Iqbal, *The Reconstruction*, pp. 125, 138.
22. Ahmed, *Khilafah in Pakistan*, p. 7.
23. Ibid., p. 8.
24. Ibid.
25. Ibid., p. 9.
26. Ibid.
27. Ibid.
28. Ibid.
29. Ibid.
30. Israr Ahmed, *Bayan-al-Qur'an* (Lahore: Qur'an Academy, 2010), vol. 6, p. 328 (also available, online, in pdf, at http://www.tanzeem.org).
31. Ibid., p. 8.
32. 'DEMOCRACY and THEOCRACY and why is VOTING … SHIRK?', Video lecture by Dr Israr Ahmed, available online at http://www.youtube.com/watch?v=mixU9H2zWAw (last accessed on 14 June 2011).
33. Ahmed, *Khilafah in Pakistan*, p. 8.
34. Ahmed, *Bayan-al-Qur'an*, vol. 2, p. 46.
35. Ibid.
36. Ahmed, *Khilafah in Pakistan*, p. 12.
37. Ibid., pp. 11–12.
38. M. Faisal Awan, 'Discussions on Democracy and Islamic States: A Study on the Discourses of Mawdudi, Israr Ahmed, and Ghamidi', in Lütfi Sunar (ed.), *The Routledge International Handbook of Contemporary Muslim Socio-Political Thought* (New York and London: Routledge, 2021), pp. 401–413.
39. Ibid., p. 408.
40. Ahmed, *Khilafah in Pakistan*, p. 12.
41. Ibid.
42. For details, see www.csss-isla.com/about-us/dr-asghar-ali-engineer and http://andromeda.rutgers.edu/~rtavakol/engineer/about.htm (last accessed on 10 May 2021); Asghar Ali Engineer, *A Living Faith: My Quest for Peace, Harmony and Social Change* (New Delhi: Oriental Blackswan, 2011); Hilal Ahmed, 'Asghar Ali Engineer (1939–2013): Emancipatory Intellectual Politics', *Economic & Political Weekly* [EPW], XLVIII, 22 (1 June 2013): 20–22; Imtiyaz Yusuf, 'Asghar Ali Engineer', in Zayn R. Kassam, Yudit Kornberg Greenberg, and Jehan Bagli (eds.), *Islam, Judaism, and Zoroastrianism* (Dordrecht, Netherlands: Springer, 2018), pp. 78–81.
43. Hassan in Hunter, *op. cit.*, p. 179.
44. Yusuf, in Kassam et al., *op. cit.*, pp. 78, 80.
45. Ahmed in *EPW*, p. 20.

46. For details on IIS, CSSS, and about biography of Engineer, see www.csss-isla.com/institute-of-islamic-studies, www.csss-isla.com/about-us and www.csss-isla.com/about-us/dr-asghar-ali-engineer (last accessed on 10 May 2021).
47. Parray in *IMS*, 2012, pp. 23–29; Idem., *AJISS*, 2012, pp. 149–151.
48. Yusuf, in Kassam et al., *op. cit.*, p. 79. Yusuf bases his assessment on these works of Engineer: Asghar Ali Engineer, *Islam and Liberation Theology: Essays on Liberative Elements in Islam* (New Delhi: Stosius Inc./Advent Books Division, 1990); Idem., *A Rational Approach to Islam*, 1st ed. (Haryana: Hope India Publications, 2001); Idem., *On Developing Theology of Peace in Islam* (New Delhi: Sterling Publishers Pvt. Ltd., [2005] 2003), p. 82.
49. Yoginder Sikand, 'Asghar Ali Engineer's Quest for an Islamic Theology of Peace and Religious Pluralism', 15 November 2006, available at http://www.svabhinava.org/MeccaBenares/YoginderSikand/AsgharAliEngineerIslamicTheology-frame.php (last accessed on 10 May 2021); also cited in Hassan in Hunter, *op. cit.*, p. 180.
50. Asghar Ali Engineer, *Islam: Challenges in 21st Century* (New Delhi: Gyan Publishing House, 2004), p. 213.
51. Ibid., pp. 213–214.
52. Engineer, *On Developing Theology of Peace in Islam*, p. 82.
53. Ibid., pp. 86–87.
54. Asghar Ali Engineer, 'Islam and Secularism', in Ibrahim M. Abu-Rabi' (ed.), *The Blackwell Companion to Contemporary Islamic Thought* (Oxford, UK: Blackwell Publishing Ltd., 2006), ch. 20, pp. 338–344, p. 340.
55. Asghar Ali Engineer, 'Islam and Secularism', in John J. Donohue and John L. Esposito (ed.), *Islam in Transition: Muslim Perspectives*, 2nd ed. (New York: Oxford University Press, 2007), pp. 136–142, pp. 137–138 [adopted from Engineer's *Rational Approach to Islam* (New Delhi: Gyan Publishing House, 2001), pp. 43–52].
56. Asghar Ali Engineer, 'What I Believe', http://andromeda.rutgers.edu/~rtavakol/engineer/belief.htm (last accessed on 10 May 2021). Originally published in *Islam and Modern Age* (July 1999), a quarterly journal of Zakir Hussain Institute of Islamic Studies, *Jamia Milia Islamia*, New Delhi.
57. Engineer, in Abu-Rabi', *op. cit.*, pp. 343–344.
58. Asghar Ali Engineer, 'Islam, Democracy and Violence', in *Indian Muslims*, 4 September 2008, available online at http://indianmuslims.in/islam-democracy-and-violence/ (last accessed on 10 May 2011).
59. Engineer, in Donohue and Esposito (ed.), *Islam in Transition*, p. 141.
60. Ibid., pp. 139–141.
61. Ibid., pp. 141, 142.
62. Engineer, *Islam*, p. 214; Engineer, *On Developing Theology*, p. 89.
63. Shirin Ebadi, 'Islam, Democracy, and Human Rights', Lecture, Syracuse University, 10 May 2004, published in *Syracuse University News*, 12 May 2004; as cited in Hashemi, *Islam Secularism, and Liberal Democracy*, p. 101.

64. Mawlana Wahiduddin Khan has written over 200 books on Islam as well as commentary on the Quran—*Tadhkir al-Qur'an*—and it has been translated into English as well. Some of his prominent books are: *The Prophet of Peace; The Quran A New Translation; A Treasury of the Quran; Tazkirul/Tadhkirul Qur'an; Indian Muslims: The Need for a Positive Outlook; Introducing Islam: A Simple Introduction to Islam; Islam Rediscovered: Discovering Islam from Its Original Sources; Islam and Peace; Islam: Creator of the Modern Age; Words of the Prophet Muhammad; The Ideology of Peace; God Arises; Muhammad: The Prophet for All Humanity*; etc. For his obituary, see Tauseef Ahmad Parray, 'A Thinker in the Eyes of Scholars', *Greater Kashmir*, 29 April 2021, p. 5.
65. Irfan A. Omar, 'Islamic Thought in Contemporary India: The Impact of Mawlana Wahiduddin Khan's al-Risala Movement' in Abu-Rabi, *op. cit.* (ch. 4, pp. 75–87), p. 76.
66. Ibid., p. 78.
67. Ibid., p. 85.
68. Mawlana Wahiduddin Khan, *God Arises* (New Delhi: Goodword Books, 2005), p. 37.
69. Ibid., p. 198.
70. Mawlana Wahiduddin Khan, *Islam: Creator of the Modern Age* (New Delhi: The Islamic Centre, 1993), p. 172 [hereafter cited as Khan, *Islam*].
71. Mawlana Wahiduddin Khan, 'The Concept of Democracy in Islam', *Insights*, 19 December 2002, available online at http://www.jammu-kashmir.com/insights/insight20021219a.html (last accessed on 15 October 2011).
72. Khan, *Islam*, p. 156.
73. Ibid., p. 173.
74. Ibid., p. 160.
75. Ibid., p. 174.
76. Rajat Malhotra, 'Democracy—An Islamic Perspective', *Salaam—Quarterly to Promote Understanding*, 37, 4 (October 2016): 178–188, p. 180.
77. Ibid., p. 188.
78. Mawlana Wahiduddin Khan, *Din-o-Shariat: Din-e Islam Ka Ek Fikri Muta'ala* [Religion and Law: An Intellectual Study of the Religion of Islam] (New Delhi: Goodword Books, 2004 [2002]), pp. 204–250. This part is a translation of a section from the chapter titled as *Taqlid Aur Ijtihad* (pp. 224–228) translated by Yoginder Sikand as 'Taqlid, Ijtihad and Democracy', 19 October 2008, available online at *Sharia Laws*, www.shariahlaws.blogspot.com/2008/10/taqlid-ijtihad-and-democracy.html?m=1 (last accessed on 25 December 2021).
79. Ibid., p. 227.
80. Ibid., pp. 227–228.
81. For details, see, 'Ijithad ki Ahmiyyat' (Significance of Independent Reasoning) and 'Fikr-I Islami ki Tashkil-i-Jadid' (The Reconstruction of Islamic Thought) in Wahiduddin Khan, *Fikr-e-Islami: Afkar-i Islami ki Tashrih wa Tawdih* (New Delhi: Goodword Books/Al-Risala Books, 2013 [1998]), pp. 20–30, 31–95.

82. Ibid., p. 32, also cited in Muhammad Qasim Zaman, *The Ulama in Contemporary Islam: Custodians of Change* (Princeton and Oxford: Princeton University Press, 2002), p. 182.
83. Ibid., p. 227.
84. Ibid., p. 228.
85. For details see, 'Former Diplomat Sadek Sulaiman Passes Away', *Muscat Daily*, 28 July 2021, retrieved from www.pressreader.com/oman/muscat-daily/20210728/28206789967721 (last accessed on 22 December 2021).
86. For details, see, 'We Lost a Great Mind: Omani Thinker Sadiq Suleiman Dies at 90', *The Arabian Stories*, 28 July 2021, retrieved from https://www.thearabianstories.com/2021/07/28/we-lost-a-great-mind-omani-thinker-sadiq-jawad-suleiman-dies-at-90/ (last accessed on 22 December 2021).
87. For details about *Al-Hewar*, see www.alhewar.com/About%20Us.html (last accessed on 20 December 2021).
88. Sulaiman, 'Democracy and Shura', in Kurzman (ed.), *Liberal Islam*, pp. 96–98.
89. Parray *in JMEISA*, 2012, pp. 68–71; Idem., *AJISS*, 2012, pp. 146–147; Idem., *Roundtable*, pp. 78.
90. Hussein Ghubash, *Oman—The Islamic Democratic Tradition*, translated from French by Mary Turton (Oxon, RN and New York: Routledge, 2006).
91. Sulaiman, in Kurzman (ed.), *Liberal Islam*, pp. 96–98. Translated from the Arabic by Dale F. Eickelman.
92. Sulaiman, in Kurzman, *Liberal Islam*, p. 97.
93. Ibid., p. 98.
94. Ibid., p. 97.
95. Ibid., p. 97.
96. Sadek Jawad Sulaiman, 'Religion, Democracy, and the Arabs' View of America', A Presentation made at *Hull University* (UK), 24 November 2003, retrieved from http://www.alhewar.net/Basket/sadek_sulaiman_religion_democracy_arabs_view_of_america.htm (last accessed on 15 December 2021).
97. Ibid.
98. Sulaiman, 'The Shura Principle in Islam', *op. cit.*
99. Ibid.
100. Ibid.
101. Ibid.
102. Ibid.
103. Ibid.
104. Ibid.
105. Parray *in JMEISA*, 2012, p.71; Idem., *AJISS*, 2012, p. 147.
106. Parray, in *Roundtable*, p. 8; Idem., *WJIHC* (2012), p. 77.
107. Ana Belén Soage, 'Shaykh Yusuf al-Qaradawi: Portrait of a Leading Islamic Cleric', *Middle East Review of International Affairs* [*MERIA*], 12, 1 (2008): 51–68, p. 51; Idem., 'Sheikh Yusuf al-Qaradawi: Moderate Voice from the Muslim World?', *Religion Compass*, 4, 9 (2010): 563–575, p. 563; Hafijur Rahman,

'Toward a Wise Political Fiqh: The Perception of State in the Political Thought of Yusuf al-Qaradawi', *ASBIDER—Akademi Sosyal Bilimler Dergisi*, 7, 21 (2020): 6–22, p. 6. See also, Sagi Polka, *Shaykh Yusuf al-Qaradawi: Spiritual Mentor of Wasati Salafism* (Syracuse, NY: Syracuse University Press, 2019); Usaama Al-Azami, *Islam and Arab Revolutions—The Ulama between Democracy and Autocracy* (London: Hurst & Co.; New York: Oxford University Press, 2021).

108. Samuel Helfont, *Yusuf al-Qaradawi, Islam and Modernity* (Tel Aviv, Israel: The Moshe Dayan Center, Tel Aviv University, 2009), p. 13.
109. Rahman, in *ASBIDER*, p. 6.
110. Yusuf al-Qaradawi, *State in Islam*, 3rd Ed. (Cairo: Al-Falah Foundation for Translation, Publication and Distribution, 2004). The book is originally in Arabic: *Min Fiqh al-Dawla fi al-Islam* (Cairo: Dar al-Shurouk, 2001 [1997]).
111. Rahman, in *ASBIDER*, pp. 8–9.
112. Qaradawi, *State in Islam*, p. 44.
113. Rahman, in *ASBIDER*, p. 17.
114. Yusuf al-Qaradawi, *Priorities of the Islamic Movement in the Coming Phase* (Cairo: Al-Dar, 1992), available online at https://www.islambasics.com/book/priorities-of-the-islamic-movement-in-the-coming-phase (last accessed on 20 August 2018) [hereinafter cited as Qaradawi, *Priorities*].
115. See, ch. 6, 'The Islamic Movement at Political and World levels', of Qaradawi's *Priorities, op. cit.*
116. Ibid.
117. Ibid.
118. Yusuf al-Qaradawi, 'Muslim World Needs Democracy', *The Muslim News* (Monthly Newspaper, UK), 8 July 2006, available online at http://www.muslimnews.co.uk/news/news.php?article=11311 (last accessed on 5 September 2010).
119. Al-Qaradawi, *State in Islam*, p. 204.
120. Ibid., pp. 204–205; Samia Rahman and Muhammad Qasim Zaman have abridged this statement as: 'we have the right to borrow from others whatever ideas, methods, and systems might be beneficial to us as long as they do not contradict the clear dictates of the foundational texts or the established principles of the shari'a[h]'. For details, see, Yuauf al-Qaradawi, 'Islam and Democracy', in *Princeton Readings in Islamist Thought: Texts and Contexts from al-Banna to Bin Laden*, Edited and Introduced by Roxanne L. Euben and Muhammad Qasim Zaman (Princeton: Princeton University Press, 2009), ch. 9, pp. 230–245, p. 237 [hereafter cited as Qaradawi, in Euben and Zaman].
121. al-Qaradawi, *State in Islam*, pp. 193–194. *Cf.* Qaradawi, in Euben and Zaman, *op. cit.*, p. 232. Zaman has translated this passage as: 'The essence of democracy—regardless of academic definitions and terminology—is that people choose who rules over them and manages their affairs; that no ruler or regime they dislike is forced upon them; that they have right to call the ruler to account if he errs and to remove him from office in case of misconduct; and that people are not forced in economic, social, cultural or political directions that

they recognize nor accept, such that if someone were to protest or oppose this, he would be punished or frightened off, tortured, even killed. This is the real essence of democracy....'

122. al-Qaradawi, *State in Islam*, p. 203. See also, Qaradawi, in Euben and Zaman, *op. cit.*, p. 236.
123. al-Qaradawi, *op. cit.*, p. 207; Cf. Qaradawi, in Euben and Zaman, *op. cit.*, p. 238 where they translate/rephrase this statement as: 'The assertion that democracy signifies the rule of the people by the people, and that this entails a rejection of the principle that sovereignty belongs to God, is not an acceptable view. For the principle of popular rule, which is the foundation of democracy, stands in opposition not to God's rule—the basis of Islamic law—but rather to the rule of the individual, which is the basis of dictatorship. A call for democracy does not necessitate a rejection of God's sovereignty over human beings. Indeed, this does not even occur to most people calling for democracy'.
124. al-Qaradawi, *State in Islam*, p. 208; Qaradawi, in Euben and Zaman, *op. cit.*, p. 238.
125. al-Qaradawi, *State in Islam*, p. 209. Euben and Zaman, *op. cit.*, p. 239 have translated these statements as: 'I would like to emphasize here that the principle of God's sovereignty (*al-hakimiyya li'llah*), is a genuine Islamic principle, affirmed by all jurists in their discourses on Islamic government and on the [position of] the ruler.... The sovereignty of God over all creatures is indisputable, then. This sovereignty is of two kinds. The first is 'universal' and determinative' (*hakimiyya kawniyya qadariyya*) ... [which] evidently means a determinative sovereignty over the cosmos rather than a legislative sovereignty. The second kind of sovereignty relates to legislation and commands (*hakimiyya tashri'yya amriyya*), that is, the authority to impose legal obligations, to command and to forbid, to make things binding or a matter of choice'.
126. al-Qaradawi, *op. cit.*, p. 209. Cf. Qaradawi, in Euben and Zaman, *op. cit.*, p. 239.
127. Sheikh Yusuf al-Qaradawi, *Ash-Sharq al-Awsat*, London, 5 February 1990, as cited by Khan in *Islamic Democratic Discourse*, p. xi; and Murad Hoffman, 'Democracy or Shuracracy', in John J. Donohue and John L. Esposito (ed.), *Islam in Transition: Muslim Perspectives*, 2nd ed. (New York: Oxford University Press, 2007), p. 296. See also Yusuf al-Qaradawi, 'Islam's Approach Towards Democracy', *The Message International*, April/May 2002, pp. 32–33, retrieved from www.messageonline.org/2002aprilmay/cover1.htm (last accessed on 10 May 2018).
128. Qaradawi, *Priorities, op. cit.*
129. al-Qaradawi, *State in Islam*, p. 218. Qaradawi, in Euben and Zaman, *op. cit.*, p. 244.
130. al-Qaradawi, *State in Islam*, p. 220. Qaradawi, in Euben and Zaman, *op. cit.*, p. 244.
131. See 'Professor Khursheed Ahmad', in Alam, *op. cit.*, pp. 295–297; Esposito and Voll, *Makers of Contemporary Islam*, p. 39.

132. See, for example, Parray, *AJISS*, 2010, pp. 14–15; Idem., *Roundtable*, p. 6; Idem., *AJISS*, 2012, 151–153.
133. Khurshid Ahmad, *The Religion of Islam* (Lahore: Islamic Publications Ltd., 1967), pp. 6–7; Idem., 'Islam: Basic Principles and Characteristics', in Khurshid Ahmad (ed.), *Islam: Its Meaning and Message*, 3rd ed. (London: Islamic Foundation, 1999 [1975]), pp. 27–30.
134. Ahmad, 'Islam: Basic Principles and Characteristics', in *IIMM, op. cit.*, p. 31.
135. Ibid., pp. 33–34.
136. Ibid., pp. 35, 36, 38.
137. Ibid., pp. 34, 37.
138. Ibid., p. 42.
139. Ibid., pp. 42–43.
140. Ibid., p. 43.
141. Ahmad, *IIMM*, fn. 24, p. 160.
142. Ahmad, *MW*, p. 19.
143. Ibid., p. 20.
144. Ibid., p. 13.
145. Ibid., pp. 11–13.
146. Khurshid Ahmad, Key Note Address on 'Economics, Islam, and Democracy', *CSID* (USA) (April 2000); reproduced in *Muslim Democrat*, 2, 2 (June, 2000): 5, 7.
147. Khurshid Ahmad and Mahmood Ahmad Ghazi, 'Religion, State and Society', *Policy Perspectives*, 5, 1 (January–June 2011), available online at http://www.ips.org.pk/islamic-thoughts/995-religion-state-and-society.html (last accessed on 15 June 2021).
148. Ibid.
149. Ibid.
150. See, Parray, *AJISS*, 2012, pp. 152–153.
151. Hassan in Hunter, *op. cit.*, 173–174.
152. Muhammad Khalid Masud, *Shatibi's Philosophy of Islamic Law*, Revised Ed. (Islamabad, Pakistan: Islamic Research Institute, 1995).
153. Hassan in Hunter, *op. cit.*, pp.173–175; Tauseef Ahmad Parray, 'Debates on Tradition and Modernity in the Subcontinent', in Lütfi Sunar (ed.), *The Routledge International Handbook of Contemporary Muslim Socio-Political Thought* (New York and London: Routledge, 2021): 59–72, p. 67.
154. Muhammad Khalid Masud, 'Defining Democracy in Islamic Polity', paper presented in the International Conference on *The Future of Islam, Democracy, and Authoritarianism in the Era of Globalization*, 5–6 December 2004, International Centre for Islam and Pluralism, Jakarta (Indonesia). Available at http://www.maruf.org/?p=69 (last accessed on 25 May 2011). This essay is also published in *ICIP Journal*, 2, 2 (2005): 1–11 [hereafter cited as Masud, 'Defining Democracy']. This essay has been referred and cited, among others, by Hassan, in Hunter, *op. cit.*, pp. 173–175; Husnul Amin, 'Post-Islamist Intellectual

Trends in Pakistan: Javed Ahmad Ghamidi and His Discourse on Islam and Democracy', *Islamic Studies* [IS], 51, 2 (2012): 169–192, pp. 169, 175–176 [hereafter cited as Amin in *IS*] . In this work, references are given from the draft (available online, 14 pages) presented in the above-mentioned conference and hence the page numbering is given of the said draft.

155. Muhammad Khalid Masud, 'Islam and Democracy in Pakistan', in Maqsudul Hasan Nuri, Muhammad Hanif, and Muhammad Nawaz Kahn (eds.), *Islam and State: Practice and Perceptions in Pakistan and the Contemporary Muslim World* (Islamabad: Islamabad Policy Research Institute, 2012), pp. 19–41.
156. Muhammad Khalid Masud, 'Religion and State Are Twin Brothers: Classical Muslim Political Theory', *Islam and Civilizational Renewal* (ICR), 9, 1 (2018): 9–26.
157. Hassan in Hunter, *op. cit.*, p. 174.
158. Ibid., pp. 173–175; Parray, in Sunar, *op. cit.*, pp. 67–68.
159. Muhammad Khalid Masud, 'Islamic Modernism', in Muhammad Khalid Masud, Alamond Salvatore, and M. Bruinessen (eds.), *Islam and Modernity: Key Issues and Debates* (Edinburgh, Scotland: Edinburgh University Press, 2009), pp. 237–260, p. 257.
160. Ibid., pp. 237–238.
161. Ibid., p. 238; also cited in Parray, in Sunar, *op. cit.*, p. 68.
162. Masud, 'Defining Democracy', p. 1.
163. Ibid.
164. Ibid., pp. 1–2.
165. Martin Kramer, 'Islam vs. Democracy', *Commentary* (magazine, New York), January 1993, pp. 35–42. This is the version revised for republication in Martin Kramer, *Arab Awakening and Islamic Revival* (New Brunswick, NJ: Transaction Publishers, 1996), pp. 265–278, available at http://www.martinkramer.org/sandbox/reader/archives/islam-vs-democracy/ (last accessed on 27 May 2011). Kramer's position, and his argument, is that Muslims cannot be democratic unless they give up Islam. For him, majority opinion, elections, participation of the masses do not count as ingredients of democracy.
166. Khalifa Abdul Hakim, *The Prophet and His Message* (Lahore: Institute of Islamic Culture, 1987), argues that the question about the compatibility of democracy with Islam continues to be problematic not because Islam is not favourable, but because democracy is not definable. For him, democracy is problematic to define in the West and in the Muslim world as well. He concludes that Islam's original vision calls for democracy.
167. Islahi, *Islami Riyasat* (trans.) *The Islamic State, op. cit.*, is of the opinion that an Islamic state (*Khilafah*) is different from western system of democracy, and as such, both parliamentary and presidential systems, as currently in vogue, against Islam.
168. Tayyib, *Fitri Hukumat* (Natural State), pp. 219–220 states that the government on earth is *Khilafat* (deputy of God), which establishes a system of government

on the pattern of the Divine natural state. Islamic caliphate is distinct from all other systems because in these systems, humans assume the Divine authority. Islamic system of government also differs from others in the following aspects. *Cf.* Masud, in *ICR*, p. 20.
169. Amin in *IS*, p. 191.
170. Masud, 'Defining Democracy', p. 12.
171. Ibid., p. 13.
172. Ibid., p. 14.
173. Ibid., p. 12. See also, M. Taufiqurrahman, 'Islam Compatible with Democracy, Scholars Say', in *The Jakarta Post*, Tuesday, 12 July 2004, available online at http://www.thejakartapost.com/news/2004/12/07/islam-compatible-democracy-scholars-say.html (last accessed on 25 June 2011).
174. Taufiqurrahman, *op. cit.*
175. Ibid., p. 13. *Cf.* Abdul Hakim, *The Prophet and His Message, op. cit.*
176. Masud, 'Islam and Democracy in Pakistan', p. 20, puts it as: 'No doubt, there are several other factors having impact on the progress of democracy in Pakistan but obviously religious arguments. Even though all the religious political parties are part of the democratic system in Pakistan yet they are foremost in expressing reservations against this system'.
177. Touqir Hussain, 'Islam and Pakistan', in Hua, *op. cit.*, p. 111 [ch. 4, pp. 89–118].
178. Parray in *WJIHC*, 2012, pp. 78–80; Idem., 'Islam-Democracy Discourse vis-à-vis the Arab Spring', in Erdoğan & Çoban (eds.), *Metamorphosis of the Arab World*, pp. 39–64; Idem., 'Islam-Democracy Discourse in the Twenty-First Century', in Mercan (ed.), *Transformation of Muslim World in the 21st Century*, pp. 63–84.
179. See 'Rashid al-Ghannoushi: Activist in Exile', in John L. Esposito and John O. Voll, *Makers of Contemporary Islam* (New York: Oxford University Press, 2001), p.117 (ch. 9, pp. 91–117) [hereafter cited as Esposito and Voll, *MCI*].
180. Azzam S. Tamimi, *Rachid Ghannouchi: A Democrat Within Islamism* (New York: Oxford University Press, Inc., 2001) [hereafter cited as Tamimi, *Rachid Ghannouchi*).
181. Mohammad Dawood Sofi, *Rashid al-Ghannushi: A Key Muslim Thinker of the 21st Century* (New York: Palgrave Macmillan, 2018).
182. Hafijur Rahman, 'The Perception of Muslim Democracy in the Political Thought of Rachid Ghannouchi', *Akademik Hassasiyetler/The Academic Elegance*, 8, 15 (2021): 361–376, p. 361.
183. See 'Rachid al-Ghannouchi', in Alam, *op. cit.*, pp. 97–100.
184. Sofi, *Rashid al-Ghannushi*, p. 82.
185. Rahman, in *The Academic Elegance*, p. 362.
186. Tamimi, *Rachid Ghannouchi*, p. vi.
187. Esposito and Voll, *MCI*, p. 113.
188. Rahman, in *The Academic Elegance*, p. 365.

189. Rashid al-Ghanushi, *al-Hurriyya al-Amma fi al-Dawla al-Islamiyyah* [Civil Liberties in an Islamic State] (Beirut: Markaz Dirasat al-Waḥdah al-'Arabiyyah, 1993).
190. Ibid., p. 77, as cited in Sofi, *Rashid al-Ghannushi*, p. 83.
191. Esposito and Voll, *MCI*, pp. 113–114.
192. Tamimi, *Rachid Ghannouchi*, p. 99.
193. *London Observer*, 19 January 1992; see also Esposito and Voll, *MCI*, p. 114.
194. Ghanushi, *al-Hurriyya*, p. 108, as cited in Sofi, *Rashid al-Ghannushi*, p. 85.
195. Rachid Ghannoushi, Interview with Esposito and Voll, London, 5 February 1993; as cited by Esposito and Voll, *loc. cit.*
196. Bustamir Khir, 'An Islamic Critique and Alternative of Democracy', *The Islamic Quarterly*, 47, 1 (2003): 73–79, p. 74.
197. Ghannoushi, Interview; as cited by Esposito and Voll, *loc. cit.*
198. Rachid Ghannouchi, 'Islam and Freedom Can Be Friends', *The Observer* (London), 19 January 1992, p. 18; as cited by Tamimi, *op. cit.*, pp. 89–90; Esposito and Voll, *MCI*, p. 114. Here it is pertinent to mention that John L. Esposito, in his *Unholy War: Terror in the Name of Islam* (New York: Oxford University Press, 2001), p. 146, puts it (a bit differently) as: 'If by democracy is meant the liberal model of government prevailing in the West, a system under which the people freely choose their representatives and leaders, in which there is an alternation of power and in which civil liberties and human rights are guaranteed, Muslims will find nothing in their religion to prevent them from applying democracy'.
199. Robin B. Wright, 'Two Visions of Reformation', in Diamond et al., *op. cit.*, p. 230 (ch. 22, pp. 220–231). Originally published in *Journal of Democracy*, 7, 2 (April 1996): 64–75. References are here given from the book.
200. Wright, *op. cit.*, p. 229.
201. Rachid al-Ghannushi, 'Self-Criticism and Reconsideration', *Palestine Times*, 94, 1999, as quoted in Graham E. Fuller, *The Future of Political Islam* (New York: Palgrave Macmillan, 2003), p. 61.
202. Rashid al-Ghanushi, 'Hukm Musharakat al-Islamiyyin fi Nizam Ghayr Islami', in 'Azam al-Tamimi (ed.), *Musharakat al-Islamiyyin fi al-Sulta* (London: Liberty for the Muslim World, 1994).
203. Ghanushi in Tamimi, pp. 16–17, as cited by Shavit, *op. cit.*, p. 356.
204. Sofi, *Rashid al-Ghannushi*, p. 109.
205. Ibid., pp. 109–110.
206. Ibid., p. 89.
207. Rahman, in *The Academic Elegance*, p. 367.
208. Tamimi, *Rachid Ghannouchi*, p. 200.
209. For details, see Maydan Editors, 'An Interview with Abdulaziz Sachedina on His Life and Scholarship', *The Maydan*, 13 September 2017, available at www.themaydan.com/2017/09/interview-abdulaziz-sachedina-life-scholarship/ (last accessed on 20 August 2018); see also Sachedina's profile at *GMU*'s

website at www.religioustsudies.gmu.edu/people/asachedi (last accessed on 20 December 2021).
210. Sonn, in Hunter, *Reformist Voices*, p. 274.
211. Abdulaziz Sachedina, *The Islamic Roots of Democratic Pluralism* (New York: Oxford University Press, 2001); See also, Tauseef Ahmad Parray, 'Muslim Reformist Thought in 21st Century and its Broad Themes: A Brief Study of 'Democratic Pluralism' in the light of A. Sachedina's *The Islamic Roots of Democratic Pluralism*', *Islam and Muslim Societies*, 4, 2, (June 2011): 12 pp., available at www.muslimsocieties.org
212. Parray in *PoV*, pp. 4–5.
213. Ibid., p. 5.
214. Abdulaziz Sachedina, 'Why Democracy and Why Now?', in Donohue and Esposito, *op. cit.*, p. 308.
215. Abdulaziz Sachedina, 'The Role of Islam in the Public Square: Guidance or Governance?', in Khan, *Islamic Democratic Discourse*, ch. 9, pp. 173–192.
216. Ibid., p. 174.
217. Sonn, in Hunter, *Reformist Voices*, p. 275.
218. Sachedina, in Donohue and Esposito, p. 308.
219. Abdulaziz Sachedina, 'Muslim Intellectuals and the Struggle for Democracy', *Global Dialogue*, 6, 1–2 (Winter/Spring 2004): 79–87, p. 81 (special issue on *Islam and Democracy*), available online at http://www.worlddialogue.org/content.php?id=301 (last accessed on 15 May 2011).
220. Ibid.
221. Ibid., p. 84.
222. See, for example, Parray in *JMEISA*, 2013, pp. 51–52.
223. Wright, *op. cit.*, p. 224.
224. See, Valla Vakili, 'Abdolkarim Soroush and Critical discourse in Iran', in Esposito and Voll, *MCI*, pp. 150–176. This is a revised version of Vakili's *Debating Religion and Politics in Iran: The Political Thought of Abdolkarim Soroush* (New York: Council on Foreign Relations, January 1996), available online at http://www.drsoroush.com/PDF/E-CMO-19960100-Debating_Religion_and_Politics_in_Iran-Valla_Vakili.pdf (last accessed on 12 March 2011). For this viewpoint of Soroush, Vakili quotes from the following sources: 'Arkan-i Farhangi-yi Dimukrasi' [The Cultural Pillars of Democracy], in *Farbih-tar az Idiuluji*, 269–272; and 'Mabani Tiorik-i Libiralizm' [The Theoretical Bases of Liberalism], in Abdolkarim Soroush, *Razdani va Raushanfikri va Dindari* [Augury and Intellectualism and Pietism], 2nd ed. (Tehran: Mu'assassah-yi Farhangi-yi Sirat, 1993), pp. 153–154. For an early discussion on democracy in the context of the Islamic Republic, see 'Musahabah-yi Duktur Surush ba Ustad Shahid Piramun-i Jumhuri Islami' [Dr Soroush's Interview with the Martyred Professor on the Islamic Republic], in Murtaza Mutahhari, *Piramun-i Inqilab-i Islami* [On the Islamic Revolution], 15th ed. (Tehran: Intisharat-i Sadra, 1995), pp. 125–141.

225. See, Mehran Kamrava, 'Introduction: Reformist Islam in Comparative Perspective', in Kamrava, *op. cit.*, p. 4.
226. 'Democracy and Rationality: An interview with Abdolkarim Soroush', *Shargh* (Daily Newspaper, Tehran, Iran), December 2003, translated by Nilou Mobasser, vide http://www.drsoroush.com, available online at http://www.drsoroush.com/English/Interviews/E-INT-20031200-1.htm (last accessed on 12 March 2011).
227. Abdulkarim Soroush, 'Democracy Is Not Summarized in Elections', Interview with *Sharqh*, Daily Newspaper, 109, 7 (January 2004), p. 4; vide http://www.drsoroush.com, available online at http://www.drsoroush.com/English/Interviews/E-INT-20040107-Sharq_Newspaper.html (last accessed on 15 March 2011).
228. Abdolkarim Soroush, 'Mudara va Mudiriyat-i Mu'minan, Sukhani dar Nisbat-i-Din va Dimukrasi' [The Tolerance and Administration of the Faithful, a Talk on the Relationship between Religion and Democracy], *Kiyan*, 4, 21 (1994): 4, as cited by Vakili, *op. cit.*, p. 161; Parray in *JMEISA*, 2013, p. 52.
229. For this, see Abdolkarim Soroush, *Hukumat-i Dimukratik-i Dini* [Religious Democratic State], as discussed in Forough Jahanbakhsh, *Islam, Democracy and Religious Modernism in Iran (1953–2000): From Bazargan to Soroush* (Leiden, Boston, Koln: Brill, 2001), pp. 154 ff.; Ali Mirsepassi, *Democracy in Modern Iran: Islam, Culture, and Political Change* (New York and London: New York University Press, 2010), pp. 87–90.
230. Forough Jahanbakhsh 'Abdolkarim Soroush: New "Revival of Religious Sciences"', *ISIM Newsletter*, 8 (2001), p. 21, available online at https://openaccess.leidenuniv.nl/bitstream/handle/1887/17496/ISIM_8_Abdolkarim_Soroush_New_Revival_of_Religious_Sciences.pdf?sequence=1
231. Abdolkarim Soroush, 'Bawar-i Dim, Dawar-i Dini' [Religious Belief, Religious Arbitrator] (1994), pp. 50–52; Idem., 'Tahlil-i Mafhum-i Hukumat-i Dini' [Analysis of the Concept of Religious Government], *Kiyan* 6, 2 (1996): p. 6, as cited in Jahanbakhsh, *Islam, Democracy and Religious Modernism*, pp. 156–157.
232. Jahanbakhsh, *Islam, Democracy and Religious Modernism*, p. 158. These views are based on following works of Soroush: 'Tahlil-i Mafhum ... ', pp. 11–13; 'Mudara wa Mudmyat-i Mu'minan: Sukhanf dar Nisbat-i Din wa Dimukrasi' [The Tolerance and Administration of the Faithful: A Remark on the Relation Between Religion and Democracy], *Kiyan*, 4, 21 (1994): pp. 11–12.
233. Vide Khan, *Islamic Democratic Discourse*, p. 166.
234. Mirsepassi, *Democracy in Modern Iran*, p. 87.
235. Ibid. Mirsepassi bases his views on Abdulkarim Soroush, *Farbeh tar az* [Loftier than Ideology] (Tehran: Saraat Press, 1997), pp. 259, 271.
236. Soroush, *Farbeh*, p. 279, as cited in Mirsepassi, *Democracy in Modern Iran*, p. 88.
237. Mirsepassi, *loc. cit.*
238. Jahanbakhsh, *Islam, Democracy and Religious Modernism*, p. 159.

# 6
# Twenty-First Century Muslim Thinkers on Islam–Democracy Compatibility—II

The relationship between Islam, democracy, and democratization—as was highlighted in the previous chapters as well—is a very important element in the contemporary political dynamics of the Muslim world. Elaborating further, as an augmentation of, the discussions set forth in the previous chapter—i.e. to present Islam–democracy compatibility discourse in the light of the views and observations of some of the globally reputed twenty-first-century intellectuals (academicians, political leaders/activists, and analysts)—the persuasive twenty-first-century Muslim voices selected for this chapter are: Javed Ahmad Ghamidi (b. 1951), Abdelwahab el-Affendi (b. 1955), Louay M. Safi (b. 1955), Khaled Abou El Fadl (b. 1963), Radwan Masmoudi (b. 1963), M. A. Muqtedar Khan (b. 1966), and Kamran Bokhari (b. 1968). This is followed by a comparative analysis between the (early) modernist thinkers (discussed in Chapters 3 and 4) and the voices of the present century (presented in Chapters 5 and in present one), to show the scope, trends, as well as relevance and significance of the discourse under discussion.

## Javed Ahmad Ghamidi (b. 1951) on '*Shura* as akin to Democracy'

Javed Ahmad Ghamidi (b. 18 April 1951, Lahore, Pakistan) is a distinguished Pakistani 'liberal'/'reformist'[1] Islamic scholar, exegete, and educator, who (claims to have) extended the work of his 'tutor', Amin Ahsan Islahi (d. 1997). Holding a significant position, he has 'attracted international attention for his pioneering role in providing a different view on the role of Islam in Pakistan'.[2] Ghamidi's ideas have been communicated through a variety of media: the list includes a series of books (like *Mizan/ Meezan* and *Burhan*); articles published in *Ishraq*,[3] the *Renaissance*,[4] Studying-Islam (magazines and online portals);[5] and numerous television, radio, and web-based interviews; and through his institute, *Al-Mawrid*, Lahore.[6] He has contributed significantly to the theme of Shura—Democracy as well.[7]

Ghamidi follows a 'text-based approach rather than an historical or sociological one' in interpreting Islam and things Islamic. For him, 'Islam's political vision is based purely on a democratic principle (in the modern sense) and not a theo-democratic one',[8] because the Qur'an (especially on the basis of Q. 42: 38) neither proposes monarchy nor dictatorship as form of government, but 'prescribes democracy as the way to run the affairs of the state'.[9]

He translates Q. 42: 38 (*Amruhum Shura Baynahum*) as '*And their system is based on their consultation*'/'*the affairs of the Muslims are run on the basis of their consultation*'; offers a linguistic analysis of this verse; and bases his entire argument within this framework in his different writings, including *Mizan/Meezan* and *Burhan*—his two major (pioneering) works—and in his exegesis '*Al-Bayan*'.[10] Using his interpretative method on this verse, the word *amr* is translated by him as 'system' or 'directive'—implying the directives which emanate from political authority as well as the state system—and argues that 'monarchy and dictatorship have often been accepted forms of government' in Muslim history, but it is wrong to proclaim that 'democracy is a concept alien to Islam'.[11] In the explanation of this verse, he further states: 'This meaning has been incorporated in it from the depth found in its general meaning 'directive'. When the word 'directive' becomes related to people, it prescribes certain limits for itself and establishes certain rules and regulations. In such cases, it implies the directives which emanate from political authority as well as the state system. A little deliberation shows that the English word 'system' is used to convey the same meaning'.[12] Since the Qur'an has not specified it by any adjective, therefore, 'all sub-systems which are part of the political system', and 'all affairs of state like the municipal affairs, national and provincial affairs, political and social directives, rules of legislation, delegation and revocation of powers, dismissal and appointment of officials, interpretation of Islam for the collective affairs of life', etc., all come under the jurisdiction of the principle laid down in this verse.[13] For him, the 'system of government of an Islamic state' is based upon this very verse.[14]

The 'style and pattern of the words' in Q. 42: 38, for him, 'demands that even the head of a state [should] be appointed' through mutual consultation of the believers and should and should conduct its affairs in all cases on the basis of a consensus or majority opinion of the believers.[15] He goes further to argue that

> Since ... the collective system of the Muslims is based on [the Qur'anic injunction of] *amruhum shura bainahum* (their system is based on their consultation), the election of their ruler as well as their representatives must take place through consultation. Also, after assuming a position of authority, they will have no right to overrule a consensus or a majority opinion of the Muslims in all the collective affairs.[16]

This verse declines, in Ghamidi's view, 'to accept the impression that it is an instruction in a situation where the society is already divided between the ruler and the ruled, whether despotic or monarchic, and they are advised to consult in state affairs.... On the contrary, this principle encompasses all three phases of governance (the process of coming into power, running of state affairs and dissolution of government)'.[17]

Though he detached himself from Mawdudi's thought and organization, he endorses (and quotes) Mawdudi's interpretation (as put forth by later in his *Tafhim al-Qur'an*)[18] of this verse, and stresses, like most modern exegetes of different schools of thought, that in Q. 3: 159 even the Prophet (pbuh) has been directed to consult others.[19] In its elucidation, Ghamidi writes:

> The principle of consultation as laid down by the Qur'an is also in accordance with the established norms of sense and reason. No Muslim can be free of faults and shortcomings. He can be the most distinguished as far as piety and knowledge are concerned; he can be the most suitable for the position of authority he holds and can even consider himself so. But even with these abilities, he cannot attain the position of head of the state [*Khilafah*] without the general opinion of the Muslims.[20]

Thus, upholding of democratic principles like *Shura* is, no doubt, emphasized by sacred texts but, for him, it does not suggest, indicate or hint towards any specific form of government. The 'form of government' is a time-space matter and depends on socio-cultural contexts. To him, democracy should be the principal means and primary end of all social and political struggles.[21] In his *Meezan* (literally 'Balance/Scale') Ghamidi mentions that in compliance with the Qur'anic injunction on *Shura*, Q. 42: 38, 'the Sunnah decreed by the Prophet (sws [pbuh]) is based on two principles: First, Muslims shall be consulted in the affairs of state through their leaders in whom they profess confidence. Second, among the various parties or groups present in an Islamic State, only that party shall assume its political authority, which enjoys the confidence of the majority'.[22] From these two principles, it is evident that 'the real essence of democracy definitely exists in an Islamic Political System'.[23]

The 'Islamic form of government is an aristocracy', he further argues, in the sense that the individuals forming 'the government are elected on the basis of their piety and political acumen and, on the other hand, it is a democracy in [the sense] that they are elected and have to run their state affairs on the basis of consultation among them'.[24] Furthermore, Ghamidi also expressed his views, in an interview with *NaseebVibes*,[25] while answering the questions related to *Ijtihad* and democracy: 'The very fact that *Muslims have accepted democracy* is an *Ijtihad*. Muslims have always put emphasis on consensus as the way to solve issues. The West has improved the idea of consensus by evolving it into a systematic approach. Be it in the form of parliamentary democracy or other political systems. That evolution is an example of *Ijtihad*. Muslims have accepted this'. (Italics added)[26]

Similarly, in reply to the question, 'Are secular ideals—the state doesn't adopt anyone's religion as a source of laws—compatible with Islam's view of how a government can be run?' Ghamidi replies:

> The importance of secularism for the West emerged as a reaction from the theocratic environment imposed by the Christian church. Since Muslims do not have the theocratic environment, there was never a need to rebel against *deen* or religion in that manner. Secondly, *Islam is pure democracy*. The majority's say in society has more significance. Thus if a people want religious laws, they are welcome to do so through a legislative process (Italics added).[27]

Furthermore, for Ghamidi, democracy is not a system or form of government founded by a Jew or a Christian or by the West, but is a system of governance that was developed by humans and thus belongs to humanity—and humanity cannot, and should not, be measured through any religious or ideological scale. The democracy, known to the world today, is basically a system of government formed by people's choice that has evolved after struggling for many centuries. Therefore, it is not problematic to accept democracy or democratic values as the Qur'an has itself described this method in Q. 42: 38. He also justifies this by adding an interesting point that when it comes to (Western) science and technology, then Muslims accept it and even make use of it, without any qualms; however, when it comes to any political concepts, philosophy, etc., Muslims point out its flaws and faults, so he suggests that it is the responsibility of the Muslims to over-come such shortcomings and fallacies of democracy and make democracy more viable by eliminating its deficiencies.[28]

Ghamidi's idea of 'Islamic democracy', thus, goes beyond 'procedural aspects' as it embraces and accepts the 'notions of rights and responsibilities of the state and its citizens',[29] and his explanation and interpretation suggest that 'the text itself appropriates new space for accommodation of western democracy'.[30] In his *Political Shari'ah of Islam*, Ghamidi has attempted to derive the political *Shari'ah* of Islam from the Qur'an and Sunnah. Therefore, one of the main conclusions—that shows both Ghamidi's stand regarding the place of democracy in Islam as well as his opinion about the Islamic form of government—is summarized as: 'the form of government envisaged by Islam is *neither a theocracy nor a monarchy. It is more akin to democracy* as a Muslim government comes into existence on the basis of a public mandate and continues to exist as long as it commands the support of the majority' (italics added).[31]

## Abdelwahab el-Affendi (b. 1955) on Democracy as a 'Stable System of Governance'

Dr Abdelwahab El-Affendi (b. 1955, Sudan)—having served as Reader in Politics at the Centre for the Study of Democracy and founder and coordinator of the Democracy and Islam Program at the *University of Westminster* (London), and presently Provost, Acting President (and formerly Dean, School of Social Sciences and Humanities) at *Doha Institute of Graduate Studies,* Qatar—is a political scientist with a special interest in areas like Islam and (its relation with) politics, modernity, democracy, multiculturalism, West, and on issues like Muslim intellectuals and Sudanese and Middle Eastern politics. In his numerous scholarly works, he has deliberated on different aspects of Islam–democracy discourse.[32]

For instance, in 'Democracy and Its (Muslim) Critics', El-Affendi argues that the 'most common counter-proposal' put forth for an authentic Islamic model of democracy is that of *Shura* (Q. 3: 159 and 42: 38).[33] Although he states that democracy, for him, means exactly 'the self-rule of the people through their freely chosen institutions and representatives'; it is neither the rule of God, or *Shura,* nor 'Islamic democracy', but only democracy;[34] but while describing the historical development of democracy, he says:

> Etymologically and historically, the term [*democracy*] (from the Greek words for people, *demos,* and rule, *kratia*) emerged to designate a certain form of governance, the rule of the people (or the many), in contrast to rival forms, such as *monarchy* (rule by one person), *oligarchy* (rule by the few) *plutocracy* (rule by the rich), or *anarchy* (rule by no one).... [In a nutshell] democracy is a system of government in which all members of the community are permitted to participate *in public decision making in some manner found acceptable to all or to the majority.* (Italics added)[35]

While describing the values of democracy, he says that however, from very early on, democracy was associated with a 'constellation of substantive values' like 'liberty, equality, tolerance, public spiritedness, respect for laws, direct participation and popular sovereignty'.[36] At the same time, he argues that an 'Islamic alternative to liberal democracy is conceivable, even desirable. However, this alternative will inevitably exhibit some of the features we ascribe today to democratic systems'.[37] El-Affendi is also of the opinion that although democracy in its normative sense has a long history as ideal, but the wave of democratization that has swept over many parts of the world during the past two decades has left the Muslim world high and dry. It is the only region where despotism appears to thrive. Some analysts, he argues, search for 'cultural' reasons for this anomaly—abnormality and irregularity. Democracy, some argue, is 'alien to the Muslim mind'. Islam emphasizes conformity and obedience, and Muslim societies have failed to develop civil society institutions. Muslim societies remain 'excessively patriarchical and rigid', while Islam has proved 'secularization-resistant'. Secularization is seen by these theorists as essential for democratization. Others point to economic and social factors, such as low literacy rates, the state's economic independence from society, and the weakness of civil organizations and of the middle class.[38]

He goes further to argue that whatever the 'Muslim mind' dictates, the fact is that the overwhelming majority of Muslims are actively demanding democracy. And while it is true that economic, political, and social factors make the fight for democracy a steep uphill struggle, yet in many Muslim countries, courageous individuals have emerged to challenge, at great risk to themselves, the monopoly of power by dominant cliques. By providing examples of Syria, Malaysia, Indonesia, and Turkey, he argues that Turkey is often cited as the only genuine democracy in the Muslim world. However, even if specifically Western models are adopted, it would be difficult to regard Turkey as a full democracy. He concludes:

> To varying degrees Malaysia, Indonesia and Tunisia show how democracy could come to the Muslim world. In all these countries a broad alliance of democratic forces, which do not exclude Islamists or anyone else, has emerged to champion democratic reforms. Success is conditional on reaching and sustaining a democratic consensus, based on inclusion for all. And of central importance will be resolving the role of Islam in the public arena.[39]

In his *Who Needs an Islamic State?* El-Affendi, very forcefully, argues that Muslim communities should give the highest priority to freedom and democracy and seek to escape the straitjacket of the modern nation-state through more creative formulas. He is of the view that Islam really has no defined political system, so modern democracy is most suitable for the Muslims today.[40] He passionately argues 'for a liberal democracy—one in which the citizens are able to actualize Islamic values into a new more viable democratic model. He believes Muslims should be aiming for a political system that is not intrusive or coercive'.[41] The 'central value governing the Islamic polity and giving it meaning', for him, is 'freedom'.[42]

He argues that human experience shows that 'democracy, broadly defined, offers the best possible method of avoiding such disappointments in rulers, and affords a way of remedying the causes for such disappointments once they occur'.[43] What is democracy if it is not a system of endless compromise, regardless of right and wrong? In fact, democracy is among the worst of systems for defending rampant injustice. It only ensures that the people accept oppression, have no real choice, yet feel that they do. It legitimizes all corruption, as a majority of a tiny minority voted for it, and it makes easy the road for all kinds of exploitation. He says that

> the tyrants lording it over the Muslims today, aided and abetted by their foreign allies, justify their existence by fear of Muslim 'fanatics' who want to coerce others into adopting an unacceptable lifestyle. This lame excuse for tyranny must be removed by affirming our commitment to democracy as the governing principle of the Muslim polity in all its states.[44]

Thus, in the end, El-Affendi proposes freedom and democracy as the solution to the Muslims' problem; and portrays a choice only between despotic rule on one side and democracy on the other. He considers the authoritarianism of the *Khilafah*—of Umayyad and Abbasid and other dynastic regimes—to be the source of corruption. This is true, if there is no accountability. We should never have to choose only between a current despot, the corrupt *Khulafa* of the past, and democracy. We choose an enlightened revival based upon the implementation of the Islamic *Shari'ah* and a righteous *Khilafah*.[45]

El-Affendi believes that values underlying democracy, such as 'justice, fairness, decency, and rational conduct', can be said to be in 'total harmony' with a certain broad and inclusive understanding of Islam. The anti-democratic thrust of much contemporary Islamic political thought is thus not a necessary outcome of Islam itself. Rather, it owes much to the fact that Islamism emerged as a response to Western colonialism and the collapse of the Ottoman Caliphate at the hands of Western powers.[46]

While defending democracy and the rights of minorities, El-Affendi does not advocate that Muslim countries uncritically adopt Western-style secular, democratic state structures. In fact, he is bitterly critical of the modern state, which, instead of serving society, demands that society serve it: 'The state should serve the ends of society and not *vice versa*'.[47]

He draws inspiration from the polity set up by the Prophet Muhammad (pbuh), which (in his terminology) was, characterized by voluntary participation, and was 'based on morality, rather than on coercion'.[48]

In theory, modernity allows for democracy, freedom (albeit one controlled by social responsibility and spiritual welfare), justice, and peaceful interaction between different peoples, thus promoting the creation of a 'truly global community', which, El-Affendi says, is in accordance with Islamic teachings.[49]

In his view, the debate over democracy, one of the most important debates in the Muslim world in the twentieth century, is still continuing without a resolution which is 'an indication of a serious crisis in the Muslim world'.[50] In the concluding part (of this essay), he ventures the following definition of democracy:

> Democracy is a stable system of governance, which seeks to guarantee the widest possible degree of political participation on equal terms and on the basis of a normatively defensible compromise acceptable to the major players in the political community, a compromise which also underpinned by a number of enforceable guarantees limiting the powers of government and the shifts which the system may undergo within a predictable range.[51]

For El-Affendi, the most sacred duty of all politically active Muslims is to try to work hard to replace these systems, and to ensure that democracy must not only prevail in all Muslim lands but must also put in deep roots.[52] But, at the same time, he accepts that 'democracy is *not a panacea* for all social and political ills. But the lessons of the evolution of modem political institutions and the way they have worked to minimize conflict needs to be studied carefully', for there is no dispute, among Muslim supporters of democracy, on 'the worth of democratic values such as freedom, justice and respect for the law'. (Italics added)[53]

## Louay Safi (b. 1955) on *Shura*—Democracy Convergences and Divergences

Dr Louay M. Safi (b. 1955, Damascus, Syria) is currently serving as Professor of Political Science and Islamic Thought in the Faculty of

Islamic Studies at *Hamad Bin Khalifa University* (HBKU; Qatar) and Senior Fellow with the 'Institute of Social Policy and Understanding' (ISPU) and 'Alwaleed Center for Muslim Christian Understanding' (ACMCU), *Georgetown University* (USA). A scholar of Islam and the Middle East, an advocate of Arab and Muslim American rights, and an activist in 'defending human rights and promoting democracy', Safi is a prolific author of a number of books and papers and he writes and lectures on globalization, democracy, human rights, and Islam and the West. Safi firmly supports reform of Islamic thought, culture, and law by engaging to the universal Islamic values; supports democratic reform in Muslim countries; discards interpretations of Islamic sources that initiate interreligious resentment; and calls for the development of more all-encompassing societies in the Muslim world.[54]

He believes that democracy as a system of self-governance, answerability of public representatives, and the rule of law is completely attuned to Islam. For the transformation of Muslim societies from autocratic rule to democracy, for him, an emphatic understanding and interpretation of Islam is essential. He further maintains that for any democratic reform, a cultural change is vital and such a change is unmanageable without alluring to more fundamental values. He further explains in the parable that as it is difficult to imagine the modern West without the 'Religious Reformation in Europe', in the same way, it is also hard to assume any kind of democratic reform in the Middle East without Islam being a big part of that.[55]

An ardent advocate of human rights and democracy, Safi believes that Islam is a set of norms and ideals that accentuates 'the equality of people, the accountability of leaders to community, and the respect of diversity and other faiths', and thus, is fully compatible with democracy. He says that 'I don't see how it could be compatible with a government that would take away those values'. Those who say that 'democracy has no place in Islam, what they really express', pronounces Safi, 'is a sense that the word "democracy" as presented in international discourse appears to be wholly owned by the West. The word itself has, for some, a connotation of cultural imperialism'.[56] In an interview with Q-News—*The Muslim Magazine*, UK (2005)—Safi claimed that the forces of reform and modernization are already in momentum in the Muslim societies, and have made, despite severe limitations, considerable advances to affect educational, cultural, and political reforms.[57] In modern times, however, the Islamic world has not been particularly fertile ground for the seeds of democracy. If it is to become such, Safi argues, changes must come from within Muslim societies. He says:

> I don't see *democracy* built without ordinary people working for that. It can't be imposed from the top down or from the outside. Definitely outsiders can help. They can apply pressure on dictatorial or authoritarian regimes as we did for example in South Africa, where outside help was essential in fostering a more *democratic regime*. But I think we have to keep in mind we can't push *democracy* down the throat of anyone. If we do that it becomes a hated concept. Nobody wants to be forced to be a democrat—that's a contradiction in terms (italics added).[58]

Safi believes that if such change is to begin, it can only happen through Islam; making the faith not only compatible and attuned, but essential and indispensable for the democratization of the Muslim societies. Across the Muslim world, governments have adopted varying degrees of self-representation in response to unique historical circumstances (such as Turkey, Indonesia, Iran, etc.) proving the fact that there is neither one-size-fits-all democracy nor is there a single interpretation of Islam. He, thus, asserts:

> Ultimately *democracy* could evolve a bit differently in different cultures. It doesn't have to be a replica of the *democracy* we have in the U.S. You can't compare what we've achieved here as a society over two centuries with an *emerging democracy*, where people are just trying to test the boundaries and find out what *democracy* means. (Italics added)[59]

The concept of consensus can provide an effective basis for accepting majority rule, and the 'legitimacy of the state', as Safi notes, 'depends upon the extent to which state organization and power reflect the will of the Ummah [the Muslim community], for as classical jurists have insisted, the legitimacy of state institutions is not derived from textual sources but is based primarily on the principle of *Ijma*'.[60]

In *Shura and Democracy: Similarities and Differences*,[61] Safi highlights that democracy and *Shura* share 'the ideal of egalitarian politics and popular political participation, but differ significantly in relating participatory government to the overall purposes of social organization and political action'. He further states that 'the ideal of democracy has been expressed in various forms, and is being implemented today through different models. It is, therefore, quite appropriate for one to speak of *Shura* as a framework for an Islamic democracy'. He is, however, attentive to the fact that 'there is no consensus among Muslim scholars on the nature and scope of a participatory government under the system of *shura*';[62] and, thus, draws the following conclusions:

1. Though Democracy and *Shura* both encounter similar challenges (including a vulnerability to various formulations and interpretations), they share the common aspiration of overcoming political elitism and preventing the control by a select few of the lives of the multitude.
2. Both diverge on three main grounds—viz., the way the two participatory systems conceive of political organization, freedom, and law.
3. Democracy is at bottom a system whose intent is to open the political process to popular participation, *Shura* is indeed a democratic system; and the principle of popular political participation is bound to undergo significant transformation in its mode of application when embraced by peoples who subscribe to an Islamic worldview.[63]

Although Safi concludes that *Shura* is indeed a democratic system, but, at the same time, for him, democracy and *Shura* diverge on the following grounds:

1. Difficulty in justifying the exclusion on ethnic and national grounds by an 'Islamic democracy', although such a democratic system will have to grabble with the question of how to prevent attempts to use religion as a tool for control and exploitation.
2. The limitation (curb and control) society may impose on individual freedom is the second area where *Shura* diverge from democracy.
3. The third area is the law: from an Islamic point of view, law is not the total sum of what rational individuals think is right and correct at any specific historical moment, but has transcendental qualities that rise above any historical community.[64]

In the wake of 'Arab Spring', Safi argued that one of the main challenges of 'establishing a democracy in many Arab countries is' due to the 'lack of tradition of the rule of law, or obeying state-enacted laws'. For him, the 'challenge today' for Muslims of the Arab world, 'is to introduce a new culture of people abiding by the rule of law under a democratic system'.[65] Though 'Arab Spring' has been described now 'as a failed attempt at democracy',[66] however, in a recent work, *Islam and the Trajectory of Globalization,* Safi has devoted a section on 'Globalization and Islamic democracy'[67] wherein he puts forth that the Arab Spring has 'shown us two things: First, that Arab societies are eager to do away with 'stable', dictatorships and embrace a democratic order and even pay the highest price for achieving it. Second, that Arab authoritarian regimes are well adept to suppress any popular objection to their inhuman governance and can rely on the outside world to keep their population in check'.[68]

## Khaled Abou El Fadl (b. 1963) on *Shura, Bay'ah,* and Modern Democracy

Dr Khaled Abou El Fadl (b. 1963, Kuwait)—a Professor of Law at the UCLA School of Law (USA)—is considered as one of the leading authorities in Islamic law globally, a prolific author, legal-theologian, and 'one of the important and influential Islamic thinkers in the modern age'.[69] A prominent scholar in the field of human rights, he is a stanch proponent of 'Islam's basically democratic and pluralistic ethos as well as Islam's protection of basic human rights'.[70] In his numerous writings, he has explored this discourse from a legal-political perspective.[71] He is also the founder of the *Institute of Advanced Usuli Studies* (The Usuli Institute), a non-profit educational institute dedicated to ethics, beauty, and critical thinking in the Islamic tradition.[72]

In his *Islam and the Challenge of Democracy,*[73] he examines the foundational texts of Islam and argues that Islam is not only compatible with democracy but that Islamic values can best expressed today in constitutional democracies (liberal democracies) that protect individual rights. For him, in a democracy, 'the people are the source of the law, and the law in turn ensures the fundamental rights that protect the well-being and interests of the individual members of the sovereignty'. Though, in his analysis, 'democracy poses a formidable challenge' for Islam, but at the same time, he sees 'democracy is an ethical good, and that the pursuit of this good does not require abandoning Islam'.[74] Emphasizing that 'the Qur'an does not specify a particular form of government', he identifies 'a set of social and political values that are central to a Muslim polity', which include ideals like 'pursuing justice through social co-operation and mutual assistance', establishing 'consultative method of governance; and institutionalizing mercy and compassion in social interactions'. These are the values that are central to (constitutional) democracy.[75]

He sees democracy as 'an appropriate system for Islam because it both expresses the special worth of human beings—the status of vicegerency—and at the same time deprives the state of any pretense of divinity by locating ultimate authority in the hands of the people', rather than in any specific group or class.[76] In his analysis, Islamic tradition is not only pluralistic in nature but integrates a number of concepts equivalent to those of modern democracies as well. Two such notions, of much significance, are the concept of consultation in government (*Shura*)—a concept deriving its legitimacy from the Islamic primary sources (Qur'an and Sunnah)—and the concept of *bay'ah* (pledge of allegiance).

Elucidating further on this theme, he offers another argument in support of democratic forms of government: that the Qur'an has charged human beings collectively to implement its principles. No doubt, he recognizes that some Muslims reject the idea of democracy on the basis of the belief that 'God is the sole legislator', but for El Fadl it is 'a fatal fiction that is indefensible from the point of view of Islamic theology'. Such arguments, for him, 'pretend that some human agents have perfect access to God's will'.[77]

Elaborating further, El Fadl argues that it is the collective responsibility of the Muslims to establish governmental structures which promote concepts and values like justice and mercy because both are among the core principles imparted by the Qur'an. In other words, divine sovereignty in a social order (government) is reflected in establishing successfully the principles of justice and mercy. Thus, the determining factor of a government reflecting divine guidance or sovereignty is not its legislative structure; rather, 'principles of mercy and justice are the primary divine charge and God's sovereignty lies in the fact that God is the authority that delegated to human beings the task of achieving justice on earth by fulfilling the virtues that approximate divinity'.[78] He, very eloquently, argues that

> Several considerations suggest that democracy—and especially a *constitutional democracy* that protects basic individual rights—is that form. My central argument ... is that democracy—by assigning equal rights of speech, association, and suffrage to all—offers the greatest potential for promoting justice and protecting human dignity.... A fundamental Qur'anic idea is that God vested all of humanity with a kind of divinity by making every person the viceroy of God on this earth: ... (2: 30). In particular, human beings, as God's vicegerents, are responsible for making the world more just. By assigning equal political rights to all adults, democracy expresses that special status of human beings in God's creation and enables them to discharge that responsibility.[79]

For Abou El Fadl, in today's world a just and merciful government is one that protects the basic human rights and protecting them must be 're-analyzed in the light of current diversity of human existence'.[80] In particular, he calls for the rights of free speech, association, and suffrage. In other words, his principal argument is that democracy offers the 'greatest potential for promoting justice and protecting human dignity'.[81] By identifying the human responsibility for pronouncing and implementing that government, divine sovereignty remains intact.

Thus, for Nader Hashemi, El-Fadl's *Islam and the Challenge of Democracy*, is 'a significant and unique contribution to advancing a democratic theory for Muslim societies';[82] for Saba Mahmood, it is 'an erudite attempt to explore those principles and values within Islamic political and legal traditions that could be made compatible with ideas of liberal democracy';[83] and for Bernard Haykel, who finds El Fadl's ideas both 'intensely stimulating and innovative', his arguments for the compatibility of Islam and democracy on the basis that 'both are premised on, and aim for, the same fundamental moral value: the pursuit of justice, which entails guaranteeing human dignity and liberty'.[84] For Noah Feldman,

> Abou El Fadl's hopeful view on the compatibility of democratic values and practices with Islam shares a familial resemblance with the writings

of such Islamic democrats as Rashid al-Ghannouchi, a Tunisian Islamist intellectual... ; [Iranian] Abdolkarim Soroush ... ; the Egyptian journalist Fahmi Huwaidi; and the Qatar-based internet and al-Jazeera phenomenon Yusuf al-Qaradawi. Though these thinkers disagree on a wide range of issues, they share a view of Islam that emphasizes justice, human dignity and equality, the rule of law, the role of the people in selecting leaders, the obligation of having consultative government, and the value of pluralism. All share a commitment to Islam as the starting place and ultimate ground for evaluating democracy, and all insist that Islam is not self-interpreting: ascertaining the will of God and coordinating quotidian social organization require human effort.[85]

In this paradigm, and by way of conclusion, for him, 'democracy is an appropriate system for Islam because it both expresses the special worth of human beings—the status of vicegerency—and at the same time, deprives the state of any pretense of divinity by locating ultimate authority in the hands of the people rather than the ulema [*ulama*: the religious scholars].'[86]

## Radwan Masmoudi (b. 1963) on Liberty, Justice, and Consultation

Dr Radwan A. Masmoudi (b. 1963, Tunisia) is the Founder and President of the Washington-based *Center for the Study of Islam and Democracy* (CSID)—a non-profit organization 'dedicated to studying Islamic and democratic political thought and merging them into a modern democratic discourse'. Established in 1999, CSID has a branch (established in 2011) in Tunisia as well.[87] Although Masmoudi (who holds Master's and PhD degrees in Mechanical Engineering and Robotics from *MIT*, USA) has been more active in organizing and conducting conferences and seminars on Islam and democracy, but he has contributed Islam–democracy discourse through academic platforms as well by writing 'on the topics of democracy, diversity, human rights, and tolerance in Islam'[88] in various journals, like *Muslim Democrat, Journal of Democracy, Future Islam*, etc. Besides, he is also a commentator and appears regularly on radio and TV shows and speaks at major public policy think tanks as well. He is an activist and expert on democracy, freedom, and human rights in Islam. He also served as editor in chief of CSID's quarterly newsletter, *Muslim Democrat*.

For Masmoudi, although the question of the relationship between the teachings of Islam and the principles of democracy is, undoubtedly, one of the most pressing issues facing the Muslim world today, but, at the same time, the principles of elected rulers, consultative bodies, accountability, tolerance, justice, equality, freedom, human rights and the rule of law are not unknown or alien to Islam but are embedded in, and promoted by, the primary sources of Islam and Islamic Law.[89] For him, majority of the Muslims (including Arabs) consider democracy as the best form of government; they want Islamic values to govern but they don't want a strict implementation of *Shari'ah*. So there is a struggle, he maintains, for the soul of Islam and it did not start yesterday or after 9/11 but has been going on for at least a century among those calling for modernizing the Muslim world. In an interview with *The Charlotte Observer*, Masmoudi said:

> We need to reinterpret Islam, but how can we do that in dictatorships where everything is controlled by the state? Democracy is the key because it will give us the opportunity to talk about all these other problems and solve them. It will take time. We need the freedom to talk about what Islam means in the 21st century.[90]

While making a passing review of the conditions of basic freedoms (including freedom for conducting free elections) and democracy in the Arab world, Masmoudi (in *Why Democracy?*, 2005) concludes with these observations: (a) the only way to resolve the crisis in the Muslim world is to end tyranny and corruption and replace them with freedom, equality, and justice—the core values of democracy; (b) democracy and democratization is the key to re-open the doors of *Ijtihad* (independent reasoning) so that an amiable environment for fostering free debate and a genuine renewal of Islamic thought; (c) values of freedom and liberty are not only compatible with, but are required by, Islam (for Islam rejects any kind of compulsion and coercion in matters of faith); and (d) genuine democracy and an honest, inclusive debate about Islam's role in society are the only ways to resolve the long-simmering problems that threaten peace and stability throughout the Muslim world.[91]

Elaborating further on the finding roots of democracy in Islam, Masmoudi is of the opinion that there are two basic political principles that are heavily emphasized in the Qur'an: *'Adl* (justice) and *Shura* (consultation). However, the problem is that there are no clear institutions or methods that are identified on how this consultation should take place in an Islamic democratic setup, as Muslims have failed in interpreting this message and in applying the idea of *Shura* (in practice).

It is within this context that Masmoudi (in his essay, 'The Silenced Majority') asserted that liberty (*Hurriyah*), justice (*'Adl*), consultation (*Shura*), and rational interpretation (*Ijtihad*) are the main pillars of 'Islamic Liberalism'—which places explicit emphasis on limited governance, individual liberty, human dignity, and human rights.[92] Liberal Islam, for Masmoudi, is a branch or school of thought in Islamic intellectual tradition accentuating on human liberty and freedom within the ambit of Islam. In this context, he thus impresses that it should be endorsed and permitted to grow, as it is the essence of democracy.[93]

Moreover, in one of his essays (published in 2007), he has focused on the future of Islamic democracy in the Middle East and claims that democracy in the Arab world and in the foreseeable future will have a more or less 'Islamic flavor', but this is normal, natural, and in the long run, a healthy development which will ultimately lead to the modernization and reinterpretation of Islamic principles for the twenty-first century. In this study, he has drawn the following conclusions, which are still relevant in the context of Arab Spring and its aftermath in the MENA: (i) democracy is the only solution to, and the only way forward to overcome, the current crisis faced by the Muslim world in general and by the Arab world in particular; (ii) democracy is perfectly compatible with Islam; and (iii) democracy cannot and/or should not exclude the moderate Islamic movements and their role in implementing it successfully (in a Muslim country).[94]

Masmoudi, while differentiating between democracy and dictatorship, believes that democracy is the only form of government that is compatible with Islam; its alternative (dictatorship) is certainly against Islam, though it has been, and is (still) practised in the Muslim societies. For him, the only solution to the current geo-political crisis faced by the Muslim world, especially the Arab countries, lies in the establishing of democracy and democratic institutions and values.

## Muqtedar Khan (b. 1966) on 3 *C*'s of Islamic Governance: *Constitution, Consensus,* and *Consultation*

Dr M. A. Muqtedar Khan (b. 1966)—an Indian-American political scientist—is Professor in the Department of Political Science and International Relations, *University of Delaware* (USA). He is also the founding Director of the Islamic Studies Program at the University of Delaware. A well-known Muslim intellectual—whose writings are widely published[95]—Khan advocates freedom of thought and independent thinking. He states that it is the inability of Muslims to sustain a dialogue with time and text that sometimes makes Islamic teachings look obsolete or chauvinistic. Khan is admired for advancing a more moderate and liberal vision of Islam.[96]

In considering Islam–democracy compatibility, Khan brings into notice that one must recognize that it is false to claim that there is no democracy in the Muslim world. Around 750 million Muslims live in democratic societies of one kind or another, including Indonesia, Bangladesh, India, Europe, North America, and even Iran.[97]

Though it is unquestionable that majority of the Muslim scholars consider the principle of *Shura* is the major source of democratic ethics in Islam, however, they recognize the differences that exist between *Shura* and democracy while advancing an Islamic conception of democracy based on *Shura*. In this context, *Shura*, for Khan, is basically a consultative decision-making process that is considered either obligatory or desirable by different scholars.[98]

Khan contends that democracy with its principles of limited government, public accountability, checks and balances, separation of powers, and transparency in governance does succeed in limiting human sovereignty. The Muslim world, for him, has been inundated badly by despots, dictators and self-regarding monarchs, and thus needs limitations, which is possible through the democratic ideals. He, thus, proposes that 'there is nothing in Islam and in Muslim practices that is fundamentally opposed to democracy—justice, freedom, fairness, equality, or tolerance'.[99]

Khan, at the same time, underscores certain differences between *Shura* and democracy. For him, the two differ in three basic ways: firstly, unlike *Shura*, democracy allows 'modification' of foundational texts; the constitution can be amended but not the Qur'an or the Sunnah. Secondly, 'Shura remains non-binding while democratic process and laws are binding and can only be reversed through a democratic process and not by unilateral and oligopolistic processes'. Finally, the way Shura is discussed in Islamic discourses, seems that it is something that the leader/ ruler initiates and is expected to do. Shura is the 'leader consulting some people'; while as in a democracy, on the other hand, it is 'people-consulting among themselves' about who will govern and how. 'Notice', argues Khan boldly, how Shura 'is top-down and democracy bottom-up [procedure]'.[100] At the same time, he claims that both Shura and democracy are deeply 'contested' notions; therefore, it is not the theoretical finessing, but the successful practice and institutionalization of these ideas that matters. He, thus, cautions:

> We must however be careful not to use the debate between the similarities and dissimilarities of Shura and democracy as a surrogate for concluding whether democracy and Islam are compatible. There is more in Islam than Shura [such as social justice, economic welfare, religious freedoms, etc.] when it comes in reflecting over the nature of good governance and best polities.[101]

Furthermore, in his *Islamic Democratic Discourse*,[102] Khan discusses in detail the 'politics' behind the discourse of Islam and democracy, emphasizing that the discourse is composed of two distinct debates: (i) one debate is primarily 'political'—and the central question that is debated is the reasons for the marked absence of democracies in the Muslim world; and (ii) the second debate is 'quasi–theological, or in a sense concerns the political theology of Islam'—and this debate is about the compatibility of Islam and democracy. In general, it explores the politics that underpins the theoretical discourse on Islam and democracy and then proceeds to evaluate the relative merits of philosophy, theology, and jurisprudence in developing an authentic Islamic discourse on democracy. While making discussion on the prospects of an Islamic democratic theory in the context of three genres of discourse—theological, jurisprudential, and philosophical (with special reference to the writings of Abdulaziz Sachedina, Khaled Abou El-Fadl, and Abdolkarim Soroush, respectively[103]—he concludes: 'while theological understanding is necessary but not sufficient, philosophical illumination is the answer but needs much more development and jurisprudence is a challenge rather than an ally of Islamic democratic theory'.[104]

Furthermore, contending that 'Political Philosophy of Islamic Governance' is based on three C's—viz., Constitution (*Mithaq al-Medina*), Consensus (*Ijmaʿ*), and Consultation (*Shura*)—Khan not only asserts that 'Democracy is indispensable', but claims that 'Consultative governance therefore is the preferred form of governance in Islam', and true Muslims 'cannot but prefer a democratic structure over all others [systems or forms of government] to realize the justice and well-being promised in Islamic sources'.[105] In the interpretation of these three *C*'s, he further writes:

> The key features of *Islamic governance* found in Islamic sources ... and contemporary Muslim discussions on the Islamic state, are *constitution, consent and consultation*.... While these principles need to be explored and articulated in the specific socio-cultural context of different Muslim societies, it is important to understand that they are essential.
>
> The Compact of Medina that the Prophet Muhammad [pbuh] adopted provides a very important occasion for the development of Islamic political theory. [ ... ] An important principle of the Constitution of Medina was that the Prophet Muhammad [pbuh] governed the city state of Medina by virtue of the consent of its citizens.... The Constitution of Medina established the importance of consent and cooperation for governance. The process of *bayah*, or the pledging of allegiance, was an important institution that sought to formalize the consent of the governed. [ ... ] The third key principle of Islamic governance is consultation, or *Shura* in Arabic. This is a very widely known concept, and many Islamic scholars have advanced the Islamic concept of *Shura* as evidence for Islam's democratic credentials. (Italics added)[106]

It is also true that Khan, though optimistic, also realizes the difficulties and barriers regarding the establishment of Islamic democratic theory; and thus, puts forth that such a form of government should first become an aspiration in Muslim minds and must dominate their discourse:

> The *barriers to democracy in the Muslim world* are both ideational and material. While political activism and even revolutionary change may become necessary to establish *democracy, Islamic democratic theory*

must precede political change in order to remove ideational barriers first. If an *authentic Islamic democracy* is to emerge, then it must first become an aspiration in Muslim minds and must dominate their discourse. Then *once the idea exists, the form can follow*. This is the challenge for Islamic political theory that has not been answered yet. (Italics added)[107]

He discerns 'much in Islamic sources and tradition that is favorable to making democracy the vehicle for delivering the products of Islamic governance, such as social justice, economic welfare, and religious freedoms'.[108] The barriers to democracy in the Muslim world, for Khan, are not limited to narrow interpretations of Islam or to the fascist tendencies (propounded by some extremist Islamic movements), but the existing 'social-political conditions, failure of states, and the negative role of foreign powers' have equally contributed to an atmosphere that dejects democracy. These barriers are both 'ideational and material'. Khan, by way of conclusion, maintains—an argument that he replicates in several of his writings—that *'Islam is not a barrier to but a facilitator of democracy, justice and tolerance* in the Muslim world' (Italics added).[109] For him, if an '*authentic Islamic democracy* is to emerge, then it must first become an aspiration in Muslim minds and dominate their discourse', and once 'the idea exists, the form can follow' (italics added).[110]

An ardent advocate and a staunch supporter of good and smart governance—as put forth in his recent work, *Islam and Good Governance*, and as underlined in the *Foreword* of this work—he has moved 'the conversation away from Islamic government to Islam and good governance placing less emphasis on ideology and more on good governance'.[111] Thus, through his prolific academic output (in the form of books, book chapters, essays, analytical pieces, etc.), Khan aspires for the possibility of an 'Islamic democracy-in-practice'.

## Kamran Bokhari (b. 1968) on Refuting 'Democracy as Disbelief'

Kamran Bokhari—presently Senior Lecturer, Security & Policy Institute of Professional Development, *University of Ottawa* (Canada); Director

(Strategy & Programs) with the *Centre for Global Policy* (a Washington-based think tank); and Director of Analytical Development at the *Newlines Institute* (a non-partisan think tank based in Washington, DC)[112]—is a political analyst who has written, and is writing, extensively on this theme. Co-author of *Political Islam in the Age of Democratization*,[113] Bokhari earned his PhD from the Department of Politics & International Relations at *University of Westminster* (UK); has written his Master's Thesis on 'Islam and Democracy in the Context of the Contemporary Islamic Political Resurgence' (at *Missouri State University* in 2002);[114] and has published a copious number of analytical, scholarly, and theoretical articles related to geopolitics of the Islamic world as well as contributed book chapters to various edited volumes. His areas of specialization include international affairs, security, counter-terrorism, comparative political systems, Islam and democracy, modern Muslim political thought, and Islamist movements.[115]

In 'Is Democracy Disbelief?'[116]—wherein he attempts to illustrate the intellectual discrepancies inherent in the notion that 'Islam is incompatible with democracy', by deconstructing the understanding that radical Islamists have regarding both Islam and democracy—he argues that the essential problem with the argument of those Islamist individuals and groups (such as *Hizb al-Tahrir, al Muhajirun,* and a host of other *Neo-Salafist* and *Jihadist* outfits) that claim democracy has nothing to do with Islam is the way in which they *define* both Islam and democracy. Most Muslim opponents of democracy construct their arguments on two false assumptions: on the one hand, they assume that 'Allah has provided a specific political system in the divine texts of the Quran and the Sunnah. At the same time, they think that the only real democracy is the western secular brand'.[117]

A major argument put forth by Bokhari is that a glance at the historical development of Islamic political thought and practice is sufficient to make one realize that there is no such thing as the 'Islamic Political System' or the 'Ruling System of Islam' or the 'Khilafah System'. He substantiates this argument by referring to the fact that one sees not only an enormous amount of variance and variation in the way the different jurists approached the subject of Islamic governance but also in the practice of the various caliphates from 632 CE (i.e. from the establishment of institution of *Khilafah*) to 1924 CE (the abolition of *Khilafah* in Turkey).

In fact, there can be 'multiple ruling systems of Islam', because the Qur'an and Sunnah do not 'privilege one particular system'; instead, the divine Texts contain only general principles regarding the issue of governance, on the basis of which scholars in any given *spatio-temporal* setting can construct political systems. Moreover, the constructs and phrases such as 'Islamic state', 'Islamic political system', 'sovereignty of Allah', etc., are the 'products of the modern age and did not exist in the 'glorious past', to which the 'radicals' advocate a return'.[118]

For Bokhari, not only do 'radical Islamists'—or, in the context of our discussion, the opponents of democracy in Islam—suffer from a misunderstanding of what Islam has to say about governance, but their tracts also betray their simplistic conceptualization of democracy. Just as they engage in the gross essentialization of the notion of Islamic governance, they exhibit a similar attitude toward democracy as well. For them, democracy is also a well-defined system in which, according to them, man as opposed to Allah enjoys the right to legislate.[119]

Like many intellectuals and political analysts, Bokhari also believes that democracy in reality is 'essentially contested concept', which means that there is not any single brand or model of democracy that is more authentic than the other. As such, democracy as a concept is universally accepted but there is no universally accepted model or brand of democracy. Hence, the argument that democracy is majority rule, they tend to disregard the role of constitutionalism and the rule of law.

Accepting that there is a single political system that Allah has ordained for the believers for all times to come, for Bokhari, such an understanding is not just superficial, but it also contradicts the belief that Islam is a way of life for all times and places.[120] He perceives democracy, when broken down to its essentials, as nothing more than the 'most efficient means of political management' available today; but the dilemma, for him, is that opponents of democracy view it as being 'synonymous with western secularism'. As the two are entirely different concepts and do not have a necessary relationship with one another, so what needs to be understood is that democracy is about providing a constitutional framework, which would ensure, 'legitimacy of the government, accountability, transparency, rule of law, regulation of state-society relations'. Also, as Islam has not provided any 'specific political system' for the believers to adopt, and democracy is nothing more than the most proficient means of organizing the political affairs of a people, then where is—Bokhari audaciously argues—the *haram* or *kufr* in this?[121]

He reaches to the conclusion that while it is true that a workable model of an Islamic democracy has yet to emerge, this is not because Islam and democracy are antithetical to one another. On the contrary, it is a function of the perpetuating condition of arrested political development in the Muslim world. Not only do radical Islamists suffer from a misunderstanding of what Islam has to say about governance, but their tracts also betray their simplistic conceptualization of democracy.[122]

Bokhari, moreover, puts forth that the 1950s and 1960s can be considered as the 'naissance of the intra-Islamist debate' over the question of Islam and democracy, but Islamists even today seem bitterly divided over the issue, and thus, there exists a 'diversity of viewpoints' ranging from 'those who view democracy as a value-neutral operational mechanism on the basis of which a modern Islamic state can be constructed', to those 'who see democracy as a value-laden concept that tries to elevate human reason above divine revelation and is hence seen as being tantamount to *kufr* (disbelief)'.[123] In other words, the disagreement is essentially about the manner in which this highly contested concept of democracy is defined and by whom. For him, the Islamist groups can be broadly categorized into two general camps, in so far as their attitude towards democracy is concerned: the *pro-democracy* camp and the *anti-democracy* camp; and the dispute between these two camps is very much rooted in the specific principles of jurisprudence or sources of legislation upon which each side bases its particular *Ijtihad*. While commenting on the relationship between Islam and democracy in theory and practice, Bokhari articulates in clear terms that:

> Islam v. [versus] Democracy debate must not continue for too long as it will only further arrest the much needed political development in the Muslim world. Muslim intellectuals must acknowledge that a feasible synthesis of Islam and democracy has yet to emerge. While the Islamist opponents of democracy are marginalized, nevertheless, the fact remains that the other side has also not been able to adequately address this issue. In order to demonstrate that Islam is compatible with democracy requires extensive work on the theoretical level.[124]

## A Comparative Analysis: Early Modernists vs. Twenty-First Century Intellectuals

Having outlined, deliberated upon, and examined the views of some prominent Muslim modernist/reformist figures of the last two-and-half-centuries (nineteenth to twenty-first)—discussed in previous chapters as well as above here—on Islam–democracy compatibility, it becomes evident that the Muslim thinkers across the globe—from Asia to MENA, and from Europe and America—are engaged in a pursuit to develop an Islamic form of democracy. They are attempting to develop it by utilizing some Islamic concepts and norms that emphasize the equality of people, the accountability of leaders to community, and the respect of diversity and other faiths. These notions—ideas and ideals—are fully compatible and well-matched with modern conceptions of democracy. Majority of them not only endorse that the principle of *Shura* (as in Q. 3: 159 and 42: 38) is the first and foremost source of democratic ethics in Islam, but also acknowledge that these verses express clearly the view that an Islamic government cannot help but be *consultative, democratic,* and *divinely inspired* (Italics added).[125] They also suggest that the concept of majority and the utilitarian aspect of the Western system are fairly comparable to Islamic principles of *Ijmaʿ* (consensus) and *Maslaha* (public interest). In a nutshell, what they argue, at least in theory, can be summarized and recapitulated in a solo statement: that Islam and democracy are unquestionably compatible on many grounds.

Theoretically, there is no ambiguity and uncertainty in this argument; or in other words, the compatibility of Islam and democracy is not in question any longer. Muslim theorists have methodologically and analytically demonstrated that Islam can co-exist with the democratic process. By highlighting and stressing the presence of democracy, of various degrees, in several Muslim countries (like Indonesia, Malaysia, Turkey, Bangladesh, etc.), and the presence of Muslims (living as minorities) in the West, European countries, or in countries like India, have drawn attention to the fact that Islam and democracy can flourish in democratic societies.[126] The challenge now is not to contend whether Islam and democracy are compatible—that debate seems settled (now), although it is being still debated, and even in the second decade of the twenty-first century, some argue and write against this—and thus it is safe to argue, in the lexis of Esposito et al., that 'the relationships between Islam and democracy are in a new phase'; and 'most Muslims around the world view democracy as desirable and see no conflict with their religious faith'.[127]

Here a crucial question that comes to the forefront here is: If the envisioned *Shura* system (*Shuracracy* or 'Islamic democracy') is established as an alternative to (western) democracy in an Islamic country, what will be the structure and procedure of this system? In other words, the challenge, at the forefront, for Muslim theorists now is to show how an 'Islamic democracy' may be conceived and what its constitutive principles and features will be? Likewise, we need to answer, at the same time, the following five core questions, so that to analyse comparatively the views of nineteenth and twentieth-century modernist thinkers (discussed in Chapters 3 and 4) and the voices of the twenty-first century (discussed in previous and this chapter as well), to determine the scope, coverage, as well as relevance and significance of the topic under discussion.

1. What are the similarities and differences among the early modernists and contemporary modernist/reformist thinkers?
2. Did the differences in the audience impact their works and ideas on the subject?
3. Were the differences in the environments (political, social, and economic context) relevant to their conclusions?
4. Given this debate has been ongoing for so long, what conclusions can be drawn, what questions have been answered, and which are still left unanswered? and
5. Why does the debate regarding compatibility continue to exist?

The main difference between the nineteenth- and twentieth-century-Muslim modernist thinkers and present-day intellectuals is that the majority audience of the former were the Muslim societies in which they lived, or the major parts of the then Muslim world (as was the case, for example, with al-Afghani). The latter are addressing a global audience, covering and encompassing the societies in which they are living, which is mainly the West, and the Muslim world (for most of them come from various regions and Muslim countries of the world—MENA to Asia). This has transformed this hotly debated topic into a globally crucial and contested discourse. Furthermore, the socio-political and intellectual milieu of the former was different, which becomes obvious from the above difference. For many thinkers in the former category, the West and its challenges were either 'new' or 'emerging', whereas these challenges are no longer new for present-day intellectuals, as Muslims have been engaged in, and responding to, these challenges from the onslaught of 'colonialism' or from the emergence of 'modernism'.

It is well-known that on the verge of completion of the second decade of the twenty-first century, the debates and deliberations over 'Islam and modernity' and the issues related to it represent almost 'two-hundred-and-fifty-year history of the encounter between Muslim societies and "modernity".'[128] Muslim modernists, from pioneering figures like Tahtawi, Afghani, and 'Abduh in the Middle East to Sir Syed, Iqbal, and Azad in the South Asia, have responded to these challenges, and thus laid the foundation of what is generally termed as 'Islamic modernism'.[129]

The thinking of early modernists was formed and fashioned by the circumstances that led to the demise of Ottoman Empire (1299–1924). They were similar, to a great extent, in their views and arguments. Although they regarded the West as *problematic*, but Islam's relation with reason and rationality, science, and scientific beliefs was not problematic for them; rather, they were in favour of the compatibility between Islam and science, revelation and reason. Besides some differences, 'their work was governed', in the words of Javed Majeed (*King's College*, London), 'by the same project, which was to show that Islam was consistent with the rationality of the European enlightenment and the development of modern science. As such, they argued that there was no fundamental incompatibility between modernity and its narrative of progress, and Islam as a [dynamic and progressive] religion'.[130]

In encountering the European colonialism and the challenges of the modernism, these influential thinkers focused, in the words of Robert Rozehnal, on a central question: How can Muslims be true to the enduring values of their own past while living in the modern world? 'Embracing the ideas of *islah* (reform), *tajdid* (renewal), and *ijtihad* (independent legal reasoning), the modernists promoted', as Rozehnal remarks, 'Muslim unity and resistance to Western culture and hegemony by adopting the fruits of science and technology while overhauling Muslim educational, legal, and political intuitions'.[131]

These early Muslim modernists were so much under pressure to reform their specific societies that they did not find enough time to imagine a great political entity, except in historical terms. The exception, of course, was al-Afghani, who was the proponent *par excellence* of 'Pan-Islamism', but, at the same time, the fact is that all these major thinkers had a major problem with power and the powerful. This situation has been beautifully summarized by Louay Safi, in his *Islam and the Trajectory of Globalization*, as:

> The European colonial intrusion into Muslim spaces was so vast and profound that it penetrated deep into the Muslim consciousness, reshaping and redefining the Muslim self-image and pushing many Muslims to reevaluate and recalibrate their place in the new modern order shaped for the first time in their collective memories by someone other than themselves. The process of reassessment was done a bit too late in the European intrusion into fragmented Muslim societies that have long lost their intellectual and scientific zeal. The transformation of Muslim societies and experiences during the colonial period and its continuation in the postcolonial Muslim societies were total and thorough, affecting all key areas of their life and society—education, culture, economy, and politics.[132]

Regarding the similarity of the thoughts, ideologies, and goals of these early modernist thinkers, Safi (in his *The Challenge of Modernity*) offered the following three main conclusions: these *modernists* (i) stood against *taqlid* (blind following/imitation) in religious sciences; (ii) were exposed to the West, and consequently all of them considered the West and its challenges problematic for Islam and Muslim countries; and (iii) believed that Islam and modern values, especially scientific values, were compatible. In this way, they defended the notion that Islam, as a system of values, could be well and alive in the modern age.[133]

Thus, despite the 'differing analyses and perceptions', all these Muslim modernists confronted one or more of the following four key issues on which the Islamic world seemed to depend: (i) morality, religious faith, and development; (ii) Islam and scientific progress; (iii) Islam and political institutions; and (iv) Islam, nationalism, and development.[134]

In comparison to these early modernist thinkers, present-day Muslim intellectuals—besides writing on various issues encircling the grand narrative of Islam and modernity—are facing scores of new challenges and they are not only writing prolifically, and answering them effectively and efficiently, on these issues, but are earnestly engaged in these debates as well. They are addressing both the Muslim world as well as the societies in which they are living—especially the Western societies. And, thus, keeping in view, the differences in their environments (socio-political, cultural, economic, and intellectual contexts), their discourses and debates on Islam and the challenges it is facing, is global in nature, as compared to early modernists.

Regarding the other last two questions posed above—questions 4 and 5—it may be argued that there are still some questions, and here in this context, the question of Islam–democracy (in) compatibility, that have not been answered yet. This is still a *challenge* both for Muslim political theorists as well as for 'Islamic political theory'.

Furthermore, the debate(s) on Islam and modernity/modernization along with its other related themes—especially Islam and the process of democratization in Muslim societies, Islam and globalization, etc.—still continue to 'exist' for the reason that in the recent decades and in the post-9/11 era especially, Islam—having its followers across the globe—has been frequently used as a 'violent/terrorist' religion having least concern with peace, human rights, justice, tolerance, pluralism, democratic values, etc. This is the main reason why such a debate is still going-on:

> The issue of the compatibility of religion and democracy has not only been discussed in the 21st century in the Islamic world, but from the final decades of the 20th century.... After the events of 9/11 and the subsequent war on terror, this issue came to be discussed with much fervor, since in this period Islam was frequently described as a violent and terrorist religion, unconcerned with peace, human rights, justice, tolerance, pluralism and democratic values.[135]

Coming back to the main question—i.e. how will be *Shura* system (*Shura-cracy* or 'Islamic democracy')—envisioned?—it may be argued that in the Islam–democracy compatibility discourse, especially *Shura* as an alternative institution and system to Western democracy, the problem is that there is lack and scarcity of literature on the practical front. Muslim thinkers and political activists/analysts have, no doubt, been sincerely and earnestly engaged in discussing the Islam–democracy compatibility on the theoretical grounds—as becomes clear from the discussions (made in the previous Chapters 3–6)—but at the same time, they have paid either less attention, or no consideration at all, to the practical aspect of this compatibility or alternative system of government. In other words, while coming to the practical aspect, one finds no guidance. There seems to be a *missing link* in turning 'political theory' into a 'political programme'—or in turning conceptualizations of the ideal government into details.

Moreover, there are certain crucial questions that are obscured, or are not addressed at all. One such issue is the structure of the *Shura* body. Should it be comprised of experts or of anyone elected through universal suffrage? And once it exists, what should be the mechanism of its operation? These questions need to be answered by these and other scholars, policy makers/political analysts, and activists, who have spent much time in debating Islam–democracy discourse in theory.

But, at the same time, it is important to highlight that although *Shura* was an important facet and feature of Islamic polity during the time of the Prophet (pbuh) and the Pious Caliphate era (622–660 CE), there is no consensus how to implement it. The problem, however, as pointed out previously, has been that the practice of *Shura* was not institutionalized. Although Caliph 'Umar (r. 634–644 CE), tried to some extent to do so, but the 'adhoc procedure', he adopted, was suitable for that small community only. Once the community expanded to span several continents, this 'procedure proved inadequate'; and as El-Affendi predicts, it will be 'equally inadequate today' as well.[136] Thus, this is the reason why the role and scope of *Shura* have been the subject of intense debate, and thus remain, along with the concept of *Khilafah*, merely the 'theoretical constructs'.[137] At the same time, it is necessary to offer a practical framework to the Islam–democracy compatibility theory: how an 'Islamic democracy' will emerge, and work, in a Muslim country is still a challenge for Islamic political theory; and it is the responsibility of Muslims (especially Muslim political theorists) to overcome this challenge.[138]

Hasan al-Turabi (1932–2016)[139]—a religious and Islamist political leader of Sudan—has been described as 'Sudan's democrat turned authoritarian'.[140] He is, perhaps, the only scholar in whose political thinking, the concept of *Shura* has played a central role and his political activity in Sudan has required him to develop material proposals about how *Shura* should be implemented. In one of his works on 'Political Jurisprudence',[141] he distinguishes between four types of *Shura*: (1) universal *Shura*, which is also the highest and strongest one, such as in referendums and general elections. This type of *Shura* constitutes *Ijma*'—a consensus within the nation, which is legally binding, but it should not contradict the Qur'an and the Sunnah; (2) *Shura* based on the people's representatives in government; (3) *Shura* based on experts; and (4) *Shura* based on opinion polls.[142] Al-Turabi seems to describe here the decision-making mechanism of Western democracies, although without committing himself to technicalities such as the frequency of elections or the balance of power between legislators and head of state. But elsewhere, he states that the principle of *Shura* is governed in accordance with knowledge, because he, who possesses more knowledge, sees things more clearly. Thus, he leaves the door open to both a theocratic and a republican form of government.[143]

In *The West and Islam*,[144] Mishal al-Sulami analyses and focuses, among others, on the similarities and differences between Western liberal democracy and *Shura* with special reference to the views of Hasan al-Turabi. A fundamental finding of al-Sulami's book is that 'the central framework of al-Turabi's *Shura system* (as it has emerged at the end of the process) is *very close in its essential elements to that of Western liberal democracy*' (italics added).[145] For Turabi—who like other (moderate) Islamist leaders 'has accepted the centrality of the notion of democracy to *shura* in modern times'[146]—it is 'not surprising' that

> seven—out of eight—of the *main elements and mechanisms of the shura system* (civil liberties, *ijma*' (consensus), election of the president of the state and members of the *shura* council, division of powers, political participation, competitive elections and multi-party or trend system), as identified in the discourse of moderate Islamist movements and prominent Islamist thinkers, *are similar to their counterparts in Western liberal democracies*[147](civil liberties, majority rule, elected representatives, separation of powers, political participation, competitive elections, and the political party system and interest groups). (Italics added)[148]

The most vital issue remaining obscure—unclear and ambiguous—goes to the heart of the distinction between *Shura* and democracy. Uriya Shavit points out, and questions, on the issues that scholars 'caution that there is no room for *shura* on issues where the Qur'an and the Sunnah have ruled, but they do not specify and/or postulate who should determine what these issues are and who will hold the authority to revoke legislation deemed un-Islamic. Should this authority be a high court, or perhaps a council of scholars? How should the authority be selected? A body entrusted with this delicate task would be the ultimate power in the envisioned Muslim state based on *Shura*. Yet not a hint is given as to its desired structure'.[149] However, Shavit here slips to take note of Turabi's 'The Islamic State' (1983), wherein he deliberates on the possible-*Shura*-structure in present times—though he too is not clear about its proper structure—in these words:

> In the period of the Prophet [pbuh] all the functions of the state were exercised by him as teacher and sovereign. He wisely but informal consulted with his companions. Later this consultative process was almost developed into an indirect representative institution called *ahl al-shura* or *majlis-i-shura* (consultative council).... Today this could very well be formulated through a parliament, a council or a *majlis-i-shura*. People may directly, through referendum, exercise their *ijma* consensus or otherwise delegate power to their deputies. There would, however, be certain rules regulating the qualifications of candidates and election campaigns for the choice of deputies or other offices of the state.[150]

Another reason for 'obscurity is the pretentiousness' of connecting and paralleling *Shura* and democracy, for Shavit, is that there is, as such, 'nothing in the Quran or the *sunna* [Sunnah] that directly supports the claim that democracy is *shura*. *Shura* implies consultation, and its interpretation as a directive to hold elections and structure a political system resembling that of Western societies is, at the very least, somewhat of a stretch. To commit that interpretation to any definite mechanisms would be another stretch—perhaps one too many'.[151] Discussing this point further—and supplementing it with the Qur'anic narration of receiving a letter from Prophet Sulaiman (AS) by Queen Saba, and its interpretations by Muhammad 'Imara and Yusuf al-Qaradawi—Shavit states:

Illustrating this fragility is the story of Queen Sheba's [or Saba] reaction to a letter she received from King Solomon [Prophet Sulaiman, referring to the Qur'an] (27: 26–35). 'Imara as well as al-Qaradawi[152], invoke it as an example for the application of *shura*. In this story, the Queen asks her ministers how she should respond to King Soloman's letter, telling them she would not make up her mind before they gave her their opinion, only to be told that the decision is hers. This tells nothing more than of a traditional monarch who holds monopoly on strategic decisions—a far cry from the type of political participation 'Imara and al-Qaradawi depict in their writings on *shura*.[153]

Mohammed Abu-Nimer puts it as:

Despite scholarly debates on when and who can be consulted in important community decisions, the fact remains that consultation and input in decision-making is expected from the whole *Ummah*, the general community and its leaders through a process of *shura*. Thus, *shura* was a hallmark of early Islamic governance.... *shura* is not merely a consultation by the rulers and their advisers only, but it is an inclusive process. *Shura* involves all matters concerning the *Ummah*, not simply those in which they might be likely to have expertise. The people of the *shura* represent all the segments of the society, differing from the people of *ijtihad* who are the Islamic *fuqaha'* (pl. of *faqih*) or experts of jurisprudence. The Prophet [pbuh] encouraged Muslims to consult with each other and with experts. He repeatedly consulted with other Muslims and followed their advice even when he disagreed with the person.[154]

Thus, given the problems persisting in the Muslim world and the neglect of practicality in the literature, two observations can be made here: (i) theoretically, more reflection, research, and reinterpretation is required to reconcile the tenets of Islam with the modern notions of democracy, liberty, justice, equality, etc.; and (ii) practically, it is now the need of the hour to translate this theory into a practical framework. By the implementation of this 'Islamic democracy', Muslims will lay the foundations of a political order that will be a blend of Islamic political principles and positive features of modern (Western) democracy.

# Notes

1. Riffat Hassan, in her 'Islamic Modernist and Reformist Discourse in South Asia' in Hunter, *Reformist Voices*, p. 176, confers/labels Ghamidi as a '*Contemporary Reformist Thinker in Pakistan*', who is 'more 'modernist' and 'reformist' than most [of the contemporary] Muslim scholars, challenging some generally prevalent interpretations in what is the most sensitive of all subjects for most Muslims'. He, and his thoughts vis-à-vis Islam and democracy, has been described by Husnul Amin as '*Post-Islamist Intellectual Trends in Pakistan*', who has emerged as 'a leading religious figure in the public and private media'. For details, see, Husnul Amin, 'Post-Islamist Intellectual Trends in Pakistan: Javed Ahmad Ghamidi and His Discourse on Islam and Democracy', *Islamic Studies* [*IS*], 51, 2 (2012): 169–192, pp. 169, 175–176.
2. Samina Yasmeen, 'Democracy for Muslims: Javed Ahmed Ghamidi' in Lily Zubaidah Rahim (ed.), *Muslim Secular Democracy: Voices from Within* (New York: Palgrave Macmillan, 2013), ch. 4, pp. 93–112, p. 93. In this chapter, Yasmeen analyses the views of Ghamidi with reference to the question of democracy in Muslim societies, arguing that Ghamidi openly supports the 'idea of democracy in Islam' as an appropriate system of government, which for him, goes beyond 'procedural aspects and encompasses notions of rights and responsibilities of the state and its citizens' (p. 104).
3. For details, see http://www.ghamidi.net/Ishraq.html
4. For details, see http://www.monthly-renaissance.com
5. For details, see http://www.studying-islam.org/
6. For details, see www.almawrid.org/ and http://javedahmadghamidi.com//
7. For details, see, Parray, *AJISS*, 2012, pp. 155–156.
8. Amin, *IS*, pp. 169–192, p. 186.
9. Javed Ahmad Ghamidi, 'Islam and the Taliban' (trans. Asif Iftikhar), *Renaissance—A Monthly Islamic Journal*, 19, 6 (June 2009), available online at http://www.monthly-renaissance.com/issue/content.aspx?id=1158 (last accessed on 25 May 2011).
10. See, Javed Ahmad Ghamidi, *Islam: A Comprehensive Introduction*, English rendering of *Mizan*, 5th edition, by Shehzad Saleem (Lahore, Pakistan: Al-Mawrid Foundation of Islamic Research and Education, 2009), p. 462 [hereafter cited as Ghamidi, *Islam*]. Shehzad Saleem has rendered a chapter of *Mizan* (4th ed., 2009, pp. 483–497) separately as 'The Political Shari'ah of Islam' (Lahore, Pakistan: Al-Mawrid Foundation of Islamic Research and Education, n.d.), with an Introduction, and some appendices as well [hereafter cited as Ghamidi, *Political Shari'ah*]. See also, Javed Ahmad Ghamidi, 'Their System Is Based on Their Consultation', in Shehzad Saleem (ed.), *Selected Essays of Javed Ahmad Ghamidi* (Lahore, Pakistan: Al-Mawrid, 2015): 183–212, also available online at http://www.javedahmadghamidi.com/meezan/view/the_state_system (last accessed on 20 August 2018). This is originally taken from the chapter 'Amruhum Shura Baynahum' in his *Burhan* (Lahore, Pakistan: Al-Mawrid, 2009), available

at http://www.javedahmadghamidi.com/burhan/view/amrohum-shoora-baena hum. Here references are given from the *Selected Essays*, and is cited as Ghamidi, 'System'.

11. Ghamidi, 'Islam and the Taliban', op. cit.
12. Ghamidi, *Islam*, p. 462; Idem., 'System', p. 185.
13. Ghamidi, *Islam*, p. 462; Idem., 'System', pp. 185–186.
14. Ghamidi, *Islam*, p. 462; Idem., 'System', p. 183.
15. Ghamidi, *Islam,* p. 462; Idem., Ghamidi, *Political Shari'ah*, p. 21; Idem., 'System', p. 187.
16. Ghamidi, *Islam*, p. 463; Idem., *Political Shari'ah*, p. 22; Idem., 'System' pp. 187–188.
17. Amin, *IS*, p. 187.
18. Syed Abul Ala Mawdudi, *Tafhim al-Qur'an* (New Delhi: Markazi Maktaba Islami Publishers, 2003), IV: 509–510.
19. Mawdudi, *Tafhim al-Quran, op. cit.*; Ghamidi, 'System', pp. 188–189; Idem., *Islam*, pp. 463–464; also cited in Amin, *IS*, p. 187.
20. Javed Ahmad Ghamidi, 'The Political Law of Islam', Shehzad Saleem (trans.), *Renaissance*, 23 December 2002; Idem., 'System', p. 190.
21. Amin, *IS*, pp. 186, 188.
22. Shehzad Saleem, 'The Political System of Pakistan: Points to Ponder' (adapted from Ghamidi's *Burhan*), *Renaissance*, http://www.monthly-renaissance.com/issue/content.aspx?id=467 (last accessed on 28 August 2018), also cited in Amin, *IS*, p. 188.
23. Saleem, *loc. cit.*
24. Javed Ahmed Ghamidi, 'Islam and the Political System in Our Society', *Studying-Islam*, 16 December 2002, available online at http://www.studying-islam.org/articletext.aspx?id=692 (last accessed on 28 December 2021).
25. An Interview with Javed Ahmad Ghamidi by *NaseebVibes*, Wednesday, 22 June 2005, available online and translated by *Studying Islam*, http://www.studying-islam.org/articletext.aspx?id=985 (last accessed on 28 December 2021).
26. Ibid.
27. Ibid.
28. See 'Ghamidi—Nizam e Jamhooriyat (democracy)' on YouTube (uploaded on 22 December 2008), available at http://www.youtube.com/watch?v=ZmAy_fq7m8c (last accessed on 9 June 2011). English translation is my own.
29. Yasmeen, 'Democracy for Muslims', op. cit., p. 104.
30. Amin, *IS*, p. 192.
31. Ghamidi, *Political Shari'ah*, p. 2.
32. For more details, see http://abdelwahab-el-affendi.net/bio.html and https://www.dohainstitute.edu.qa/EN/About/Pages/OOTP.aspx (last accessed on 20 June 2021); see also, Tauseef Ahmad Parray, 'Three Living Western [Muslim] Academicians on Islam-Democracy Discourse: Analyzing the Views of Prof(s) Abou El Fadl, El-Affendi, and Sachedina', *Point of View* [*PoV*]: Centre for Mediterranean, Middle East & Islamic Studies [CEMMIS], University of Peloponnese, Greece (28 January 2015): 1–7, pp. 2–3.

33. Abdelwahab El-Affendi, 'Democracy and Its (Muslim) Critics: An Islamic Alternative to Democracy', in M. A. Muqtedar Khan (ed.), *Islamic Democratic Discourse: Theory, Debates and Philosophical Perspectives* (Lanham, MD: Lexington Books, 2006), pp. 227–256, p. 232.
34. Abdelwahab El-Affendi, 'Rationality of Politics and Politics of Rationality: Democratization and the Influence of Islamic Religious Traditions', in Azzam Tamimi and John L. Esposito (eds.), *Islam and Secularism in the Middle East* (London: C. Hurts and Co., 2000), pp. 151–169, p. 168.
35. Affendi, 'Democracy and Its (Muslim) Critics', in Khan (ed.), *Islamic Democratic Discourse*, op. cit., p. 247.
36. Ibid., p. 243.
37. Ibid., p. 254.
38. Abdelwahab El-Affendi, 'Do Muslims Deserve Democracy?', available online at http://www.newint.org/features/2002/05/01/do-muslims-deserve-democracy/#key (last accessed on 25 May 2011).
39. Ibid.
40. Abdelwahab El-Affendi, *Who Needs an Islamic State?* 2nd ed. (UK: Malaysia Think Tank London, 2008 [1991]). The first edition of this was published in 1991 by Grey Seal Books, London.
41. See Wan Saiful Wan Jan, 'Preface', in Affendi, *Who Needs an Islamic State? op. cit.*, p. 14.
42. Ibid.
43. El-Affendi, *Islamic State, op. cit.*, p. 139.
44. Ibid., p. 140.
45. Ibid.
46. Ibid., p. 30.
47. Ibid., p. 49.
48. Ibid., p. 60.
49. Ibid., p. 122.
50. Abdelwahab El-Affendi, 'The Modern Debate(s) on Islam and Democracy', available online at http://www.ndid.org.my/web/wp-content/uploads/2010/04/The-Modern-Debate-on-Islam-and-DemocracyAbdelwahab-El-Affendi-4.htm#_ftn1 (last accessed on 25 May 2011).
51. Ibid.
52. El-Affendi, in Tamimi and Esposito, *Islam and Secularism*, p. 162.
53. El-Affendi, *Islamic State*, p. 152.
54. Louay M. Safi is the author of about twenty books in Arabic and English— including *The Challenge of Modernity* (1994), *The Foundation of Knowledge* (2014 [1996]), *Truth and Reform* (1998), *Peace and the Limits of War* (2001), *Tensions and Transitions in the Muslim World* (2003), *Blaming Islam: Examining the Religion Building Enterprise* (2006), *Islam and the Trajectory of Globalization* (2021)—and numerous papers (presented in various international forums and conferences, and published in various academic journals). He maintains his own

website www.louaysafi.com also. Besides, he has also appeared on numerous radio and TV programmes, including CNN, BBC, Monte Carlo, Fox News, PBS, Middle East TV (MBC), Al-Jazeera TV, Voice of America, Malaysian Television, etc. For details, see http://louaysafi.com//index.php?option=com_content&task=view&id=9&Itemid=37 and https://hbku.edu.qa/en/cis/staff/louaysafi (last accessed on 28 December 2021).
55. Louay M. Safi, 'Can Islam and Democracy Coexist?' *National Geographic News*, 24 October 2003, available online at http://news.nationalgeographic.com/news/2003/10/1021_031021_islamicdemocracy.htm (last accessed on 5 September 2010) [hereafter cited as Safi, *NGN*]; also available at http://www.onthewing.org/user/Islam%20-%20Can%20Islam%20and%20Democracy%20Coexist.pdf (last accessed on 5 December 2021).
56. Safi, *NGN, op. cit.*
57. Louay M. Safi, 'Democracy Inside Out: The Case of Egypt', *Q-News—The Muslim Magazine*, March 2005, 17, 361, available online at http://www.q-news.com/361-Egypt.html (last accessed on 5 September 2010) [hereafter cited as Safi, *Q-News*, 2005].
58. Ibid.
59. Ibid.
60. Safi, *AJISS*, p. 233.
61. Louay Safi, 'Shura and Democracy: Similarities and Differences', 6 November 1999, available online at http://louaysafi.com//index.php?option=com_content&task=view&id=51&Itemid=22 (last accessed on 20 August 2018). Originally presented as a paper at the Annual Meeting of the *Middle East Studies Association* (MESA), Washington, on 19 November 1999.
62. Ibid.
63. Ibid.
64. Ibid.
65. Louay M. Safi, 'Arab Democracy Is a Work in Progress', 2 April 2012, available online at http://louaysafi.com//index.php?option=com_content&task=view&id=118&Itemid=7. The article is based on a public lecture delivered by Dr Safi at Doha on 22 February 2012 under the title 'From Sultanic Rule to Democracy'.
66. Louay M. Safi, *Islam and the Trajectory of Globalization: Rational Idealism and the Structure of World History* (New York: Routledge, 2021), p. 214.
67. Safi, *Islam and the Trajectory of Globalization*, pp. 214–218.
68. Ibid., p. 214.
69. See, 'About Dr. Khaled Abou El Fadl', *Scholar of the House*, available online at www.scholarofthehouse.org/abdrabelfadl.html (last accessed on 20 June 2017).
70. Tamara Sonn, 'Voices of Reformist Islam in the United States' in Hunter (ed.), *Reformist Voices of Islam, op. cit.*, pp. 267–286, p. 276.
71. Parray in *PoV*, 2015, pp. 1–2.
72. See its website www.usuli.org (last accessed on 20 December 2021).

73. Khaled Abou El Fadl, *Islam and the Challenge of Democracy* (Princeton: Princeton University Press, 2004).
74. Ibid., pp. 4, 5.
75. Ibid., p. 5.
76. Ibid., p. 36.
77. Ibid., p. 9.
78. Ibid., p. 22.
79. Ibid., pp. 5–6.
80. Ibid., p. 27.
81. Ibid., pp. 5–6.
82. Nader A. Hashemi, 'Change from Within', in Abou El Fadl, *Islam and the Challenge of Democracy*, pp. 49–54, p. 50.
83. Mahmood, 'Is Liberalism Islam's only Answer?', in Abou El Fadl, *Islam and the Challenge of Democracy*, pp. 74–77, p. 74.
84. Bernard Haykel, 'Popular Support First', in Abou El Fadl, *Islam and the Challenge of Democracy*, pp. 78–80, p. 78.
85. Feldman, 'The Best Hope', in Abou El Fadl, *Islam and the Challenge of Democracy*, pp. 59–62, pp. 59–60.
86. Abou El Fadl, *Islam and the Challenge of Democracy*, p. 36.
87. For details, see www.csidonline.org/about (last accessed on 5 December 2021).
88. For details, see www.csidonline.org/people/radwan-masmoudi (last accessed on 5 December 2021).
89. Radwan Masmoudi, ['Editorial'] *Muslim Democrat*, 1, 2 (September 1999): 1.
90. Radwan Masmaudi, 'Muslims Do Want Democracy', *The Charlotte Observer* (Fri, October 2006), available online at www.charlotte.com/mld/observer/news/opinion/15691590.htm (last accessed on 5 September 2010).
91. Radwan Masmoudi 'Why Democracy?', *Muslim Democrat*, 7, 1 (April 2005): 1–2.
92. Radwan Masmoudi, 'The Silenced Majority', in Larry Diamond et al. (eds.), *Islam and Democracy in the Middle East* (Baltimore: John Hopkins University Press, 2003), pp. 258–262, pp. 258–259.
93. Ibid., p. 260.
94. Radwan Masmoudi, 'The Future of "Islamic Democracy" in the Middle East–Islamists and Democracy: Friends or Foes?', *Future Islam*, September–October 2007, available online at http://www.futureislam.com/20070901/insight/radwan_a_masmoudi/The%20Future%20of%20Islamic%20Democracy%20in%20the%20Middle%20East.asp (last accessed on 9 December 2010).
95. M. A. Muqtedar Khan has written extensively on the Islam–democracy compatibility theme. For details, see, M. A. Muqtedar Khan, *American Muslims: Bridging Faith and Freedom* (Maryland, Amana Publications, 2002); Idem., 'Islamic Democratic Theory: Between Political Philosophy and Jurisprudence', *Global Dialogue* [GD], 6, 1 and 2 (Winter 2004): 44–52; Idem., 'Islamic Democracy and Moderate Muslims: The Straight Path Runs Through the Middle' in (the Special Issue on *Debating Moderate Islam* of) *AJISS*, 27, 2 (Summer 2005): 39–50;

Idem., 'The Politics, Theory and Philosophy of Islamic Democracy', in Khan (ed.), *Islamic Democratic Discourse* (2006), ch. 8, pp. 149–171; Idem., *Debating Moderate Islam* (Utah, 2007); Idem., 'Islamic Democratic Theory: Between Political Philosophy and Jurisprudence', in Nadeem Hasnain (ed.), *Beyond Textual Islam* (New Delhi: Serial Publications, 2008), pp. 27–41; Idem., 'Islamic Governance and Democracy' in Shiping Hua (ed.), *Islam and Democratization in Asia* (New York: Cambria Press, 2009), pp. 13–27; Idem., 'Democracy is Indispensable: A Political Philosophy of Islamic Governance', *The Roundtable*, 9, 1 (2011–2012): 11–14; Idem., 'Three Dimensions of the Emerging Political Philosophy of Islam', in Shahram Akbarzadeh (ed.), *Routledge Handbook of Political Islam* (New York: Routledge, 2012), ch. 3, pp. 27–34, also available online at https://works.bepress.com/muqtedar_khan/25/ (last accessed on 20 August 2018); Idem., 'Political Authority in Islam', in M. Kabir Hassan and Mervyn K. Lewis (eds.), *Handbook on Islam and Economic Life* (Cheltenham, UK and Northampton, MA: Edward Elgar, 2014), ch. 26, pp. 520–540; Idem., 'What Is Islamic Democracy? The Three Cs of Islamic Governance', in Timothy Poirson and Robert Oprisko (eds.), *Caliphates and Islamic Global Politics* (UK: E-International Relations Publications, 2015), pp. 94–99, also available at: http://works.bepress.com/muqtedar_khan/36/ (last accessed on 20 August 2018). Besides these, he has authored a good number of articles on this theme, including, 'Islam's Compatibility with Democracy'; 'Shura and Democracy'; 'The Compact of Medina: A Constitutional Theory of the Islamic State'; etc., all available on his (personal) websites www.ijtihad.org and/or www.Glocaleye.org. Hereafter all these works are cited in abbreviated and/or shortened forms.

96. Professor Muqtedar Khan is regarded as one of the 'rising stars among Muslim intellectuals' in the West (*The Daily Star*); 'Voice of Moderate Islam' (*Los Angeles Times* and *The Boston Globe*); 'A Rare Moderate Voice' (*The Daily Times*); a scholar who brings 'passion, eloquence and intellectual power to bear on his subject' (Dr Ali Mazrui); and an 'intelligent, reasoned, self-critical, impassioned and provocative Muslim voice [who] makes a distinctive and significant contribution to the process of reexamination and reform' (John L. Esposito). For details, see Khan's personal website www.ijtihad.org

97. M. A. Muqtedar Khan, 'Compatibility of Islam and Democracy', in *United States Institute of Peace (USIP) Special Report on 'Islam and Democracy'* (Washington, DC) 93 (September 2002), pp. 3–4, p. 3 [hereafter cited as Khan, *USIP*].

98. Khan, *American Muslims*, pp. 105–106; see also, Khan, *USIP*, p. 4. The book *American Muslims* also contains a collection of essays that Khan wrote over the years and subsequently published in various magazines, and international newspapers, like Washington Report on Middle East Politics, Mirror International, Muslim Observer, and the Globalist, etc. Some of these essays are also available on his personal website www.ijtihad.org, so the references are made of both, book and the website.

99. Khan, *American Muslims*, pp. 96–97; Idem., 'Islam's Compatibility with Democracy', online at www.ijtihad.org/isladem.htm, 11 April 2001 (last accessed on 26 August 2010).
100. Khan, *American Muslims*, p. 107; Idem., 'Shura and Democracy', *Muslim Democrat*, 1, 2 (September 1999): 5; Idem., in Hua, *op. cit.*, p. 25.
101. Khan, *American Muslims*, loc. cit.
102. Khan, 'The Politics', p. 151. In this book, he attempts to accelerate the development of the gradually emerging philosophical and theological discourse on Islamic democratic theory. Making a systematic effort to link contemporary Muslim ideas on Islam and democracy with classical Islamic theories and profound theological concepts and issues, it opens new avenues to seriously build authentic Islamic theory/theories of democracy. See, for example, Tauseef Ahmad Parray, 'Review: M. A. Muqtedar Khan. Ed. *Islamic Democratic Discourse: Theory, Debates and Philosophical Perspectives*. Lanham, MD: Lexington Books, 2006 …', *Insights* (Pakistan), 1, 3 (2009): 171–176.
103. Khan builds his analysis on the basis of these works: Abdulaziz Sachedina, *The Islamic Roots of Democratic Pluralism* (New York: Oxford University Press, 2001); Abdul Karim Soroush, 'Tolerance and Governance: A Discourse on Religion and Democracy', in M. Sadri and S. Sadri (trans and eds.), *Reason, Freedom and Democracy in Islam; Essential Writings of Abdul Karim Soroush* (New York: Oxford University Press, 2000), pp. 131–155; Abou El-Fadl, *Islam and the Challenge of Democracy*, op. cit.
104. Khan, 'The Politics', p. 166. *Cf.* Idem., in Akbarzadeh, p. 33.
105. Khan, in *Roundtable*, pp. 11, 14; Idem., 'Political Authority in Islam', p. 537.
106. Khan, 'Political Authority in Islam', *op. cit.*, pp. 535–537. *Cf.* Idem., 'What Is Islamic Democracy?', pp. 94–99.
107. Khan, 'The Politics', p. 166; Idem., 'Islamic Democratic Theory' in Hasnain, pp. 37–38.
108. Khan in *Roundtable*, p. 14; Idem., in Hua, *op. cit.*, p. 25.
109. See, for example, Khan in *Roundtable*, p. 14; Idem., in Hua, *op. cit.*, p. 25; Idem., 'The Politics', p. 166; Idem., in Hasnain, loc. cit.
110. See, for example, Khan, in Hua, *loc. cit.*; Idem., 'The Politics', p. 166.; Idem., in Hasnain, loc. cit. Idem., in *GD*, p. 52.
111. See M. A. Muqtedar Khan's 'Foreword' in this book. Idem., *Islam and Good Governance: Political Philosophy of Ihsan* (New York: Palgrave Macmillan, 2019). See also, Tauseef Ahmad Parray, 'Ihsan as the basis of "Good Governance"', *Greater Kashmir*, 5 March 2020, p. 9.
112. For more details, see his profile at Newlines Institute website at https://newlinesinstitute.org/people/kamran-bokhari/ (last accessed on 29 December 2021).
113. See, Kamran Bokhari and Farid Senzai, *Political Islam in the Age of Democratization* (New York: Palgrave Macmillan, 2013), p. 11, in which they offer a comprehensive view of the complex nature of contemporary political Islam and its relationship to democracy, by focusing on the process of

democratization vis-à-vis political Islam. For details, see, Tauseef Ahmad Parray, 'Political Islam, Islamists, and Democratization', *Kashmir Reader*, 21 August 2015, p. 7; Idem., 'Recent Scholarship on "Islamism" Discourse: An Evaluation and Assessment', *Analisa*, 1, 1 (June 2016): 1–17, pp. 13–14.

114. The Abstract of this work states: 'During the last quarter of a century, much has been said and written about the correlation between Islam and democracy, in both Muslim as well as non-Muslim circles. In so far as the former group is concerned, the debate has generally been amongst Islamists and certain academic quarters, whereas in the latter it has been amongst academicians, journalists, and policy analysts. While the Non-Muslim contribution to this debate has indeed played a significant role in shaping modern Islamic political philosophy, however, this thesis will focus essentially on the Islamist perceptions of democracy. Although the dominant Islamist point of view is that Islam is wholly compatible with democracy, however, there remain a significant number of Islamists who view democracy as being antithetical to Islam. The more recent literature on this issue indicates that the locus of debate is slowly shifting to the question of just how much is Islam compatible with democracy. The purpose of this thesis is to examine the debate over Islam and democracy within the framework of the contemporary global movement towards Islamic revival, and to suggest future contemplative trends in this regard'. For details, see Kamran Bokhari, 'Islam & Democracy in the Context of the Contemporary Islamic Political Resurgence' (2002). *MSU Graduate Theses*, 2232, retrieved from https://bearworks.missouristate.edu/theses/2232 (last accessed on 29 December 2021).

115. For more details, see his profile at Newlines Institute website at https://newlinesinstitute.org/people/kamran-bokhari/ (last accessed on 29 December 2021).

116. Kamran Bokhari, 'Is Democracy Disbelief?', *Q-News*, 352 (December 2003): 34–35, available online at http://www.q-news.com/352.pdf

117. Ibid.

118. Ibid., p. 34.

119. Ibid.

120. Ibid., p. 35.

121. Ibid.

122. Ibid.

123. Kamran A. Bokhari, 'Islamist Attitudes Toward Democracy', in *Islam, Democracy and the Secularist State in the Post-Modern Era* (Conference Proceedings of *Center for the Study of Islam and Democracy Second Annual Conference* (Burtonsville, MD: CSID, 2001), p. 174.

124. Ibid. p. 175.

125. Mahdi Bazargan, 'Religion and Liberty', in Charles Kurzman (ed.), *Liberal Islam—A Sourcebook* (New York: Oxford University Press, 1994), pp. 73–84, p. 79.

126. For this argument, see, among others, Abou El-Fadl, *Islam and the Challenge of Democracy*; Khan (ed.), *Islamic Democratic Discourse*; Hasan (ed.), *Democracy*

in *Muslim Societies*; Hua (ed.), *Islam and Democratization in Asia*; Hashemi, *Islam Secularism, and Liberal Democracy*; Kubicek, *Political Islam and Democracy in the Muslim World*; Esposito et al., *Islam Democracy after the Arab Spring*.

127. Esposito et al., *Islam and Democracy after the Arab Spring*, p. 239.
128. Ali Paya, *Islam, Modernity, and a New Millennium: Themes from a Critical Rationalist Reading of Islam* (London and New York: Routledge, 2018), p. 8; see also, Tauseef Ahmad Parray, *Mediating Islam and Modernity: Sir Sayyid, Iqbal and Azad* (New Delhi: Viva Books, 2019).
129. Some of the pioneering works, of past and present, on this theme are: Charles C. Adams, *Islam and Modernism in Egypt: A Study of the Modern Reform Movement Inaugurated by Muhammad 'Abduh* (New York: Russel and Russel, 1933; reissued 1968); Albert Hourani, *Arabic Thought in the Liberal Age* (Cambridge: Cambridge University Press, 1962; reissued 1983); Aziz Ahmad, *Islamic Modernism in India and Pakistan—1857-1964* (London: Oxford University Press, 1967); Fazlur Rahman, *Islam and Modernity: Transformation of an Intellectual Tradition* (Chicago: University of Chicago Press, 1982); Louay M. Safi, *The Challenge of Modernity: The Quest for Authenticity in the Arab World* (Lanham: University Press of America, 1994); Kurzman, *Liberal Islam*; John Cooper Ronald Nettler, and Mohamed Mahmoud (eds.), *Islam and Modernity: Muslim Intellectuals Respond* (London and New York: I. B. Tauris, 2000) Charles Kurzman (ed.), *Modernist Islam:1840-1940—A Sourcebook* (New York: Oxford University Press, 2002); Mansoor Moaddel, *Islamic Modernism, Nationalism, and Fundamentalism: Episode and Discourse* (Chicago: University of Chicago Press, 2005); Mehran Kamrava (ed.), *The New Voices of Islam: Reforming Politics and Modernity—A Reader* (New York and London: I. B. Tauris, 2006); Shireen T. Hunter (ed.), *Reformist Voices of Islam—Meditating Islam and Modernity* (New York: M.E. Sharpe, Inc., 2009); Muhammad Khalid Masud, Armando Salvatore, and Martin van Bruinessen (eds.), *Islam and Modernity: Key Issues and Debates* (Edinburgh: Edinburgh University Press, 2009); Safdar Ahmed, *Reform and Modernity in Islam: The Philosophical, Cultural and Political Discourses among Muslim Reformers* (New York: I. B. Tauris, 2013).
130. See, among others, Javed Majeed, 'Modernity', in Richard C. Martin (ed.), *Encyclopedia of Islam and Modern World* [*EIMW*] (New York: Macmillan, 2004), II: 456-458.
131. Robert Rosehnal, 'Debating Orthodoxy, Contesting Tradition: Islam in Contemporary South Asia', in R. Michael Feener (ed.), *Islam in World Cultures: Comparative Perspectives* (California: ABC-CLIO, Inc., 2004), ch. 8, 103-131, p. 111.
132. Safi, *Islam and the Trajectory of Globalization*, p. 192.
133. Safi, *The Challenge of Modernity*, p. 111.

134. Tareq Y. Ismael and Jacqueline S. Ismael, *Government and Politics in Islam* (London: Frances Pinter Publishers, 1985), p. 30.
135. For details, see Tauseef Ahmad, Parray, 'Islam and Democracy in the Age of Democratization'. *Daily Sabah* (Turkey), 17 September 2015, https://www.dailysabah.com/op-ed/2015/09/17/islam-and-democracy-in-the-age-of-democratization (last accessed on 20 December, 2021).
136. El-Affendi, 'Democracy and Its (Muslim) Critics', in Khan, *op. cit.*, p. 235.
137. Ibid., p. 237.
138. This insight/idea is borrowed, among others, from Khan, in Hasnain, *op. cit.*, pp. 30, 38.
139. For the life, legacy, thought, and activities of Hasan al-Turabi see, Abdelwahab El-Affendi, *Turabi's Revolution: Islam and Power in Sudan* (London: Grey Seal, 1991); Millard Burr, *Revolutionary Sudan: Hasan al-Turabi and the Islamist State, 1989–2000* (Boston, MA: Brill, 2003).
140. W. J. Berridge, 'Hassan al-Turabi: Sudan's democrat turned authoritarian (1932–2016)', *African Arguments*, 3 August 2016, available online at www.africanarguments.org/2016/03/08/hassan al-turabi-sudans-democrat-turned-authoritarian-1932-2016/ (last accessed on 20 August 2018).
141. Hasan al-Turabi, *Nazrat fi al-Fiqh al-Siyasi* (Um al-Fahim: Markaz al-Dirasat al Mu'asira, 1997) [hereafter cited as Turabi, *Nazarat*].
142. Turabi, *Nazrat*, pp. 117–118, as cited by Uriya Shavit, 'Is *Shura* a Muslim Form of Democracy? Roots and Systemization of a Polemic', *Middle Eastern Studies* [*MES*], 46, 3 (2010): 356.
143. Hasan al-Turabi, *Tajdid al-Fikr al-Islami*, 3rd ed. (Jeddah: Al-Dar al-Saudiyya lil-Nashr wal-Tawzi', 1993), p. 87, vide Shavit in *MES*, p. 356.
144. Mishal Fahm Al-Sulami, *The West and Islam: Western Liberal Democracy versus the System of Shura* (New York: Routledge Curzon, 2003).
145. Ibid., p. 199.
146. Ibid.
147. It is pertinent to mention that Turabi here refers to, among others, Larry Diamond et al., *Democracy in Developing Countries* (London: Adamantine Press, 1988), pp. 218–260, who has mentioned that there are seven features common to any democracy: individual freedoms and civil liberties; rule of the law; sovereignty resting upon the people; equality of all citizens before the law; vertical and horizontal accountability for government officials; transparency of the ruling systems to the demands of the citizens; and equality of opportunity for citizens.
148. Al-Sulami, *op. cit.*, p. 199.
149. See Shavit in *MES*, 349–374, p. 357.
150. Hassan Turabi, 'The Islamic State', in Esposito (ed.), *Voices of Resurgent Islam*: ch. 12: 241–251, p. 248.
151. Shavit in *MES*, p. 357.

152. Shavit, *op. cit.,* here refers to these works: Muhammad 'Imara, *al-Islam wa Huquq al-Insan Darurat La Huquq* (Damascus and Cairo: Markaz al-Raya, Dar al-Islam, 2004-2005 [1985]), pp. 45-46; Yusuf al-Qaradawi, *Malamih al-Mujtama' al-Islami alladhi nanshuduhu* (Beirut: al-Risala, 1996), pp. 135-146.
153. Shavit in *MES*, p. 357.
154. Mohammed Abu-Nimer, 'Framework for Nonviolence and Peacebuilding in Islam', in Abdul Aziz Said et al. (eds.), *Contemporary Islam:Dynamic, Not Static* (Oxon and New York: Routledge, 2006), pp. 131-172, pp. 159-160.

# 7

# Democracy and Its Muslim Critics

## Objections and Observations of the 'Opponents'

In the discourses on Islam–democracy relation, there are two broad trends/poles: The Proponents (or Compatibility pole) and Opponents (or Incompatibility pole). Though the major focus of this work is to highlight the 'compatibility' pole—as outlined in the preceding chapters—however, for the purpose of maintaining equilibrium and equipoise, it is necessary to provide a brief assessment of the second trend/pole as well. The preceding chapters make it ample clear that in the discourses on Islam–democracy relation, it is the compatibility trend which is dominant and prevailing; however, what is true is, in the lexis of Kamran Bokhari:

> There exists a diversity of viewpoints ranging on one hand from those who view democracy as a value-neutral operational mechanism on the basis of which a modern Islamic state can be constructed, to those who see democracy as a value-laden concept that tries to elevate human reason above divine revelation and is hence seen as being tantamount to *kufr* (disbelief).[1]

The issues of (in)compatibility of democracy and the process of democratization, therefore, 'continue to remain the subject of vigorous debate'.[2] The Opponents—or supporters of *Rejectionist Theses*[3] and/or the *Muslim Isolationists*[4]—stress that democracy is a Western product and as such it has to be avoided at all cost. This trend, represented mainly by the conservative and some radical religious figures, takes on a negative view of any shape or form of democracy and democratic system; or as Azzam Tamimi puts it: 'the opposition, or hostility, to democracy [comes, both from] some Islamic quarters, within factions as well as within academia. The grounds for hostility range from considering democracy antithetical to Islam to considering it a Western design against it. The dispute within Islamic circles over democracy has had serious ramifications.[5] They regard democracy as forbidden (*haram*) and something which contradicts the Islamic concept of Divine Sovereignty. Besides, it is pertinent to mention here that the 'concept of sovereignty in Islam is one that has vexed scholars', both in medieval and, especially, in the modern era.[6] But this group is marginal, in comparison to the proponent trend (or compatibility pole), having 'limited grassroots support, as their view does not reflect the opinion of the majority of Muslim people'.[7] Many thinkers, including Ghannouchi, consider this opposition and this 'rejectionist attitude toward democracy an obstacle that undermines the endeavor of mainstream Islamic movements', throughout the Muslim world, 'to bring about peaceful political reform' in Muslim societies.[8]

In this backdrop, this chapter will review the opinions of some of the opponents of democracy. It first highlights the views and approaches of some 'hard-core'/'radical' Islamist intellectuals and groups favouring the 'rejectionist' trend, or falling in the 'incompatibility pole'—arguing that Islam and democracy are totally incompatible. Some of these include: Sayyid Qutb (d. 1966); Taqi al-Din al-Nabhani (d. 1977); and Abd al-Qadim Zallum (d. 2003)—both associated with *Hizb al-Tahrir*. This is followed by a brief overview of the views of the academicians like Abdul Rashid Moten (Malaysia) and analysts like Canada-based Abid Ullah Jan. This trend—rejecting the theory that Islam and democracy *are,* or *can be,* compatible—argues that democracy is an ideology alien to Islam, therefore, has no recognition at all. This is followed by a succinct overview of 'Islam and democracy: What Is the Real Question', with special reference to the views/perspectives, among others, of Asef Bayat (*University of Illinois,* USA), Nader Hashemi (*University of Denver,* USA), Amr G. E. Sabet (*University of Helsinki,* Finland), etc.

## Democracy and Its Muslim Critics: Objections and Observations of the 'Opponents'/Rejectionists'

In this section, an assessment of the views and approaches of some selected 'hard-core'/'radical' Islamist intellectuals and groups is presented.[9] Generally, what they argue is that Islam is totally incompatible with democracy: i.e. they are enlisted in the category of the 'rejectionist' trend or the 'incompatibility pole'. Rejecting the theory that Islam and democracy are, or can be, compatible, this group/trend considers democracy as an ideology alien to Islam, and thus needs to be avoided at all costs. 'The Islamic hostility towards democracy', for Fatih Abdel Salam, 'ranges from considering democracy antithetical to Islam to considering it a Western conspiracy against Islam'.[10]

## Sayyid Qutb (d. 1966) on Sovereignty, *Shura*, and Opposition to Democracy

Sayyid Qutb (1906–1966)—the leading intellectual of the Egyptian Muslim Brotherhood in the 1950s and '60s—occupies a 'central position in the scholarly output on what is usually labeled as Islamic fundamentalism',[11] or as 'Islamism'/'Political Islam'. Qutb is considered as 'the most significant thinker of Islamic resurgence in the modern Arab world',[12] 'Intellectual ideologue of Islamic Revival',[13] 'the influential Egyptian ideologue of Islamism',[14] and 'one of the most influential architects of contemporary Islamist political thought'.[15] He is 'one of the few thinkers who, after his ordeal and death, still influenced several generations of Islamically committed intellectuals'.[16] In the realm of 'Political Islam', 'Qutb's name has achieved near iconic status'.[17]

Qutb believed that mankind was 'on the brink of a precipice' because it sought refuge in Western civilization, which is 'devoid of those vital values which are necessary not only for its healthy development, but also for its real progress'.[18] In his view, Western beliefs, institutions (including democracy), and way of life are inconsistent with Islam, for 'Western civilization is unable to present any healthy values for the guidance of mankind'; and 'it does not possess anything', for Qutb, 'which will satisfy its own conscience and justify its existence'.[19] Maintaining that only Islam owns such values and also the real way of life,[20] Qutb, hence, makes it obligatory for the Muslims that: 'If Islam is again to play the role of the leader of mankind, then it is necessary that the Muslim community be restored to its original form';[21] and that 'to abolish [all] those oppressive political systems' which prevent people 'from expressing their freedom to choose whatever beliefs they want'.[22]

Qutb strongly objected to any notion of popular sovereignty as incompatible with God's sovereignty (*hakimiyah*).[23] Although he stressed that Islamic state be based on the Qur'anic principle of Consultation (Q. 3: 159 and 42: 38),[24] but he believed that *Shari'ah*, as a legal and moral system, is so complete that no further legislation is possible. In addition, he believed that for one group of people to legislate for others was contrary to the equality and absolute dignity of believers. For him, the Islamic political system has three important components: 'justice on the part of rulers; obedience on the part of followers; and consultation between leaders and followers'.[25] He is of the opinion that as the 'main value is not democracy but the implementation of the *Shari'ah*', therefore, any political system—be it monarchy, republican form of government, or a just dictatorship—is acceptable in Islamic perspective, on the condition that in enforces the Shari'ah.[26] 'It is necessary', Qutb believes, 'that the believers in this faith be autonomous and have power in their own society, so that they may be able to implement this system and give currency to all its laws'.[27] Being very critical of Western democracies, he suggests that it was naive to think that sovereignty and power were really vested in the people, since elites and those who fund elections exercise real power. Islam recognizes God as sovereign, not people or elected governments.

On the issue of Islamic governance, Qutb differed from many modern Muslim intellectuals who claimed democracy was Islamic because the Qur'anic institution of *Shura* supported elections and democracy. In his exegesis, *Fi Zilal al-Qur'an*,[28] Qutb pointed out that Surah *Shura* (Q. 42) was revealed during the Makkan period, 'long before the establishment of the Islamic state', and thus means that 'this quality is characteristic of Muslim community in all situations'.[29] Qutb, while interpreting Q. 3: 159, writes that in this verse, we find not only 'the basic principle governing the life of the Muslim community, namely, consultative government' but it gives 'a clear order to implement this principle of consultation'.[30] He further stresses that it is a 'definitive statement which leaves the Muslim community in no doubt that consultation is central to Islamic government. Without it, no system is truly Islamic'.[31] Furthermore, he points out that in the organization and procedure *Shura* will keep changing, for there are no definite rules about it:

What form this consultation takes and how the principle is implemented are matters which can be adapted to the prevailing conditions of any particular Islamic society. Any forms and mechanisms which ensure that consultation is really, not superficially, practised are acceptable to Islam.[32]

In the explanation of Q. 42: 38, he writes: 'The way to conduct is left for every generation and environment to decide. It is not cast in a rigid form that must always be followed'.[33] The position of Qutb on God's sovereignty, Islamic conception of governance, and on Islam–democracy relationship, is summarized, laudably, by Khattab and Bouma in these lines:

> Faced with a crisis of government augmented by the despotic and corrupt conduct of Muslim rulers, Qutb sought to limit governmental power through a constitutional rule based on what he called *hakimiyyah* (sovereignty), that is, practically Islamic law [*Shari'ah*]. The law, in Islamic state, is the highest legal and governmental authority. The state and its government derive its sovereignty from the activity of facilitating the application of law. He ... thought his analysis of *hakimiyyah* not only illustrated Islam's compatibility with democracy, but also demonstrated how the Islamic system's inclination and capacity could work the democratic values better than democracy itself. Qutb provides *Islamic system of government as an alternative system of democracy*. Qutb ... called for a *parliamentary government of any form based on Islamic principles of shurah* (consultation). But, the state, to him, cannot be called by any title other than 'Islamic'. He argued that some of the Western democratic values are based on materialistic conceptions of the universe, life and humanity. Such conceptions ... are unacceptable to Islam. With this, he also does not reject ... the *'positive' features of democracy*. In this sense, he distinguishes between the *'term'* and the *'concept' of democracy*. He is of the view that there is similarity between Islam and democracy to some degree, but this similarity does not mean Islam should change its name and identity. To him, *Islam is Islam and democracy is democracy*. With this, Muslims can also borrow from the West ideas that are in harmony with Islam and not in conflict with it (italics added).[34]

## *Hizb al-Tahrir* on Western Democracy as Idolatrous System (*Nizam-i-Kufr*)

*Hizb al-Tahrir al-Islami* or *Hizb ut-Tahrir* (The Islamic Liberation Party/ HT)[35] is an international pan-Islamic political organization founded by Taqi al-Din al-Nabhani (1909–1977: a Palestinian Islamic scholar) in 1953 in Jerusalem. The founding members of this organization reject Western system of democracy by calling it un-Islamic political system. For them, democracy is a system of blasphemy/disbelief (*Nizam al-Kufr*). Democracy has neither any connection nor any relation with Islam. According to this group, the genuine Islamic alternative system of rule is the *Khilafah* system. This system is fundamentally different from democratic systems and in actual conflict with it. While democracy is a man-made system premised on the sovereignty of the people, the ruling system in Islam is based on divine revelation and supremacy in it is for the *Shari'ah* and not for the people.[36]

Having written extensively on establishing an Islamic state (*Khilafah*/ Caliphate), Nabhani strongly rejects democracy and democratic system. In his *Political Thoughts*, he calls democracy a man-made 'fanciful idea' propagated by the West.[37] The adoption of democracy, which is nothing but an 'idea laid down by the West for the cultural invasion of Muslim lands',[38] not only leads to disaster but more importantly amounts to the rejection of the system of Allah. Democracy, wherein man's fallibility is given precedence over Allah's infallibility, is a system of *Kufr*, and ruling by the democratic system is tantamount to calling for a system of *Kufr*. Democracy, and 'the democratic system contradicts the ruling system of Islam, and therefore, it is *haram* [unlawful/forbidden] to adopt it or call for it'.[39] For him, democracy and democratic procedures are forbidden for three (3) reasons: (i) it's an idea propagated by the West for the 'cultural invasion' of the Muslim lands; (ii) it is 'a fanciful idea that cannot be implemented'; and (iii) 'democracy is man-made. It is laid down by humans for humans', which contradicts the 'system that is from Allah'. Therefore, 'the democratic system is a system of *Kufr*' and 'Islam has nothing to do with democracy'.[40]

In his *The System of Islam*, Nabhani is of the opinion that *Shura* differs from Western representative democracy in that while part of 'the ruling structure' of the Islamic caliphate, it's 'not one of its pillars'. For him, this is 'because the *Shura* (consultation) in Islam is for seeking the opinion and not for ruling. This is contrary to the parliamentary system in democracy'.[41]

In Article 104 of their 'Draft Constitution',[42] *Shura* is defined, and placed, as: 'Consultation (Shura) and the *mashura* (sic. *Mashwara*) are the seeking of views in absolute terms. The views are not binding in legislation, definitions, [and] intellectual matters such as discovering the facts and the technical and scientific matters'.[43]

Abdul Qadeem Zalloom, sometimes as Zalloum (d. 2003)—one of the founding members of *Hizb al-Tahrir* and a vehement critic of democracy—in his '*Democracy is a System of Kufr*' strengthens the view that Islam and democracy are totally incompatible.[44] For him, democracy 'completely contradicts the rules of Islam whether in the comprehensive or partial issues, in the source from which it came, in the '*Aqeedah* [belief] from which it emanated, in the basis on which it is established and in the thoughts and systems it has brought'.[45] Commenting on the genesis of the term democracy, Zalloom is of the opinion that

> Democracy is a Western word and a Western term applied to 'ruling of people, for the people by the legislation of the people'. Thus the people are the absolute master and they possess the sovereignty.... Each and every individual [in Western democracy] has the same right as everyone else in terms of establishing the state, appointing the rulers and enacting the systems and laws.[46]

For him, Western democracy is the 'antithesis' of Islamic ideas and ideals, and thus is 'forbidden for the Muslims to adopt it, call for it or establish [political] parties on its basis, or to take its viewpoints about life, to apply it, to take it as the basis or source for the Constitution and laws or to make it a basis for education or objectives'.[47] He warns, by way of conclusion, all the Muslims to discard democracy completely, and implement Islam, as a whole:

> It is obligatory on the Muslims to completely discard democracy. It is filth. It is the rule of *Taghut*. It is *Kufr*, thoughts of *Kufr*, systems of *Kufr*, [and] laws of *Kufr*, which have no connection to Islam whatsoever.

It is also obligatory on them to implement and enforce the whole of Islam in life, state, and society.[48]

On *HT*'s overall approach to western concepts such as democracy, capitalism, nation-states, etc., Mohamed Nawab Bin Mohamed Osman (*Australian National University*) sums up their stand in these lines:

> As in the case of many jihadist groups (and diametrically opposed to MB [Muslim Brotherhood]), HT staunchly rejects many concepts related to modernity such as democracy, capitalism and the nation-state, deeming these concepts as un-Islamic. For An-Nabhani the concept of democracy is contrary to the teachings of Islam due to the fact that the final power within the state rests in the hands of human beings so that all individuals, regardless of religion, have equal rights with regard to establishing the state, appointing rulers and making laws as well as anything else that is related to governance and the state. An-Nabhani's main argument against democracy is the fact that its laws are man-made, as opposed to the divine rules in the shari'a, which are ordained by God for all humans.[49]

## Abdul Rashid Moten (b. 1947) on Islam–Democracy Compatibility as a 'Western Construct'

Abdul Rashid Moten (b. 1947) is a Bangladeshi political scientist who served in the Department of Political Science at *International Islamic University, Malaysia* (IIUM). He has served as editor of *Intellectual Discourse* (Malaysia) and is currently the editor of *International Journal of Islamic Thoughts* (Bangladesh). He has authored/edited dozens of books and has published a large number of book chapters and research articles on Islam and politics, Islamic movements, and good governance in Islamic perspective, etc.

Moten criticizes democracy as well as expresses its incompatibility with Islam, by calling it 'a Western construct'.[50] In Moten's analysis, the West is making efforts constantly and earnestly to enforce and impress upon the Muslim countries the value of democracy, representing their programme of extending and strengthening its cultural imperialism/hegemony.

Therefore those who stand for democracy and call people to embrace this value—whom Moten brands as 'westernized Muslim thinkers', and includes in his list the pioneering figures like Afghani, 'Abduh, Sir Sayyid, and (among the contemporary voices) Soroush and Ghannouchi—do no service to the Muslims, rather represent and serve the interests of the West at large. For him, their advocacies of Islam–democracy compatibility 'lend further credence to the false belief in the eminence of the democratic system'.[51] He rejects this theory on the grounds that Islam already has a system of governance that is superior to democracy; and he charges the proponents of Islam–democracy compatibility for having 'trivialized' the fundamental principles of an Islamic political system:

> The practice of *shura*, meaning people's participation in governing themselves, was turned into parliamentary democracy; *ijma'*, denoting the consensus of the umma [*Ummah*] or of the leading '*ulama*' on a regulation was held to be synonymous with public opinion; and *maslaha*, referring to the adoption of a course which is considered to be in the best interest of the community, was developed into die liberal notion of utility.[52]

Moten has also expressed similar views in his *Political Science: An Islamic Perspective*,[53] wherein he makes distinction and differentiation between the *Shari'ah* (divine Law) and the man-made law; between *ijtihad* (independent reasoning) and complete freedom of independent action; and in between *Shura* and a liberal democratic structure. He writes:

> Muslims generally agree that the Islamic political system is based upon the interrelated concepts of *tawhid*, Shari'ah, shura, justice, equality and freedom. These principles set the Islamic polity apart from both capitalist and Marxist systems. [ ... ] The principles, values and the structural features the Islamic polity cannot be categorized as either parliamentary or presidential democracies. The superficial affinities in terms of election, consultation and the rule of law notwithstanding, the Islamic way of life is irreconcilable with the Western democratic philosophy. Shari'ah is not the same as the man-made law, *ijtihad* does not mean complete freedom of independent action, and *shura* is not compatible with a liberal democratic structure of authority. Democracy

is the product of the overall evolution of Western civilization; its secular content is the result of centuries of conflict be-tween the church and the state in which the latter won; its emphasis on suffrage, political freedom and voluntary association is the consequence of the demands made by the rising industrial proletariat in the nineteenth century.... In short, democracy is the product of the materialistic philosophy which considers man as the measure of everything whose work is weighed in absolute material terms to the utter neglect of his spiritual aspects [which goes contrary to the Islamic teachings on establishing a political order].... Democracy is, as such, antithetical to the Islamic way of life.[54]

## Abid Ullah Jan (b. 1965) on 'Islamic Democracy' as a 'Myth'

Abid Ullah Jan (b. 1965) is a prolific writer, political analyst, and community development specialist, based in Ottawa, Canada. Basically from Pakistan, he graduated from the *University of London*, and is the author of a number of books on international affairs. He writes extensively on Islam and contemporary political issues, and he features in Esposito and Donohue's *Islam in Transition* as well.[55]

Jan regards 'Islamic democracy' as no more than a 'myth',[56] and is of the opinion that 'Democracy is not a challenge to Islam. It is rather Islam that has become challenge to the most exploited concept of democracy'. Despite the most promoted question of Islam's compatibility with democracy, those who understand the core of Islam would agree that 'Islam is, in fact, a challenge to the kind of democracy we see around us'. While criticizing Western democracy, Jan goes further to argue that with the 'collapse of democratic values in the West', Islamic political movements, gaining increasing support in the Muslim world, will result in presenting a 'convincing alternative' not only to the 'authoritarian regimes in the world of Islam', but it will establish 'democracies in the West for the way they practice democracy today'.[57] 'Democracy in itself', for Jan, 'has nothing to do with compatibility and incompatibility with Islam'.[58] He is of the viewpoint that the 'secular democracy' is no longer for the present world, because many countries have fallen either under 'domination of squalid oligarchs' or are 'reduced to anarchy'.[59] He further asserts that

> Discussing the compatibility of Islam with democracy is misleading because it takes the focus away from the fact that we did not witness the miracle of secular democracy as a political system with its godless institutional mechanisms to call the unjust to account.... As far as the idea of popular vote, equal rights, special status of human beings etc. is concerned, no one has any quarrel with the idea of democracy in the Muslim world. It is the idea of the sovereign people flouting Qur'anic injunctions and the Sunnah that is a matter of concern for Muslims.[60]

Thus, radical Islamists and some hardcore voices are repeatedly denouncing democracy as godless. Their subject matter, in this regard, signifies that Islam and democracy are inherently antithetical. For these groups, democracy is *Shirk* (idolatry or assigning partners with Allah) and a system of *Kufr* contradicting Islam's core in all matters, major or minor. The ideology and doctrines of these movements evince that Muslims have to liberate themselves from the ideas, systems, and laws of other civilization if they envision for re-establishing the Islamic society established by the Last Messenger of God (pbuh).[61] Or as Khattab and Bouma put it: 'all militants do not trust Western ideas, including democracy. They attempt to find whatever in their religion and culture to support their position against democracies which supports despotism and dictatorship'. This is mainly because of their 'understandings of Islamic government to mean "government by God" or "God's rule"'—or theocracy.[62] They further state that

> The concept of *hakimiyyah* lies at the heart of the militants' [radical Islamists] argument against Islam's compatibility with democracy, and they try to draw strength from [Sayyid] Qutb.... [These] groups argue that democracy recognizes the sovereignty of the people, but in Islam the sovereignty is for God. They claim that democracy's recognition of the sovereignty of the people would have to mean the denial of God's 'sovereignty'. Therefore, democracy and democratic process are 'forbidden', and those who participate in it are 'apostates' and 'infidels'.[63]

Deliberating thoroughly on the Muslim opponents' criticism to (western) democracy, especially on the concept of God's sovereignty (*hakimiyyah*) as contradicting with the foundations of democracy (sovereignty of people), Khattab and Bouma conclude that

> Modern opposition to democracy, in the Muslim world, is not of *religious basis* but *politically motivated*. Religion is used by some only to enforce their rejection which, in a sense, stems mainly from the fact that the Western democracies, which provided inspiration and were greatly admired by reformists in the East, had colonized much of the Muslim world, and divided its territories among themselves as booties. (Italics added)[64]

Furthermore, King Fahd of Saudi Arabia, as quoted by *Mideast Mirror*, declared that democracy is a Western institution foreign to Islam, which has its own forms of participation: The 'democratic system prevalent in the world is not appropriate in this region' because the 'election system has no place in the Islamic creed, which calls for a government of advice and consultation and for the shepherd's openness to his flock, and holds the ruler fully responsible before his people'.[65] Furthermore, King Fahd (as quoted in *Middle East International*) stated:

> Islam is our social, political, and economic system and Islamic law is its own comprehensive constitution ... comprising social justice, economic justice, the judiciary, everything.... The democratic system prevailing in the world does not suit us in this region.[66]

## Islam and Democracy: What Is the Real Question?

In the context of the discussion of Islam–democracy discourse, it is necessary to remember that democracy is, after all, a 'contested concept': its meanings, practices, and outcomes have been, and may be, very different.[67] Ahrar Ahmad puts it as: 'Authoritarian regimes may describe themselves as "people's democracies", and various western systems of governance may witness democracy's coexistence with economic disparity, judicial inequity, racial prejudice, social pathology, and feelings of alienation and apathy on the part of many of their citizens'.[68] He further states that it is possible, indeed necessary, 'to deconstruct the concept of democracy into its procedural and substantive aspects. In this sense, it may be considered as a set of practical, legal, and institutional arrangements that ensures constitutional/majority rule, but also, as a political system inspired by a conception of the "common good", attempts to lay the foundations of a discursive, deliberative, communicative "community" and assumes a commitment to normative and humanistic ideals ("deep democracy" [69])'.[70]

Consequently, on the one hand, democracy focuses on such essential procedural elements as holding free, fair, and regular elections; functioning political parties; separating the powers of different branches of government (executive, legislative, and judicial); the possibility of judicial review to uphold constitutional supremacy, and so on. On the other hand, it emphasizes on such substantive components as respecting the rule of law, tolerating debate, encouraging cultural inclusiveness, promoting intellectual and aesthetic excellence, embracing the idea of consultation in major decisions affecting the community, insisting on the preeminence of the public interest, pursuing social justice, and ensuring the individual's dignity, security, and moral integrity. Therefore, considering the 'spirit' than merely the 'process' of democracy, as Ahrar Ahmad suggests, 'the relationship between Islam and democracy ... is not inherently problematic even by Western standards'.[71]

At the same time, it may be pointed out that scholars like Asef Bayat (the prominent Iranian-American scholar; Professor of Sociology and Middle Eastern Studies, *University of Illinois*, USA),[72] argue that it is 'wrong question to pose in the first place' that '*is Islam and democracy compatible?*' because this debate of '*Islam vs. democracy*' then 'centers almost exclusively on one side of the equation, Islam, as if, the other side, democracy is free from complexities' and could be easily applied to any socio-political setting (italics added).[73] He emphasizes, and questions the meaning of the term 'democracy': is it equal to Robert Dahl's 'polyarchy'[74] ('a consensual government by competing elites representing different social interests in a pluralist framework')? If so, then where do the economic and socio-culture domains of public life stand? For him, these 'questions are as old as the history of democracy itself'.[75]

Bayat makes it clear that the question should not be whether 'Islam is or is not compatible with democracy' because democracy is after all a complicated and 'convoluted' concept—or in Gallie's words, an 'essentially contested concept'[76]—but rather the question, as Bayat suggests, should be

> *how and under what conditions* Muslims can *make* Islam embrace democratic ethos. Nothing intrinsic to Islam—or any other religion—makes it inherently democratic or undemocratic, peaceful or violent. It depends on the intricate ways in which the living faithful perceive, articulate, and live through their faiths: some deploy their religions in exclusive, authoritarian, and violent terms, while others read in them *justice, peace, equality, representation, and pluralism.* (Italics added)[77]

These questions, for Bayat, are deep-rooted in the history of democracy, and they have been raised by a 'host of movements and critiques which have sought to make democracy democratic'. For example, Marxism has highlighted the 'conflict of economic liberalism and democratic ideals', social Democracy and 'associationalism' have emphasized citizenship and equality'.[78] For Bayat, 'the question is not whether Islam is or is not compatible with democracy or by extension modernity, but rather under what conditions Muslims can *make* them compatible. Because there is nothing intrinsic in Islam, and for that matter, any other religion, which makes them *inherently* democratic or undemocratic. *We*, the social agents, determine the inclusive or authoritarian thrust of religion'. Thus, in the discourses on Islam and democracy, Bayat suggests that we should 'mediate between discourse and power, [and] between the word and the world'. (Italics in original)[79] In short, for Bayat,

> [T]he compatibility or incompatibility of a religion, including Islam, with democracy is *not* a matter of merely philosophical speculations, but of *political struggle*. It is not as much the question of texts as the balance of power between those who want a democratic religion and those who pursue an authoritarian version. *Islamism* and *post-Islamism* tell the story of these two social forces (Italics in original).[80]

In an interview with Jahandad Memarian (of *Medium*),[81] Bayat puts forth these views with regard to Islam, democracy, Muslims, and the Muslim world: that 'Islam is inherently undemocratic' is a false interpretation; 'there is nothing inherent about Islam that make[s] it either democratic or authoritarian; rather it is the (Muslim) citizens who, ... , can make their religion democratic or otherwise'. He also opines that 'post-Islamist' movements and discourses 'do not see Islam and democracy as necessarily incompatible', and are trying to 'make their Islam compatible with electoral democracy'.

Are Islam and Democracy Compatible? To this intriguing question, Graham E. Fuller, in his *The Future of Political Islam*, echoes almost similar views (as that of Bayat), when he argues: 'No religion is inherently "compatible" with democracy: Judaism, Christianity, Buddhism, and Islam are all concerned with issues that have little to do with democracy'. But, at the same time, he argues that with reference to 'just governance', 'Islam explicitly talks about the necessity for the ruler to 'consult with the people"' (Q. 3: 159; 42: 38), and indeed, Muslims 'find in this concept of consultation its modern functional equivalent in representative institutions like parliament'. For him, indeed, 'the real question is not whether *Islam is compatible with democracy* but rather what is the relationship between *Muslims and democracy*'. (Italics added)[82] *We are discussing*, he stresses, *not what Islam is, but what Muslims want* (Italics in original).[83] Irfan Ahmad also puts it as: 'the question "Is Islam compatible with democracy" is theoretically flawed. An interesting question ... is: what interpretation of Islam? What form of democracy; democracy for whom?'[84] Nader Hashemi, in his 'Islam and Democracy', puts it differently as:

> Religion is not a monolithic and unchanging category that speaks with one voice throughout history. It is shaped by changing political and socio-economic contexts and can be interpreted in a myriad of different ways.... Like other religious traditions..., *Islam is neither more nor less compatible with modern democracy* than Christianity or Judaism.... The key interpretive point here is that *religious traditions* are a highly complex body of ideas, assumptions, and doctrines that ... contain sufficient ambiguity and elasticity to be read in a variety of different ways— *both in support of and in opposition to democracy* (italics added).[85]

Gudrun Krämer (*University of Berlin*, Germany), in 'Islamist Notions of Democracy', has perceptively noted that 'it is not possible to talk about Islam and democracy in general but only about Muslims living and theorizing under specific historical circumstances'. In the debate on Islam and democracy, encountering such arguments as 'the Islamic position is' such-and-such regarding democracy, human rights or pluralism, etc., is 'misleading' because while all religions have basic tenets, the rest is subject to debate and interpretation, particularly the structure of a modern political system and the role of religion within it.[86] Amr G. E. Sabet (*University of Helsinki*, Finland), in his *Islam and the Political*, goes some steps further while discussing the 'challenging implications' associated with the way the issue of the compatibility of Islam and democracy is formulated, or that hinder the question of the compatibility Islam–democracy relationship:

> First Islam, a worldview, is reduced to the level of a democratic concept. Second, it is then linked in this reduced and particularized re-conception, in a de-privileged *contingent* relationship to the alternatively universalized and *necessary* democratic tenet. If democracy, broadly and substantively speaking, is understood here as a secular legitimizing conceptual principle, then we have an interesting process where Islam is reduced to a concept, then linked to another concept belonging to an alternative secular worldview, as a means of subsuming the Islamic worldview under secular principles. Third, it mystifies first by obscuring that worldviews and concepts ought to be compared and contrasted with their respective counterparts, not with each other; Islam *vis-à-vis* secularism, and *Shura*, for instance, *vis-à-vis* democracy (Italics in original).[87]

Therefore, in such a situation, what is needed is, as Hashemi recommends, 'a sense of history', so that to understand that the 'development of democracy is a historical process that is evolutionary and gradual'. It thus, requires 'patience', because

> In Muslim societies, the debate on Islam and democracy is relatively recent and the topic does not emerge as a major theme in its own right before 1980s. In this sense, the journey is just beginning for Muslims. In contrast to the Western experience with democracy [for example the development of democracy in United States of America], the Muslim experience—of which there are many—is unfolding in a rapidly different and more complicated domestic, regional and international

context. In the end it should be remembered that ... [t]here are no easy formulas to follow or exact models to emulate. Trial, error and experimentation are the only ways forward.[88]

Hashemi's viewpoint is also shared, among others, by Imtiyaz Yusuf (who served for many years at *Mahidol University*, Thailand and is presently working at *International Institute of Islamic Thought and Civilization* [ISTAC], Malaysia), who argues that the development of democracy, in Western societies especially, is a historical process that is evolutionary and gradual. Democracy, in other words, requires patience: 'Democracy is a fragile thing, it needs to be nurtured and learned'; establishing democracy in the Middle East, for Yusuf, 'requires the tolerance of difference and the practice of patience' (*Sabr*)—and *Sabr* is one of the core teachings of the Qur'an.[89]

## Notes

1. Kamran A. Bokhari, 'Islamist Attitudes Toward Democracy', in *Islam, Democracy and the Secularist State in the Post-Modern Era* (Conference Proceedings of *Center for the Study of Islam and Democracy Second Annual Conference* (Burtonsville, MD: CSID, 2001), p. 174.
2. Mohammad Dawood Sofi, *Rashid al-Ghannouchi: A Key Muslim Thinker of the 21st Century* (New York: Palgrave Macmillan, 2018), p. 78.
3. See, Azzam Tamimi, *Rachid al-Ghannouchi: A Democrat within Islamism* (New York: Oxford University Press, 2001), p. 182.
4. See, M. A. Muqtedar Khan, 'The Politics, Theory, and Philosophy of Islamic Democracy', in M. A. Muqtedar Khan (ed.), *Islamic Democratic Discourse: Theory, Debates and Philosophical Perspectives* (Lanham, MD: Lexington Books, 2006), pp. 149–171, p. 153.
5. Tamimi, *Rachid al-Ghannouchi*, p. 182.
6. Sayed Khattab and Gary D. Bouma, *Democracy in Islam* (New York: Routledge, 2007), p. 12.
7. Jawad, 'Islam and Democracy in the Twenty-First Century', p. 66.
8. Tamimi, *Rachid al-Ghannouchi*, op. cit., p. 182.
9. This phrase is used by Abdelwahab El-Affendi, 'Democracy and Its (Muslim) Critics: An Islamic Alternative to Democracy', in Muqtedar Khan (ed.), *Islamic Democratic Discourse*, pp. 227–256.
10. Fatih A. Abdel Salam, 'Islam, Democracy and Secularism: The Question of Compatibility', *Insight Islamicus: An Annual Journal of Studies and Research in Islam*, 5, 1 (2005): 85–101, p. 93.

11. Khattab and Bouma, *Democracy in Islam, op. cit.*, p. 73.
12. Ibrahim Abu Rabi', *Intellectual Origins of Islamic Resurgence* (New York: State University of New York Press, 1996), p. 93.
13. Yvonne Y. Haddad, 'Sayyid Qutb: Intellectual Ideologue of Islamic Revival', in John L. Esposito (ed.), *Voices of Resurgent Islam* (New York: Oxford University Press, 1983), pp. 67–98, p. 67.
14. John Calvert, *Sayyid Qutb and the Origins of Radical Islamism* (New York: Oxford University Press, 2013).
15. Euben and Zaman (eds.), *Princeton Readings in Islamist Thought*, p. 129.
16. Khattab and Bouma, *Democracy in Islam, op. cit.*, p. 73.
17. Shahrough Akhavi, 'Sayyid Qutb', in John L. Esposito and Emad El-Din Shahin (eds.), *Key Islamic Political Thinkers* (New York: Oxford University Press, 2018), pp. 67–84, p. 67.
18. Sayyid Qutb, *Milestones*, 1st ed. (Delhi: Markazi Maktaba Islami, 1981), p. 7.
19. Ibid.
20. Ibid., p. 9.
21. Ibid.
22. Ibid. p. 12.
23. For this, see, Haddad, in Esposito, *Voices*, pp. 89–90; Sayed Khatab, *The Power of Sovereignty: The Political and Ideological Philosophy of Sayyid Qutb* (London and New York: Routledge, 2006); Khattab and Bouma, *Democracy in Islam, op. cit.*, pp. 81–90.
24. Sayyid Qutb, *In the Shade of the Qur'an,* English Translation of *Fi Zilal (Dhilal) al-Quran*, Adil Salahi, 18 Volumes. I have consulted volumes II and XV, from the pdf version available online at www.sunniconnect.con/m3/download/pdf-in-the-shade-of-the-quran-fi-dhilal-al-quran-sayyid-qutb-18-vol/ (last accessed on 20 August 2018). The verses Q. 3: 159 and 42: 38 are translated, respectively, as: *and consult with them in the conduct of public affairs* (II: 217) and *conduct their affairs by mutual consultation* 42: 38 (XV: 175).
25. For this viewpoint of Qutb, see Esposito, 'Contemporary Islam', *loc. cit.*; M. Muslih, 'Democracy', in John L. Esposito (ed.), *The Oxford Encyclopedia of the Modern Islamic World* [OEMIW] (New York: Oxford University Press, 1995), I: 356–360, p. 359.
26. Vide M. Muslih, 'Democracy', in *OEMIW*, I: 356–360, p. 359.
27. Qutb, *Milestones*, p. 58.
28. Sayyid Qutb, *In the Shade of the Qur'an* (trans.) Adil Salahi, 18 vols., available in pdf, online at www.sunniconnect.con/m3/download/pdf-in-the-shade-of-the-quran-fi-dhilal-al-quran-sayyid-qutb/ (last accessed on 20 August 2018),Vols. II, XV.
29. Ibid., XV: 193; *Cf.* XV: 186: 'Although these verses [Q. 42: 36–43] were revealed in Makkah, long before the establishment of the Muslim state in Medina, we note that one of these qualities is that its affairs are conducted on the basis of mutual consultation'.

30. Qutb, *In the Shade of the Qur'an,* II: 218.
31. Ibid., II: 220.
32. Ibid.
33. Ibid., XV: 194.
34. Khattab and Bouma, *Democracy in Islam, op. cit.,* pp. 91–92.
35. For details, see its website, www.hizb-ut-tahrir.org/EN; For the history of *HT*, see Suha Taji-Farouki, *The Fundamental Quest: Hizb al-Tahrir and the Search for the Islamic Caliphate* (London: Grey Seal, 1996); Mohamed Nawab Bin Mohamed Osman, 'Hizb ut-Tahrir', in Shahram Akbarzadeh (ed.), *Routledge Handbook of Political Islam* (Oxon, RN; New York and London: Routledge, 2012), pp. 89–104.
36. See, for example, 'Democracy Is a System of Kufr', ch. 23 in Taqiuddin an-Nabhani, *Political Thoughts* (London: Al-Khilafah Publications, 1999), pp. 114–118; Abdul Qadeem Zalloom, *Democracy Is a System of Kufr*, 2nd ed. (London: Al-Khilafah Publications, 1995 [1990]). This booklet, originally published in Arabic under the title *Al-Dimiqratiyyah Nizam al-Kufr*, has been translated into English and Urdu (among others) as well [hereafter cited as Zalloom, *Democracy*].
37. Nabhani, *Political Thoughts*, p. 117.
38. Ibid., p. 114.
39. Ibid., p. 118.
40. Ibid., pp. 116–117.
41. Taqiuddin an-Nabhani, *Nidham ul Islam/The System of Islam* (London: Al-Khilafah Publications, 2002), p. 62.
42. Ibid., pp. 115–146. Articles 101–107 (pp. 141–144) are related to 'The Ummah Assembly' (*Majlis al-Ummah*).
43. Ibid., p. 142.
44. Zalloom, *Democracy, op. cit.*
45. Ibid., p. 5.
46. Ibid., p. 6.
47. Ibid., p. 49.
48. Ibid.
49. Osman, 'Hizb ut-Tahrir', in Shahram Akbarzadeh (ed.), *Routledge Handbook of Political Islam*, pp. 93–94.
50. Abdul Rashid Moten, 'Democratic and Shura-Based Systems: A Comparative Analysis', *Encounters: Journal of Inter-Cultural Perspectives*, 3, 1 (March 1997): 3–20, p. 17, as cited in Tamimi, *op. cit.*, p. 184; Sofi, *op. cit.*, p. 81.
51. Moten, *loc. cit.*, p. 11.
52. Moten, *loc. cit.*, p. 11; Tamimi, *op. cit.*, p. 185.
53. For details, see '*Khilafah*: The Islamic Political Order', ch. 6 in Moten, *Political Science: An Islamic Perspective, op. cit.*, 82–106.
54. Moten, *Political Science*, pp. 104, 106.
55. For details, see Abid Ullah Jan, 'Compatibility: Neither Required Nor an Issue', in John J. Donohue and John L. Esposito (eds.), *Islam in Transition: Muslim Perspectives*, 2nd ed. (New York: Oxford University Press, 2007), pp. 319–331.

56. Abid Ullah Jan, *After Fascism: Muslims and the Struggle for Self-determination* (Ottawa, Canada: Pragmatic Publishing, 2006), p. 13, 111.
57. Abid Ullah Jan, *The End of Democracy* (Canada: Pragmatic Publishing, 2003), p. 67.
58. Jan, *After Fascism*, p. 116.
59. Ibid., p. 109.
60. Jan, 'Compatibility: Neither Required Nor an Issue', in Donohue and Esposito (eds.), *Islam in Transition*, p. 326.
61. Khattab and Bouma, *Democracy in Islam*, op. cit., p. 80; Sofi, *op. cit.*, p. 81.
62. Khattab and Bouma, *Democracy in Islam*, op. cit., p. 80.
63. Ibid., p. 82.
64. Ibid., p. 91.
65. *Mideast Mirror*, 30 March 1992, p. 12, as quoted in Esposito, *Unholy War*, p. 145; Esposito, 'Contemporary Islam', p. 677. Haifaa Jawad quotes this statement in favour of the trend adopted by 'conservative and some radical religious forces' that adopt a negative view of any shape or form of democratic system, stressing that democracy is a 'Western product' and as such it has to be avoided at all cost. For details, see, Jawad, *op. cit.*, p. 65.
66. (King) Fahd ibn Abd al-Aziz, as quoted in *Middle East International*, 29 May 1992; p. 28; also cited by Sonia Alianak, *Middle East Leaders and Islam: A Precarious Reading* (New York: Peter Lang Publishing Inc., 2007), p. 60.
67. The sub-heading is taken from the title of Bayat's *Islam and Democracy*, op. cit.
68. Ahrar Ahmad, 'Islam and Democracy: Text, Tradition, and History', *American Journal of Islamic Social Sciences* [AJISS], 20, 1 (2003): 20–45, p. 22.
69. The concept of 'deep democracy' is mentioned and broached in Judith M. Green, *Deep Democracy: Community, Diversity, and Transformation* (London: Rowman and Littlefield, 1999), pp. v–xv.
70. Ahmad in *AJISS*, p. 22.
71. Ahmad in *AJISS*, p. 22.
72. Bayat, *Islam and Democracy*; Idem., *Life as Politics: How Ordinary People Change the Middle East* (Amsterdam: Amsterdam University Press, 2010), p. 242.
73. Bayat, *Islam and Democracy*, p. 9.
74. Robert Dahl, *Democracy and Its Critiques* (Ithaca: Yale University Press, 1989).
75. Bayat, *Islam and Democracy*, p. 9.
76. Gallie, *Philosophy and the Historical Understanding*, p. 158.
77. Bayat, *Life as Politics*, p. 242.
78. Bayat, *Islam and Democracy*, pp. 9–10. Bayat bases his argument on David Held, *Models of Democracy*, 3rd ed. (Cambridge, UK: Polity Press, 2006).
79. Bayat, *op. cit.*, pp. 10, 13.
80. Ibid., p. 13.
81. Jahandad Memarian, 'Asef Bayat: A Critique of the Eurocentric Vision of the Middle East', *Medium*, 30 August 2018, available online at www.medium.com/@jahandad/asef-bayat-a-critique-of-eurocentric-vision-of-the-middle-east-699f16f9562 (last accessed on 20 September 2018).

82. Graham E. Fuller, *The Future of Political Islam* (New York: Palgrave Macmillan, 2003), pp. 121–122.
83. Fuller, *The Future of Political Islam*, loc. cit.
84. Irfan Ahmad, 'Democracy and Islam', *Philosophy and Social Criticism* [PSC], 37, 4 (2011): 459–470, p. 461.
85. Hashemi in Esposito and Shahin, *op. cit.* p. 83.
86. Gudrun Krämer, 'Islamist Notions of Democracy', in Joel Beinin and Joe Stork (eds.), *Political Islam: Essays from Middle East Report* (Berkeley: University of California, 1997), pp. 71–82, p. 72.
87. Amr G. E. Sabet, *Islam and the Political: Theory, Governance and International Relations* (London: Pluto Press 2008), p. 186.
88. Hashemi in Esposito and Shahin, *op. cit.*, p. 84.
89. Imtiyaz Yusuf, 'Second Chance?', *The Nation*, 13 July 2013, available online at http://www.nationmultimedia.com/opinion/Second-chance-30210276.html (last accessed on 15 July 2013).

# Epilogue

In this work, it has been argued that speaking of democracy and the concept of democratic participation does not mean that the word democracy is a Qur'anic term or a term covered by the Sunnah. It only means that the Islamic legacy—both cultural and intellectual—contains many conceptions and institutions—perceptions and principles, ideas and ideals, as well as notions and values—that show resemblance and similarity with the democratic principles and values. Some of these key concepts and values of Islamic political order—rule of law, accountability of the ruler, responsibility of the government, general will, public welfare, constitutionalism, freedom, justice, equality, human rights, etc. (among others)—are compatible and in harmony with the positive features and values of modern democracy.[1] These concepts also provide evidence that the Islamic system of government, in the concrete sense, is democratic. Thus, it is much feasible and reasonable to propose that considering the 'spirit' than merely the 'process' of democracy, the relationship between Islam and democracy—'complex and nuanced' as it may be—is not inherently problematic even by Western standards.

Arguably, democracy is both a universally accepted theory and an 'essentially contested concept'; therefore, its meaning, practices, and outcomes have been very different. There is some dispute and disparity, centred on such concepts, as there is no universally accepted model of democracy. In other words, the term 'democracy' has multiple interpretations and applications—a fact that leads to the recognition that there can be alternative uses of this term. Taking advantage of this space, most of the contemporary Muslim scholars see no problem and difficulty in accepting the term democracy when conceived from a particular Islamic perspective. There is no surprise, then, that not only throughout the Muslim world, but in the West and the rest of the world as well, various scholars and intellectuals are actively engaged in defining 'Islamic democracy' with the help of various traditional concepts and institutions of Islamic polity, like *Shura* and *Khilafah*, *Ijma'* and *Ijtihad*, *Bay'ah* and *Maslaha*, *Mithaq al-Madina*, etc. Especially, the principle of *Shura*—which is perceived, and interpreted, as the principal source of democratic ethics in Islam—is regarded at times as a substitute for describing democracy in the Islamic context.

The views and observations presented by numerous Muslim scholars/intellectuals—discussed in Chapters 3–6 especially—establish and determine that there is, speaking theoretically, much harmony and consistency between Islam and the supposedly true 'participatory' and/or 'liberal' democracy. Democracy is not only as a set of practical, legal, and institutional arrangements that ensures constitutional/majority rule, but also, a political system inspired by the conception of the 'common good', that attempts to lay the foundations of a discursive, deliberative, communicative community and assumes a commitment to normative and humanistic ideals.

Consequently, it is also clear that in the discourses of Islam–democracy compatibility, scholars also focus on essential procedural elements of democracy, such as holding free, fair, and regular elections; separating the powers of different branches of government, etc. They also emphasize such substantive components as respecting the rule of law, tolerating debate, encouraging cultural inclusiveness, promoting intellectual excellence, embracing the idea of consultation in major decisions affecting the community, insisting on the preeminence of the public interest, pursuing social justice, and ensuring the individual's dignity, security, and moral integrity. Therefore, in the debates and discourses revolving around Islam–democracy compatibility, it is the *spirit*, not merely the *process* of democracy, which is being highlighted and taken into consideration.

Moreover, the advocacy of democracy by these Muslim intellectuals may not be seen as an imitative, derivative, or clichéd adoption of modernity. Fairly, it appears to be a creative and innovative envisioning of the Islamic principles of freedom, equality, justice, and human dignity in the modern situation. For, these scholars maintain that the notion of democratic participation is innate in Islamic tradition, which is ordained by the noble Qur'an and practiced by the holy Prophet (pbuh) himself and the pious Caliphs especially. This study also reveals that the nature of Islamic concepts, especially *Shura*, and their relation to democracy requires a great deal of further reflection and re-interpretation as the Islamic primary sources throw sufficient light and guidance on these concepts and values. The views of the intellectuals and political analysts also indicate that although there are some basic differences between Islam and democracy, many similarities exist between the two systems of political thought.

The concept of *Shura* (mutual consultation)—which is considered both as an alternate as well as synonymous in spirit for democracy in Islam—is interpreted both in the historical context (with examples, specifically, from the Prophetic period and the era of Pious Caliphs) as well as with modern (re)interpretations, to lay down the foundations of democracy in Islam. In other words, democracy is advocated with special stress laid on the concept of *Shura*, which is taken to allow or require the expression of the popular will in matters of state. Thus, if democracy is broadly understood as to refer to a decision taken by the people after deliberation, then democracy becomes almost identical to *Shura*, which, in turn, suggests that there is nothing in the primary or extended meaning of democracy that makes it intrinsically Western or secular. If *Shura* can take a secular form, as Dr Jaafar Sheikh Idris (b. 1931; a Sudanese Muslim scholar) points out, so can democracy take an Islamic form; and as *Shura* was practiced in the pre-Islamic period as well, there is nothing in the concept which makes it entirely and 'intrinsically Islamic'.[2]

Indeed, in Islam, there is, among others, freedom of popular participation in politics—explicitly and unambiguously expressed in the Qur'an as *Shura* (consultation)—which clearly goes back to the principle of 'tribal democracy', as practiced in the pre-Islamic period—e.g. the *Dar al-Nadwah*. As discussed in Chapter 2, the Arabs of the pre-Islamic period engaged in practices of social and political deliberation and a number of tribes had their own 'councils' for discussing and settling the affairs of common interest, and adjudicating the intra- and inter-tribal matters through the process of consultation. The tribal chief (*al-Shaykh*) was a *primus inter pares* ('first among equals') and the one who took final responsibility for executing decisions arrived at through consultation between the elders. By the same token, one also has to study how the Prophet (pbuh)—he who least needed to consult men, as he had God instructing him! But even he was told: *Shawirhum fil amr* (3: 159) in order, precisely, to exhort all leaders that they must consult those over whom they have power. But, here, it may be pointed out that one only has to study how the Prophet and, later, the first four Caliphs ruled, whose caliphate was 'open to criticism'; there was broad participation and involvement in political life, public accountability, concern about human rights in terms of justice, and equality before the law, as well as respect for differences of opinion.

Thus, the practice of *Shura*—or the consulting and the soliciting of opinions—especially during the early period of Islamic history, is a clear illustration of the Islamic system of government signifying the principle of people's participation in their own affairs, their 'self-determination'—in the modern phraseology, 'the national sovereignty'. Also, the Prophetic Tradition states: 'Every one of you is a shepherd (of the community) and is responsible for his flock. The leader of people is a guardian and is responsible for his subject' (*Sahih Bukhari* and *Sahih Muslim*)—besides expressing a shared responsibility and public involvement, and in a sense, 'sovereignty of the people over the people'—articulates that the Islamic government cannot help but be at once consultative, democratic, and divinely inspired.

The assessment of the views of the Muslim thinkers of East and West, who are engaged in their quest and pursuit to develop an Islamic programme/formula of democracy, use Islamic ideas and institutions that emphasize the equality of people, the accountability of leaders to community, and the respect of diversity and other faiths—those concepts that are fully compatible with modern democracy. It is also true and needs to be pointed out here again that as across the world, millions of Muslims live in various democratic societies of one kind or another (like India, Europe, North America), it is comparable and equivalent to a misunderstanding to deny, in totality, Islam–democracy compatibility. It is equally questionable to claim that there are more differences and contradictions between the two systems of political thought.

Thus, in this context, this study proposes the *theory of 5R's*, which states that with more *reflection* and *research*, *(re)interpretation* and *(re)understanding* are essential to *reconcile* and merge together Islamic socio-political concepts with the modern notion of democracy—as the Islamic primary sources throw sufficient light and guidance on these concepts and values. Also, throughout the Muslim world, a demand and desire for democracy is evidently seen, and while using several important concepts from within the Islamic heritage, Muslims have been trying to lay the foundations of a political order that merges Islamic principles with a democratic system of government.

Thus, keeping in view the whole discussion, there is no reason at all why, one should object to the acceptance and adoption of certain democratic procedures (elections, polls, parliamentary system, etc.) together with such principles as the rule of law, constitution, and others within an Islamic polity. This is indispensable because Islamic law is a clearly defined entity, whereas there is not any clearly defined or specific or prescribed Islamic political system: there are different political systems claiming to be derived from Islam, but none of them has a 'canonical' or absolute status. The need for *Shari'ah* as the foundation for the judiciary, is both crucial and central, while leaving the legislature and executive spheres to be determined in accordance both with the universal principles of the *Shari'ah* and the conditions of the times. And as one of these conditions, today is precisely the widespread expectation and desire for democracy, for freedom, for political and civil rights, etc., therefore, any successful political system will have to 'accommodate' these legitimate expectations while simultaneously upholding 'Islamic principles'; and, in Haifa Jawad's terminology, the democracy is the kind of 'government wished for by [the] majority of the moderate Muslims' all over the world.[3]

It sounds very logical—and is reasonable as well—to propose that a combination of Islamic principles and democratic procedure is the best formula for moderation in the Muslim world. The relevance of a politically open, democratic system, within which Islam will be the dominant socio-religious force for law-making in harmony with the wishes of the majority is essential. The 'sovereignty of people' is maintained properly: the wish of the majority dictates the framework; and the framework chosen freely by the people is one in which 'God reigns supreme as the true 'sovereign'', that is, the *Shari'ah* becomes the source of authority, and within the *Shari'ah*, the specific weight given to different *Maqasid* (objectives) will again be dictated by a combination of religious and human sources: scholarly *Ijtihad*, on the one hand, and *Shura*, consulting different communities, and their representatives, on the other. Thus, a democratic expression of the Islamic law or vice-versa can thus be envisaged.

Similarly, both—the Qur'an and *Sunnah* of the Prophet (pbuh)— demonstrate that Islam provides a rich resource for the development of societies that promote the good of all and are diverse, that recognize the need for consultation, and respect the human dignity of all persons and groups; and to find a way forward that leads to peace, internal security, the development of sustainable values and a richly nourishing religious and spiritual life is all that is needed.

At the same time, it is also necessary here to highlight, as pointed out in Chapter 6 as well, that a number of 'gaps' and 'cavities' remain to be filled within the thought of the proponents of 'Islamic democracy'. That is, little effort has been made as to what the modern 'democratic state' would look like. The Muslim intellectuals, in other words, have paid much attention to the discussions revolving around Islam–democracy compatibility on theoretical and academic grounds, but have given very little consideration to the practical and realistic implementation of 'Islamic democracy'. How an 'Islamic democracy' will work in a Muslim country is still a 'challenge' for Islamic political theory as well as the responsibility of Muslim political theorists mainly in the twenty-first century. Thus, it is the need of the hour to mould and turn this theory into a practical framework. By the implementation of this 'Islamic democracy', in any Muslim country, Muslims will, therefore, lay the foundations of a political order/form of government that will be an amalgamation of Islamic political principles based on Qur'an and *Sunnah* and those positive features and notions of modern Western democracy that are neither in disagreement with Islam, its law and essence, nor contradict and oppose the limits prescribed by Islam.

Furthermore, Islam and democracy are compatible and companionable for the reason that there are various institutions and mechanisms, models and forms of government possible in Islam. There are many forms, models, and variants, of democracy—which the world has experienced in the past, is experiencing presently, and will practice in the future as well—and each country can determine its own political destiny and embrace the various characteristics that will be suited to them. Muslims have a rich history and tradition that will lend itself to look ahead and make mature choices for political activity. Thus, Muslims today can 'embrace' those forms of democracy that are more compatible with Islam and, in the future, they could very well develop 'ideas for post-democracy'— a 'social[ly] just and egalitarian [democratic] society'; and being rich in tradition, Muslims should develop a political framework, 're-organized and re-constructed' that includes, among others, the 'idea of democracy' as well.[4]

Undoubtedly, in Islam, there is not any explicitly prescribed form of governance, but it does provide guidelines for establishing the political system and has left it open to the *Ummah* to develop different forms, institutions and mechanisms of governance/political setups, suitable for different socio-historic conditions. A variety of governmental forms and arrangements are possible within this dynamic framework of Islam. Some of these systems and models have been experienced in the past. New experiments and arrangements can be made today and tomorrow by implementing them within a particular Muslim society and/or country. This is the exquisiteness, prospective, and potential of Islam—its law, intellectual and cultural legacy, and its dynamic and vibrant character—and this has been the distinctive feature of the Muslim historical experience spread over more than fourteen centuries.

At the same time, it cannot be ignored that Islam is, on some grounds, incompatible with, and in opposition to, a Western liberal democracy that rests on individualism and secularism, but it is not incompatible with democratic ideals such as basic human rights, respect for human dignity, social justice, and other such concepts and values. To wrap up, there is no ambiguity or vagueness in the argument that Islam and democracy are compatible on many counts, and majority of the Muslim intellectuals are engaged in discussing and debating this discourse—and none of them is calling for a wholesale acceptance of any Western model. Nor are they overlooking the basic differences that occur between Islam and democracy—but, at the same time, while there are rich sources of Islamic thought on democracy, practically an 'Islamic democracy' has not emerged yet, and this is still a *challenge* for Muslim political theorists in particular in the twenty-first century.

The crucial issue and the challenge ahead—for Muslim scholars in general, and Muslim political theorists in particular—that needs much attention is that the theory of 'Islamic democracy' needs to be explored, deliberated, and discussed, from the realistic perspective and from the vantage point of practicality. In other words, a broad framework and structure of an *Islamic-democracy-in-practice* are required, because the entire discourse revolving around 'Islam-democracy compatibility'—on which, the Muslim thinkers have spent, as this study has revealed now, a great deal of time and energy for many decades—will look a mere *'illusion'* and 'hypothetical vision'. Also, as it is necessary for the materialization of an 'authentic Islamic democracy' that it must first become an aspiration and a target in Muslim minds and must dominate their discourse—and both these phases have been effectively passed by Muslim intelligentsia—and thus, as the idea/formula exists, but what is required is the practical shape of this model. This is a challenge—for Islamic political theory and theorists—that has not been answered yet. It is now time to knit and interlace this vision of Islamic democratic theory into the fabric of reality.

# Notes

1. I have been making such kind of arguments for more than a decade now, and I have put forth these, and other such arguments, in many writings, cited and referred to in different chapters of this work. All these appear in the Bibliography as Parray, Tauseef Ahmad, 2010–2021.
2. Jaafir Idris [Dr Jaafar Sheikh Idris], 'Shura and Democracy: A Conceptual Analysis', *Al-Jumuah*, 6 December 2021, available at www.aljumuah.com/shurah-and-democracy-a-conceptual-analysis/?utm_source=rss&utm_medium=rss&utm_compaign=shurah-and-democracy-a-conceptual-analysis (last accessed on 28 December 2021).
3. Haifaa Jawad, 'Islam and Democracy in the 21st Century', in Gabriele Marranci (ed.), *Muslim Societies and the Challenge of Secularization: An Interdisciplinary Approach* (London: Springer, 2010), pp. 65–81, p. 78.
4. AbuBakr Karolia, 'Islam and Democracy: Political thought towards post-democracy' (Study of Islam Program, *University of Johannesburg*, South Africa), *Academia.edu*, 19 October 2010: 1–21, p. 19, available at www.academia.edu/775684/Islam_and_Democracy_Political_thought_towards_post_democracy (last accessed on 28 December 2021).

# Book Description (Publisher's Description)

In the twenty-first century, Islam as a religion has been in a position of precarious co-existence with the modern democratic world system. The resultant portrayal of Islam as a necessarily violent religion has led the author to question this binary relation between Islamic political thought and the Western concept of democracy from a theoretical perspective. He creates a discursive terrain for positing the notions of convergence vis-à-vis the notions of divergence inherent in the debates surrounding Islam and democracy. In such an attempt, the author treads through diverse theoretical Islamic texts like the *Qur'an* and the *Sunnah* and other more contemporary works by eminent scholars on this issue. The author further provides interesting insight regarding the practicality of the concept of 'Islamic democracy'. The book is an important document for understanding the theoretical relationship between Islam and Western concept of democracy and also for contextualizing the notion of Islamic democratic theory in reality.

# About the Book (Author's Description)

This book attempts to analyse and examine, on theoretical grounds, the relationship between Islam and its socio-political concepts and institutions and the principles of (modern) democracy, in the views of (selected) prominent Muslim scholars of the last two-and-half centuries—of the Arab world and South Asia. A crucial question that *has* highly intensified since 1980s, gained momentum in post-9/11 era, and again came to the limelight with the inception of 'Arab Spring' is: *Is Islam compatible with democracy?* It seeks to address this very crucial question by highlighting key concepts and figures that have been essential in framing the contemporary debates surrounding Islam and democracy. It:

- Attempts to tread through diverse theoretical Islamic texts like the Qur'an, Sunnah, and other more contemporary works by eminent scholars on the hotly debated issue of Islam–democracy (*in*)compatibility;
- Endeavours to create a discursive terrain for theorizing the notions of convergence vis-à-vis the notions of divergence inherent in the debates surrounding Islam and democracy;
- Provides an assessment of some operational key concepts/institutions of democracy in Islam, including *Shura* (Mutual Consultation), *Bay'ah* (Oath of Allegiance), and *Mithaq al-Medina* (the Constitution of Medina), etc.;
- Provides an assessment of the views and visions of some selected Muslim scholars (from the nineteenth to twenty-first centuries) on Islam–democracy compatibility, globally (Proponents);
- Deliberates, very succinctly, on the objections and observations of the 'Opponents' of Islam–democracy relation.

It is a helpful source for the students and scholars of Islamic Political Thought, Comparative Politics, and Islamic Studies, and is equally fascinating for the readers interested in knowing the contemporary political dynamics of the Muslim world.

# About the Author

### Brief Profile

Dr Tauseef Ahmad Parray is presently working as Assistant Professor, Islamic Studies, in Higher Education Department, Jammu and Kashmir (India). He is the author of six books on Islamic intellectual tradition, Islam and Modernity, and Quranic scholarship. His major areas of interest are: Islam and Democracy; Modernist/Reformist Thought in South Asia; and Recent Trends and English Scholarship in the Qur'anic Studies.

### Detailed Profile

Dr Tauseef Ahmad Parray is presently working as Assistant Professor, Islamic Studies, in Higher Education Department, Jammu and Kashmir (J&K) (India). He holds a Masters, PhD, and post-doctorate in Islamic Studies from *University of Kashmir* (2008), *Aligarh Muslim University* (2014), and 'IRD', *International Islamic University Islamabad,* Pakistan (2015), respectively. He is the author of six books, viz., *Towards Understanding the Qur'anic Terms, Concepts, and Themes* (2017), *Muslim Intellectual Deficit: Reasons and Remedies* (2018), *Mediating Islam and Modernity: Sir Sayyid, Iqbal and Azad* (2019), *Exploring the Qur'an: Concepts and Themes* (2019), *Recent Trends in Qur'anic Scholarship* (2020), and *Decadence of Muslim Intellectualism: Reasons, Ramifications, and Remedies* (2021). He has published in numerous reputed academic journals, magazines, and newspapers, from over a dozen countries, around the world. He has contributed encyclopaedia entries in *The Oxford Encyclopedia of Islam and Politics* (2 Vols.; 2014) and *Islam: A Worldwide Encyclopedia* (4 Vols.; 2017) and many book chapters in edited volumes, like *Metamorphosis of the Arab World* (2015), *Transformation of Muslim World in the 21st Century* (2016), *Contemporary Thought in Muslim World* (4 Vols.; 2020), *Oxford of the East: Aligarh Muslim*

*University 1920–2020* (2020) and *The Routledge International Handbook of Contemporary Muslim Socio-Political Thought* (2022). His major areas of interest are: Islam and Democracy; Modernist/Reformist Thought in South Asia; and Recent Trends and English Scholarship in the Qur'anic Studies. Email: tauseef.parray21@gmail.com

# Bibliography

Abd al-Salam, Faruq. *Al-Ahzab al-Siyasiyah Fi al-Islam* [Political Parties in Islam] (Cairo: Qalyub Publishing House, 1978).

Abdel Haleem, M. A. S. *The Qur'an: A New Translation* (Oxford: Oxford World Classics, 2004, 2005).

Abdel Salam, Fatih A. 'Islam, Democracy and Secularism: The Question of Compatibility', *Insight Islamicus: An Annual Journal of Studies and Research in Islam*, 5, 1 (2005): 85–101.

Abdel Salam, Fatih A. 'The Questions of Compatibility between Islam, Democracy and Secularism', *Tafhim: IKIM Journal of Islam and International Relations*, 1, 3 (2004): 107–127.

Abed, Shukri B. 'Islam and Democracy', in David Garnham and Mark Tessler (eds.), *Democracy, War, and Peace in the Middle East* (Bloomington: Indiana University Press, 1995): 116–132.

Abou El Fadl, Khaled. 'Islam and the Challenge of Democracy', *Boston Review*, 28, 2 (2003), available online at https://bostonreview.net/issue/aprilmay-2003/ (last accessed on 5 June 2010).

Abou El Fadl, Khaled. *Islam and the Challenge of Democracy: A Boston Review Book*, edited by Joshua Cohen and Deborah Chasman (Princeton, NJ: Princeton University Press, 2004).

About Dr. Khaled Abou El Fadl, *Scholar of the House*, available online at www.scholarofthehouse.org/abdrabelfadl.html (last accessed on 20 June 2017).

Abu 'Ubayd. *Kitab al-Amwal* (Cairo: Maktabba al-Kulliyya al-Azhariyyah, 1395/1975).

Abu Rabi', Ibrahim M. *Intellectual Origins of Islamic Resurgence in the Modern Arab World* (New York: State University of New York Press, 1996).

Abu Yusuf. *Kitab al-Kharaj* (Cairo: Maktabba al-Salaffiyyah, 1976).

Abu-Nimer, Mohammed. 'Framework for Nonviolence and Peacebuilding in Islam', in Abdul Aziz Said, Mohammed Abu-Nimer, and Meena Sharify-Funk (eds.), *Contemporary Islam: Dynamic, not Static* (Oxon and New York: Routledge, 2006), pp. 131–172.

Adamec, Ludwig W. *Historical Dictionary of Islam*, 2nd ed. (Lanham, MD: The Scarecrow Press, 2009).

Adams, Charles C. *Islam and Modernism in Egypt: A Study of the Modern Reform Movement Inaugurated by Muhammad 'Abduh* (New York: Russel and Russel, 1933; reissued 1968).

Adams, Charles J. 'Mawdudi and the Islamic State', in John L. Esposito (ed.), *Voices of Resurgent Islam* (New York: Oxford University Press, 1983), pp. 99–133.

Afsaruddin, Asma. 'Mawdudi's "Theo-Democracy": How Islamic Is It Really?', *Oriente Moderno*, 87, 2 (2007): 301–325.

# BIBLIOGRAPHY

Afsaruddin, Asma. 'The "Islamic State": Genealogy, Facts, and Myths', *Journal of Church and State* [*JCS*], 48, 1 (2006): 153–173.

Afsaruddin, Asma. 'Theologizing about Democracy: A Critical Appraisal of Mawdudi's Thought', in Asma Afsaruddin (ed.), *Islam, the State, and the Political Authority: Medieval Issues and Modern Concerns* (New York: Palgrave Macmillan, 2011), pp. 131–154.

Afsaruddin, Asma. *Contemporary Issues in Islam* (Edinburgh: Edinburgh University Press, 2015).

Afsaruddin, Asma. *The First Muslims: History and Memory* (Oxford: Oneworld Publications, 2008).

Afsarududin, Asma. 'Consultation, or *Shura*', in Josef W. Meri (ed.), *Medieval Islamic Civilization: An Encyclopedia* (New York: Routledge, 2006), I: 171.

Ahmad, Aziz. 'India and Pakistan', in P. M. Holt, A. K. S. Lambton, and Bernard Lewis (eds.), *The Cambridge History of Islam* (Cambridge: Cambridge University Press, 1970), 2A: 97–119.

Ahmad, Aziz. *An Intellectual History of Islam in India* (Edinburgh: Edinburgh University Press, 1969).

Ahmad, Aziz. *Islamic Modernism in India and Pakistan—1857–1964* (London: Oxford University Press, 1967).

Ahmad, Mumtaz. 'Islam And Democracy: The Emerging Consensus', *The Journal of Turkish Weekly*, 20 June 2005, http://www.iiu.edu.pk/wp-content/uploads/downloads/ird/downloads/Islam-&-Democracy-Emerging-Concensus.pdf (last accessed on 15 June 2018).

Ahmad, Irfan. 'Democracy and Islam', *Philosophy and Social Criticism* [*PSC*], 37, 4 (2011): 459–470.

Ahmad, Irfan. 'Islam and Politics in South Asia', in John L. Esposito and Emad El-Din Shahin (eds.), *The Oxford Handbook of Islam and Politics* (New York: Oxford University Press, 2013), pp. 324–339.

Ahmad, Irfan. 'The Categorical Revolution: Democratic Uprising in the Middle East', *Economic and Political Weekly*, xlvi, 44–45 (5 November 2011): 30–35.

Ahmad, Irfan. *Islamism and Democracy in India: The Transformation of the Jamaat-e-Islami in India* (Princeton, NJ: Princeton University Press, 2009).

Ahmad, Kassim. 'A Short Note on the Medina Charter', available online at https://www.dinmerican.wordpress.com/2015/12/09/kassim-ahmad-on-the-medina-charter/ (last accessed on 18 January 2011).

Ahmad, Khurshid, and Ghazi, Mahmood Ahmad. 'Religion, State and Society', *Policy Perspectives*, 5, 1 (Jan-June 2011), available online at http://www.ips.org.pk/islamic-thoughts/995-religion-state-and-society.html (last accessed on 10 December 2021).

Ahmad, Khurshid. (ed.), *Islam: Its Meaning and Message*, 3rd ed. (London: Islamic Foundation, 1999 [1975]).

Ahmad, Khurshid. (ed.), *Islamic Perspectives: Studies in Honour of Sayyid Abdul A'la Mawdudi* (Leicestershire: Islamic Foundation, 1979).

Ahmad, Khurshid. (ed.), *Mawdudi: An Introduction to His Life and Thought* (Leicestershire: Islamic Foundation, 1979).

Ahmad, Khurshid. 'Islam and Democracy: Some Conceptual and Contemporary Dimensions', *The Muslim World* [*MW*], 90, 1&2 (Spring 2000): 1–21.

Ahmad, Khurshid. 'Islam: Basic Principles and Characteristics', in Khurshid Ahmad (ed.), *Islam: Its Meaning and Message*, 3rd ed. (London: Islamic Foundation, 1999 [1975]), pp. 27–44.

Ahmad, Khurshid. 'Key Note Address on 'Economics, Islam, and Democracy', *Centre for the Study of Islam and Democracy* [*CSID*], April 2000; reproduced in *Muslim Democrat*, 2, 2 (June 2000): 5, 7.

Ahmad, Khurshid. *The Religion of Islam* (Lahore: Islamic Publications, 1967).

Ahmad, Manzooruddin. 'Classical Muslim State', *Islamic Studies*, 1, 3 (September 1962): 83–104.

Ahmad, Mohammad Ashfaq (trans.). *The Noble Qur'an: Tafsir-e-Usmani*, 3 vols. (New Delhi: Idara Impex, 2008).

Ahmad, Mubasher. *Khilafat and Caliphate*: 1–13, available online at https://www.alislam.org/topics/khilafat-and-caliphate/ (last accessed on 20 May 2010).

Ahmad, Mumtaz. 'In Memoriam: Prof. Fazlur Rahman 1919–1988', *The American Muslim* [*TAM*], 1 October 2005, available online at http://www.theamericanmuslim.org/tam.php/features/articles/rahman_prof_fazlur_in_memorium_1919_1988 (last accessed on 25 December 2021).

Ahmad, Rifa'at Sayyid. *Al-Din Wa al-Dawlah Wa al-Thawrah* [Religion, State and Revolution] (Cairo: al-Dar al-Sharqiyah, 1989).

Ahmed, Ahad M. *The Theological Thought of Fazlur Rahman: A modern Mutakkalim* (Kuala Lumpur, Malaysia: Islamic Book Trust, 2017).

Ahmed, Ahad M. *The Theological Thought of Fazlur Rahman: A modern Mutakkalim* (Kuala Lumpur, Malaysia: Islamic Book Trust, 2017).

Ahmed, Israr. 'Democracy and Islam' (Video), available online at http://www.youtube.com/watch?v=OC9HFYwMKU0 (last accessed on 14 June 2011).

Ahmed, Israr. 'DEMOCRACY and THEOCRACY and why is VOTING … SHIRK?' (Video), available online at http://www.youtube.com/watch?v=mixU9H2zWAw (last accessed on 14 June 2011).

Ahmed, Israr. *Bayan-al-Qur'an* (Lahore: Qur'an Academy, 2010), also available online at http://www.tanzeem.org (last accessed on 16 August 2018).

Ahmed, Israr. *Khilafah in Pakistan: What, Why and How?* A collection of two articles written by Dr Israr Ahmad, compiled by Shoba Samo Basr (Lahore, Pakistan: Markazi Anjuman Khuddam-ul-Qur'an, 2006 [2001]).

Ahmed, Hilal. 'Asghar Ali Engineer (1939-2013): Emancipatory Intellectual Politics', *Economic & Political Weekly* [*EPW*], XLVIII, 22 (1 June 2013): 20–22.

Ahmed, Safdar. *Reform and Modernity in Islam: The Philosophical, Cultural and Political Discourses among Muslim Reformers* (New York: I. B. Tauris, 2013).

Akhavi, Shahrough. 'Sayyid Qutb', in John L. Esposito and Emad El-Din Shahin (eds.), *Key Islamic Political Thinkers* (New York: Oxford University Press, 2018), pp. 67–84.

Al-'Alwani, Taha Jabir. 'Taqlid and Ijtihad', *American Journal of Islamic Social Sciences*, 8, 1 (1991): 129–142.

Al-'Imara, Muhammad. *A'mal al-Kamila lil-Imam Muhammad 'Abduh* (Beirut: al-Mu'assasa al-'Arabiyya lil Dirasat wal-Nashr, 1972).

Al-Afghani, Jamal al-Din, and 'Abduh, Muhammad. *Al-'Urwa al-Wuthqa wa al-Thawrah al-Tahririyyah al-Kubra*, 1st ed. (Cairo: Dar al-Arab, 23 July 1957).

Al-Afghani, Jamal al-Din. 'Al-Hukumah al-Istibdadiyah' [The Despotic Government], in Abdulbasit Hasan (ed.), *Jamal al-din al-Afghani* (*Biography of al-Afghani*) (Cairo: Maktabatul Wahbah, 1982) [first published in *Misr* journal 14 February 1879], pp. 267–268.

Al-Azami, Usaama. *Islam and Arab Revolutions—The Ulama between Democracy and Autocracy* (London: Hurst & Co.; New York: Oxford University Press, 2021).

Azzam, Abd al-Rehman. 'The Islamic State', in Salem Azzam (ed.), *Concept of Islamic State* (London: Islamic Council of Europe, 1979), pp. 11–18.

Al-Baghdadi, Ahmad Mubarak. 'Consultation', (trans.) Brannon M. Wheeler, in Jane Dammen McAuliffe (ed.), *The Encyclopedia of Qur'an [EQ]* (Leiden: E. J. Brill, 2001–2006), I: 406–410.

Al-Baladhuri, Ahmad b. Yahya. *Futuh al-Buldan* (Cairo: Dar al-Nashr li al-Jamein, 1957).

Al-Dajani, Ahmad Sudqi. 'Tatawur Mafahim al-Dimuqratiyah Fi al-Fikr al-'Arabi al-Hadith' [The Development of the Concepts of Democracy in the Modern Arab Thought], in Saad Eddin Ibrahim (ed.), *Azmat al-Dimuqratiyah Fi al-Watan al-'Arabi* [The Crisis of Democracy in the Arab Homeland] (Beirut: Arab Unity Studies Centre, 1984), pp. 115–125.

Al-Darmi, Muhammad b. Abdullah. *Al-Sunnan* (Kanpur, India: al-Matba al-Nizami).

Al-Faruqi, Isma'il Raji'. *Al-Tawhid: Its Implications for Thought and Life*, 2nd ed. (Herndon, VA: International Institute of Islamic Thought [IIIT], 1992 [1982]).

Al-Ghannouchi, Rachid. 'Hukm Musharakat al-Islamiyyin fi Nizam Ghayr Islami', in 'Azam al-Tamimi (ed.), *Musharakat al-Islamiyyin fi al-Sulta* (London: Liberty for the Muslim World, 1994), pp. 12–24.

Al-Ghannouchi, Rachid. 'Islam and Freedom Can Be Friends', *The Observer* (London), 19 January 1992, p. 18.

Al-Ghannouchi, Rachid. 'Self-Criticism and Reconsideration', *Palestine Times*, 94, 1999.

Al-Ghannouchi, Rachid. *Al-Hurriyya al-Amma fi al-Dawla al-Islamiyyah* [Civil Liberties in an Islamic State] (Beirut: Markaz Dirasat al-Waḥdah al-'Arabiyyah, 1993).

Al-Ghazali, Abu Hamid. *Al-Mustaf min 'Ilm al-Usul* (Baghdad: Muthana, 1970).

*Al-Hewar (Dialogue) Centre*—The Centre for Arab Culture and Dialogue (Washington, D.C.), www.alhewar.com/About%20Us.html (last accessed on 20 December 2021).

Al-Hibri, Azizah Y. 'Islamic Constitutionalism and the Concept of Democracy', *Case Western Reserve Journal of International Law*, 24, 1 (1992): 1–27. It was published in book form as well by American Muslim Foundation, New York, 1992.

Ali, Abdullah Yusuf. *The Glorious Qur'an: Text, Translation and Commentary*, 2nd ed. (Plainfield, IN: American Trust Publications, 1977).

Ali, Muhammad Mumtaz. 'Political Thought of Iqbal and Contemporary Islamic Resurgence', *Dr Iqbal Society of North America [DISNA]*, 18 March 2011, available online at http://disna.us/allamaiqbal/2011/03/18/political-thought-of-iqbal-and-contemporary-islamic-resurgence (last accessed on 28 May 2011).

Ali, Syed Ameer. *A Short History of Saracens*, 4th ed. (New Delhi: Adam Publishers and Distributors, 2010 [1898]).

Alianak, Sonia. *Middle East Leaders and Islam: A Precarious Reading* (New York: Peter Lang Publishing, 2007).

Al-Mawardi, Abu al-Hasan. *Al-Ahkam al-Sultaniyyah* (Beirut: Dar al-Fikr, 1966).

Al-Mawardi, Abu al-Hasan. *The Ordinances of Government* (trans.) W. H. Wahba (Reading: Garnet Publishing, 1996).

*Al-Mawrid*, www.almawrid.org/.

Al-Qaradawi, Yusuf. 'Islam and Democracy', in *Princeton Readings in Islamist Thought: Texts and Contexts from al-Banna to Bin Laden*, Edited with an Introduction by Roxanne L. Euben and Muhammad Qasim Zaman (Princeton: Princeton University Press, 2009), pp. 230–245.

Al-Qaradawi, Yusuf. 'Muslim World Needs Democracy', in *The Muslim News*, 8 July 2006, available online at http://www.muslimnews.co.uk/news/news.php?article=11311 (last accessed on 5 September 2010).

Al-Qaradawi, Yusuf. *Al-Khasa'is al-'Ama lil-Islam* (Cairo: Maktabat Wahhaba, 1977).

Al-Qaradawi, Yusuf. *Malamih al-Mujtama' al-Islami alladhi nanshuduhu* (Beirut: al-Risala, 1996).

Al-Qaradawi, Yusuf. *Min Fiqh al-Dawla fi al-Islam* (Cairo: Dar al-Shurouk, 2001 [1997]).

Al-Qaradawi, Yusuf. *Priorities of the Islamic Movement in the Coming Phase*, available online at https://www.islambasics.com/book/priorities-of-the-islamic-movement-in-the-coming-phase (last accessed on 20 August 2018).

Al-Qaradawi, Yusuf. *State in Islam*, 3rd ed. (Cairo: Al-Falah Foundation for Translation, Publication and Distribution, 2004).

Al-Raysuni, Ahmad. *Al-Shura: The Qur'anic Principle of Consultation* (trans.) Nancy Roberts, Abridged by Alison Lake (Herndon, VA: The International Institute of Islamic Thought [IIIT], [2011] 2012).

Al-Shatibi, Abu Ishaq. *Al-I'tisam* (Cairo: 1331 AH).

Al-Solh, R. 'Islamist Attitudes Towards Democracy: A Review of the Ideas of al-Ghazali, al-Turabi and Amara', *British Journal of Middle Eastern Studies [BJMES]*, 20, 1 (1993): 57–63.

Al-Sulami, Mishal Fahm. *The West and Islam: Western Liberal Democracy versus the System of Shura* (New York: Routledge Curzon, 2003).

Al-Suyuti, Jalal ud Din Abdul Rehman b. *Al-Durr al-Manthur fi Tafsir bi al-Mathur* (Beirut: Dar al-Thaqafah, n.d.).

Al-Tahtawi, Rifa'a Rafi'. *An Imam in Paris: Account of a Stay in France by an Egyptian Cleric (1826–1831)*, Translated and Introduced by Daniel L. Newman, 2nd ed. (London: Saqi Books, 2011 [2004]).

Al-Turabi, Hasan. 'Islamic State', in John L. Esposito (ed.), *Voices of Resurgent Islam* (New York: Oxford University Press, 1983), pp. 241–251.

Al-Turabi, Hasan. *Nazrat fi al-Fiqh al-Siyasi* (Um al-Fahim: Markaz al-Dirasat al Mu'asira, 1997).

Al-Turabi, Hasan. *Tajdid al-Fikr al-Islami*, 3rd ed. (Jeddah: Al-Dar al-Saudiyya lil-Nashr wal-Tawzi', 1993).

Alusi, Syed Mahmud. *Ruh al-Ma'ani* (Beirut: Mu'assassat al-Risalah, n.d.).

Al-Waqidi. *Kitab al-Maghazi* (Oxford: Oxford University Press, 1966).

Amin, Ahmad. *Zu'ama' al-Islah* [The Leaders of Reform] (Cairo: Lajnat al-Ta'lif wa al-Tarjamah, 1948).

Amin, Husnul. 'Post-Islamist Intellectual Trends in Pakistan: Javed Ahmad Ghamidi and His Discourse on Islam and Democracy', *Islamic Studies* [IS], 51, 2 (2012): 169–192.

An Interview with Abdulaziz Sachedina on His Life and Scholarship, *The Maydan*, 13 September 2017, available online at www.themaydan.com/2017/09/interview-abdulaziz-sachedina-life-scholarship/ (last accessed on 20 August 2018).

An Interview with Javed Ahmad Ghamidi by *NaseebVibe*s, Wednesday, 22 June 2005, available online, and translated by *Studying Islam*, http://www.studying-islam.org/articletext.aspx?id=985 (last accessed on 28 May 2011).

An-Nabhani, Taqiuddin. *Nidham ul Islam/The System of Islam* (London: Al-Khilafah Publications, 2002).

An-Nabhani, Taqiuddin. *Political Thoughts* (London: Al-Khilafah Publications, 1999).

Asad, Muhammad. *The Message of the Qur'an* (Gibraltar: Dar al Andalus, 1980).

Asad, Muhammad. *The Principles of State and Government in Islam* (Barkley and Los Angeles: University of California Press, 1961).

Ashour, Omar. 'Democratic Islam? Assessing the Bases of Democracy in Islamic Political Thought', *McGill Journal of Middle East Studies* [MJMES], 9, 1 (2008): 7–27.

Awan, M. Faisal. 'Discussions on Democracy and Islamic States: A Study on the Discourses of Mawdudi, Israr Ahmed, and Ghamidi', in Lütfi Sunar (ed.), *The Routledge International Handbook of Contemporary Muslim Socio-Political Thought* (New York & London: Routledge, 2021), pp. 401–413.

Awan, Muzaffar K. 'Reconciling Democracy and Islam', *Renaissance*, available online at http://www.monthly-renaissance.com/issue/content.aspx?id=84 (last accessed on 10 March 2011).

Ayalon, A. 'Shura: In the Modern Arab World', in C. E. Bosworth et al. (eds.), *The Encyclopedia of Islam* [EI2], New Edition (Leiden: E. J. Brill, 1960–2001), IX: 506.

Ayubi, Nazih N. *Political Islam: Religion and Politics in the Arab World* (London and New York: Routledge, 1993 [1991]).

Azad, Abul Kalam. '[*Qaul-i-Faisal*: The Last Word:] Statement of Maulana Azad before the Presidency Magistrate' [dated 11 January 1922, Calcutta] (trans.) Durlab Singh, in *Famous Trials of Mahatma Gandhi, Jawaharlal Nehru, Maulana Abul Kalam Azad* (Lahore: Hero Publications, 1944), pp. 41–67.

Azad, Abul Kalam. 'The Last Word' [*Qaul-i-Faisal*], in Charles Kurzman (ed.), *Modernist Islam: 1840–1940—A Sourcebook* (New York: Oxford University Press, 2002), pp. 325–333.

Azad, Abul Kalam. 'Al-Hilal ki Political Taleem', *Al-Hilal*, Weekly Magazine (Calcutta, India), 1, 8 (1 September 1912): 9.

Azad, Abul Kalam. 'Al-Hilal ke Maqsad aur Political Taleem ki Nisbat Eik Khat aur iska Jawab', *Al-Hilal*, Weekly Magazine (Calcutta, India), 9, 1 (8 September 1912): 4–8.

Azad, Abul Kalam. 'Wa'az-e Yusufi [Prophet Joseph's Preaching]', *Al-Hilal*, Weekly Magazine (Calcutta, India), 23, 1 (18 December 1912): 5–11.

Azad, Abul Kalam. *Islami Jamhurriyah* [Islamic Democracy] (Lahore: Al Hilal Book Agency, 1956).

Azad, Abul Kalam. *Mas'la Khilafat* [The Issue of Caliphate] (Lahore: Maktaba Ahbab, n.d.).

Azad, Abul Kalam. *Tarjaman al-Qur'an* (New Delhi: Sahitya Academy, 1966).

Azad, Abul Kalam. *The Tarjuman al-Quran*, 5 vols. (edited and trans.), Syed Abdul Latif (Hyderabad: Dr Syed Abdul Latif Trust for Quranic Cultural Research, 1962–1978; New Delhi: Sahitya Academy, 1966).

Azhar, Zahoor Ahmad. 'Shura', in Mahmudul Hasan Arif (Editor-in-Chief), *Urdu Dai'rahMa'arif-i- Islamiya*, 24 Vols. (Lahore: Danishgah Punjab, 1975), XI: 810–812.

Badawi, Elsaid M., and Abdel Haleem, Muhammad. *Arabic-English Dictionary of Qur'anic Usage* (Leiden and Boston: Brill, 2008).

Badry, Roswitha. "'Democracy' versus 'Shura-cracy': Failures and Chances of a Discourse and Its Counter-Discourse," in Tzvetan Theophanov et al. (eds.), *30 Years of Arabic and Islamic Studies in Bulgaria* (Sofia: University Press St. Kliment Ohridski, 2008), pp. 329–345.

Barber, Benjamin. *Jihad vs. McWorld: How Globalism and Tribalism Are Reshaping the World* (New York: Ballantine Books, 1996).

Baron de Montesquieu. *The New Encyclopedia Britannica*, 15th ed. (Chicago: Encyclopedia Britannica, 1985–2010 [1768-7]), VIII: 284.

Bayat, Asef. *Islam and Democracy: What Is the Real Question?* (Leiden: Amsterdam University Press, 2007).

Bayat, Asef. *Life as Politics: How Ordinary People Change the Middle East* (Amsterdam: Amsterdam University Press, 2010).

Bazargan, Mahdi. 'Religion and Liberty', in Charles Kurzman (ed.), *Liberal Islam—A Sourcebook* (New York: Oxford University Press, 1994), pp. 73–84.

Becker, Carl L. *Modern Democracy*, 10th ed. (New Haven: Yale University Press, [1941] 1951).

Beg, Abdullah Anwar. *Poet of the East* (Lahore: Qaumi Kutub Khana, 1939).

Bennabi, Malek. *La Democratie en Islam* [Islam and Democracy] (Alger: Mosquee de Beni Messous, n.d.).

Bennett, Clinton 'Iqbal, Allamah Sir Muhammad', in Zayn R. Kassam, Yudit Kornberg Greenberg, and Jehan Bagli (eds.), *Islam, Judaism, and Zoroastrianism* (Dordrecht, The Netherlands: Springer, 2018), pp. 312–321.

Berridge, W. J. 'Hassan al-Turabi: Sudan's Democrat Turned Authoritarian (1932–2016)', *African Arguments*, 3 August 2016, available online at www.africanarguments.org/2016/03/08/hassan al-turabi-sudans-democrat-turned-authoritarian-1932-2016/ (last accessed on 20 August 2018).

Bhat, Abdur Rashid. *Iqbal's Approach to Islam—A Study* (New Delhi: Islamic Book Foundation, 1996).

Black, Antony. *The History of Islamic Political Thought: From the Prophet to the Present* (New York: Oxford University Press, 2001; South Asian Edition by OUP Karachi, 2004).

Blaug, Ricardo, and Schwarzmantel, John (eds.), *Democracy: A Reader* (New York: Columbia University Press, 2000).

Bokhari, Kamran, and Senzai, Farid. *Political Islam in the Age of Democratization* (New York: Palgrave Macmillan, 2013).

Bokhari, Kamran. 'Is Democracy Disbelief?', *Q-News*, 352 (December 2003): 34–35.

Bokhari, Kamran. 'Islamist Attitudes Toward Democracy', in Radwan A. Masmoudi, Ali A. Mazrui, John L Esposito et al. (eds.), *Islam, Democracy and the Secularist State in the Post-Modern Era*, Conference Proceedings of Center for the Study of

*Islam and Democracy Second Annual Conference* (Burtonsville, MD: CSID, 2001), pp. 173–175.

Bokhari, Kamran. http://www.post-islamist.info/5152.html (last accessed on 9 December 2012).

Bosworth, C. E. 'Shura: In Early Islamic History', in C. E. Bosworth et al. (eds.), *The Encyclopedia of Islam*, New Edition (Leiden: E. J. Brill, 1960–2001), IX: 505.

Bryce, James. *Modern Democracies* (New York: Macmillan, 1931).

Bulac, Ali. 'The Madina Document', in Charles Kurzman (ed.), *Liberal Islam—A Sourcebook* (New York: Oxford University Press, 1994), pp. 169–178.

Burr, Millard. *Revolutionary Sudan: Hasan al-Turabi and the Islamist State, 1989–2000* (Boston, MA: Brill, 2003).

Butt, Khalid Manzoor, and Siddiqui, Naeema. 'Compatibility between Islam and Democracy', *South Asian Studies—A Research Journal of South Asian Studies*, 33, 2 (July–December 201): 513–527.

Çaha, Ömer. 'Islam and Democracy: A Theoretical Discussion on the Compatibility of Islam and Democracy', *Alternatives: Turkish Journal of International Relations*, 2, 3&4 (2003): 106–134.

Calvert, John. *Sayyid Qutb and the Origins of Radical Islamism* (New York: Oxford University Press, 2013).

Campanini, Massimo. 'Democracy in the Islamic Political Concept', *Oriento Moderno*, 24 (85), 2/3 (2005): 343–352.

Center for Study of Society and Secularism (CSSS): www.csss-isla.com/about-us (last accessed on 10 May 2021).

Choueiri, Youssef M. 'The Political Discourse of Contemporary Islamist Movements', in Abdel Salam Sidahmed and Anoushiravan Ehteshami (eds.), *Islamic Fundamentalism* (Oxford: Westview Press, 1996), pp. 19–33.

Cook, Michael. *Commanding Right and Forbidding Wrong in Islamic Thought* (Cambridge: Cambridge University Press, 2002).

Cooper, John, Nettler, Ronald, and Mahmoud, Mohamed (eds.), *Islam and Modernity: Muslim Intellectuals Respond* (London and New York: I. B. Tauris, 2000).

Cragg, Kenneth. *The Pen and the Faith: Eight Modern Muslim Writers and the Quran* (London: George Allen & Unwin, 1985).

Dahl, Robert. *Democracy and Its Critiques* (Ithaca: Yale University Press, 1989).

Dahl, Robert A. *A Preface to Democratic Theory* (Chicago: University of Chicago Press, 2006).

Daryabadi, Abdul Majid. *Tafsir-i-Qur'an: Tafsir-i-Majidi*, 2nd ed. (Urdu) (Lucknow, India: Academy of Islamic Research and Publications, 2003).

Daryabadi, Abdul Majid. *Tafsir-i-Qur'an: Translation and Commentary of the Holy Qur'an*, 4 vols. (Karachi: Darul Ishaat, 1991).

Daryabadi, Abdul Majid. *The Glorious Qur'an: Text, Translation, and Commentary* (Leicester, Mark.: The Islamic Foundation, 2001).

*Dawn*. 'Prominent scholar Dr Israr Ahmed dies'. 15 April 2010, available online at http://www.dawn.com/news/857508/prominent-scholar-dr-israr-ahmed-dies (last accessed on 14 June 2021).

Declaration of Independence [1789], in *The New Encyclopedia Britannica*, 15th ed. (Chicago: Encyclopedia Britannica, 1985–2010 [1768–7]), VI: 283–284.

Declaration of the Rights of Man and of the Citizen [1789], in *The New Encyclopedia Britannica*, 15th ed. (Chicago: Encyclopedia Britannica, 1985–2010 [1768–7]), X: 7.

Democracy and Rationality: An interview with Abdolkarim Soroush, *Shargh* (Daily Newspaper, Tehran), December 2003 (trans.) Nilou Mobasser, available online at http://www.drsoroush.com/English/Interviews/E-INT-20031200-1.htm (last accessed on 12 March 2011).

Democracy, in *The New Encyclopedia Britannica*, 15th ed. (Chicago: Encyclopedia Britannica [1768–7], 1985–2010), IV: 5.

Denli, Ozlem. 'An Islamic Quest for a Pluralistic Political Model: A Turkish Perspective', in M. A. Muqtedar Khan (ed.), *Islamic Democratic Discourse: Theory, Debates and Philosophical Perspectives* (Lanham, MD: Lexington Books, 2006), pp. 85–103.

Dhulipala, Venkat. *Creating a New Madina: State Power, Islam, and the Quest for Pakistan in Late Colonial North India* (New Delhi: Cambridge University Press, 2015).

Diamond, Larry et al. (eds.), *Democracy in Asia* (New Delhi, India: Vistaar Publications [a division of Sage], 1989).

Diamond, Larry et al. (eds.), *Democracy in Developing Countries* (London: Adamantine Press, 1988).

Diamond, Larry et al. (eds.), *Islam and Democracy in the Middle East* (Baltimore: John Hopkins University Press, 2003).

Diamond, Larry. 'Why Are There No Arab Democracies?', *Journal of Democracy*, 21, 1 (2010): 93–104.

Doi, Abdul Rehman I. 'Maslaha', in John L. Esposito (ed.), *The Oxford Encyclopedia of Modern Islamic World* (New York: Oxford University Press, 1999), III: 63–65.

Douglas, Ian Henderson. Gail Minault, and Christian W. Troll (eds.), *Abul Kalam Azad—An Intellectual and Religious Biography* (Delhi: Oxford University Press, 1988).

Ebadi, Shirin. 'Islam, Democracy, and Human Rights', Lecture, Syracuse University, 10 May 2004, published in *Syracuse University News*, 12 May 2004.

El-Affendi, Abdelwahab. *Turabi's Revolution: Islam and Power in Sudan* (London: Grey Seal, 1991).

El-Affendi, Abdelwahab. 'Democracy and Its (Muslim) Critics: An Islamic Alternative to Democracy', in M. A. Muqtedar Khan (ed.), *Islamic Democratic Discourse: Theory, Debates and Philosophical Perspectives* (Lanham, MD: Lexington Books, 2006), pp. 227–256.

El-Affendi, Abdelwahab. 'Democracy and the Islamist Paradox', in Roland Axtmann (ed.), *Understanding Democratic Politics* (London: Sage, 2003), pp. 311–320.

El-Affendi, Abdelwahab. 'Do Muslims Deserve Democracy?', *New Internationalist*, 345 (May 2002), available online at http://www.newint.org/features/2002/05/01/do-muslims-deserve-democracy/#key (last accessed on 25 May 2011).

El-Affendi, Abdelwahab. 'On the State, Democracy and Pluralism', in Suha Taji-Farouki and Basheer Nafi (eds.), *Islamic Thought in the Twentieth Century* (New York: I. B. Tauris, 2004), pp. 180–203.

El-Affendi, Abdelwahab. 'Rationality of Politics and Politics of Rationality: Democratization and the Influence of Islamic Religious Traditions', in

Azzam Tamimi and John L. Esposito (eds.), *Islam and Secularism in the Middle East* (London: C. Hurts and Co., 2000), pp. 151–169.

El-Affendi, Abdelwahab. 'The Elusive Reformation', *Journal of Democracy*, 14, 2 (2003): 34–39.

El-Affendi, Abdelwahab. 'The Modern Debate(s) on Islam and Democracy', available online at http://www.ndid.org.my/web/wp-content/uploads/2010/04/The-Modern-Debate-on-Islam-and-DemocracyAbdelwahab-El-Affendi-4.htm#_ftn1 (last accessed on 25 May 2011).

El-Affendi, Abdelwahab. 'The Modern Debate(s) on Islam and Democracy', *The Asia Foundation*, 2010, available online at https://westminsterresearch.westminster.ac.uk/item/90331/the-modern-debate-s-on-islam-and-democracy-a-literature-review (last accessed on 15 June 2021).

El-Affendi, Abdelwahab. *Who Needs an Islamic State?* 2nd ed. (UK: Malaysia Think Tank London, 2008 [1991]).

El-Affendi, Abdelwahab. *Who Needs an Islamic State?* 1st ed. (London: Grey Seal Books, 1991).

El-Awa, Muhammad Saleem. *On the Political System of Islamic State* (Indianapolis: American Trust Publications, 1980).

Elliot, Florence, and Summerskill, Michael. *A Dictionary of Politics* (UK and USA: Penguin Books, 1981).

Elliot, W. Y., and McDonald, N. A. *Western Political Heritage* (New York: Prentice-Hall, 1949).

Enayat, Hamid. *Modern Islamic Political Thought* (Austin: University of Texas Press, 1988).

*Encyclopædia Britannica (EB)*, available online at https://www.britannica.com/ (last accessed on 20 August 2018).

Engineer, Asghar Ali. 'Islam and Secularism', in Ibrahim Abu-Rabi' (ed.), *The Blackwell Companion to Contemporary Islamic Thought* (Oxford, UK: Blackwell Publishing, 2006), pp. 338–344.

Engineer, Asghar Ali. 'Islam and Secularism', in John J. Donohue and John L. Esposito (ed.), *Islam in Transition: Muslim Perspectives*, 2nd ed. (New York: Oxford University Press, 2007), pp. 136–142.

Engineer, Asghar Ali. 'Islam, Democracy and Violence', in *Indian Muslims*, 4 September 2008, available online at http://indianmuslims.in/islam-democracy-and-violence/ (last accessed on 10 May 2011).

Engineer, Asghar Ali. 'What I Believe', available online at http://andromeda.rutgers.edu/~rtavakol/engineer/belief.htm (last accessed on 20 December 2021). Originally published in *Islam and Modern Age* (July 1999), a quarterly journal of Zakir Hussain Institute of Islamic Studies, *Jamia Milia Islamia*, New Delhi.

Engineer, Asghar Ali. *A Living Faith: My Quest for Peace, Harmony and Social Change* (New Delhi: Oriental Blackswan, 2011).

Engineer, Asghar Ali. *A Living Faith: My Quest for Peace, Harmony and Social Change* (New Delhi: Oriental Blackswan, 2011).

Engineer, Asghar Ali. *A Rational Approach to Islam*, 1st ed. (New Delhi: Gyan Publishing House; Haryana: Hope India Publications, 2001).

Engineer, Asghar Ali. *Islam and Liberation Theology: Essays on Liberative Elements in Islam* (New Delhi: Stosius/Advent Books Division, 1990).

Engineer, Asghar Ali. *Islam: Challenges in 21st Century* (New Delhi: Gyan Publishing House, 2004).
Engineer, Asghar Ali. *On Developing Theology of Peace in Islam* (New Delhi: Sterling Publishers [2005] 2003).
Eshkevari, Hasan Yusofi. 'Hokumat-e Demokratik-e Eslami' [Democratic Islamic Government], in Ali Muhammad Izadi et al. (eds.), *Din va Hokumat* [Religion and Government] (Tehran: Rasa, 1377 AH/1998 CE), pp. 285–328.
Esposito John L., and Piscatori, James P. 'Democratization and Islam', *The Middle East Journal* [*MEJ*], 45, 3 (1991): 427–440.
Esposito, John L. 'Contemporary Islam: Reformation or Revolution?', in John L. Esposito (ed.), *The Oxford History of Islam* (New York: Oxford University Press, 1999), pp. 643–690.
Esposito, John L. 'Muhammad Iqbal and the Islamic State', in John L. Esposito (ed.), *Voices of Resurgent Islam* (New York: Oxford University Press, 1983), pp. 175–190.
Esposito, John L. 'Practice and Theory', in Khaled Abou El Fadl, *Islam and the Challenge of Democracy: A Boston Review Book*, edited by Joshua Cohen and Deborah Chasman (Princeton, NJ: Princeton University Press, 2004), pp. 93–100.
Esposito, John L., and Voll, John O. 'Islam and Democracy', *Humanities*, 22, 6 (November/December 2001), available online at www.artic.ua.es/biblioteca/u85/documentos/1808.pdf (last accessed on 25 May 2022).
Esposito, John L., and Voll, John O. 'Islam's Democratic Essence', *Middle East Quarterly* [*MEQ*], 1, 3 (1994): 3–11, available online at http://www.meforum.org/151/islams-democratic-essence (last accessed on 15 June 2010).
Esposito, John L., and Voll, John O. *Islam and Democracy* (New York: Oxford University Press, 1996).
Esposito, John L., and Voll, John O. *Makers of Contemporary Islam* (New York: Oxford University Press, 2001).
Esposito, John L. *Islam and Politics*, 3rd ed. (Syracuse: Syracuse University Press, 1991).
Esposito, John L. *Islam: The Straight Path*, 5th ed. (New York: Oxford University Press, 2016 [1988]).
Esposito, John L. *The Future of Islam* (New York: Oxford University Press, 2010).
Esposito, John L. *The Islamic Threat: Myth or Reality?* (New York: Oxford University Press, 1988).
Esposito, John L. *Unholy War: Terror in the Name of Islam* (New York: Oxford University Press, 2001).
Esposito, John L. *What Everyone Needs to Know about Islam*, 2nd ed. (New York: Oxford University Press, 2011 [2002]).
Euben, Rozzane L., and Zaman, Muhammad Qasim (eds.), *Princeton Readings in Islamist Thought: Texts and Contexts from al-Banna to Bin Laden* (Princeton: Princeton University Press, 2009).
Fahad, Obaidullah. *Islamic Shura: State, Religion and Government* (New Delhi: Serials Publications, 2007).
Fahad, Obaidullah. *Redefining Islamic Political Thought: A Critique in Methodological Perspective* (New Delhi: Serials Publications, 2006).
Fahmi, Mustafa Abu Zayd. *Fann al-Hukm fi al-Islam* [The Art of Government in Islam] (Cairo: Al-Maktab al-Misri al-Hadith, 1981).

Farooq, Mohammad Omar. 'Islam and Democracy: Perceptions and Misperceptions', 2002, available online at www.papers.ssrn.com/sol3/papers.cfm?abstract_id=1772541/ (last accessed on 20 Aug 2018).

Faruqi, Imadulhasan Azad [I. H. A.]. *The Tarjuman al-Quran: A Critical Analysis of Maulana Abul Kalam Azad's Approach to the Understanding of the Quran* (New Delhi: Vikas, 1982 [1991]).

Faruqi, Muhammad Yusuf. 'The Institution of *Shura*: Views of Early *Fuqaha'* and the Practices of the *Rashidun Khulafa*', *Jihat al-Islam*, 1, 2 (June–July 2008): 9–30.

Feldman, Noah. 'The Best Hope', in Khaled Abou El Fadl, *Islam and the Challenge of Democracy: A Boston Review Book*, edited by Joshua Cohen and Deborah Chasman (Princeton and Oxford: Princeton University Press, 2004), pp. 59–62.

Feldman, Noah. *After Jihad: America and the Struggle for Islamic Democracy* (New York: Farrar, Straus and Giroux, 2003).

Feldman, Noah. *The Aab Winter: A Tragedy* (Princeton: Princeton University Press, 2020).

Feldman, Noah. *The Fall and Rise of the Islamic State* (Princeton: Princeton University Press, 2012 [2008]).

Forrest, G. B. *The Emergence of Greek Democracy: The Character of Greek Politics, 800–400 B.C.* (London: World University Library, 1966).

French Revolution: 1787–1799, *Encyclopædia Britannica (EB)*, available online at https://www.britannica.com/event/French-Revolution (last accessed on 20 August 2018).

Fukuyama, Francis. *The End of History and the Last Man* (New York: Free Press, 1992).

Fuller, Graham E. *The Future of Political Islam* (New York: Palgrave Macmillan, 2003).

Gallie, W. B. *Philosophy and the Historical Understanding* (London: Chatto and Windus, 1964).

Gauhar, Altaf. 'Islam and Secularism', in Altaf Gauhar (ed.), *The Challenge of Islam* (London: Islamic Council of Europe, 1978), pp. 298–310.

Ghamidi, Javed Ahmad. 'Islam and the Taliban', (trans.) Asif Iftikhar, *Renaissance—A Monthly Islamic Journal*, 19, 6 (June 2009), available online at http://www.monthly-renaissance.com/issue/content.aspx?id=1158 (last accessed on 25 May 2011).

Ghamidi, Javed Ahmad. 'The Political Law of Islam', (trans.) Shehzad Saleem, *Renaissance*, 23 December 2002.

Ghamidi, Javed Ahmad. *The Political Shari'ah of Islam*, (trans.) Shehzad Saleem, 4th ed. (Lahore: Al-Mawrid Foundation of Islamic Research and Education, 2009).

Ghamidi, Javed Ahmad. 'Their System Is Based on Their Consultation', in Shehzad Saleem (ed.), *Selected Essays of Javed Ahmad Ghamidi* (Lahore: Al-Mawrid, 2015), pp. 183–212.

Ghamidi, Javed Ahmad. *Burhan* (Lahore: Al-Mawrid, 2009), available at http://www.javedahmadghamidi.com/burhan/view/amrohum-shoora-baenahum (last accessed on 28 August 2018).

Ghamidi, Javed Ahmad. *Islam: A Comprehensive Introduction*, English rendering of *Mizan* by Shehzad Saleem, 5th ed. (Lahore: Al-Mawrid Foundation of Islamic Research and Education, 2009).

Ghamidi, Javed Ahmed. 'Islam and the Political System in Our Society', *Studying-Islam*, 16 December, 2002, available online at http://www.studying-islam.org/articletext.aspx?id=692 (last accessed on 28 May 2011).

Ghamidi—Nizam e Jamhooriyat (democracy), Video on YouTube, uploaded on 22 December 2008, available at http://www.youtube.com/watch?v=ZmAy_fq7m8c (last accessed on 9 June 2011).

Ghubash, Hussein. *Oman—The Islamic Democratic Tradition*, translated from French by Mary Turton (Oxon, RN and New York: Routledge, 2006).

Gibb, H. A. R. 'Ahl al-Hall w'al-'Akd', in C. E. Bosworth et al. (eds.), *The Encyclopedia of Islam*, New Edition (Leiden: E. J. Brill, 1960–2001), I: 263–264.

Glasse, Cyrill. *Concise Encyclopedia of Islam* (London: Stacey International, 1989).

Glorious Revolution, *Encyclopædia Britannica (EB)*, available online at https://www.britannica.com/event/Glorious-Revolution (last accessed 20 August 2018).

Green, Judith M. *Deep Democracy: Community, Diversity, and Transformation* (London: Rowman and Littlefield, 1999).

Grimes, William. 'Fathi Osman, Scholar of Islam, Dies at 82', *The New York Times*, 19 September 2010, available online at http://www.nytimes.com/2010/09/20/us/20osman.html?_r=1 (last accessed on 25 February 2011).

Guillaume, A. *The Life of Muhammad: A Translation of Ishaq's Sirat Rasul Allah*, Introduction and Notes by A. Guillaume (Oxford and Delhi: Oxford University Press, 1955).

Haddad, Yvonne Y. 'Sayyid Qutb: Intellectual ideologue of Islamic Revival', in John L. Esposito (ed.), *Voices of Resurgent Islam* (New York: Oxford University Press, 1983), pp. 67–98.

Hadenius, Axel. *Democracy and Development* (Cambridge: Cambridge University Press, 1992).

Hakim, Khalifa Abdul. *Fikr-i-Iqbal* [The Thoughts of Iqbal], 4th ed. (Lahore: Bazm-i-Iqbal, 1968).

Hakim, Khalifa Abdul. *Islam and Communism* (Lahore: Institute of Islamic Culture, 1969).

Hakim, Khalifa Abdul. *The Prophet and His Message* (Lahore: Institute of Islamic Culture, 1987).

Hallaq, Wael B. 'Ahl al-Hall wa al-'Aqd', in John L. Esposito (ed.), *The Oxford Encyclopedia of Modern Islamic World* (New York: Oxford University Press, 1999), I: 53–54.

Hallaq, Wael B. *A History of Islamic Legal Theories* (Cambridge: Cambridge University Press, 1997).

Hallaq, Wael. B. 'Was the Gate of Ijtihad Closed?', *International Journal of Middle East Studies [IJMES]*, 16, 1 (1984): 3–41.

Hamidullah, Muhammad. *Introduction to Islam*, New and Enlarged Edition (Gary, IN: International Islamic Federation of Student Organizations, 1969).

Hamidullah, Muhammad. *The First Written Constitution in the World* (Lahore: Sheikh Muhammad Ashraf, 1968 [England, 1941]).

Haq, Abdul. 'Iqbal: Concept of Spiritual Democracy', *Iqbal Review*, 27, 3 (1986): 67–73.

Haque, Munawar. 'Sayyid Abul Ala Mawdudi's Views on Ijtihad and their Relevance to the Contemporary Muslim Society', *Journal of Islam in Asia [JIA]*, 6, 2 (2010): 123–151.

Hartung, Jan-Peter. *A System of Life: Mawdudi and the Ideologisation of Islam* (London: Hurst and Co., 2020 [2013]).

## BIBLIOGRAPHY

Hasan, Abd al-Basit. *Jamal al-Din al-Afghani wa- atharuhu fi al-'alam al-Islami al-Hadit* (Cairo: Maktabat Wahbah, 1982).

Hasan, Masudul. *Sayyid Abul A'ala Maududi and His Thought*, 2 vols. (Lahore: Islamic Publications, 1984).

Hasan, Zoya. (ed.), *Democracy in Muslim Societies: The Asian Experience* (New Delhi: Sage Publications, [in association with] Observation Research Foundation, 2007).

Hashemi, Nader. 'Change from Within', in Khaled Abou El-Fadl (ed.), *Islam and the Challenge of Democracy: A Boston Review Book*, edited by Joshua Cohen and Deborah Chasman (Princeton, NJ: Princeton University Press, 2004), pp. 49–54.

Hashemi, Nader. 'Islam [and Democracy] since 9/11', in Benjamin Isakhan and Stephen Stockwell (eds.), *The Edinburgh Companion to the History of Democracy* (Edinburgh: Edinburgh University Press, 2012), pp. 441–451.

Hashemi, Nader. 'Islam and Democracy', in John L. Esposito and Emad El-Din Shahin (eds.), *The Oxford Handbook of Islam and Politics* (New York: Oxford University Press, 2013), pp. 68–88.

Hashemi, Nader. *Islam, Secularism, and Liberal Democracy: Toward a Democratic Theory for Muslim Societies* (New York: Oxford University Press, 2009).

Hashmi, Sohail H. 'Reform: Arab Middle East and North Africa', in Richard C. Martin (ed.), *Encyclopedia of Islam and Modern World*, 2 vols. (New York: Macmillan, 2004), II: 574–577.

Hassan, Riffat. 'Iqbal's View of Democracy', *Dawn*, 11 June 2010.

Hassan, Riffat. 'Islamic Modernist and Reformist Discourse in South Asia', in Shireen T. Hunter (ed.), *Reformist Voices of Islam—Mediating Islam and Modernity* (New Delhi: Pentagon Press, 2009), pp. 159–186.

Haykal, Muhammad Hasanayn. *Kharif al-Ghadab* [The Autumn of Anger], 2nd ed. (Cairo: Sharikat al-Matbu'at, 1983).

Haykal, Muhammad Husayn. *Hayat-i-Muhammad (The Life of Muhammad)*, English translation by Ismail Raji al-Faruqi, 8th ed. (Indianapolis: American Trust Publications, 1976).

Haykel, Bernard. 'Popular Support First', in Khaled Abou El-Fadl (ed.), *Islam and the Challenge of Democracy: A Boston Review Book*, edited by Joshua Cohen and Deborah Chasman (Princeton, NJ: Princeton University Press, 2004), pp. 78–80.

Helal, Abdul Aleem. *Social Philosophy of Sir Muhammad Iqbal* (New Delhi: Adam Publishers and Distributors, 1995).

Held, David. *Models of Democracy*, 3rd ed. (Cambridge, UK: Polity Press, 2006).

Helfont, Samuel. *Yusuf al-Qaradawi, Islam and Modernity* (Tel Aviv, Israel: The Moshe Dayan Center, Tel Aviv University, 2009).

Hizb-ut- Tahrir, www.hizb-ut-tahrir.org/EN.

Hobbes, Thomas, in *The New Encyclopedia Britannica*, 15th ed. (Chicago: Encyclopedia Britannica, 1985–2010 [1768-7]), V: 959–960.

Hoffman, Murad. 'Democracy or Shuracracy', in John J. Donohue and John L. Esposito (eds.), *Islam in Transition: Muslim Perspectives*, 2nd ed. (New York: Oxford University Press, 2007), pp. 296–306.

Hourani, Albert. *Arabic Thought in the Liberal Age* (Cambridge: Cambridge University Press, 1983 [1962]).

Hua, Shiping (ed.). *Islam and Democratization in Asia* (New York: Cambria Press, 2009).

Hunter, Shireen T. (ed.). *Reformist Voices of Islam—Meditating Islam and Modernity* (New York: M. E. Sharpe, 2009).

Huntington, Samuel. 'Democracy's Third Wave', *Journal of Democracy* [*JoD*], 2, 2 (1991): 12–34.

Huntington, Samuel. *The Clash of Civilizations and the Remaking of World Order* (New York: Simon and Schuster, 1996).

Husaini, S. A. 'The Shura', *Journal of the Pakistan Historical Society*, III, II (1955): 151–165.

Husaini, S. Waqar Ahmed. *Islamic Environmental Engineering Systems* (USA: American Trust Publications; UK: Macmillan, 1980).

Husayn, M. Muhammad. *Al-Islam wa al-Hadarah al-Gharbiyyah* [Islam and Western Civilization] (Beirut: Al-Risalah, 1985).

Hussain, Touqir. 'Islam and Pakistan', in Shiping Hua (ed.), *Islam and Democratization in Asia* (Amherst, NY: Cambria Press, 2009), pp. 89–118.

Ibn al Sa'ad. *al-Tabaqat al-Kubra* (Beirut: Dar Sader, 1957).

Ibn Hisham, Abd al-Malik. *al-Sirah al-Nabawiyyah* [The Prophetic History], 1st ed., 4 vols. (Beirut: Dar Ihya' al-Turath, 1995).

Ibn Manzur. *Al-Lisan al-Arab* (Beirut: Dar Sadir, 1968).

Ibrahim, Urooj Sadeq. *'Uthman bin 'Affan* (Cairo, 1947).

Idris, Jaafir [Sheikh Jafar Idris]. 'Shura and Democracy: A Conceptual Analysis', *Al-Jumuah*, 6 December 2021, available online at www.aljumuah.com/shurah-and-democracy-a-conceptual-analysis/?utm_source=rss&utm_medium=rss&utm_compaign=shurah-and-democracy-a-conceptual-analysis (last accessed on 28 December 2021).

Imarah, Muhammad. *Al-Islam wa Huquq al-Insan Darurat La Huquq* (Damascus and Cairo: Markaz al-Raya, Dar al-Islam, 2004–5 [1985]).

Imarah, Muhammad. *Al-Islam wa Huquq al-Insan: Daruriyyat la Huquq* [Human Rights in Islam Are Obligatory: Necessities, Not Merely Rights], 1st ed. (Cairo: Dar al-Shuruq, 1989).

Ingram, Brannon. 'Ashraf Ali Thanawi', in Zayn R. Kassam, Yudit Kornberg Greenberg, and Jehan Bagli (eds.), *Islam, Judaism, and Zoroastrianism* (Dordrecht, The Netherlands: Springer, 2018), pp. 82–84.

Institute of Islamic Studies (IIS). www.csss-isla.com/institute-of-islamic-studies (last accessed on 10 May 2021).

Iqbal, Javed. 'Iqbal's Concept of *Ijtihad*', *QLCian*, 2009: 16–21.

Iqbal, Muhammad. 'Islam as a Moral and Political Ideal' (Part-I), *Hindustan Review* (Allahabad, India), 20, 119 (July 1909): 29–38.

Iqbal, Muhammad. 'Islam as a Moral and Political Ideal' (Part-II), *Hindustan Review*, 20, 120 (August 1909): 166–171.

Iqbal, Muhammad. *Asrar-i-Khudi/Secrets of the Self*, English translation with an Introduction by R. A. Nicholson (Dr Iqbal Society of North America [DISNA], n.d.), available online at http://disna.us/files/SECRETS_OF_THE_SELF.pdf.

Iqbal, Muhammad. *Bang-i-Dara/The Call of the Caravan Bell*, (trans.) M. A. K. Khalil, available online at http://disna.us/files/The_Call_of_The_Caravan_Bell.pdf (last accessed on 28 May 2011).

Iqbal, Muhammad. *Kulliyat-i-Iqbal* (Lahore: Shaykh Ghulam Ali & Sons, 1973).

Iqbal, Muhammad. *Payam-i-Mashriq* (trans.) M. Hadi Husain, *A Message from the East*, available online at http://disna.us/files/A_MESSAGE_FROM_THE_EAST. pdf (last accessed on 28 May 2011).

Iqbal, Muhammad. *The Reconstruction of Religions Thought in Islam* (Lahore: Shaikh Muhammad Ashraf, 1962 [1930 and 1934]).

Iqbal, Muhammad. *The Reconstruction of Religious Thought in Islam*, Edited and Annotated by M. Saeed Sheikh, 2nd ed. (Lahore: Iqbal Academy Pakistan and the Institute of Islamic Culture, 1986).

Iqbal, Muhammad. *The Reconstruction of Religious Thought in Islam*, Edited and Annotated by M. Saeed Sheikh, With a new Introduction by Javed Majeed (Stanford, California: Stanford University Press, in collaboration with Iqbal Academy Pakistan, Lahore, 2012).

Isbell, Thomas. 'Separate and Compatible? Islam and Democracy in Five North African Countries', *AFRO Barometer*, Dispatch no. 118 (14 February 2018): 1–11.

*Ishraq*, http://www.ghamidi.net/Ishraq.html.

Ishrat, Waheed. 'Iqbal and Democracy—I' (trans.) M. A. K. Khalil, *Iqbal Review (Journal of the Iqbal Academy Lahore)*, 34, 3 (1993): 51–77.

Ishrat, Waheed. 'Iqbal and Democracy—II' (trans.) M. A. K. Khalil, *Iqbal Review (Journal of the Iqbal Academy Lahore)*, 35, 1 (1994): 16–47.

Isik, Harun. 'Malek Bennabi's Approach to decadence and Democracy in Muslim World', *The Islamic Quarterly*, 53, 4 (2009): 343–354.

Islahi, Amin Ahsan. 'The Institution of Consultation during the Reign of Rightly Guided Caliphs' (trans.), Jhangeer Hanif, available online at http://www.amin-ahsan-islahi.com/?=136 (last accessed on 20 May 2011).

Islahi, Amin Ahsan. *Islami Riyasat* (Lahore: Anjuman Khuddamul Qur'an, 1977).

Islahi, Amin Ahsan. *Tadabbur al-Qur'an* (Delhi: Taj Company, 1989).

Islahi, Amin Ahsan. *The Islamic State* (trans.) Tariq Mahmood Hashmi (Germany: Lambert Academic Publishing, 2012).

Islam, Md Nazrul, and Islam, Md Saidul. 'Islam and Democracy: Conflicts and Congruence', *Religions*, 8, 6 (2017): 1–19.

Islam, Md Nazrul, and Islam, Md Saidul. *Islam and Democracy in South Asia: The Case of Bangladesh* (Cham, Switzerland: Palgrave Macmillan/Springer Nature, 2020).

Ismael, Tareq Y., and Ismael, Jacqueline S. *Government and Politics in Islam* (London: Frances Pinter Publishers, 1985).

Jackson, Roy. *Fifty Key Figures in Islam* (London: Routledge, 2006).

Jackson, Roy. *Mawlana Mawdudi and Political Islam: Authority and the Islamic State* (Oxon, New York, and Canada: Routledge, 2011).

Jahanbakhsh, Forough. 'Abdolkarim Soroush: New 'Revival of Religious Sciences', *ISIM Newsletter*, 8 (2001): 21, available online at https://openaccess.leidenuniv.nl/bitstream/handle/1887/17496/ISIM_8_Abdolkarim_Soroush_New_Revival_of_Religious_Sciences.pdf?sequence=1 (last accessed on 12 March 2011).

Jahanbakhsh, Forough. *Islam, Democracy and Religious Modernism in Iran (1953–2000): From Bazargan to Soroush* (Leiden, Boston, Koln: Brill, 2001).

Jan, Abid Ullah. 'Compatibility: Neither Required nor an Issue', in John J. Donohue and John L. Esposito (eds.), *Islam in Transition: Muslim Perspectives*, 2nd ed. (New York: Oxford University Press, 2007): 319–331.

Jan, Abid Ullah. *After Fascism: Muslims and the Struggle for Self-determination* (Canada: Pragmatic Publishing, 2006).

Jan, Abid Ullah. *The End of Democracy* (Canada: Pragmatic Publishing, 2003).

Jansen, G. H. 'Islam and Democracy: Are They Compatible?', *Middle East International* [*MEI*], 42, 6 (May 1992): 18-19.

Javed Ahmad Ghamidi. http://javedahmadghamidi.com/.

Jawad, Haifaa. 'Islam and Democracy in the 21st Century', in Gabriele Marranci (ed.), *Muslim Societies and the Challenge of Secularization: An Interdisciplinary Approach* (London: Springer, 2010), pp. 65-81.

Kamali, Mohammad Hashim. 'The *Shariʿa*: Law as the Way of God', in Vincent J. Cornell (General Editor), *Voices of Islam*, 5 vols.; Vol. I: Voices of Tradition (Westport, CT: Praeger Publishers, 2007), pp. 149-181.

Kamali, Muhammad Hashim. 'Islam and Democracy', *Islam and Civilizational Renewal* [*ICR*], 4, 3 (July 2013): 437-439.

Kaminski, Joseph J. *The Contemporary Islamic Governed State: A Reconceptualization* (London: Palgrave Macmillan, 2017).

Kamrava, Mehran (ed.). *The New Voices of Islam: Reforming Politics and Modernity—A Reader* (New York and London: I. B. Tauris, 2006).

Kamrava, Mehran. 'Introduction: Reformist Islam in Comparative Perspective', in Mehran Kamrava (ed.), *The New Voices of Islam: Reforming Politics and Modernity—A Reader* (New York and London: I. B. Tauris, 2006), pp. 1-27.

Kamrava, Mehran. 'Shiʿism at the Gates of Historic Change', in Mehran Kamrava (ed.), *Innovation in Islam: Traditions and Contributions* (Berkeley, Los Angeles, and London: University of California Press, 2011), pp. 58-81.

Kaplan, Robert. *The Coming Anarchy: Shattering the Dreams of the Post-Cold War* (New York: Vintage Books, 2000).

Karolia, AbuBakr. 'Islam and Democracy: Political Thought Towards Post-democracy' (Study of Islam Program, *University of Johannesburg*, South Africa), Academia.edu, 19 October 2010: 1-21, available online at www.academia.edu/775684/Islam_and_Democracy_Political_thought_towards_post_democracy (last accessed on 28 December 2021).

Kausar, Zeenat. 'Iqbal on Democracy: Acceptance or Rejection?', *Iqbal Review*, 42, 4 (2001): 33-60.

Kausar, Zeenat. 'Mawdudi on Democracy: A Critical Appreciation', *The Islamic Quarterly*, 47, 4 (2003): 301-333.

Keane, John. *The Life and Death of Democracy* (London: Simon and Schuster, 2009).

Keddie, Nikkie R. 'Afghani, Jamal-al-Din', in *Encyclopedia Iranica*, 15 December 1983, available online at http://www.iranica.com/articles/afgani-jamal-al-din (last accessed on 5 January 2011).

Kedourie, Elie. *Democracy and Arab Political Culture* (Washington: The Washington Institute for Near East Policy, 1992).

Kerr, Malcolm H. *Islamic Reform: The Political and Legal Theories of Muhammad Abduh and Rashid Rida* (Berkeley, University of California Press, 1966).

Khadduri, Madjid. 'Maslaha', in C. E. Bosworth et al. (eds.), *The Encyclopedia of Islam*, New Edition (Leiden: E. J. Brill, 1960-2001), vi: 738-739.

Khalid, Khalid Muhammad. Interview in *Mayu*, 8 March 1982.

Khan, Ali. 'Commentary on the constitution of Medina', in Hisham M. Ramadan (ed.), *Understanding Islamic Law: From Classical to Contemporary* (New York: AltaMira Press, 2006), pp. 205–208.

Khan, M. A. Muqtedar. 'Compatibility of Islam and Democracy', in *United States Institute of Peace (USIP) Special Report on 'Islam and Democracy'*, prepared by David Smock (Washington, DC), 93 (September 2002), pp. 3–4.

Khan, M. A. Muqtedar. 'Democracy is Indispensable: A Political Philosophy of Islamic Governance', *The Roundtable*, 9, 1 (2011–2012): 11–14.

Khan, M. A. Muqtedar. 'Islam's Compatibility with Democracy', 11 April 2001, available online at www.ijtihad.org/isladem.htm (last accessed on 26 August 2010).

Khan, M. A. Muqtedar. 'Islam's Compatibility with Democracy'; 'Shura and Democracy'; 'The Compact of Medina: A Constitutional Theory of the Islamic State', available online at www.ijtihad.org and www.Glocaleye.org (last accessed on 26 August 2010).

Khan, M. A. Muqtedar. 'Islamic Democracy and Moderate Muslims: The Straight Path Runs Through the Middle', *American Journal of Islamic Social Sciences*, 27, 2 (2005): 39–50 [Special Issue on *'Debating Moderate Islam'*].

Khan, M. A. Muqtedar. 'Islamic Democratic Theory: Between Political Philosophy and Jurisprudence', *Global Dialogue [GD]*, 6, 1&2 (2004): 44–52.

Khan, M. A. Muqtedar. 'Islamic Democratic Theory: Between Political Philosophy and Jurisprudence', in Nadeem Hasnain (ed.), *Beyond Textual Islam* (New Delhi: Serial Publications, 2008), pp. 27–41.

Khan, M. A. Muqtedar. 'Islamic Governance and Democracy' in Shiping Hua (ed.), *Islam and Democratization in Asia* (Amherst, NY: Cambria Press, 2009), pp. 13–27.

Khan, M. A. Muqtedar. 'Political Authority in Islam', in M. Kabir Hassan and Mervyn K. Lewis (eds.), *Handbook on Islam and Economic Life* (Cheltenham, UK and Northampton, MA, USA: Edward Elgar, 2014), pp. 520–540.

Khan, M. A. Muqtedar. 'Shura and Democracy', *Muslim Democrat*, 1, 2 (1999): 5.

Khan, M. A. Muqtedar. 'The Compact of Medina: A Constitutional Theory of the Islamic State', *The Mirror International*, 30 May, 2001. Also available online at http://www.Ijtihād.org/compact.htm (last accessed on 25 May 2010).

Khan, M. A. Muqtedar. 'The Politics, Theory, and Philosophy of Islamic Democracy', in M. A. Muqtedar Khan (ed.), *Islamic Democratic Discourse: Theory, Debates and Philosophical Perspectives* (Lanham, MD: Lexington Books, 2006), pp. 149–171.

Khan, M. A. Muqtedar. 'The Priority of Politics—A response to *'Islam and the Challenge of Democracy'*', *Boston Review*, April–May 2003, available online at http://bostonreview.net/BR28.2/khan.html (last accessed on 25 May 2010).

Khan, M. A. Muqtedar. 'Three Dimensions of the Emerging Political Philosophy of Islam', in Shahram Akbarzadeh (ed.), *Routledge Handbook of Political Islam* (New York: Routledge, 2012), pp. 27–34.

Khan, M. A. Muqtedar. 'What Is Islamic Democracy? The Three Cs of Islamic Governance', in Timothy Poirson and Robert Oprisko (eds.), *Caliphates and Islamic Global Politics* (Bristol, UK: E-International Relations Publications, 2015), pp. 94–99.

Khan, M. A. Muqtedar. *American Muslims: Bridging Faith and Freedom* (Beltsville, MD: Amana Publications, 2002).

Khan, M. A. Muqtedar. *Debating Moderate Islam: The Geopolitics of Islam and the West* (Utah: University of Utah Press, 2007).

Khan, M. A. Muqtedar. *Islam and Good Governance: Political Philosophy of Ihsan* (New York: Palgrave Macmillan, 2019).

Khan, Majid. *The Pious Caliphate* (Kuwait: Karamatullah Sheikh, 1982).

Khan, Mawlana Wahiduddin. 'Taqlid, Ijtihad and Democracy' (trans.) Yoginder Sikand, 19 October 2008, available online at Sharia Laws, www.shariahlaws.blogs pot.com/2008/10/taqlid-ijtihad-and-democracy.html?m=1 (last accessed on 25 December 2021).

Khan, Mawlana Wahiduddin. 'The Concept of Democracy in Islam', *Insights*, 19 December 2002, available online at http://www.jammu-kashmir.com/insights/insight20021219a.html (last accessed on 15 October 2011).

Khan, Mawlana Wahiduddin. *Din-o-Shariat: Din-e Islam Ka Ek Fikri Muta'ala* [Religion and Law: An Intellectual Study of the Religion of Islam] (New Delhi: Goodword Books, 2003).

Khan, Mawlana Wahiduddin. *Fikr-e-Islami: Afkar-i Islami ki Tashrih wa Tawdih* (New Delhi: Goodword Books/al-Risala Books, 2013 [1998]).

Khan, Mawlana Wahiduddin. *God Arises* (New Delhi: Goodword Books, 2005).

Khan, Mawlana Wahiduddin. *Islam: Creator of the Modern Age* (New Delhi: The Islamic Centre, 1993).

Khatab, Sayed, and Bouma, Gary D. *Democracy in Islam* (New York: Routledge, 2007).

Khatab, Sayed. *The Power of Sovereignty: The Political and Ideological Philosophy of Sayyid Qutb* (London and New York: Routledge, 2006).

Khir, Bustamir. 'An Islamic Critique and Alternative of Democracy', *The Islamic Quarterly*, 47, 1 (2003): 73–79.

Kidwai, Abdur Raheem. 'Foreword', in Wani, Gowhar Quadir and Choughley, Abdul Kader (eds.), *Abdul Majid Daryabadi's Tafsir-ul-Qur'an: A Critical Study* (Aligarh: Brown Books, in association with KAN-CQS, AMU and Ahsan Academy of Research, Springs, South Africa, 2021), pp. ix–xi.

Kidwai, Abdur Raheem. *From Darkness into Light: Life and Works of Mawlana Abdul Majid Daryabadi* (Springs, South Africa: Ahsan Publication, 2013).

Krämer, Gudrun. 'Democracy and *Shura*', in Nissim Rejwan (ed.), *The Many Faces of Islam: Perspectives on a Resurgent Civilization* (Florida: University Press of Florida, 2000), pp. 127–130.

Krämer, Gudrun. 'Islamist Notions of Democracy', in Joel Beinin and Joe Stork (eds.), *Political Islam: Essays from Middle East Report* (Berkeley: University of California Press, 1997), pp. 71–82.

Krämer, Gudrun. 'Islamist Notions of Democracy', *Middle East Report* [*MER*], 183 (July–August 1993): 2–8; also reproduced in Joel Beinin and Joe Stork (eds.), *Political Islam: Essays from Middle East Report* (Berkeley: University of California Press, 1997), pp. 71–82.

Kramer, Martin. 'Islam vs. Democracy', *Commentary* (New York) (January 1993): 35–42; also reproduced in Martin Kramer, *Arab Awakening and Islamic Revival* (New Brunswick, NJ: Transaction, 1996), pp. 265–278.

Kramer, Martin. *Arab Awakening and Islamic Revival* (New Brunswick, NJ: Transaction Publishers, 1996), available online at http://www.martinkramer.org/sandbox/reader/archives/islam-vs-democracy/ (last accessed on 27 May 2011).

# BIBLIOGRAPHY

Kubicek, Paul. *Political Islam and Democracy in the Muslim World* (Boulder, CO: Lynne Rienner Publishers, 2015).

Kurzman, Charles (ed.). *Liberal Islam: A Sourcebook* (New York: Oxford University Press, 1998).

Kurzman, Charles (ed.). *Modernist Islam:1840–1940—A Sourcebook* (New York: Oxford University Press, 2002).

Kutelia, Murman. 'Egyptian Enlightener Rifa'a at-Tahtawi', *International Black Sea University Scientific Journal [IBSUSJ]*, 5, 1 (2011): 83–92.

Larsson, Goran. 'Yusuf al-Qaradawi and Tariq Ramadan on Secularization: Differences and Similarities', in Gabriele Marranci (ed.), *Muslim Societies and the Challenge of Secularization: An Interdisciplinary Approach* (London: Springer, 2010), pp. 47–63.

Laski, Harold J. 'Democracy', in Edwin R. A. Seligman (ed.), *Encyclopedia of the Social Sciences*, Rep. (New York: The Macmillan Company, 1935 [1923]), V: 76–84.

Lewis, Bernard. 'Islam and Liberal Democracy', *Atlantic Monthly*, 271 (February 1993): 89–98.

Lewis, Bernard. '*Mashwara*', in C. E. Bosworth et al. (eds.), *The Encyclopedia of Islam*, New Edition (Leiden: E. J. Brill, 1960–2001), VI: 725.

Lewis, Bernard. 'Shura', in C. E. Bosworth et al. (eds.), *The Encyclopedia of Islam*, New Edition (Leiden: E. J. Brill, 1960–2001), IX: 504.

Lewis, Bernard. 'The Roots of Muslim Rage', *Atlantic Monthly*, 266 (September 1990): 47–60.

Lewis, Bernard. *The Shaping of the Modern Middle East* (New York: Oxford University Press, 1994).

Lincoln, Abraham. 'The Gettysburg Address', in Ricardo Blaug and John Schwarzmantel (eds.), *Democracy: A Reader* (New York: Columbia University Press, 2000), p. 91.

Locke, John. *The New Encyclopedia Britannica*, 15th ed. (Chicago: Encyclopedia Britannica, 1985–2010 [1768-7]), VII: 435.

*Magna Carta (The Great Charter)*, available online at http://www.constitution.org/eng/magnacar.pdf (last accessed 30 December 2012).

Mahmood, Saba. 'Is Liberalism Islam's Only Answer?', in Khaled Abou El Fadl (ed.), *Islam and the Challenge of Democracy: A Boston Review Book*, edited by Joshua Cohen and Deborah Chasman (Princeton, NJ: Princeton University Press, 2004), pp. 74–75.

Majeed, Javed. 'Modernity', in Richard C. Martin (ed.), *Encyclopedia of Islam and Modern World* (New York: Macmillan, 2004), II: 456–458.

Malhotra, Rajat. 'Democracy—An Islamic Perspective', *Salaam—Quarterly to Promote Understanding*, 37, 4 (October 2016): 178–188.

Malik, Hafeez, and Hashemi, Sohail. 'Iqbal, Muhammad', in John L. Esposito (ed.), *The Oxford Encyclopedia of Modern Islamic World* (New York: Oxford University Press, 1999), I: 509–512.

Malik, Hafeez (ed.). *Iqbal: Poet-Philosopher of Pakistan* (New York: Columbia University Press, 1971).

Malik, Rizwan. 'Muslim Nationalism in India: Ashraf Ali Thanawi, Shabbir Ahmad Usmani and the Pakistan Movement', *Pakistan Journal of History and Culture*, XVIII, 2 (1997): 73–82.

Martin, Richard C. 'Maslaha', in Richard C. Martin (ed.), *Encyclopedia of Islam and Modern World*, 2nd ed. 2 vols. (New York: Macmillan, 2016 [2004]), II: 440.

Masmaudi, Radwan. 'Muslims Do Want Democracy', *The Charlotte Observer* (Fri, October 2006), available online at www.charlotte.com/mld/observer/news/opinion/15691590.htm (last accessed on 5 September 2010).

Masmoudi, Radwan. 'Editorial', *Muslim Democrat*, 1, 2 (1999): 1.

Masmoudi, Radwan. 'The Future of 'Islamic Democracy' in the Middle East–Islamists and Democracy: Friends or Foes?', *Future Islam*, September–October 2007, available online at http://www.futureislam.com/20070901/insight/radwan_a_masmoudi/The%20Future%20of%20Islamic%20Democracy%20in%20the%20Middle%20East.asp (last accessed on 9 December 2010).

Masmoudi, Radwan. 'The Silenced Majority', in Larry Diamond et al. (eds.), *Islam and Democracy in the Middle East* (Baltimore & London: The Johns Hopkins University Press, 2003), pp. 258–262.

Masmoudi, Radwan. 'Why Democracy?', *Muslim Democrat*, 7, 1 (2005): 1–2.

Masud, Muhammad Khalid, Salvatore, Armando, and Bruinessen, Martin van (eds.), *Islam and Modernity: Key Issues and Debates* (Edinburgh: Edinburgh University Press, 2009).

Masud, Muhammad Khalid. 'Defining Democracy in Islamic Polity', paper presented in the International Conference on '*The Future of Islam, Democracy, and Authoritarianism in the Era of Globalization*', 5–6 December 2004, International Centre for Islam and Pluralism, Jakarta, available online at http://www.maruf.org/?p=69 (last accessed on 25 May 2011); also published in *ICIP Journal*, 2, 2 (2005): 1–11.

Masud, Muhammad Khalid. 'Islam and Democracy in Pakistan', in Maqsudul Hasan Nuri, Col. Muhammad Hanif, Muhammad Nawaz Kahn (eds.), *Islam and State: Practice and Perceptions in Pakistan and the Contemporary Muslim World* (Islamabad: Islamabad Policy Research Institute, 2012), pp. 19–41.

Masud, Muhammad Khalid. 'Islamic Modernism', in Muhammad Khalid Masud et al. (eds.), *Islam and Modernity: Key Issues and Debates* (Edinburgh: Edinburgh University Press, 2009): 237–260.

Masud, Muhammad Khalid. 'Religion and State are Twin Brothers: Classical Muslim Political Theory', *Islam and Civilizational Renewal* [*ICR*], 9, 1 (2018): 9–26.

Masud, Muhammad Khalid. *Iqbal's Reconstruction of Ijtihad* (Lahore: Iqbal Academy, 2003).

Masud, Muhammad Khalid. *Shatibi's Philosophy of Islamic Law*, Revised Edition (Islamabad, Pakistan: Islamic Research Institute, 1995).

Matthews, D. J. *Iqbal: A Selection of Urdu Verse* (ed. and trans.) (New Delhi: Heritage Publishers, 1993).

Mawdudi, Abu'l Ala. 'Political Theory of Islam', in Khurshid Ahmad (ed.), *Islam: Its Meaning and Message,* 3rd ed. (London: Islamic Foundation, 1999 [1975]), pp. 147–171.

Mawdudi, Syed Abul Ala. *Islami Riyasat* [Islamic State] (New Delhi: Islamic Book Foundation, 1991).

Mawdudi, Syed Abul Ala. *Islamic Law and Constitution* (trans. and ed.) Khurshid Ahmad (Lahore: Islamic Publications, 1960).

Mawdudi, Syed Abul Ala. *Islamic Way of Life* (trans.) Khurshid Ahmad (Delhi: Markazi Maktaba Islami, 1967).

Mawdudi, Syed Abul Ala. *Tafhim al-Qur'an* (New Delhi: Markazi Maktaba Islami Publishers, 2003).

Mawdudi, Syed Abul Ala. *Tafhim al-Qur'an/Towards Understanding the Qur'an* (trans.) Zafar Ishaq Ansari, assisted by A. R. Kidwai (Markfield, Leices., London: Islamic Foundation, 1989; also published and reprinted in New Delhi by Markazi Maktaba Islami Publishers, 1999).

Mawdudi, Syed Abul Ala. *Tafhim al-Qur'an—The Meaning of the Qur'an*, available online at www.englishtafsir.com.

McDermott, Leina. 'Exploring the Compatibility of Political Islam and Democracy', *World Outlook* [*WO*], 56 (Fall 2019): 110–115.

Memarian, Jahandad. 'Asef Bayat: A Critique of the Eurocentric Vision of the Middle East', *Medium*, 30 August 2018, available online at www.medium.com/@jahandad/asef-bayat-a-critique-of-eurocentric-vision-of-the-middle-east-699f16f9562 (last accessed on 20 September 2018).

Mernissi, Fatema. *Islam and Democracy: Fear of the Modern World* (trans.) Mary Jo Lakeland (New York: Addison-Wesley Publishing Company, 1992).

Mir, Mustansir. 'Iqbal, Muhammad', in Gerhard Bowering et al. (eds.), *The Princeton Encyclopedia of Islamic Political Thought* (Princeton and Oxford: Princeton University Press, 2013), pp. 259–260.

Mir, Mustansir. *Iqbal: Makers of Islamic Civilization* (London: I. B. Tauris, 2007).

Mir-Hosseini, Ziba, and Tapper, Richard. *Islam and Democracy in Iran: Eshkevari and the Quest for Reform* (New York: I. B. Tauris, 2006).

Mirsepassi, Ali. *Democracy in Modern Iran: Islam, Culture, and Political Change* (New York and London: New York University Press, 2010).

Mirza, Mahan. 'Ahmad, Israr (1932–2010)', in Gerhard Bowering et al. (eds.), *The Princeton Encyclopedia of Islamic Political Thought* (Princeton and Oxford: Princeton University Press, 2013), pp. 23–24.

Moaddel, Mansoor. *Islamic Modernism, Nationalism, and Fundamentalism: Episode and Discourse* (Chicago: University of Chicago Press, 2005).

Moten, Abdul Rashid. 'Democratic and Shura-Based Systems: A Comparative Analysis', *Encounters: Journal of Inter-Cultural Perspectives*, 3, 1 (March 1997): 3–20.

Moten, Abdul Rashid. *Political Science: An Islamic Perspective* (London: Macmillan Press, 1996).

Mubarak, Abdulkadir. 'Democracy from Islamic Law Perspective', *Kom: Journal of Religious Sciences*, V, 3 (2016): 1–18.

Munawwar, Muhammad. 'Iqbal's Idea of Democracy', *Iqbal Review: Journal of the Iqbal Academy Pakistan*, 26, 1 (1985): 120–139.

Musahabah-yi Duktur Surush ba Ustad Shahid Piramun-i Jumhuri Islami (Dr. Soroush's Interview with the Martyred Professor on the Islamic Republic), in Murtaza Mutahhari, *Piramun-i Inqilab-i Islami* [On the Islamic Revolution], 15th ed. (Tehran: Intisharat-i Sadra, 1995), pp. 125–141.

Muslehuddin, Mohammad. *Islam and Its Political System* (Islamabad, Pakistan: Dr Muslehuddin Islamic Trust, IIUI, 1988).

Muslih, M. 'Democracy', in John L. Esposito (ed.), *The Oxford Encyclopedia of the Modern Islamic World* (New York: Oxford University Press, 1995), I: 356–360.

Nadeem, Khursheed Ahmad. 'Barr-e Sagheer ki Chand Aham Tafaseer: Ek Taqabuli Jayezah [Some Prominent Quran Exegesis of the Subcontinent: A Comparative Study]', *Fikr-o-Nazr*, 32, 3&4 (1999): 323-351.

Najjar, Fauzi M. 'Democracy in Islamic Political Philosophy', *Studia Islamica*, 51 (1980): 107-122.

Najjar, Fauzi M. 'Islam and Modern Democracy', *The Review of Politics*, 20, 2 (April 1958): 164-180.

Nakhleh, Emile A. 'Bay'ah', in John L. Esposito (ed.), *The Oxford Encyclopedia of the Modern Islamic World* (New York: Oxford University Press, 1995), I: 205-206.

Nasr, Seyyed Vali Raza. 'Mawdudi, Sayyid Abu Al-Ala', in Emad El-Din Shahin (ed.), *The Oxford Encyclopaedia of Islam and Politics*, 2 vols. (New York: Oxford University Press, 2014): II: 43-47.

Nasr, Seyyed Vali Raza. *Mawdudi and the Making of Islamic Revivalism* (Oxford: Oxford University Press, 1996).

Nasr, Seyyed Vali Raza. *The Vanguard of Islamic Revolution: The Jama'at-i Islami of Pakistan* (Berkeley: University of California Press, 1994).

Nasr, Vali R. 'The Rise of Muslim Democracy', *Journal of Democracy*, 16, 2 (2005): 13-27.

Nayar, Sushila. 'Mawlana Abul Kalam Azad and National Integration', in Subhash C. Kashyap (ed.), *Mawlana Abul Kalam Azad—A Centenary Volume* (New Delhi: National Publication House, 1989), pp. 67-77.

Newman, Daniel L. 'Rifa'a Rafi' al-Tahtawi (1801-1873)', in Richard C. Martin (ed.), *Encyclopedia of Islam and Modern World*, 2nd ed. 2 vols. (New York: Macmillan, 2016 [2004]), II: 1178-1179.

Nu'mani, Allama Shibli. *Al-Farooq* (Azamgarh: Ma'arif Press, 1376/1956).

Okvath, Csaba, and Iqbal, Muzaffar. 'Consultation (Shura)', in Muzaffar Iqbal (General Editor), *The Integrated Encyclopedia of Qur'an [IEQ]*, Vol. 1 (Sherwood Park, Canada: Centre for Islamic Sciences, 2013), available online at www.iequran.com/articles/C/85 (last accessed on 15 July 2021).

Omar, Abdul Mannan. *Dictionary of the Holy Qur'an: Arabic Words-English Meanings* (Hockessin, New Castle: Noor Foundation International, 2010 [2003]).

Omar, Irfan A. 'Islamic Thought in Contemporary India: The Impact of Mawlana Wahiduddin Khan's al-Risala Movement', in Ibrahim M. Abu Rabi' (ed.), *The Blackwell Companion to Contemporary Islamic Thought* (UK, USA, and Australia: Blackwell Publishing, 2006), pp. 75-87.

Osman, Fathi. *Islam in a Modern State: Democracy and the Concept of Shura*. Occasional Papers Series (Washington, DC: Center for Muslim-Christian Understanding: History of International Affairs, Edmund A. Walsh School of Foreign Services, Georgetown University, 2001).

Osman, Fathi. 'Islam Should be Recognized as Dynamic, Flexible Religion', *Al-Hewar Center* (Washington, DC), 6 May 1998, available online at http://www.alhewar.com/FathiOsman.html.

Osman, Fathi. 'Shura and Democracy', in John J. Donohue and John L. Esposito (eds.), *Islam in Transition: Muslim Perspectives*, 2nd ed. (New York: Oxford University Press, 2007), pp. 288-295.

Osman, Fathi. '*Shura* in Islamic Life', *Muslim Democrat [MD]*, 1, 2 (1999): 6-7.

Osman, Mohamed Nawab Bin Mohamed. 'Hizb ut-Tahrir', in Shahram Akbarzadeh (ed.), *Routledge Handbook of Political Islam* (Oxon, RN, New York, and London: Routledge, 2012), pp. 89–104.

Paret, R. 'Dar al-Nadwah', in C. E. Bosworth et al. (eds.), *The Encyclopedia of Islam*, New Edition (Leiden: E. J. Brill, 1960–2001), II: 128.

Parray, Tauseef Ahmad. 'A Thinker in the Eyes of Scholars', *Greater Kashmir*, 29 April 2021, p. 5.

Parray, Tauseef Ahmad. 'Ihsan as the Basis of 'Good Governance'', *Greater Kashmir*, 5 March 2020, p. 9.

Parray, Tauseef Ahmad. "Islamic Democracy' or Democracy in Islam: Some Key Operational Democratic Concepts and Notions', *World Journal of Islamic History and Civilization* [*WJIHC*], 2, 2 (2012): 66–86, http://idosi.org/wjihc/wjihc2(2)12/2.pdf.

Parray, Tauseef Ahmad. 'A Survey of Four Indo-Pakistani Scholars' Perspectives on the Islam-Democracy Discourse', *American Journal of Islamic Social Sciences* [*AJISS*], 29, 1 (2012): 146–159.

Parray, Tauseef Ahmad. 'Allama Iqbal on Islam-Democracy Discourse: A Study of his Views on Compatibility and Incompatibility', *Islam and Muslim Societies—A Social Science Journal* [*IMS*], 4, 2 (2011): 9 pp.

Parray, Tauseef Ahmad. 'Articulating an 'Islamic Democracy' in 21st Century: Views and Visions of Some Living Muslim Intellectuals of Indo-Pak Subcontinent', in *Islamic Academic Conference Proceedings* (Calicut, India: Students Islamic Organization, Kerala, 2012), pp. 267–274.

Parray, Tauseef Ahmad. 'Debates on Tradition and Modernity in the Subcontinent', in Lütfi Sunar (ed.), *The Routledge International Handbook of Contemporary Muslim Socio-Political Thought* (New York and London: Routledge, 2021), pp. 59–72.

Parray, Tauseef Ahmad. 'Democracy and Democratization in the Muslim World: An Evaluation of some Important Works on Democratization in South/Southeast Asia', *Analisa: Journal of Social Science & Religion*, 2, 1 (2017): 79–101.

Parray, Tauseef Ahmad. 'Democracy in Islam: Views of Modern Muslim Scholars', *The Roundtable*, 9, 1 (2011–2012): 4–10.

Parray, Tauseef Ahmad. 'Democracy in Islam: Views of Several Modern Muslim Scholars', *American Journal of Islamic Social Sciences*, 27, 2 (2010): 140–148.

Parray, Tauseef Ahmad. 'Exploring Nejatullah Siddiqi's Contribution to the *Maqasid al-Shari'ah* in the Urdu Literature', *American Journal of Islamic Social Sciences*, 34, 1 (2017): 80–103.

Parray, Tauseef Ahmad. 'Global Muslim Voices on Islam-Democracy Compatibility and Co-existence: A Study of Sadek J. Sulaiman, Louay Safi, Radwan Masmoudi, and Muqtedar Khan', *Journal of Middle Eastern and Islamic Studies in Asia* [*JMEISA*], 6, 1 (2012): 53–86.

Parray, Tauseef Ahmad. 'Globalization, Democracy, and Muslim World: Some Contemporary (Theoretical) Perspectives', *Journal of Society in Kashmir*—Annual Journal of Department of Sociology, Kashmir University [*JSK*], 4 (2014): 1–20.

Parray, Tauseef Ahmad. '*Ijtihad*: Connotation and Implication', *Pakistan Observer*, 27 March 2015, p. 5.

Parray, Tauseef Ahmad. 'Importance of *Ijtihad* for Muslims in 21st century', *Kashmir Reader*, 13 March 2015, p. 7.

Parray, Tauseef Ahmad. 'Introducing Iqbal's 'Less-explored' Prose Works', *Pakistan Observer*, 21 April 2018, p. 5.

Parray, Tauseef Ahmad. 'Iqbal's *Reconstruction* vis-à-vis 'Religion-Modernity Encounter", *Greater Kashmir*, 23 April 2020, p. 5.

Parray, Tauseef Ahmad. 'Iqbal's *Reconstruction*: Reception, Responses, & Reactions', *Greater Kashmir*, 9 November 2017, p. 9.

Parray, Tauseef Ahmad. 'Iranian Intellectuals on 'Islam and Democracy' Compatibility: Views of Abdulkarim Saroush and Hasan Yousuf Eshkevari', *Journal of Middle Eastern and Islamic Studies in Asia*, 7, 3 (2013): 43–64.

Parray, Tauseef Ahmad. 'Islam and Democracy in the Age of Democratization'. *Daily Sabah* (Turkey), 17 September 2015, https://www.dailysabah.com/op-ed/2015/09/17/islam-and-democracy-in-the-age-of-democratization.

Parray, Tauseef Ahmad. 'Islam-Democracy Discourse in 21st Century: Views of 2 Indo-Pak Intellectuals—Prof Khurshid Ahmad and Asghar Ali Engineer', *Encompassing Crescent* (Magazine, New York), 2 July 2011: 61–71.

Parray, Tauseef Ahmad. 'Islam-Democracy Discourse in the Twenty-First Century: From Post 9/11 to the Post Arab Spring Era', in Muhammad Huseyn Mercan (ed.), *Transformation of Muslim World in the 21st Century* (Lady Stephenson Library, Newcastle upon Tyne, UK: Cambridge Scholars Publishing, 2016), pp. 63–84.

Parray, Tauseef Ahmad. 'Islam-Democracy Discourse vis-à-vis the Arab Spring', in Barış Erdoğan and Barış Çoban (eds.), *Metamorphosis of the Arab World: The Social and Political Impact of the Arab Spring* (Turkey: Iskenderiye Kitap, 2015), pp. 39–64.

Parray, Tauseef Ahmad. 'Islam-Democracy Reconciliation in the Thought/Writings of Asghar Ali Engineer', *Islam and Muslim Societies*, 5, 1 (2012): 23–29.

Parray, Tauseef Ahmad. 'Modern Muslim Scholars' on Islam-Democracy Discourse: Views of Azad, Iqbal, and Maududi', *Journal of the Institute of Islamic Studies* [*JIIS*], 40 (2011): 27–50.

Parray, Tauseef Ahmad. 'Muslim Reformist Thought in 21st Century and Its Broad Themes: A Brief Study of 'Democratic Pluralism' in the Light of A. Sachedina's *The Islamic Roots of Democratic Pluralism*', *Islam and Muslim Societies*, 4, 2 (2011): 12 pp.

Parray, Tauseef Ahmad. 'Muslim Reformist Thought in 21st Century and its Broad Themes: A Brief Study of 'Democratic Pluralism' in the light of A. Sachedina's *'The Islamic Roots of Democratic Pluralism"*, *Islam and Muslim Societies*, 4, 2 (2011): 12 pp.

Parray, Tauseef Ahmad. 'On the Reception & Responses to Allama Iqbal's Masterpiece: *Reconstruction*', *Kashmir Reader*, 9 November 2017, p. 7.

Parray, Tauseef Ahmad. 'Operational Concepts of Islamic Democracy: *Khilafah, Shura, Ijma', and Ijtihad*', *Journal of Humanity and Islam* [*JHI*] 1, 1 (2011): 11–27.

Parray, Tauseef Ahmad. 'Political Islam, Islamists, and Democratization', *Kashmir Reader*, 21 August 2015, p. 7.

Parray, Tauseef Ahmad. 'Recent Scholarship on 'Islamism' Discourse: An Evaluation and Assessment', *Analisa*, 1, 1 (2016): 1–17.

Parray, Tauseef Ahmad. 'Review of the Literature on Islam–Democracy Compatibility Theme: 1990 to 2009', *Islam & Muslim Societies*, 4, 2 (2011): 31 pp., available online at http://www.muslimsocieties.org/Vol4-2/Review_of_the_Literature_on_the_Islam.pdf.

Parray, Tauseef Ahmad. 'Review: M. A. Muqtedar Khan. Ed. *Islamic Democratic Discourse: Theory, Debates and Philosophical Perspectives.* 2006', *Insights*, 1, 3 (2009): 171–176.

Parray, Tauseef Ahmad. 'The Legal Methodology of '*Fiqh al-Aqalliyyat*' and Its Critics: An Analytical Study', *Journal of Muslim Minority Affairs* [*JMMA*], 32, 1 (2012): 88–107.

Parray, Tauseef Ahmad. 'The Less Studied Iqbal: Allama Iqbal's Prose Works on Islam/Muslims vis-à-vis Socio-Politico-Economic Issues', *Greater Kashmir*, 21 April 2019, p. 9.

Parray, Tauseef Ahmad. 'Three Living Western [Muslim] Academicians on Islam-Democracy Discourse: Analyzing the Views of Prof(s) Abou El Fadl, El-Affendi, and Sachedina', *Point of View:* Centre for Mediterranean, Middle East & Islamic Studies [CEMMIS] (*University of Peloponnese*, Greece, www.cemmis.edu.gr), 28 January 2015, pp. 1–7.

Parray, Tauseef Ahmad. 'Tools for Reformation in Islam', *The Islamic Quarterly* [*IQ*], 60, 2 (2016): 231–245.

Parray, Tauseef Ahmad. *Exploring the Qur'an: Concepts and Themes* (Srinagar, J&K: Kitab Mahal Publishers, 2019).

Parray, Tauseef Ahmad. *Mediating Islam and Modernity: Sir Sayyid, Iqbal and Azad* (New Delhi: Viva Books, 2019).

Parray, Tauseef Ahmad. *Recent Trends in Qur'anic Scholarship* (New Delhi: Viva Books, in association with K. A. Nizami Centre for Quranic Studies, AMU, Aligarh, 2020).

Parray, Tauseef Ahmad. *Towards Understanding Some Qur'anic Terms, Concepts, and Themes* (Karachi: Qirtas Books, 2017).

Paya, Ali. *Islam, Modernity, and a New Millennium: Themes from a Critical Rationalist Reading of Islam* (London and New York: Routledge, 2018).

Polka, Sagi. *Shaykh Yusuf al-Qaradawi: Spiritual Mentor of Wasati Salafism* (Syracuse, NY: Syracuse University Press, 2019).

Prakash, Pranav. 'Abu'l Kalam Azad', in Zayn R. Kassam, Yudit Kornberg Greenberg, and Jehan Bagli (eds.), *Islam, Judaism, and Zoroastrianism* (Dordrecht, The Netherlands: Springer, 2018), pp. 7–15.

Profile Introduction: Dr Israr Ahmed, available online at http://www.drisrarahmed.com/ (last accessed on 14 June 2011).

Qutb, Sayyid. *In the Shade of the Qur'an,* (trans.) Adil Salahi, 18 vols., available, in pdf, online at www.sunniconnect.con/m3/download/pdf-in-the-shade-of-the-quran-fi-dhilal-al-quran-sayyid-qutb/ (last accessed on 20 August 2018).

Qutb, Sayyid. *Milestones*, 1st ed. (Delhi: Markazi Maktaba Islami, 1981).

Rahman, Fazlur. 'Implementation of the Islamic Concept of State in the Pakistani Milieu', *Islamic Studies*, vi, 3 (1967): 205–223.

Rahman, Fazlur. 'Revival and Reform in Islam', in Holt et al. (eds.), *Cambridge History of Islam* (Cambridge: Cambridge University Press, 1970), II: 632–656.

Rahman, Fazlur. 'The Principle of *Shura* and the Role of the Umma in Islam', *American Journal of Islamic Studies* [*AJIS*] (now *American Journal of Islamic Social Sciences* [*AJISS*]) 1, 1 (1984): 1–9.

Rahman, Fazlur. *Islam and Modernity: Transformation of an Intellectual Tradition* (Chicago: University of Chicago Press, 1982).

Rahman, Fazlur. *Major Themes of the Qur'an* (Minneapolis: Bibliotheca Islamica, 1980).
Rahman, Fazlur. *Major Themes of the Qur'an*, 2nd ed. (Kuala Lumpur: Islamic Book Trust, 1999).
Rahman, Fazlur. *Revival and Reform in Islam: A Study of Islamic Fundamentalism*, Edited and with an Introduction by Ebrahim Moosa (Oxford: Oneworld Publications, 2000).
Rahman, Hafijur. 'The Perception of Muslim Democracy in the Political Thought of Rachid Ghannouchi', *Akademik Hassasiyetler/The Academic Elegance*, 8, 15 (2021): 361–376.
Rahman, Hafijur. 'Toward a Wise Political Fiqh: The Perception of State in the Political Thought of Yusuf al-Qaradawi', *ASBIDER—Akademi Sosyal Bilimler Dergisi* 7, 21 (2020): 6–22.
Rahman, Mawlana Gauhar. *Islami Siyasat [Islamic Politics]* (Rampur, India: Maktaba Zikra, 1982).
Rahman, Mujibur. 'Iqbal's Critique of Democracy', *Dr Iqbal Society of North America [DISNA]*, 15 October 2010, available online at http://disna.us/allamaiqbal/2010/10/15/iqbal%E2%80%99s-critique-of-democracy/#more-119 (last accessed on 28 May 2011).
Raja, Masood A. 'Muhammad Iqbal: Islam, the West, and the Quest for a Modern Muslim Identity', *The International Journal of the Asian Philosophical Association [IJAPA]*, 1, 1 (2008): 37–49.
Ramadan, Tariq. 'Ijtihad and Maslaha: The Foundations of Governance', in Muqtedar Khan (ed.), *Islamic Democratic Discourse* (Lanham, MD: Lexington Books, 2006), pp. 3–20.
Ramadan, Tariq. 'Notion of Shura: Shura and Democracy', *The American Muslim [TAM]*, 1 September 2002, http://www.theamericanmuslim.org/tam.php/features/articles/notion_of_shr_shr_or_democracy/.
Ramadan, Tariq. *Islam, the West and the Challenges of Modernity* (Leicester, UK: The Islamic Foundation, 2004).
Ramadan, Tariq. *Western Muslims and the Future of Islam* (New York: Oxford University Press, 2004).
Rane, Halim. 'Democracy and Muslims', in Ronald Lukens-Bull and Mark Woodward (eds.), *Handbook of Contemporary Islam and Muslim Lives*, 2 vols. (Switzerland: Springer Nature, 2021), Chapter 52, pp. 1067–1088.
Reckinger, Carole. 'Islam and Democracy, an Oxymoron? *Politik*, Forum 272 (December 2007): 21–23.
Rehman, Afzalur (ed.). *Muhammad: Encyclopedia of Seerah* (London: Seerah Foundation, 1998).
Rejai, Mostafa. *Democracy: The Contemporary Theories* (New York: Atherton Press, 1967).
*Renaissance*. http://www.monthly-renaissance.com.
Renowned Religious Scholar Dr Israr Ahmed Passes Away, *Daily Times* (Pakistan), 15 April 2010, http://www.dailytimes.com.pk/default.asp?page=2010%5C04%5C15%5Cstory_15-4-2010_pg13_7 (last accessed on 14 June 2011).
Rida, Muhammad Rashid. *Tarikh al-Ustadh al-Imam al-Shaykh Muhammad 'Abduh*, 1st ed. (Cairo: al-Manar, 1931).

## BIBLIOGRAPHY

Declaration of the Rights of Man and of Citizen. *The New Encyclopedia Britannica*, 15th ed. (Chicago: Encyclopedia Britannica, 1985-2010 [1768-7]), X: 68.
Declaration of the Rights of Man and of the Citizen. *The New Encyclopedia Britannica*, 15th ed. (Chicago: Encyclopedia Britannica, 1985-2010 [1768-7]), X: 69.
Rizvi, S. A. A. 'The Breakdown of Traditional Society', in P. M. Holt et al. (eds.), *The Cambridge History of Islam* (Cambridge: Cambridge University Press, 1970), 2A: 67-97.
Rousseau, Jean Jacques. *The New Encyclopedia Britannica*, 15th ed. (Chicago: Encyclopedia Britannica, 1985-2010 [1768-7]), X: 210.
Roy, Oliver. *Secularism Confronts Islam* (New York: Columbia University Press, 2007).
Rozehnal, Robert. 'Debating Orthodoxy, Contesting Tradition: Islam in Contemporary South Asia', in R. Michael Feener (ed.), *Islam in World Cultures—Comparative Perspectives* (Santa Barbara, CL: ABC-CLIO, 2004), pp. 103-131.
Rubin, U. 'Mala', in C. E. Bosworth et al. (eds.), *The Encyclopedia of Islam*, New Edition (Leiden: E. J. Brill, 1960-2001), XII: 573-574.
Sabet, Amr G. E. *Islam and the Political: Theory, Governance and International Relations* (London: Pluto Press, 2008).
Sabine, George H. *A History of Political Theory*, 3rd ed. (New York: Holt, Rinehart, and Winston, 1961).
Sachedina, Abdulaziz. 'Muslim Intellectuals and the Struggle for Democracy', *Global Dialogue*, 6, 1-2 (2004): 79-87 (special issue on *Islam and Democracy*), available online at http://www.worlddialogue.org/content.php?id=301 (last accessed on 15 May 2011).
Sachedina, Abdulaziz. 'The Role of Islam in the Public Square: Guidance or Governance?', in M. A. Muqtedar Khan (ed.), *Islamic Democratic Discourse: Theory, Debates and Philosophical Perspectives* (Lanham, MD: Lexington Books, 2006), pp. 173-192.
Sachedina, Abdulaziz. 'Why Democracy and Why Now?', in John J. Donohue and John L. Esposito (eds.), *Islam in Transition: Muslim Perspectives*, 2nd ed. (New York: Oxford University Press, 2007), pp. 307-310.
Sachedina, Abdulaziz. *The Islamic Roots of Democratic Pluralism* (New York: Oxford University Press, 2001).
Saeed, Abdullah. 'Fazlur Rehman: A Framework for Interpreting the Ethico-Legal content of the Qur'an', in Suha Taji-Farouki (ed.), *Modern Muslim Intellectuals and the Qur'an* (New York: Oxford University Press; in association with The Ismaili Institute, London, 2004), pp. 37-66.
Saeed, Abdullah. 'Trends in Contemporary Islam: A Preliminary Attempt at a Classification', *Muslim World* [*MW*], 97 (2007): 395-404.
Saeed, Abdullah. *Islamic Thought: An Introduction* (London: Routledge, 2006).
Saeed, Abdullah. *Reading the Quran in the Twenty-First Century: A Contextualist Approach* (New York: Routledge, 2013).
Saeed, Abdullah. *The Qur'an: An Introduction* (London: Routledge, 2008).
Safi, Louay M. "Shura and Democracy: Similarities and Differences', 6 November 1999, available online at http://louaysafi.com//index.php?option=com_content&task=view&id=51&Itemid=22 (last accessed on 20 August 2018). Originally presented as a paper at the Annual Meeting of the *Middle East Studies Association* (MESA), Washington, on 19 November 1999.

## BIBLIOGRAPHY 351

Safi, Louay M. 'Arab Democracy is a Work in Progress', 2 April 2012, available online at http://louaysafi.com//index.php?option=com_content&task=view&id=118&Itemid=7. The article is based on a public lecture delivered by Dr. Safi at Doha on 22 February 2012 under the title 'From Sultanic Rule to Democracy'.

Safi, Louay M. 'Can Islam and Democracy Coexist?' *National Geographic News*, 24 October 2003, available online at http://news.nationalgeographic.com/news/2003/10/1021_031021_islamicdemocracy.htm (last accessed on 5 September 2010); also available at http://www.onthewing.org/user/Islam%20-%20Can%20Islam%20and%20Democracy%20Coexist.pdf (last accessed on 5 December 2021).

Safi, Louay M. 'Democracy Inside Out: The Case of Egypt', *Q-News—The Muslim Magazine*, 361 (March 2005): 17, available online at http://www.q-news.com/361-Egypt.html (last accessed on 5 September 2010).

Safi, Louay M. 'The Islamic State: A Conceptual Framework', *American Journal of Islamic Social Sciences*, 8, 2 (1991): 221–234.

Safi, Louay M. *Islam and the Trajectory of Globalization: Rational Idealism and the Structure of World History* (New York: Routledge, 2021).

Safi, Louay M. *The Challenge of Modernity: The Quest for Authenticity in the Arab World* (Lanham: University Press of America, 1994).

Salame, Ghassan (ed.). *Democracy without Democrats? The Renewal of Politics in the Muslim World* (London and New York: I. B. Tauris, 1994).

Saleem, Shehzad. 'The Political System of Pakistan: Points to Ponder' (Adapted from Ghamidi's '*Burhan*'), *Renaissance*, available online at http://www.monthly-renaissance.com/issue/content.aspx?id=467 (last accessed on 28 August 2018).

Saleem, Muhammad Mubeen. '*Bayan al-Qur'an* by Ashraf Ali Thanwi' in Nazeer Ahmad Ab. Majeed (ed.), *Quran Interpretation in Urdu: A Critical Study* (New Delhi: Viva Books, in association with K. A. Nizami Center for Quranic Studies, AMU, 2019), pp. 64–82.

Saleem, Muhammad Mubeen. '*Ma'arif-ul-Qur'an* by Muhammad Shafi', in Nazeer Ahmad Ab. Majeed (ed.), *Quran Interpretation in Urdu: A Critical Study* (New Delhi: Viva Books, in association with K. A. Nizami Center for Quranic Studies, AMU, 2019), pp. 152–164.

Sardar, Ziauddin. 'What Do We Mean by Islamic Future?' in Ibrahim Abu Rabi' (ed.), *The Blackwell Companion to Contemporary Islamic Thought* (Malden, MA, Oxford, UK, and Victoria, Australia: Blackwell Publishing, 2006), pp. 562–586.

Sardar, Ziauddin. *Reading the Qur'an: The Contemporary Relevance of the Sacred Text of Islam* (Gurgaon, India: Hachette Book Publishing India, 2011).

Sartori, Giovanni. 'Rethinking Democracy: Bad Polity and Bad Politics', *International Social Science Journal*, 43 (1991): 437–450.

Schacht, Joseph. *An Introduction to Islamic Law* (Oxford: Clarendon Press, 1964).

Schimmel, Annemarie *Gabriel's Wing: A Study of the Religious Ideas of Sir Muhammad Iqbal* (Leiden: E. J. Brill, 1963).

Sedgwick, Mark. *Muhammad Abduh* (London: Oneworld Publications, 2014).

Shafi, Mufti Muhammad. *Ma'ariful-Qur'an* (trans.) Muhammad Hasan Askari and Muhammad Shamim, Revised by Justice Mufti Muhamad Taqi Usmani, 8 vols. (Karachi: Maktaba-i-Dar al-'Ulum, 1996–2004; New Delhi: Farid Book Depot, 2008).

Shahroor, Muhammad. 'A Proposed Charter for Muslim Activists', August 1999, as cited in Graham E. Fuller, *The Future of Political Islam* (New York: Palgrave Macmillan, 2003), p. 61 and Abdullah Saeed, *Reading the Quran in the Twenty-First Century: A Contextualist Approach* (New York: Routledge, 2013), p. 155.

Shakir, Moin. 'Political Ideas of Mawlana Azad', in *Azad, Islam and Nationalism, Essays by Moin Shakir and others* (New Delhi: Kalamkar Prakashan, n.d.), pp. 9-39.

Shavit, Uriya. 'Is *Shura* a Muslim Form of Democracy? Roots and Systemization of a Polemic', *Middle Eastern Studies* [MES], 46, 3 (2010): 349-374.

Shaw, Stanford J. *History of the Ottoman Empire and Modern Turkey* (Cambridge: Cambridge University Press, 1976).

Shepard, William. 'The Diversity of Islamic Thought: Toward a Typology', in Taji-Farouki and Nafi (eds.), *Islamic Thought in the Twentieth Century* (New York: I. B. Tauris, 2004), pp. 61-103.

Sherwani, H. K. *Studies in Muslim Political Thought and Administration*, 2nd and Revised ed. (Lahore: Sheikh Mohd. Ashraf, 1945).

Siddiqi, Mazharrudin. *Modern Reformist Thought in the Muslim World* (New Delhi: Adam Publishers and Distributors, 2014 [1982]).

Siddiqi, Mazharuddin. *Concept of Muslim Culture in Iqbal* (Islamabad: Islamic Research Institute, 1983).

Sikand, Yoginder. 'Asghar Ali Engineer's Quest for an Islamic Theology of Peace and Religious Pluralism', 15 November 2006, available online at http://www.svabhinava.org/MeccaBenares/YoginderSikand/AsgharAliEngineerIslamicTheology-frame.php (last accessed on 10 May 2021).

Sisk, Timothy D. *Islam and Democracy: Religion, Politics, and Power in the Middle East* (Washington, DC: United States Institute of Peace, 1992).

Smith, Wilfred Cantwell. *Modern Islam in India: A Social Analysis* (Lahore: Minerva Book Shop, 1943).

Soage, Ana Belén. 'Shaykh Yusuf al-Qaradawi: Portrait of a Leading Islamic Cleric', *Middle East Review of International Affairs*, 12, 1 (2008): 51-68.

Soage, Ana Belén. 'Sheikh Yusuf al-Qaradawi: Moderate Voice from the Muslim World?', *Religion Compass*, 4, 9 (2010): 563-575.

Soage, Ana Belén. '*Shurà* and Democracy: Two Sides of the Same Coin?', *Religion Compass*, 8, 3 (2014): 90-103.

Sofi, Mohammad Dawood, and Parray, Tauseef Ahmad. 'Reinterpreting *Mithaq al-Madina* [Madina Constitution]: A Study of Some Contemporary Scholars', *The Journal of Rotterdam Islamic & Social Sciences* [JRISS], 7, 1 (2016): 75-90.

Sofi, Mohammad Dawood. *Rashid al-Ghannushi: A Key Muslim Thinker of the 21st Century* (New York: Palgrave Macmillan, 2018).

Sonn, Tamara. 'Voices of Reformist Islam in the United States', in Shireen T. Hunter (ed.), *Reformist Voices of Islam—Mediating Islam and Modernity* (New Delhi: Pentagon Press, 2009), pp. 267-286.

Soroush, Abdulkarim. 'Bawar-i Dim, Dawar-i Dini' [Religious Belief, Religious Arbitrator], pp. 45-78, and 'Arkan-i-Farhangi-yi Dimukrasi' [The Cultural Pillars of Democracy], pp. 269-283 (both) in Abdulkarim Soroush, *Farbihtar az Idiuluzhi* [More Comprehensive than Ideology], 2nd ed. (Tehran: Sirat, 1373/1994).

Soroush, Abdulkarim. 'Democracy Is Not Summarized in Elections', Interview with *Sharqh, Daily Newspaper*, 109, 7 (January 2004): 4, available online at http://www.drsoroush.com/English/Interviews/E-INT-20040107-Sharq_Newspaper.html (last accessed on 15 March 2011).

Soroush, Abdulkarim. 'Mabani Tiorik-i-Libiralizm' [The Theoretical Bases of Liberalism], in Abdulkarim Soroush, *Razdani va Raushanfikri va Dindari* [Augury and Intellectualism and Pietism], 2nd ed. (Tehran: Mu'assassah-yi Farhangi-yi Sirat, 1993).

Soroush, Abdulkarim. 'Mudara va Mudiriyat-i Mu'minan, Sukhani dar Nisbat-i-Din va Dimukrasi' [The Tolerance and Administration of the Faithful, a Talk on the Relationship between Religion and Democracy], *Kiyan* 4, 21 (1994): 4.

Soroush, Abdulkarim. 'Mudara wa Mudmyat-i Mu'minan: Sukhanf dar Nisbat-i Din wa Dimukrasi' [The Tolerance and Administration of the Faithful: A Remark on the Relation Between Religion and Democracy], *Kiyan* 4, 21 (1994): 11–12.

Soroush, Abdulkarim. 'Tahlil-i Mafhum-i Hukumat-i Dini' [Analysis of the Concept of Religious Government], *Kiyan* 6, 2 (1996): 6.

Soroush, Abdulkarim. 'Tolerance and Governance: A Discourse on Religion and Democracy', in Mahmoud Sadri and Ahmad Sadri (translated, edited, and with a Critical Introduction), *Reason, Freedom and Democracy in Islam; Essential Writings of Abdul Karim Soroush* (New York: Oxford University Press, 2000), pp. 131–155.

Soroush, Abdulkarim. *Farbeh tar az* [Loftier than Ideology] (Tehran: Saraat Press, 1997).

Stepan, Alfred (ed.). *Democratic Transitions in the Muslim World: A Global Perspective* (New York: Columbia University Press, 2018).

*Studying Islam.* http://www.studying-islam.org/.

Sulaiman, Sadek J. 'Democracy and Shura', in Charles Kurzman (ed.), *Liberal Islam— A Sourcebook* (New York: Oxford University Press, 1998), pp. 96–98.

Sulaiman, Sadek J. 'Shura Principle in Islam', available online at http://www.alhewar.com/SadekShura.htm (last accessed on 25 December 2021).

Sulaiman, Sadek J., 'Religion, Democracy, and the Arabs' View of America', A Presentation made at *Hull University* (UK), 24 November 2003, available online at http://www.alhewar.net/Basket/sadek_sulaiman_religion_democracy_arabs_view_of_america.htm (last accessed on 15 December 2021).

Taji-Farouki, Suha. *The Fundamental Quest: Hizb al-Tahrir and the Search for the Islamic Caliphate* (London: Grey Seal, 1996).

Tamimi, Azzam. 'Democratic Synergies and Oppositions in the Muslim World: Arab Democracy and Islamic Democracy', paper presented at the PSA Conference, Leicester University, Wednesday, 16 April 2003.

Tamimi, Azzam. 'Islam and Democracy from Tahtawi to Ghannouchi', *Theory, Culture & Society*, 24, 2 (2007): 39–58.

Tamimi, Azzam. *Rachid al-Ghannouchi: A Democrat within Islamism* (New York: Oxford University Press, 2001).

Tariq, A. R. (Compiler). *Speeches and Statements of Iqbal* (Lahore: Sheikh Ghulam Ali & Sons, 1973).

Taufiqurrahman, M. 'Islam Compatible with Democracy, Scholars Say', *The Jakarta Post*, Tuesday, 12 July 2004, available online at http://www.thejakartapost.com/news/2004/12/07/islam-compatible-democracy-scholars-say.html (last accessed on 25 June 2011).

Tayyib, Qari Muhammad. *Fitri Hukumat* [The Natural State] (Lahore: Idara Islamiyyat, 1963).

Tessler, Mark. 'Islam and Democracy in the Middle East: Impact of Religious Orientations on Attitudes toward Democracy in Four Arab Countries', *Comparative Politics* 34, 3 (2002): 337–354.

Thanawi, Mawlana Muhammad Ashraf Ali. *Tafsir Bayan al-Qur'an*, 3 vols. (Lahore: Maktaba Rahmaniya, 1934).

*The Arabian Stories*. 'We Lost a Great Mind: Omani Thinker Sadiq Suleiman Dies at 90', 28 July 2021, available online at https://www.thearabianstories.com/2021/07/28/we-lost-a-great-mind-omani-thinker-sadiq-jawad-suleiman-dies-at-90/ (last accessed on 22 December 2021).

*The New Encyclopedia Britannica*, 32 vols., 15th ed. (Chicago: Encyclopedia Britannica [1768–1771], 1985–2010).

Tibi, Bassam. 'Major Themes in the Arabic Political Literature of Islamic Revivalism, 1970–1985: The Islamic System of Government (*al-nizam al-islami*), *shura* Democracy and the Implementation of the *Shari'a* as Opposed to Secularism ('*ilmaniyya*)', *Islam and Christian–Muslim Relations* [*ICMR*], 3, 2 (1992): 183–121 and 4, 1 (1993): 83–99.

Tiruneh, Gizachew. 'Democracy', in William A. Darity Jr. (ed.), *International Encyclopedia of the Social Sciences*, 2nd ed. (Macmillan Reference USA/Thomson Gale Group, 2008), II: 272–276.

Tocqueville, Alexis de. *Democracy in America*, (trans.) Henry Reeve (New York: Vintage Books, 1990).

Turabi, Hassan. 'The Islamic State', in John L. Esposito (ed.), *Voices of Resurgent Islam* (New York: Oxford University Press, 1983), pp. 241–251.

Tyan, E. 'Bay'a', in C. E. Bosworth et al. (eds.), *The Encyclopedia of Islam*, New Edition (Leiden: E. J. Brill, 1960–2001), I: 1113.

United States Institute of Peace, 'The Problem of Democracy in the Muslim World' and 'Compatibility of Islam and Democracy', *Special Report: Islam and Democracy*, Report prepared by David Smock, 93 (September 2002): 2–3, 3–5.

Uthmani, Mufti Shabbir Ahmad. *Qur'an Majeed* (New Delhi: Taj Company, n.d.).

Uthmani, Muhammad Taqi. 'Hakim al-Ummat ke Siyasi Afkar', *Al-Balagh* (Karachi), 25 (March 1990): 23–53, reprinted in Muhammad Ishaq Multani (ed.), *Islam awr Siyasat* [Islam and Politics] (Multan: Idara-yi Ta'li-fat-i Ashrafiyya, 1998): 21–76.

Vahid, Syed Abdul (ed.). *Thoughts and Reflections of Iqbal* (Lahore: Sheikh Muhammad Ashraf, 1992).

Vahid, Syed Abdul. *Iqbal: His Art and Thought* (New Delhi: Deep and Deep Publications, 1988).

Vakili, Valla. *Debating Religion and Politics in Iran: The Political Thought of Abdolkarim Soroush*. Occasional Paper Series No. 2 (New York: Council on Foreign Relations, 1996), available online at http://www.drsoroush.com/PDF/E-CMO-19960100-Debating_Religion_and_Politics_in_Iran-Valla_Vakili.pdf (last accessed on 12 March 2011).

Vernon, Bogdanor (ed.). *The Blackwell Encyclopedia of Political Institutions* (Oxford and New York: Blackwell Reference, 1987).

Vida, G. Levi Della. 'Kusayy', in C. E. Bosworth et al. (eds.), *The Encyclopedia of Islam*, New Edition (Leiden: E. J. Brill, 1960–2001), V: 519–520.

# BIBLIOGRAPHY 355

Waki, Muhammad ibn Khalaf. *Akhbar al-Qudat* (Cairo: 'Alam al-Kutub, n.d.).
Waliullah, Shah. *Hujjatullah al-Balighah*, 1st ed. (Lahore: Maktabah al-Salafiyyah, 1975).
Wallace, Willard M. 'American Revolution', in *Encyclopædia Britannica [EB]*, available online at https://www.britannica.com/event/American-Revolution (last accessed on 20 August 2018).
Wani, Gowhar Quadir, and Choughley, Abdul Kader (eds.). *Abdul Majid Daryabadi's Tafsir-ul-Qur'an: A Critical Study* (Aligarh: Brown Books, in association with KAN-CQS, AMU and Ahsan Academy of Research, Springs, South Africa, 2021).
Wasey, Akhtarul, and Kidwai, Abdur Raheem (eds.). *Journey of Faith: Maulana Abdul Majid Daryabadi* (New Delhi: Shipra Publications, 2016).
Watt, W. Montgomery. *Muhammad: Prophet and Statesman* (London: Oxford University Press, 1961).
White, Joshua T., and Siddiqui, Niloufer. 'Mawlana Mawdudi', in John L. Esposito and Emad El-Din Shahin (eds.), *The Oxford Handbook of Islam and Politics* (New York: Oxford University Press, 2013): 144–155.
Woo, Elaine. 'Fathi Osman Dies at 82; Voice for Modernism in Islam', *Los Angeles Times*, 15 September 2010, available online at http://articles.latimes.com/2010/sep/15/local/la-me-fathi-osman-20100915 (last accessed on 25 February 2011).
Wright, Robin B. 'Two Visions of Reformation', in Diamond et al. (eds.), *Islam and Democracy in the Middle East* (Baltimore and London: The Johns Hopkins University Press, 2003), pp. 220–231 [originally published in *Journal of Democracy*, 7, 2 (1996): 64–75].
Yasmeen, Samina. 'Democracy for Muslims: Javed Ahmed Ghamidi', in Lily Zubaidah Rahim (ed.), *Muslim Secular Democracy: Voices from Within* (New York: Palgrave Macmillan, 2013), pp. 93–112.
Yusuf, Imtiyaz. 'Second chance?', *The Nation*, 13 July 2013, available online at http://www.nationmultimedia.com/opinion/Second-chance-30210276.html (last accessed on 15 July 2013).
Yusuf, Imtiyaz. 'Asghar Ali Engineer', in Zayn R. Kassam, Yudit Kornberg Greenberg, and Jehan Bagli (eds.), *Islam, Judaism, and Zoroastrianism* (Dordrecht, The Netherlands: Springer, 2018), pp. 78–81.
Zafar, S. M. 'Accountability, Parliament, and *Ijtihad*', in Charles Kurzman (ed.), *Liberal Islam—A Sourcebook* (New York: Oxford University Press, 1994), pp. 67–72.
Zalloom, Abdul Qadeem. *Democracy Is a System of Kufr*, 2nd ed. (London: Al-Khilafah Publications, 1995 [1990]).
Zaman, Muhammad Qasim. *Ashraf Ali Thanawi: Islam in Modern South Asia* (Oxford: Oneworld Publications, 2007).
Zaman, Muhammad Qasim. *The Ulama in Contemporary Islam: Custodians of Change* (Princeton and Oxford: Princeton University Press, 2002).
Zoubir, Yahia H. 'Algerian Islamists' Conception of Democracy', 1996, available online at http://www.thefreelibrary.com/Algerian+Islamists'+conception+of+democracy-a019129732 (last accessed on 20 January 2011).
Zoubir, Yahya H. 'Democracy and Islam in Malek Bennabi's Thought', *American Journal of Islamic Social Sciences*, 15, 1 (1998): 107–111.
Zoubir, Yahya H. 'State, Civil Society and the Question of Radical Fundamentalism in Algeria', in Ahmad S. Moussali (ed.), *Islamic Fundamentalism: Myths and Realities* (Reading, UK: Ithaca Press, 1998), pp. 123–167.

# Index

*For the benefit of digital users, indexed terms that span two pages (e.g., 52–53) may, on occasion, appear on only one of those pages.*

Abbasid caliphate, 66
Abbasid dynasty, 66
Abbasids, 65–66, 69, 194, 195, 250
Abduh, Muhammad, 14–15, 37–38, 69, 91–92, 115, 116–17, 120, 121–25, 204–5, 221, 270, 295–96
Abu Bakr, 55, 58–59, 62–63, 75, 78, 89, 150, 153–54, 162, 164
Abu Yusuf, 61
*Adl* (justice), 119–20, 121
Affendi, Abdelwahab el-
    on authoritarianism of the Khilafah, 250
    on democracy as a stable system of governance, 247–48
    on essentials of democracy, 39, 248–49
    on liberal democracy, 248–49
    on meaning of democracy, 39
    on Muslim attitudes towards democracy, 29–30
    on rights of minorities, 250–51
    on Shura as an authentic Islamic model of democracy, 248
Afghani, Jamal al-Din al-, 5, 14–15, 37–38, 70, 115, 116–17, 120–22, 269–70, 271, 295–96
Afsaruddin, Asma, 49, 55, 56, 75, 79, 80–81, 160–61
*Ahl al-Din* (experts in Religion), 71
*Ahl al-Hall wa al-'Aqd* (the 'Wise Ones'), 12–13, 14, 47, 71, 77–78, 92–93, 153
*Ahl al-'Ilm* (people of knowledge), 71
*Ahl al-Ray* (people of opinion), 153
*Ahl al-Shura*, 275
*Ahl Al-Sunnah wa Al-Jama'ah* (the mainstream Muslim stance on things Quranic), 165–66

Ahmad, Ahrar, 39, 48, 300
Ahmad, Irfan, 4, 5, 302
Ahmad, Khurshid, 9, 15, 23, 36, 37–39, 40, 83, 86–87, 115, 159, 184, 210
Ahmad, Mumtaz, 9
Ahmed, Israr, 15, 156, 184, 187–88, 191
Al-Ghazali, 90–91, 135–36
Ali, Syed Ameer, 62–63, 65–66, 95
Al-Mamun, 66
*al-Maslaha al-Mursalah* (Public Interest), 123, 125–26
*al-Urwah al-Wuthqa*, 121–22
Alwani, Taha Jabir al-, 86–87, 88
Amin, Qasim, 120, 122–23
Amir, 71, 89, 168, 170, 190–91
*Amr bil Ma'ruf wa nahi an al-Munkar*, 65, 83, 125–26, 185
anarchy, 61–62, 170, 248, 297
Arab Spring, 1, 4–5, 7, 10–11, 112–13, 255, 260, 319
aristocracy, 5–6, 25–26, 141, 147, 246
Ashour, Omar, 9, 78–79
Awwa, M. Saleem El-, 37–38, 115
Azad, Abul Kalam
    as an advocate of democratization of Islam, 5
    his *al-Balagh*, 149
    his exegesis, *Tarjuman al-Qur'an*, 149, 151, 153–54
    on the French Revolution (of 1789), 152
    on government as the possession of Public (Jumhur), 152, 153
    his *al-Hilal*, 5, 149, 151, 152
    as Indian liberal theologian-philosopher, 149

Azad, Abul Kalam (*cont.*)
  his interpretation of Shura,
    55, 150–51
  on/ his Islami Jumhuriyya, 149, 153–54
  on Islamic Democracy, 5
  Pranav Prakash on al-Hilal, 151
  on significance of the institution of
    Shura, 54
  on Shura as an substitute for
    democracy, 149
Aziz, Umar bin Abd al-, 64, 65–66

Badry, Roswitha, 4–5, 9
Baghdadi, Ahmad Mubarak Al-, 52
*Baihaqi*, 57
Bakar, Osman, 37–38, 115
Banna, Hasan al-, 37–38, 115
Banu Ummayya, 64–66, 69, 194–95, 250
*Bay'ah* (Oath of Allegiance), 37, 58–59,
    64–65, 90, 220, 256, 263
Bayat, Asef ( 9, 15–16, 289, 300–2
Bennabi, Malek, 14–15, 36, 116, 127–
    29, 219
Berber, Benjamin, 11
Bokhari, Kamran, 15, 184, 243, 264–
    67, 288
Buddhism, 2, 302

Caliph 'Ali, 57, 58–59, 60, 61–62, 64, 66
Caliph Umar, 58–59, 60–61, 62–63, 70–
    71, 75, 259, 273
Caliph Uthman, 60, 61–63
capitalism, 144, 145, 295
Christian (or Christians/Christianity),
    2, 96, 142–43, 247, 302
Christian church, 246
Christian liberation theology, 193
citizenship, 95, 192, 225, 301
constitutionalism, 94–95, 116–17, 125–
    26, 204, 266, 309
contested term (or contested concept),
    24–25, 27, 36–37, 39, 215, 266,
    267, 299–301, 309–10
critical Islam, 31

Dahl, Robert, 300
Daryabadi, Abdul Majid

  Abdur Raheem Kidwai on
    Daryabadi, 170
  a prominent voice of the Traditional
    bent, 135, 170
  representative of Ahl Al-Sunnah wa
    Al-Jama'ah, 165–66
democratization, 5–6, 7, 9, 10, 12, 13,
    28–29, 31, 32, 35, 38–39, 83,
    87, 94, 112, 129, 141, 183, 197,
    212–13, 219, 243, 248–49, 253,
    259, 272
Deoband school of thought (or
    Deobandi), 165–66, 169, 217, 220
despotism, 25–26, 56, 67–68, 123, 126,
    128–29, 153–54, 206–7, 248–
    49, 298
Diamond, Larry, 6, 7–8, 9, 26

elections (*Intikhabat*), 153–54
El Fadl, Khaled Abou, 8, 15, 28, 40,
    113, 114, 184, 243, 255, 256–
    58, 262–63
Engineer, Asghar Ali, 15, 184, 192–
    97, 258–59
Eshkevari, Hasan Yousefi, 113, 114
Esposito, John L., 4, 7, 8, 28–29, 30, 35,
    38, 67, 68, 76, 83, 84, 94, 137, 138,
    147, 148, 156, 221, 268–69, 297

Feldman, Noah, 4–5, 8, 257
*Fiqh* (Islamic jurisprudence), 161–62,
    200, 201, 206, 229
*Fiqhi* (Islamic/ jurisprudential), 88, 228
French Revolution, 25–26, 39–40, 117–
    18, 149, 152, 153–54
  *See also* Abul Kalam Azad: Revolution
    of 1789
Fukuyama, Francis, 11
Fuller, Graham E., 2, 302
fundamentalism, 86

Gallie, G. B., 27, 36–37, 300–1
Ghamidi, Javed Ahmad, 15, 184, 191,
    243–44, 245, 246, 247
Ghannoushi, Rachid al-, 9, 15, 28,
    37–38, 115, 184, 219–20, 221,
    222, 223

## INDEX

globalization, 32, 94, 251–52, 255, 272
Greek (or Greek democracy), 23, 24, 26–27, 40, 117–18, 248

Hakim, Khalifa Abdul, 146, 217, 218
*Hakimiyyah* (or *hakimiya*), 29, 158, 209, 291, 292, 298–99
Hanafi, Hasan, 37–38, 115
hard-core Islamists (or radical Islamists), 12, 15–16, 265, 266, 267, 289–90, 298
Hasan, Mohammad Kamal, 115
Hashemi, Nader, 1–2, 4–5, 8, 9, 15–16, 41, 257, 289, 302, 303, 304
Hassan, Riffat, 136–37, 192–93
Hibri, Azizah Y. Al-, 6–7, 28, 92, 93, 98
*Hisba*, 65
*Hizb al-Tahrir*, 15–16, 265, 289, 293, 294
Hobbes, Thomas, 25–26
Huntington, Samuel P., 11

*Iblees ki Majlis-e-Shura*, 145
Ibrahim, Anwar, 37–38, 115
*Ijma'* (community consensus or consensus), 2–3, 5–6, 12–13, 14, 29, 34–35, 47, 63, 73, 74, 84–85, 87, 114–15, 125–26, 140, 183, 220, 221, 223, 253, 263, 268, 273–74, 275, 296, 309–10
*Ijtihad* (Independent Interpretive Reasoning) 2–3, 5–6, 12–13, 14, 29, 30–31, 32, 34–35, 37, 47, 67, 73, 74, 77–79, 84, 85–87, 88, 91–92, 114–15, 122, 124–26, 140, 141, 142, 183, 188, 198, 200–1, 208, 212–13, 220, 222, 223, 246, 259, 260, 267, 270, 276, 296–97, 309–10, 313
*Ikhlitaf* (disagreement), 64–65
Imperialism (or anti-imperialism), 120, 143, 144, 252–53, 295–96
*Infaq*, 213–14
Iqbal, Javed, 142
Iqbal, Muhammad, 5–6, 14–15, 37–38, 86–87, 115, 135–38, 139–40, 141, 142–43, 144, 145–46, 147, 148, 159, 188, 193, 270

Isbell, Thomas, 9
Ishrat, Waheed, 143, 144, 145–46
*Islah* (reform), 31, 270
Islahi, Amin Ahsan, 14–15, 49, 135, 243–44
  on differentiating between Islamic State and the (modern) secular democracy, 165
  on institution of Shura (Shuraiyat), 54, 164
  on Khilafah (Islamic state), 164–65
  his Tadabbur al-Qur'an, 163–64
  his works
    Islami Riyasat/ The Islamic State, 163–64, 217
Islam, Md Nazrul and Saidual, Md, 9, 10, 11
Islam and modernity, 33, 93–94, 116, 165–66, 270, 272, 321
Islamic constitutionalism, 6–7, 98
Islamic fundamentalism, 7, 30, 290
Islamic Heritage, 14, 68, 137, 138, 312–13
Islamic liberalism, 260
Islamic modernism, 120, 122, 137, 216, 270
Islamic modernists, 32–33, 91–92
Islamism, 250, 290, 301
  *See also* fundamentalism; Islamic fundamentalism; political Islam
*Istislah*, 90

Jan, Abid Ullah, 15–16, 289, 297
Jawad, Haifaa, 9, 28–29, 33–34, 313
Jiahdist, 265
Jihadist groups, 295
Jihad Vs MCWorld, 11
Judaism, 302

Kamali, Muhammad Hashim, 9, 84
Kamrava, Mehran, 30, 85–86
Kaplan, Robert, 11
Kausar, Zeenat, 160
Khalid Butt and Naeema Siddiqui, 9
Khan, M. A. Muqtedar, 8, 15, 31–32, 86–87, 97, 113, 141, 184, 243, 261
Khan, Mawlana Wahiduddin 15, 184, 197–99, 200

Khan, Sir Syed Ahmad, 24, 115, 270
Khatab, Sayed and Bouma, Gary D., 9, 113, 124–25
Khatib Baghdadi, 57
*Khilafah* (Caliphate), 12–13, 14, 34–35, 36, 37, 47, 58, 59, 65–66, 81–82, 83, 85, 114–15, 155–57, 158–59, 160, 164–65, 169–70, 183, 187–89, 190, 192, 203, 211, 214, 245, 246, 250, 265–66, 273, 293, 309–10
Kramer, Gudrun, 4, 302–3
*Kufr* (disbelief), 266–67, 288, 293, 294, 298

liberal democracy (or Western liberal democracy), 7–8, 9, 39, 141, 148, 218, 226, 248–49, 257, 274, 315
Liberal Islam, 31, 260
liberalization, 28–29, 31, 32
Lincoln, Abraham, 24, 185–86
Locke, John, 25–26

Madjid, Nurcolish, 37–38, 115
Madni, Ali Abbassi al-, 37–38, 115
Magna Carta, 25, 94–95
Mahmood, Saba, 8, 28, 257
*Majlis* (or *mala*), 50, 51
*Majlis al-Shura* (or *Majlis-i-Shura*), 60, 62–63, 69, 77, 275
*Mashwara* (or *Mashawarat*), 49, 66, 68, 69, 70–71, 150, 157, 168, 294
*Maslaha* (Public Interest), 2–3, 12–13, 14, 29, 37, 47, 90–92, 123, 125–26, 215–16, 268, 296, 309–10
Masmoudi, Radwan A., 15, 184, 243, 258–59, 260
Masud, Muhammad Khalid, 15, 85, 184, 215–16, 217, 218
Mawdudi, Mawlana Syed Abu'l 'Ala, 14–15, 37–38, 54, 81, 82, 83, 135, 154–56, 158, 159, 160–61, 188–89, 191, 210, 245, 275, 276
McDermott, Leina, 9
Medi, Sadiq al-, 37–38, 115
Middle East, 4, 5–6, 11, 12, 37–38, 66–67, 79, 112–13, 115, 116, 117–18, 120, 205–6, 251–52, 260, 270, 304, 319
Middle East and North Africa (and MENA), 7–8, 34–35, 112, 115, 260, 268, 269–70
*Mithaq al-Madina*, 12–13, 14, 47, 48, 89, 94–95, 96, 97–98, 142–43, 263, 309–10, 319
moderate Islamists (or moderate Islamic/Islamist movements), 2–3, 260, 274
modernist Islam, 31
monarchy, 25–26, 28–29, 64, 121–22, 153–54, 157, 194–96, 200, 206–7, 218, 244–45, 247, 248, 291
Montesquieu, Baron de, 25–26, 117–18
Moten, Abdul Rashid
  on formulating the most suitable form of government, 113
  on Islam-democracy compatibility as a 'Western construct', 295–96
  on Maslaha, 296
  as one of the opponents of democracy, 289
  on practice of Shura, 296
  on Shura and a liberal democratic structure, 296
  on selection and election of the four caliphs, 58
  on westernized Muslim thinkers, 295–96
Muslim Brotherhood, 290, 295
*Muslim Democrat*, 259
Muslim Democrats, 2–3, 14, 31–32

Nabhani, Taqiuddin al-, 15–16, 289, 293–94
*Nasiha/nasihah* (advice), 64–65, 185, 207
*Niyabah*, 153–54
*Nizam-i-Kufr* (system of *Kufr*), 293, 294
Numani, Shibli, 60, 61

oligarchy, 248
Omar, Irfan A., 197
opponents, 14, 15–16, 28, 265, 266–67, 288–89, 298–99, 319
Osman, Mohamed Fathi, 15, 37–38, 184–85, 186, 187

INDEX 361

Ottoman (or Ottoman empire), 68, 69, 194

parliament, 23, 50–51, 69, 75–76, 77–78, 93, 145, 160, 206, 207, 223, 275, 302
parliamentary democracy, 72, 73, 117, 125, 246, 296–97
parliamentary form of government, 160
parliamentary government (or parliamentary governance), 27, 116–17, 141, 147
See also parliamentary governance; parliamentary system/ parliamentary form of government
parliamentary system/ parliamentary form of government, 51, 116–17, 124–25, 149, 160, 217, 220, 293–94, 313
pluralism (or political pluralism), 11, 32, 33–34, 62, 74, 77, 89, 94–95, 97, 116–17, 118–19, 124–25, 126, 149, 184–85, 195, 198, 204–6, 212–13, 215–16, 219–20, 221, 222, 223–24, 257–58, 272, 301, 302–3
plutocracy, 248
political Islam, 7, 10–11, 203, 290, 301
polyarchy, 300
process of democratization, 2–3, 7, 9, 14, 33, 114, 127–28, 183, 272, 288–89, 310
progressive islam, 31
Prophet Sulaiman, 275, 276
Prophet Yusuf (Joseph), 201

Qaradawi, Yusuf al-, 15, 73, 184, 205–6, 207, 208, 209, 210, 219, 257–58, 275, 276
Queen Saba, 275, 276
Qutb, Sayyid, 37–38, 115, 289, 290–91, 292, 298

Rahman, Fazlur, 14–15, 64–65, 70, 86, 135, 161–63, 215–16
Raja, Masood, 145, 148
Rane, Halim, 9, 10, 73

Ra'y (opinion of Ummah), 153
Raysuni, Ahmad al-, 52
Reckinger, Carole, 9
Reformist Islam, 31, 161–62
religious resurgence (or Islamic resurgence), 35, 154–55, 290
resurgence, 93–94
Rida, Rashid, 14–15, 69, 91–92, 93, 116, 120, 122–23, 125, 126, 186, 204–5
Risalat/Risalah (Prophethood), 139–40, 147, 155–56
Rousseau, Jean Jacques, 25–26, 117–18, 198–99
Rumi, Jalal ud Din, 138

Sabet, Amr (Sabet, Amr G. E.), 15–16, 289, 302–3
Sachedina, Abdulaziz
  on democracy and democratic ideals, 225, 226
  on democratic ideals within an Islamic framework, 225
  on democratic pluralism, 223–24, 226
  his The Islamic Roots of Democratic Pluralism, 7–8, 223–24
  a keen proponent of democracy as an Islamic value, 223–24
  one of major voices of pluralism in Islam, 223–24
  on Quranic philosophy, 223–24
Sadd al-dharai (blocking the means), 123, 125–26
Safi, Louay M., 15, 85, 184, 243, 251–54, 255, 271
Sahih Bukhari, 312
Sahih Muslim, 185, 312
Salah, 54
Salam, Fatih A. Abdel, 9, 289–90
secular (or secularists), 2–3, 28–29, 30, 32–33, 35, 87, 112–13, 127, 128–29, 148, 155–56, 195–96, 199, 214, 220, 221–22, 246, 250–51, 265, 296–97, 303, 311
secularism, 6, 32, 34, 144, 196, 200, 218, 226, 246, 266–67, 303, 315

Shafi, Mufti Muhammad, 49, 53, 54, 135, 158, 165–67, 168–69
Shah Waliullah, 61, 137, 138
Shari'ati, Ali, 37–38, 115
Shavit, Uriya, 4, 5, 9, 222, 275
*Shirk,* 298
Soage, Ana Belén, 9
social contract (or *The Social Contract*), 25–26, 94–95, 97–98, 117–18, 198–99
Soroush, Abdolkarim
  on the constitutive principles of democracy, 228
  on democracy as a method of governance, 227
  on democracy as the rejection of tyranny, 227
  on democracy as a sociological construct, 228–29
  on democracy as a value system, 227
  a distinguished voice on Islam-democracy compatibility, 226
  as Islamic democrat, 257–58
  on religious democratic state, 227
spiritual democracy, 5–6, 142–43, 144
Stepan, Alfred, 9
substantive democracy, 48
Sulaiman, Sadek J., 15, 74, 83, 184, 201–3, 204, 205
Sulami, Mishal Fahm Al- (or al-Sulami), 7–8, 50–51, 66, 274
Sultan, 66–67, 68
sultanates, 29, 112
*Sunnah* (*or Sunna*), 3, 31–32, 34–35, 56, 58, 59, 64, 67, 80, 84, 91, 93, 94–95, 113–14, 126, 162, 164–65, 167–68, 189, 190, 191, 192, 197–98, 211, 212–13, 246, 247, 256, 261–62, 265–66, 273–74, 275, 298, 309, 313–14

Tahtawi, Rifa'a Badawi Rafi al-, 9, 14–15, 116–20, 270
*Tajdid* (renewal), 270
Taqlid (blind following/ imitation), 91–92, 122, 136–37, 201, 271
*Tawhid* (*or Tawheed*), 47, 83, 139–40, 155–56, 210, 296–97

Tayyib, Qari Muhammad, 14–15, 135, 165–66, 169–70, 217
Tessler, Mark, 9, 11
Thanawi, Maulana Ashraf Ali, 14–15, 135, 165–68
theocracy, 140, 155–56, 188–89, 190, 221, 247, 298
theo-democracy, 112, 113, 155–56, 158, 160–61, 188–89, 244
Tocqueville, Alexis de, 1–2
traditionalist(s), 14–15, 30–31, 56, 74, 116–17, 135, 165–66
Turabi, Hassan al-, 37–38, 219, 273–74, 275

Ulama (or Ulema) (the religious scholars), 31–32, 35, 68, 74, 77, 91–92, 166–67, 258, 296
*Ummah al-Wahida* (or *Ummat-ul-Wahida*), 95, 142–43
ummah, 47, 54, 57, 58–59, 62, 67, 69, 81–82, 83, 84, 85, 88, 95, 96, 136–37, 153–54, 157–58, 203, 206, 212–13, 218, 253, 276, 296, 315
U.S. Constitution (or Constitution of U.S/ American constitution), 25–26, 98
Uthmnai, Mufti Shabbir Ahmad , 14–15, 55, 135, 158, 165–66, 167–68

Voll, John O., 4, 7, 29, 38, 67, 68, 76, 83, 94, 156, 221

Wahid, Abdurrahman, 37–38, 115
*waqf,* 213–14
wave of democratization, 7, 248–49
Western democracy, 4–5, 6, 26–27, 99, 115–16, 126–27, 141, 144, 145–46, 148, 155–56, 158–59, 160, 161, 169, 206, 207, 212, 220, 247, 272–73, 294, 297, 314

Yusuf, Imtiyaz, 192–93, 304

Zakat (or Zakah), 54, 129, 170, 213–14
Zallum, Abd al-Qadim, 15, 289
  his association with Hizb al-Tahrir, 15–16, 289, 294